A MONSTER OF VOICES
SPEAKING FOR H. P. LOVECRAFT

Robert H. Waugh

Hippocampus Press

New York

Published by Hippocampus Press
P.O. Box 641, New York, NY 10156.
http://www.hippocampuspress.com

Cover art by Philip Fuller.
Cover design by Barbara Briggs Silbert.
Hippocampus Press logo by Anastasia Damianakos.

First Edition
1 3 5 7 9 8 6 4 2

ISBN 978-0-9844802-2-7

A Monster of Voices: Speaking for H. P. Lovecraft

Contents

Introduction

In 2005, in my introduction to *The Monster in the Mirror*, my first collection of essays on H. P. Lovecraft's work, I addressed the question, "Why H. P. Lovecraft? Why do we care for him, and why does he insist on our care?" Now in 2011 I believe the answer is less hesitant, in part because of such publications as the selection of his work in the Library of America series. Whether or not Lovecraft is truly a part of that will-o'-the-wisp called the canon, which has become so much more porous in the last forty years, he is certainly a part of our ongoing conversation, both in popular culture and in professional circles, on the literature of the 1920s and its relation to us now. If any quantitative test is necessary, consider the recent quantitative analysis that Candace R. Benefiel has conducted and her conclusion that the impact Lovecraft exerted upon his readers in the 1920s and 1930s and the following generation was weighty and pervasive (459–63). We have not been able to hold him back. He has entered into our persistent conversation, whether in the arts—consider his popularity in heavy metal, punk rock, and rockabilly circles—in criticism, or in our everyday lives. Turn where you will, Lovecraft is liable to loom there.

Like my earlier collection, this book is made up of essays previously published and now revised and expanded and of essays written for this occasion. The first section begins with two studies of Lovecraft's perhaps most esteemed story, "The Colour out of Space." The first essay considers it in relation to *Macbeth* and *Paradise Lost*, the second more speculatively considers it in relation to D. H. Lawrence's novella *St. Mawr* and to other works of the period devoted to the mythic figure of Pan. I hope that they demonstrate how resonant Lovecraft's story remains. The third essay treats of "The Rats in the Walls" as Lovecraft's World War I story; the poets of the war could not leave the rats of the trenches out of their verses, and Lovecraft was compelled to accept the rats too. And with beasts in mind, the next essay takes up the problem of one of Lovecraft's least respected stories, "The Hound," which returns us to one of the major themes of *The Monster in the Mirror*, the hero as ghoul; this essay also concerns the relation of this story to Arthur Conan Doyle's most famous novel, *The Hound of the Baskervilles*, as well as to Francis Thompson's poem "The Hound of Heaven." The last essay, with a great debt to Plato and Josef Pieper, deals with the erotic ecstasis

7

of "The Thing on the Doorstep," "Medusa's Coil," "The Dreams in the Witch House," and "The Whisperer in Darkness."

The second section takes up Lovecraft's work a bit more freely. The first essay looks at Fritz Leiber's late novel, *Our Lady of Darkness*, in the framework of its several references to many literary figures, among them of course H. P. Lovecraft; and in its conclusion the essay takes up the close, intentional connections between Leiber's novel and Lovecraft's late story "The Haunter of the Dark," with attention also to their relations with Robert Bloch's three stories, the early "The Shambler from the Stars" in which he tried to kill Lovecraft off, "The Dark Demon" in which he tried to kill him off again, and the later "The Shadow from the Steeple" in which he tried to reconfigure the conversation he and Lovecraft had been leading; the three men could not let off their conversations. The next essay is interested in the way that Lovecraft in *The Case of Charles Dexter Ward* and other stories and Sarah Clarke in her recent novel *Jonathan Strange and Mr Norell* treat the problem of the weird tale as an historical fiction as Georg Lukacs understood it. Then we consider Lovecraft's use of the dramatic monologue in several of his stories, especially "The Picture in the House," "The Tomb," "The Call of Cthulhu," "Pickman's Model," *The Dream-Quest of the Unknown Kadath*, "The Dunwich Horror," "The Shadow over Innsmouth," "The Whisperer in Darkness," and "The Thing on the Doorstep," as well as a few minor examples. So pervasive is this technique that we may consider it a significant aspect of Lovecraft's style, both technically and thematically. The next essay deals with the nature of Lovecraft's imagination as it exists in an intricate relation with the imaginations of C. S. Lewis and J. R. R. Tolkien, which are so different from one another. The last essay considers several of Lovecraft's stories within the framework of three German Romantic operas, *Der Freischütz, Der Vampyr,* and *Der Fliegende Holländer;* this is an essay in which I must most ask the indulgence of the reader, but I promise that it shall deal with Lovecraft in both a broad and detailed fashion, not because those operas have influenced his work—not this unmusical gentleman—but because his affinities with those operas are so strong.

The last section deals with several influences that Lovecraft felt in his creative life, especially his reactions to Latin and French literature. These two essays are very different in their approaches; but in their conclusions they deal especially with Lovecraft's Roman dream, out of which he had hoped to write a story but never did, and with "The Shunned House" and "Medusa's Coil." The last essay deals with Lovecraft's relation to Eugene O'Neill, taking up once more the theme of Lovecraft's position within American Modernism and the remarkable congruities of the two men's work.

In this work I make a peculiar use of dictionaries. Playing upon America's revolt from England, Lovecraft at times claimed to loathe Webster and to use only the language of Dr. Johnson in his works (with a bit of Poe sprinkled through); hence it is a colour out of space, in the full panoply of the English spelling "colour," that invades the American landscape of the Gardners. So I will on occasion appeal to meanings culled from Johnson's dictionary. The *Oxford English Dictionary* is of course useful as a context for Johnson's work, but we must not ignore Webster, for Lovecraft did swear by its treatment of etymologies (SL 5.233); so despite himself Lovecraft's mother tongue was inescapably American and surrounded him from his first years in Providence. Lovecraft's style is American masquerading as English.

Many years ago I approached Lovecraft as an intellectual problem, attempting to see in him the difference between horror fiction and science fiction. I cannot say that I ever came to a conclusion on that problem, but that introduction to his fiction slowly took hold of me, so that when I had the opportunity in 1987 to host a Lovecraft Forum at SUNY New Paltz I was ready to consider his fiction upon its own terms with both a critical eye and with affection. In this present enterprise I of course owe much to the Lovecraft community, Peter Cannon, Steven J. Mariconda, Norm Gayford, Judith Johnson, David E. Schultz, and S. T. Joshi, to whom every Lovecraftian owes so much; to the librarians of Sojourner Truth Library, SUNY New Paltz, and the John Jay Library, Brown University; to Louise van Santen for help in Dutch translation; to Derrick Hussey for his faith in my project and to him, S. T. Joshi, and David E. Schultz for their careful editorial work; and to my colleagues, Carley Bogarad, Jan Schmidt, Dan Kempton, Tom Olsen, and Alex Bartholomew; and to students of more than twenty-five years, especially John Langan. I am very grateful to Barton Levi St. Armand for his appreciation and good wishes. I owe more than I can say to the patience and support of my wife Kappa.

ABBREVIATIONS

D   *Dagon and Other Macabre Tales* (Arkham House, 1986)

DH   *The Dunwich Horror and Others* (Arkham House, 1984)

LL   *Lovecraft's Library: A Catalogue* (Hippocampus Press, 2002)

MM   *At the Mountains of Madness and Other Novels* (Arkham House, 1985)

MW   *Miscellaneous Writings* (Arkham House, 1995)

OED   *Oxford English Dictionary*

SL   *Selected Letters* (Arkham House, 1965–76; 5 vols.)

—Are you to have all the pleasure quizzing on me? I didn't say it aloud, sir. I have something inside of me talking to myself. (Joyce, *Finnegans Wake* 523)

Ars erat esse patrem; vidit natura periclum
et pariter iuvenem somnoque ac morte levavit
tunc iterum natum et fato per somnia raptum.
[Art was to be a father; nature saw the danger
and lifted the youth from sleep and death
reborn and rapt from sleep by fate] (Manilius 5.308–10)

[. . .] like the black pebble on the enraged beach. (Blake, *Milton* 30/28.35)

But, bejees, something ran over me! Must have been myself, I guess. (O'Neill, *The Plays* 3.691)

Further Sorties

The Blasted Heath in "The Colour out of Space"

Why this is hell, nor am I out of it:
Think'st thou that I, that saw the face of God,
And tasted the eternal joys of Heaven,
Am not tormented with ten thousand hells,
In being deprived of everlasting bliss? (Marlowe, *Faust* 1.3)

At a number of points in "The Colour out of Space" the narrator refers to the area around the Gardner house as "the blasted heath," and once he refers to "a poet" as the authority for the phrase. The identity of this poet, however, is in some doubt, since two well-known poets use the phrase, Shakespeare in *Macbeth* and Milton in *Paradise Lost,* perhaps with some debt to the playwright.[1] Which of them is the source of the narrator's phrase? S. T. Joshi believes that the description of Hell in the epic is the source ("Introduction and Notes" 399n2); but I believe that the tragedy provides substantial grounds to be considered as well, since a number of other details from the tragedy are probably at work in Lovecraft's story, some of them trivial and some of them profound. Nevertheless, I do not deny that Lovecraft was aware of the phrase in Milton's epic; on the contrary, several passages in the epic are also at work in the story. Both *Macbeth* and *Paradise Lost,* in some tension with each other, contribute to Lovecraft's achievement.[2]

---

1. Lovecraft was of course familiar with both authors. He attributed the appearance of his night-gaunts to Doré's illustrations of *Paradise Lost* (SL 1.35) and could quote passages of the poem from memory (SL 3.19 and 4.287); his praise of Milton is not perfunctory (SL 4.158). As for Shakespeare, one letter deals with *Hamlet* at length (SL 1.76–77), another argues passionately for the immediacy of the plays (SL 3.60–62), and another attests to Lovecraft's frequent presence at productions (SL 5.340). He quotes passages with ease (SL 1.118, 1.184, 1.298, 5.279, and 5.432).

2. Donald R. Burleson deals with this problem but only to reach the conclusion that "what is called into question [by the phrase "blasted heath" and the reference to its poet] is the notion of origins, of recoverable intentions, of authorial presence" (*Lovecraft* 113); from the point of view of deconstruction theory the question of the two poets' influence remains undecidable.

As we read *Paradise Lost* and *Macbeth*, however, we must try to read them as Lovecraft did. It would be misleading to say that he read Milton as Blake did, because Lovecraft was not of the party of Satan but of the party of Chaos. More precisely, he believed that the existence of chaos, not the existence of divinity, was the basis of the universe, but he did not believe that humanity should betray its attachments or traditions or morality because of that chaos; Lovecraft sets God and Satan aside, but does not elevate Azathoth in their place, and thus he reads *Paradise Lost* as a qualified humanist would. He reads *Macbeth* not only as a drama but as an example of the belief in witches that according to Margaret Murray has its own basis in a submerged fertility cult. According to these two readings the blasted heath is not a fanciful image; it is a potent symbol of the human condition, an infected fertility and an infectious chaos that must, for the sake of human sanity, be opposed. It is a nightmare theodicy.

A preliminary orientation of the story vis-à-vis Milton and Shakespeare involves examining how the phrase "the blasted heath" appears in the story. The narrator first introduces it as part of a neutral description: "There was once a road over the hills and through the valleys, that ran straight where the blasted heath is now" (*DH* 54). In the next paragraph the phrase is more charged: "When I went into the hills and vales to survey for the new reservoir they told me the place was evil. They told me this in Arkham, and because that is a very old town full of witch legends I thought the evil must be something which grandams had whispered to children through centuries. The name 'blasted heath' seemed to me very odd and theatrical, and I wondered how it had come into the folklore of a Puritanical people" (*DH* 54). The interpretation of this passage points in two directions. The narrator considers the phrase "theatrical" because he recognizes that it originates in Shakespeare's play—and Lovecraft, therefore, recognizes that also. A touch of the atmosphere of the play is contained in the gesture toward the witches of Arkham. But the narrator's puzzlement over how a Puritan culture came to use the phrase receives a rather direct answer in the reader's recognition that the Puritan poet Milton used the phrase, perhaps in imitation of his Elizabethan master whom he profoundly admired.

Two paragraphs later, after a description of the broader landscape of the story, the narrator returns to the phrase:

Though I am attracted by his suggestion that the opening of the story owes a debt to "Il Penseroso," the two passages do not convince me (112).

> But even all this was not so bad as the blasted heath. I knew it the moment I
> came upon it at the bottom of a spacious valley; for no other name could fit
> such a thing, or any other thing fit such a name. It was as if the poet had
> coined the phrase from having seen this one particular region. It must, I
> thought as I viewed it, be the outcome of a fire; but why had nothing new
> ever grown over those five acres of grey desolation that sprawled open to the
> sky like a great spot eaten by acid in the woods and fields? (DH 55)

This passage refers to "the poet" who "coined the phrase"; but unless we accept
the previous passage as evidence that Lovecraft was aware of the phrase in
Shakespeare, as I think we can, no detail here directly points to the play. Instead, as we shall see, this passage has some affinity to the Miltonic landscape.
The phrase next occurs at the beginning of the following paragraph: "In the
evening I asked old people in Arkham about the blasted heath, and what was
meant by that phrase 'strange days' which so many evasively muttered" (DH
55). Here the phrase is once more neutral, though connected with another
phrase that recurs in the story, "strange days." After this passage only two other
uses of the phrase occur. One is three paragraphs later, after the narrator has
heard the story of the Gardners from Ammi Pierce, again in a fairly neutral description: "I could not go into that dim chaos of old forest slope again, or face
another time that grey blasted heath where the black well yawned deep beside
the tumbled bricks and stones" (DH 56). But despite its neutrality the passage
has some point in the fact that in *Paradise Lost* God carves Hell from Chaos;
and this passage contains the second mention of the well that plays so important a part in the events. After this opening cluster, the final mention of the
phrase occurs near the end of the story and repeats significant details from the
third passage: "Five eldritch acres of dusty grey desert remained, nor has anything ever grown there since. To this day it sprawls open to the sky like a great
spot eaten by acid in the woods and fields, and the few who have ever dared
glimpse it in spite of the rural tales have named it 'the blasted heath'" (DH 80).
It is difficult not to recall the words of Lady Macbeth, "Out, damned spot! Out,
I say!" (5.1.35). We shall have much more to say of those words, but this glance
at Lovecraft's specific use of the phrase makes it probable that Shakespeare's
play is a part of the background of the story.

Before we investigate the tragedy more closely, however, let us review the
scene in the epic. It follows upon the catalogue of the fallen angels, like Satan "Hurled headlong flaming from th'ethereal sky / With hideous ruin and
combustion down / To bottomless perdition" (1.45–47). Marshaled before
their leader they stand

> [. . .] condemned
> For ever now to have their lot in pain,
> Millions of Spirits for his fault amerc't
> Of Heav'n, and from Eternal Splendours flung
> For his revolt, yet faithful how they stood,
> Thir Glory withered. As when Heaven's Fire
> Hath scath'd the Forest Oaks, or Mountain Pines,
> With singed top thir stately growth though bare
> Stands on the blasted Heath. (1.608–15)

A number of details from this passage reappear in Lovecraft's story, besides that telling phrase itself: the fall from heaven, the indeterminate nature of those fallen (for it is unclear whether the entity of the Colour is one or many), the colors, the lightning, the woods on fire, and the possibility that this fall means a punishment (whether upon the fallen entity or upon the ground upon which it falls is not clear). Clearly there is good reason to believe that Milton's lines may have sparked Lovecraft's imagination in a number of ways.

These details, however, and a number of others appear when we turn to what actors prefer to call the Scotch play. Shortly after the three weïrd sisters announce to Macbeth and Banquo their ambiguous prophecy, Macbeth conjures them:

> [. . .] Say from whence
> You owe this strange intelligence, or why
> Upon this blasted heath you stop our way
> With such prophetic greeting. Speak, I charge you. (1.3.75–78)

That question reverberates through the play. Whence and why have they come, what kind of intelligence—knowledge or message—do they exhibit, and can they or shall they say more than they do? These questions directly concern Lovecraft's story, questions which at the end of the story the narrator still feels unable to answer: "Do not ask me for my opinion," he concludes, "I do not know—that is all" (*DH* 81). But another question may be asked of the play: why is the heath upon which Macbeth meets the weïrd sisters blasted? The only answer offered is that it has just suffered an ambiguous battle, one in which "fair is foul, and foul is fair" (1.1.12), one in which "the battle's lost and won" (1.1.4). The chiasmus and paradox set the tone for Shakespeare's tragedy and Lovecraft's story.

This theme of paradoxical language becomes most explicit in the words of the porter. To him the gate of Macbeth's castle is the gate to hell, which stands open to equivocators "that could swear in both scales against either scale; who committed treason enough for God's sake, yet could not equivo-cate to heaven" (2.3.8–10); most commentators agree that these are the people implicated in the Gunpowder Plot, an attempt at a violent overthrow of the parliament and king. Macbeth, when he begins "To doubt th'equivocation of the fiend / That lies like truth" (5.5.43–44), identifies the weïrd sisters as equivocators. His experience confronts the paradox that truth itself may lie or, at the least, omit an important element of the truth.

In Johnson's dictionary the historical context of the Gunpowder Plot de-fines an equivocator as "one who uses mental reservation." The wealth of ci-tations that Johnson mobilizes to illustrate the sense of "equivocator," "equivocal," "equivocally," and "equivocalness" suggests a wide scope and also, two hundred years after the crisis that occurred early in the reign of James I, indicates his judgment of equivocation's dire nature. According to Stillingfleet whom Johnson cites, "Words of different significations, are of an equivocal sense; but being considered with all their particular circumstances, they have their sense restrained." Certainly in *Macbeth* the equivocations of the witches are restrained by their outcomes, albeit not in ways restrained by Macbeth's hopes; but in "The Colour out of Space" the meaning of the stone is never restrained, in part because it has been ripped out of its context. It is out of space. To Dennis's question, whether "two or three equivocals have the force to corrupt us," both the play and the story reply in the affirmative. But the nature of that corruption may be understood in a variety of ways. In the eyes of Shakespeare's audience and in the eyes of the Catholic equivoca-tors the signifier and the signified are so closely bound together that one must use extreme care not to corrupt the one through the corruption of the other. In the eyes of the equivocators a silence or reservation is only admissible when performed *in ordine ad Deum* (Wills 94–96), as though, like Bishop Berkeley's tree in the forest, truth can only be preserved as long as God ob-serves and preserves it; in the eyes of most Englishmen, however, equivoca-tion strains the bond between the signifier and the signified, as though the restrained silence introduced a discontinuity into the world. To return to Johnson's citations, South asserts that "words abstracted from their proper sense and signification, lose the nature of words, and are only equivocally so called." So the message of the stone may not be the only equivocal element of the story—the narrator's need to call the stone a messenger may itself be an equivocation, albeit one in which most readers connive. Finally Norris's in-sight that the equivocalness of the word may be considered its "lassitude" points up the fact that both Macbeth and the Gardners suffer from an increasing, radical despondency, one against which Macbeth rouses himself in the final scenes of the play but to which the Gardners ultimately succumb. An equivocation is a corruption that in wearing down distinctions of the word and the world also wears down the mind that distinguishes them.

In Lovecraft's story equivocal language is represented by those flames that tip "each bough like the fire of St. Elmo or the flames that came down on the apostles' heads at Pentecost" (DH 76); these are, however, "tongues of foul flame" (DH 78), perhaps more resembling the tongues of fire within which Dante's evil counselors, equivocators themselves, are enveloped (Inf. 26–27). Although Pier delle Vigne is not in the circle of the equivocators and thus not guilty of their sin, his seductive language with its play on "infiammare" and "disdegnoso" (13.67–72) yet suggests the power and suicidal danger of a playful language. Once the Colour has totally engulfed the farm its resemblance to St Elmo's fire must be seen as ambiguous[3] and its resemblance to a perverse descent of the Holy Spirit renders difficult any communication; no gospel follows from this descent.

It is difficult in the play to resolve equivocal language. No sooner does Macbeth ask what the witches are than they disappear. To Banquo's words, "The earth hath bubbles as the water has, / And these are of them. Whither are they vanished?" Macbeth responds, "Into the air, and what seemed corporal melted / As breath into the wind. Would they had stayed!" (1.3.79–82). Banquo's mystification resembles that which troubles the professors from Miskatonic University. When they chip into the stone they discover a peculiar emptiness that

> seemed to be the side of a large coloured globule imbedded in the substance. The colour [. . .] was almost impossible to describe; and it was only by analogy that they called it a colour at all. Its texture was glossy, and upon tapping it appeared to promise both brittleness and hollowness. One of the professors gave it a smart blow with a hammer, and it burst with a nervous little pop. Nothing was emitted, and all trace of the thing vanished with the puncturing. It left behind a hollow spherical space about three inches across [. . .] (DH 59)

The chips that they obtain, however, melt and leave nothing behind, and the Miltonic lightning destroys the stone next to the Gardners' well.

This emptiness of the messenger, which is only present through the Col-

---

3. In Moby-Dick St. Elmo's fire plays ambiguously upon the three masts like a "lofty tri-pointed trinity of flames" and upon Ahab's harpoon "like a serpent's tongue" (496, 497; ch. 119).

our that is no color, resembles the pervasive theme of hallucination in the play. The language with which Banquo challenges the weird sisters, "Are ye fantastical, or that indeed / Which outwardly ye show?" (1.3.53–54), a language that Macbeth echoes toward the end of the same scene when he refers to his "thought, whose murder yet is but fantastical" (1.3.139), foreshadows how much in the play is imaginary or not what it seems, a condition that he seems to will when he concludes that "nothing is / But what is not" (1.3.141–42). The dagger that he sees before he murders Duncan, the voice that he hears after the murder, the appearance of the dead Banquo at the feast, the spot that Lady Macbeth cannot wash away—each of these moments emphasizes the fantasmal nature of the play and corresponds to the fantasmal nature of the threat in Lovecraft's story.

That spot that Lady Macbeth cannot wash away bears a rich significance for the story because of the weight that it bears in the play. Twice the story refers to the spot in the landscape, "eaten by acid," which the stony messenger had left, and the sample in the laboratory leaves "only a charred spot" (*DH* 58); in the play the theme of the hand-washing is introduced shortly after the murder with her words, "Go get some water / And wash this filthy witness from your hand" (2.2.49–50), and reiterated by her confident words at the end of the scene, "A little water clears us of this deed" (2.2.70). Macbeth, however, is not at all so confident:

> Will all great Neptune's ocean wash this blood
> Clean from my hand? No, this my hand will rather
> The multitudinous seas incarnadine,
> Making the green one red. (2.2.63–66)

His anxiety is repeated in the story, for the narrator is very doubtful that the "spot" of the heath shall ever be cleansed by the reservoir that shall flood the area. Though he says, "I shall be glad to see the water come" (*DH* 81), the story leaves a powerful suspicion that the Colour shall not be erased by the water but will instead infect it. Landscape and mind have been infected by the Colour, and the Colour is as unseen as the blood within our human body that is inhumanly released in the play—in no other Shakespearean play, not even *Titus Andronicus*, do such words as "blood" and "bloody" so often occur. But if that hopelessness of the story is significant, if the rising waters of the reservoir can do nothing to wash away the Colour that has invaded the New England landscape, we cannot help but recall Macbeth's hopelessness: "I am in blood / Stepped in so far that, should I wade no more, / Returning were as tedious as go o'er" (3.4.137–39). The few references in the story to the exodus of Israel from Egypt, following the pillar of a cloud by day and the pillar of fire by night (cf. Ex. 13.21 and *DH* 57), suggest that from the viewpoint of the story this imagery of the rising waters recalls the Red Sea in which Pharaoh's army is drowned.[4] The two colors, the Colour distinctive of the story and the blood distinctive of the play, correspond.

But the Colour and blood are like no other color and blood. Lady Macbeth's words, "Out, damned spot!" echo in Macbeth's words, "Out, out, brief candle, / Life's but a walking shadow . . ." (5.5.23–24). In these two half-lines, which form a pentameter, the parataxis allows a variety of readings. Perhaps it implies that the candle casts the shadow, or that because life is a shadow the candle of life should be extinguished. But nothing precludes a reading based upon the trochaic rhythm of the two words, underlined by their falling at the end of the one line and at the end of the first clause in the second, a rhythm that asserts an identity between the candle and the shadow, between the brightness and the darkness. This contradictory language is exploited by Lovecraft to suggest the ineffable nature of the Colour. "It burns . . . cold an' wet," Nahum says, just before he dies (*DH* 71). It is a rainbow, an iridescence (*DH* 78, 75), the color of blood, yes, but that blood is hot and cold, bright and dark, a "chiaroscuro" (*DH* 54). It is also plural, "moving colours" that refuse to stay fixed (*DH* 66).

The closest connection between the play and the story, of course, originates in the witches' prophecy, "Macbeth shall never vanquished be until / Great Birnam Wood to high Dunsinane Hill / Shall come against him" (4.1.14–16), lines fulfilled when the Messenger reports, "As I did stand my watch upon the hill, / I looked toward Birnam, and anon methought / The wood began to move" (5.5.33–35). In the story the trees do more than move, taking their motion from the "moving colours"; they burn, and do not burn. But we should not be surprised that they burn since in the play they are the woods of Birnam. The pun heightens the apparition, which Lovecraft further expands into the apocalyptic imagery of the Pentecostal fire.

But Lovecraft's trees do more than burn and move: "They were twitching morbidly and spasmodically, clawing in convulsive and epileptic madness at the moonlit clouds; scratching impotently in the noxious air as if jerked by

---

4. In a perceptive article Robert M. Price argues that another source of this imagery and of Ammi's name lies in the biblical account of the destruction of Sodom by fire from heaven that resulted in the Dead Sea and in the incestuous continuation of Lot's line (23–25).

some alien and bodiless line of linkage with terrene horrors writhing and struggling below the black roots" (*DH* 76). The sight resembles "a monstrous constellation of unnatural light, like a glutted swarm of corpse-fed fireflies dancing hellish sarabands over an accursed marsh" (76). Three paragraphs later "the column of unknown colour flared suddenly and began to weave itself into fantastic suggestions of shape which each spectator later described differently" (77). Though we can point to no verbal reminiscence in these passages, this column of trees, streaming in an unknown color, may recall a passage upon the fallen angels that occurs only a few lines earlier than those we are most concerned with:

> All in a moment through the gloom were seen
> Ten thousand Banners rise into the Air
> With Orient Colours waving: with them rose
> A Forest huge of Spears: and thronging Helms
> Appear'd, and serried Shields in thick array
> Of Depth immeasurable. (1.544–49)

That is to say, though each person perceives the shape of the trees in a different fashion, the truth of the matter is that they are encountering a spiritual entity that resembles the fallen angels. Next to these passages, however, we need to align the conclusion of the epic. Comparable to the banner of the fallen angels which "Shone like a Meteor streaming to the Wind" (1.537) is the appearance of the Cherubim who at the will of God the Father descend to the gate of Eden to defend it against banished humanity:

> [. . .] on the ground
> Gliding meteorous, as Ev'ning Mist
> Ris'n from a River o'er the marish glides,
> And gathers round fast at the Laborer's heel
> Homeward returning. High in Front advanc't,
> The brandisht Sword of God before them blazed
> Fierce as a Comet [. . .] (12.628–34)

The images of the fallen angel and the penal angel converge in Milton's epic. The Colour that tortures and expresses itself through the moving trees is neither demonic nor divine (at least we have no conclusive proof on either side of the question), but it combines within itself both the pursuer and the pursued, the revolt and that against which it revolts, that which doubly casts humanity out of its Eden. The resemblance between the Gardners and Adam and Eve in their garden becomes significant in the light of these passages, though in the case of the Gardners they are not exiled from their Eden but destroyed; and Eden is destroyed also. In this aspect the story and the play once more converge, for it is not difficult to see in the play parallels to the story of Eden: "a beneficent divine father, feminine temptations of the hero to aspire high, an act of disobedience that generates disorder in nature as well as guilt and vulnerability in fallen man," and a regicide in the play that is equivalent to deicide insofar as the king is the representative of God (Calderwood 91). The narrator asserts that "this was no fruit of such worlds" as the astronomers view (*DH* 81), but it is a bad fruit. Before Nature sickens the Gardners hope to profit by the fall of the meteor from Heaven; Nahum vows "that his orchards were prospering as never before" (60). These hopes are dashed when "into the fine flavour of the pears and apples had crept a stealthy bitterness and sickishness" (60), words suggestive of Satan's stealthy entrance into Paradise. The result is that next spring "the bad fruit of the fall before was freely mentioned, and it went from mouth to mouth that there was poison in Nahum's ground" (62). This punning passage parodies the fruit of Adam's Fall that corrupts the human race, as the blight in the ground threatens to do at the end of the story, not only the New England neighborhood of Arkham. Both the oak trees surrounding the house and the apple and pear trees of the orchard have an influence far beyond the farm. Parody does not necessarily mean denial; it may also imply a grotesque intensification of the original story.

With all this said, Lovecraft's trees are not granted the locomotion of Birnam Wood, for the trees of the Gardners' farm never leave the earth to which they are rooted, though at the end of the story the narrator alludes to a rumor "about fat oaks that shine and move" (*DH* 81). The trees wish to move; the torture of their writhing originates in the tension between the energy that the entity pours into them and the impossibility of their uprooting. The watchers are too terrified to grant them the grace of lopping their branches. Instead, like the fallen angels in Hell and like the cherubim with the sword at the gate of Eden, they are fixed in place to fulfill the powerful wrath of God the Father.

Other objects are in motion in the play, and speak in the play, which we must consider in motion in the story also. As Macbeth walks to the slaughter of Duncan he appeals to the earth, "Hear not my steps which way they walk, for fear / Thy very stones prate of my whereabout / And take the present horror from the time" (2.1.58–60). The stones do not speak, unless we believe that the insistent knocking on the gate represents such a preternatural voice.

De Quincey, as Lovecraft was aware, certainly felt that the knocking had an effect disproportionate to its cause, framing the condition of Macbeth and his wife who through their murder "are taken out of the region of human things, human purposes, human desires" (393); the knocking attests to the terror of transcending and abolishing the human. And Macbeth hears another voice that cries, "Macbeth does murder sleep" (2.2.39). Whatever those voices may be, he comes to believe that stones and trees may bear witness against him:

> It will have blood, they say: blood will have blood.
> Stones have been known to move and trees to speak;
> Augurs and understood relations have
> By maggotpies and choughs and rooks brought forth
> The secret'st man of blood. (3.4.123–27)

Leaving aside the reference to such stories as the cranes of Ibycus, we cannot but be fascinated by the notion that stones and trees share the world of motion and speech, although this passage reverses the usual order that stones speak and trees move; Macbeth speaks here before the witches speak of the motion that shall animate Birnam Wood. In "The Colour out of Space" those motions and speeches are ambiguous, but they are no less ambiguous in the play.

The prating stones in *Macbeth* also recall Jesus' reply when the Pharisees ask him to forbid the people to praise him: "if these should hold their peace, the stones would immediately cry out" (Luke 19:40). These stones, however, shall testify to innocence. In the story the stone is often called a messenger, but the nature of the message is in profound question. It would be futile to recall all the words of the angels in *Paradise Lost* ("messenger" *graece* is "angel"), but one message truly concerns an ambiguity, a conscious equivocation on the part of Raphael, who is silent concerning the Copernican universe, when Adam asks him to explain the motion of the planets and "is doubtfully answer'd" (8.arg.) by the observation how men

> [. . .] will wield
> The mighty frame, how build, unbuild, contrive
> To save appearances, how gird the Sphere
> With Centric and Eccentric scribbl'd o'er,
> Cycle and Epicycle, Orb in Orb [. . .] (8.80–84)

Whatever the truth of the matter, Raphael is reticent, ascribing to mere human effort the language and geometries of the Ptolemaic and Copernican systems. This combination of satire and reticence matches Lovecraft's fascination with astronomical detail as well as his growing skepticism about human constructs, which in "The Colour out of Space" becomes radical. Though the stone is lethal, its message remains inscrutable to all efforts to read it.

This ambiguity infects another theme of the play, the difficult nature of the three weïrd sisters. They themselves, Macbeth, and Banquo call them—what? Are they the "weyward sisters" as the Folio would have it (cf. 1.3.32, 1.5.8, and 2.1.20), or the "weïrd sisters" as so many commentators agree? Hecate calls Macbeth "wayward," but in a scene of dubious authority. Either the weïrd sisters have a true insight into fate, or as wayward old women they have no insight at all, except that given them by the devil.[5] "You should be women," Banquo says, "And yet your beards forbid me to interpret / That you are so" (1.3.45–47). A pallid version of them may be those three wise men from Miskatonic University who hurry out to investigate "the weird visitor from unknown interstellar space" (DH 57). But however we understand the three women it is Mrs. Gardner who is reduced to a "blasphemous monstrosity" that moves and crumbles as Ammi watches (70). Nothing of her identity or sexuality remains, except that classic identity of the madwoman in the attic. It is an identity that she shares with Lady Macbeth, who invokes the spirits of the air to unsex her (1.5.40) and who kills herself to escape the sickness of the mind she suffers.

This is the point at which we need to read Lovecraft, Shakespeare, and Milton in the light of Margaret Murray's theory that witches celebrated a god "found in Italy (where he was called Janus or Dianus) [...]. The feminine form of the name, Diana, is found throughout Western Europe as the form of the female deity" (12). The double-faced deity presides over Macbeth and "The Colour out of Space" insofar as the theme of equivocation and ambiguity is present. As a fertility god or goddess (the ambiguity is not surprising), the deity can raise storms (51) and promote or destroy human, animal, and agricultural potency (169–85); the weïrd sisters raise storms (1.3.11–25) and compose their cauldron from several symbols of potency, and two of the most striking effects of the Colour are its sapping of the en-

---

5. Though most editors emendate the Folio's "weyward" as "weïrd," the argument continues; Wills believes that "weyward" is justified by the witches' condition as outcasts, marginal to the human world (46, 161). Richard Grant White, the editor of the Shakespeare which Lovecraft possessed (LL #787), annotates "weird sisters" thus: "supposed supernatural creatures like the Fates, controlling destiny. Their name is pronounced wayrd [...] and is spelled weyward in the folio" (3.452n).

ergy of the orchard, the animals, especially the hogs, and the people, and its raising of a storm when it departs. Murray does not, however, discuss the classical ability of witches to control the moon, which is directly under the provenance of the Roman goddess Diana; in Ovid's *Metamorphoses* Medea threatens to draw the moon (7.207), and a hag in Horace's *Epodes* "lunam [. . .] caelo deripit" (5.46). Milton follows this tradition when he compares his monster Sin to the Night-Hag Hecate or Lilith who flies "Lur'd with the smell of infant blood, to dance / With *Lapland* Witches, while the laboring Moon / Eclipses at their charms" (2.664–66). Witches invoke Hecate, the triceps goddess (Ovid 7.194), and through her cast the beneficent or maleficent influence of the moon across the earth.

Given the prominence of this motif, we may wonder who in the story draws down the meteor to the destruction of the Gardner farm. Is it the three wise men? At this point the fluid identity of the weïrd sisters and their deity once more comes into play, for there are several triads in the story. Gardner has three sons. Three officers and three medical men accompany Ammi to the farm. Three women occupy the margins of the story: Mrs. Gardner, whose body is reduced to chaos; Mrs. Pierce, Ammi's wife, who avoids the farm after the first day when the meteor has fallen and who has died by the end of the story; and the entity in the well described by details associated with Tsathoggua and Azathoth, that is to say with Chaos (Waugh, "Landscapes" 237–38). Finally, the story has three protagonists closely linked to one another, Nahum, Ammi, and the anonymous narrator. If anyone draws down the meteor it would seem to be these three, for in terms of the plot they slowly internalize each other and the Colour, and in terms of the narrative it is they who are unimaginable as characters, personae worthy of a narrative interest, unless the meteor descends; insignificant if it does not come down, they are made by the meteor.

This fluidity of identity in both the tragedy and the story occurs in an atmosphere of sleeplessness which releases nightmare into the waking world; like "blood" and "bloody," "sleep" and its various permutations appear frequently. Nightmare appears implicitly in the four invocations to night that is the domain of witchcraft and horror (Wills 57–59); following his fantasmal dagger to the murder of Duncan, Macbeth asserts that "Now o'er the one half-world / Nature seems dead, and wicked dreams abuse / The curtained sleep" (2.1.50–52). Macbeth kills more than Duncan; he kills sleep and is thereby condemned either to sleeplessness (2.2.45–46) or to "the affliction of those terrible dreams / That shake us nightly" (3.2.19–20). But after the

murder of Banquo he enters a new condition in which he lives within his
unconscious in his waking hours. Perhaps referring to the attack on
Macduff's house, he says to Lady Macbeth: "Strange things I have in head,
that will to hand, / Which must be acted ere they may be scanned"
(3.4.140–41). He not only does not consult her; he no longer consults himself, unable any longer to bear the pain of reflecting upon his purposes. He
reconfirms this decision when he hears of Macduff's escape: "The very firstlings of my heart shall be / The firstlings of my hand" (4.1.169–70), the only
children he shall have. Lady Macbeth begins to walk her nightmares also until, like Mrs. Gardner screaming from nightmares, she dies.

The nightmares of the play and the story have a number of details in
common. One of the first consequences of Duncan's murder is the frenzy of
his horses that break out of their stalls and eat one another (2.4.14–18); in
Lovecraft's story Nahum's horses stampede from the barn and have to be shot
because "something had snapped in their brains" (DH 65); in the climax of
the story Ammi's horse Hero goes mad and dies from the shock of being so
near to the well when the Colour shows forth its power. In the waking world,
as Banquo remarks, we are able to restrain those thoughts to which nature
yields when asleep (2.1.6); but in the "eldritch dream-world" that Ammi experiences on the farm (DH 70), the landscape awakens to an aggressive sexuality: "The Dutchman's breeches became a thing of sinister menace, and the
bloodroots grew insolent in their chromatic perversion" (63). Released from
dream the nightmare is unrestrained and exorbitant, just as the equivocal
word is exorbitant when released from its restraints. And just as most nightmares seem to have no conclusion except a repetitious horror, Macbeth's
nightmare of repetitious, meaningless tomorrows is echoed by the reduction
of the Gardner family to "thankless and monotonous chores through the aimless days, [. . .] as if they walked half in another world between lines of nameless guards to a certain and familiar doom" (66). In the dénouement of the
story the narrator says that foreigners who have come to the area, despite
"their wild, weird stores of whispered magic," have left because of the horror
of their dreams (80), and he himself confesses in the last sentence his unease
at the thought of Ammi "as the grey, twisted, brittle monstrosity which per-
sists more and more in troubling my sleep" (82). Rather than presenting a series of events that take place in the waking world, the play, the epic, and the
story are concerned with events that much more resemble the condensed,
discontinuous world of the dream. The instinctual life has been released
through the lifting of material and moral restraints.

This release of nightmare into the waking world may account for the decision of the farmers in the area to refer to the destruction of the Gardners as
an event of "the strange days," a phrase that becomes as incantatory as the
blasted heath. It occurs three times in the story (*DH* 55, 56, 62), never in a
context particularly charged, and the phrase itself does not appear in either
Shakespeare or Milton; but its very repetition draws our attention to it. Certainly the word "strange" is important for the story. In *Paradise Lost*, when
Moloch argues for a direct attack on God, he uses these words:

> [. . .] he shall hear
> Infernal Thunder, and for Lightning see
> Black fire and horror shot with equal rage
> Among his Angels; and his Throne itself
> Mix'd with *Tartarean* sulphur and strange fire,
> His own invented Torments. (2.65–70)

Moloch contemplates turning the Father's anger back on Him, but it is not
clear whether the fire is strange in its creation or in its perversion.

In *Macbeth* the word "strange" is employed repeatedly. In reporting the
battle Ross wants to describe "things strange" (1.2.47) and later claims that
in battle Macbeth makes "strange images of death" (1.3.97). Macbeth calls
the witches' prophecy "a strange intelligence" (1.3.76), as does Banquo
(1.3.122), who later comments that the news sits ill on them, as would "our
strange garments" (1.3.145), an early enunciation of the theme of ill-fitting
clothes that Caroline Spurgeon found so telling in the play (325–26). This ill
fit is translated into another mode when Lady Macbeth says that "strange
matters" (1.5.62) can be read in Macbeth's face. During the night of the
murder "strange screams" are heard (2.3.56); and the days thereafter contain
"Hours dreadful and things strange" (2.4.3), among them the violence of
Duncan's horses, "a thing most strange" (2.4.14). In a moment of indirection
Macbeth accuses Malcolm and Donalbain of a "strange invention" (3.1.32).
Banquo's ghost occasions an eruption of strangeness. Macbeth says that the
ghost is "more strange" than anything known before it (3.4.83), while Lady
Macbeth excuses her husband's frenzy as a "strange infirmity" (3.4.87), to
which Macbeth retorts, facing everyone who cannot see the ghost, "You
make me strange" (3.4.113). As the scene ends he has "strange things in
mind" (3.4.140), perhaps referring to the attack upon Macduff's house, and
more cryptically glances at and away from his own "strange and self-abuse"
(3.4.143). After this scene it is as though no more strangeness can be at-

tained; Macbeth has arrived at a point where the strange becomes humdrum, as commonplace as he would claim his crimes are. As far as he is concerned nothing is strange hereafter, not Birnam Wood and not the
revelation of Macduff's birth. The only further use of the word is in Malcolm's reference to King Edward's ability to heal scrofula as a "strange virtue" (4.3.156), the only positive use of the word in the play. Strangeness
enters the play early in the action and slowly corrupts our perception of the
events, often touching upon or highlighting the nightmare.

The reason for the emphasis in the story upon the bottomless well is located within this atmosphere of the strange and the walking nightmare. The
well becomes important when it is clear that Merwin and Zenas may have disappeared into it. After the police empty the water they discover that "the ooze
and slime at the bottom" is "inexplicably porous and bubbling," through which
a long pole sinks "to any depth in the mud of the floor without meeting any
solid obstruction" (DH 73). Later the man who went down into the well says,
"There was no bottom at all" (77). The bottom turns out to have no bottom,
though out of "the black pit" the odd Colour begins "to shoot up" as though
possessed of an immense power, one that has obviously killed at least some of
the Gardners (74). We must not imply, however, that this well is the origin of
the Colour, for it came from space—it is out of space—and to that space it returns, "the great outside" (59). The stone is "a frightful messenger from unformed realms of infinity beyond all Nature as we know it; from realms whose
mere existence stuns the brain and numbs us with the black extra-cosmic gulfs
it throws open before our frenzied eyes" (81). There is no bottom, neither in
the well nor in the sky; infinity stretches in both directions, an infinity with
which the Colour and its degeneration are closely associated.

In several plays Shakespeare appears reticent to explain evil. Why does as
Iago act as he does? How shall we answer the question Lear asks, lost in the
storm on his heath, "Is there any cause in nature that makes these hard
hearts" (3.6.75–76)? In Macbeth the question is externalized as the problem
about the three weïrd sisters, deflecting us from the problem of identifying
the origin of the evil in Macbeth (Calderwood 49–51). But the question also
arises in Malcolm's self-representation:

> [. . .] But there's no bottom, none,
> In my voluptuousness. Your wives, your daughters,
> Your matrons, and your maids could not fill up
> The cistern of my lust. (4.3.60–63)

And neither can the well at the Gardner farm be filled. The only solution is to let the reservoir fill the valley, but by the end of the story this solution is not satisfactory, for it cannot fill the bottomless. In *Paradise Lost* Milton constructs a complex apparatus to justify God's ways to men; but because the universe in which this justification proceeds is bottomless, because Hell is a "bottomless perdition" (1.47) or a "bottomless pit" (6.866), the universe remains inconclusive. On the other hand, Satan asserts that God has fixed the fallen angels "to the bottom of this Gulf" (1.329), as though Hell did have a limit, describing Chaos as the "dark unbottom'd infinite Abyss" (2.405) through which he will have to wander to the new world that God has created. From the perspective of Heaven, however, Chaos is a "vast immeasurable Abyss / Outrageous as a Sea, dark, wasteful, wild, / Up from the bottom turn'd by furious winds" (7.211–13). But if any category is implied by these passages, it is shattered by that word "abyss," which means "without bottom." The indeterminate nature of Milton's universe offers evil an immense play, which only the worsening nature of his Satan places a limit to: "horror and doubt distract / His troubl'd thoughts, and from the bottom stir / The Hell within him" (4.19–21).

One further theme of the play needs to be investigated, a theme more apparent in its cumulative effect than explicit. In arguing with her husband Lady Macbeth suddenly exclaims:

> [. . .] I have given suck, and know
> How tender 'tis to love the babe that milks me:
> I would, while it was smiling in my face,
> Have plucked my nipple from his boneless gums
> And dashed the brains out, had I so sworn as you
> Have done to this. (1.7.54–59)

Coming as it does 30 lines after the famous passage about pity, "like a newborn babe / Striding the blast" (1.7.21–22), it is possible to read her words allegorically, for Macbeth slays pity as well as Duncan. The witches casually mention the "finger of birth-strangled babe / Ditch-delivered by a drab" (4.1.30–31) and the sow "that hath eaten / Her nine farrow" (4.1.86–87). A Bloody Child rises in the necromantic scene. Lennox recognizes that Macbeth threatens both Fleance, the son of Banquo, and Malcolm and Donalbain, the sons of Duncan, simply because they are sons. And the audience witnesses the murder of the son of Macduff; though Macduff has other children whom Macbeth murders, it is the son that is foregrounded by the action. And at the end of the play Macbeth kills young Siward, whose father does not mourn him overmuch. Far from it. Urged to mourn, he replies simply, "They say he parted well and paid his score, / And so, God be with him" (5.8.52–53). Everyone justifies this violence against the sons by political considerations. But the language of Lady Macbeth and the witches is in excess of that justification, just as the language of Siward is deficient. The violence in part stems from Macbeth's own childless state, which the prophecy of the witches to Banquo aggravates:

> They hailed him father to a line of kings.
> Upon my head they placed a fruitless crown
> And put a barren scepter in my grip,
> Thence to be wrenched with an unlineal hand,
> No son of mine succeeding. (3.1.60–64)

It is no good thing to be a son in this play.

For the sake of contrast we may glance for a moment at *King Lear*. Children die in that play, Edmund, Goneril, Regan, and Cordelia; but only the death of the youngest daughter gives us pause, and the other three die of sibling rage, not paternal. Only Edgar is threatened by his father, a threat that does have some effect upon the imagery of the play when Gloucester enters during the storm with a lantern, to be greeted by the Fool with the words, "Look, here comes a walking fire" (3.4.106). Edgar, playing the madman, transfigures this walking fire into "the foul Flibbertigibbet," who "gives the web and the pin, squints the eye, and makes the harelip; mildews the white wheat, and hurts the poor creature of earth" (3.4.108–111). Only in this passage can we sense the atmosphere of Lovecraft's story, focused at the moment when a son fears for his life.

Though like the source of Macbeth's murderous thoughts it is difficult to identify the source of this theme, James Calderwood's investigation of the theme of increase and augmentation may help us. Given that in many Shakespeare's works, especially the sonnets, increase, the begetting of children who extend the mortal self into an immortality, is fruitfully opposed to an augmentation of the mere mortal self (63–64), we may understand why so much of the play turns against the sons whose very existence reveals Macbeth's own mortality; he stakes his existence on self-inflation and fails. In the story fecundity usurps increase; fertilized by the stone from heaven the harvest is too much and becomes hollow. The sexuality is perverse because it gives the mere appearance of increase, and so the children that it produces, orchard, flocks, and people, surrender to their own brittle condition and crumble away. Macbeth suffers a similar inflation and deflation, one measured by the distance between Lady Macbeth's expostulation, "Glamis thou art, and Cawdor, and shalt be / What thou art promised" (1.5.14–15), and Banquo's words, "Thou hast it now—king, Cawdor, Glamis, all" (3.1.1). Together the two moments form a chiasmus that emphasizes Glamis, the title Macbeth held at the beginning of the play by his own right. But in his own eyes he becomes a walking shadow, even less than Glamis. In the same way the Gardner farm expands for a short time and then contracts to dust.

The theme of the death of children unrolls further in Lovecraft's story; and this aspect is arresting, since so often in his stories the Oedipal theme plays out from the side of the child. In "The Colour out of Space" the theme plays out from the side of the father as the three sons of Nahum die their various deaths. But I do not believe that the deaths of Thaddeus, Merwin, and Zenas—rather dim characters who die dim deaths, absorbed into the "dusty death" (5.5.23) that overtakes the entire family—are the most significant examples of the theme. More interesting is the consideration that in the light of the story of Eden the entire family represents the sons of God. But the merciful God and the just God do not exist in this story. Nahum's puzzlement indicates that absence when he ruminates, "It must all be a judgment of some sort; though he could not fancy what for, since he had always walked uprightly in the Lord's ways so far as he knew" (*DH* 68). But is Nahum so guiltless? He exhibits a certain amount of pride at the fecundity of his farm, perhaps a pride at being singled out by the meteorite, and in autumn when "the pears and apples slowly ripened [. . .] Nahum vowed that his orchards were prospering as never before" (60). Nevertheless, despite his pride and despite the possible allusion to Adam's apple and Augustine's pear, the punishment is still too much. The book of Job seems more appropriate to the situation than the book of Genesis. It is hard not to apply Macbeth's words, "It is a tale / Told by an idiot, full of sound and fury, / Signifying nothing" (5.5.26–27), to Lovecraft's story. The central God of Lovecraft's theodicy is the idiot God Azathoth, who personifies the material universe shaped only by cause and effect, not purpose. This is, of course, not a universe that signifies nothing. If we were to paraphrase the meaning of the play it would not be in these words of Macbeth but in his earlier fears that it might be impossible to "trammel up the consequence" (1.7.3); the play demonstrates the existence of a moral coherence by which trespass draws after itself its own consequence. Lovecraft on occasion, following such thinkers as

Ernst Haeckel and Hugh Elliot, dreams of universes in which the Humean skepticism of cause and effect is realized, meta-universes of the idiot God Azathoth which truly signify nothing. In "The Colour out of Space" we read how a messenger from those universes invades the garden of this world and how thereby the sons of God, the people who believe in a just God who assures coherence, are destroyed.

The justice of Milton's God, however, is the very point that has been in contention among the readers of the epic almost as soon as it was written. The proem to the epic reverses the Pauline task to explain God's justification of man. Milton's task, to "justify the ways of God to men" (1.26) has become a critical difficulty, for rather than achieving that justification his attempt has lead such readers as Blake and Empson to charge God the Father with an "infinite malice" (38) because the Father's actions appear "intended to lead [Satan] into greater evil" (42). The problem with the defense of Milton's God, as in Hugh MacCallum's study *The Sons of God*, is that the author says very little about Satan and the rebel angels as such sons. Yet they remain sons by creation as much as the angels whose sonship is confirmed by their fidelity. Though MacCallum emphasizes Milton's denial of the equality of the Son and examines closely how the Christ becomes the Son only through the will of the Father (39–47), he denies Satan by omission and thereby perpetuates the divine anger. The acts of mediation, so important a part of the doctrine of the Son as he takes part in the creation and chooses to become the redeemer of fallen humanity through "the renewal of the image of God in man" (7, 29, 57), are broken in the case of Satan, who attempts to undo creation, disgusted at being replaced by the human flesh (79–81). This theme is carried over in Lovecraft's story by the fact that the message that the stone bears cannot be read; mediation is broken and the image of coherence in the human flesh destroyed. From another point of view, however, the messenger does renew the image of humanity by reducing the Gardners to their real existence as they sink back into the material chaos that composes the universe; but their true existence, that of the affectional life, reveals and accuses the anger that is turned upon them, hence the tone of lament that permeates the story.

With that lament in mind we can ask whether anything in the theme of the sons destroyed by the father appealed to Lovecraft's own situation, and the answer may lie in the words with which Lady Macduff refers to her son: "Fathered he is, and yet he's fatherless" (4.2.27). Though the son rejects her joke, her insistence is disturbing; and *pace* Donald R. Burleson's book it disturbs more than the universe. The scene is played for wit, but the audience is perfectly aware, as the mother and son are not, that the hand of the bad father, the sonless Macbeth, is about to reach out and kill her and her son. From this point of view we may regard the description of Mrs. Gardner's and Thaddeus's screams in the attic "from behind their locked doors," as though "in some terrible language that was not of this earth" (DH 66), as an expressive hyperbole for the period during which Lovecraft and his mother lived alone with one another, when she was going insane and he was suffering a breakdown that is still obscure. Since in the deaths of his father and grandfather so much of the agony of the family can be located, but located without explanation and without excuse, those deaths may themselves seem dooms upon him and his mother, impossible to deal with except through the mediation of art.

The pervasiveness of this theme, the destruction of the sons of God, sheds a further light upon the allusion to the Christmas story that Burleson noted ("Prismatic Heroes" 14). If Lovecraft is indeed playing upon the descent of Jesus from heaven to earth to be born in a humble stable in Bethlehem, the doctrine of the kenosis by which the divine empties itself into the human (Phil. 2:5–11), an event greeted by the "glory of the Lord" that shines around the shepherds and terrifies them in the appearance of angels (Luke 2:9) and also greeted by the epiphany of a star to the three wise men, then he may also be playing upon the story of Herod whose reaction to the message of the wise men is to slay "all the children that were in Bethlehem, and in all the coasts thereof, from two years and under" (Matt. 2:16). In Lovecraft's story the innocent die, the Pentecostal fire destroys, and the inner Parousia slowly visits a judgment upon the sanity of the narrator.

But though the Christmas story seems crucial to "The Colour out of Space," we need to reiterate that the fall of the angels, the fall of Adam and Eve, and the crucifixion story are also crucial; for if as Burleson says the stone suffers various trials at the hands of the scientists, the wise of this world ("Prismatic Heroes" 15–16[6]), it also descends to the Hell that the "nefandous well" (DH 80), a "black pit" (74), represents. Once Milton refers to the "Pit of Hell" (1.381), three times to the "infernal pit" (1.657, 2.850, 4.964), and once to the "bottomless pit" (6.866). Perhaps more apt to "The

---

6. In justice to Burleson's argument, he regards the chemical tests as an initiation rite and the underground of the story as the presence of the entity at the roots of the trees; I use his analysis of a generalized monomyth as a guide to how the story works in terms of the several other doctrinal parodies and inversions to be found in Lovecraft's story.

Colour out of Space" than the kenosis narrative, in the light of these passages, is Milton's story of Satan's descent upon earth, his entrance into Eden
through an underground river and fountain (9.74–75), his first temptation of
Eve, "Squat like a Toad, close at [her] ear" as she sleeps (4.800), his departure from earth as his nature becomes slowly degraded, yet in the Fall the
world-wide extension of his influence. The word "pit" indicates the infernal
background of the story.

   Another passage is also telling. At the end of the story the farm where
"the blight is spreading" is called "the dark realm" (*DH* 80), surely a remarkable hyperbole for the modest farm, all the more striking when three paragraphs later the stone is referred to as a messenger "from unformed realms of
infinity beyond all Nature as we know it; from realms whose mere existence
stuns the brain and numbs us with the black extra-cosmic gulfs it throws
open before our frenzied eyes" (81). In *Paradise Lost* two passages seem apt.
Belial speculates that the angels of Heaven may pursue the fallen hosts "far
and wide into the Realm of night" (2.133). Upon his return from earth Satan
announces to Sin and Death that he has "made one Realm / Hell and this
World, one Realm, one Continent / Of easy thorough-fare" (10.391–93).
Behind all this language lies the complaint of Mephistophilis in Marlowe's
Faust; the stone cast out of the outside space that is inconceivable to human
categories suffers this hell of earth and longs to escape it. Thus Lovecraft's
language is especially telling because it suggests that once the entity leaves
its proper place beyond our universe and comes to earth it becomes hellish,
or at least is perceived as such, and slowly spreads, since under the aspect of
eternity no place is safe from the possible infection of an outside. If in *Macbeth* murder has the consequence of delusion, insanity, and isolation, and if
in *Paradise Lost* rebellion and fall have the consequence of suffering, world
history, and redemption, so in "The Colour out of Space" the constitution of
the universe implies that nothing is safe from chaos; we cannot read the
message of the messenger, but we can detect its activity and effects, insanity,
isolation, and ruin, a Hell on earth into which one may descend but which
no one can harrow and no one fully leave. Thus in its ascension the entity
leaves a part of itself still on earth, a perverse spirit that causes a blight to
creep across the land and that disrupts the dreams of the narrator. And that
narrator, the most immediate messenger of the story, cannot say like the
messengers who reported the deaths of his children to Job, "And I only am
escaped alone to tell thee" (1.19), for the narrator realizes that any survey is
hopeless in the face of the chaos that the blight represents and through his

diseased dreams he knows that his pious hopes for the purification of the
blasted heath are futile. The lassitude of this equivocal place is disordered
and disordering. Thus the chiasmic pattern of the kenosis narrative and the
Satan narrative is partially broken in Lovecraft's story.

What is the world reflected in these blasted heaths? The world of Hell,
inhabited by fallen angels, the rebel sons of God the Father, and also inhabited by those angels through whom the Father exerts his anger. Milton's
blasted heath silhouettes those angels as trees upon which a punishing lightning plays, as well as those angels as trees that lift their swords against God;
it is a field of battle. Shakespeare's blasted heath is a field of battle also, a
battle of rebellion, upon which the witches speak equivocal words. Through
its fecundity Lovecraft's blasted heath confuses the categories of plenitude
and emptiness. Caught between these various forces that so far exceed them,
unable to rebel although they believe that they can and unable to protect
themselves, the sons of God are destroyed—not without reason, however,
for their mere presumption of innocence, a category that does not exist in
the universe of the story, lays them open to destruction. They know just
enough, something of the witch in them, to bring them to call for that destruction. We cannot avoid the implications of these references in "The
Colour out of Space." Though the Colour may be indifferent to human concerns, it creates a Hell that energizes and undermines everything it touches;
the paradoxes and equivocations destabilize and revolt against conventional
hierarchies and thereby become an expression of anger and retribution. But
the retribution is not for any one trespass that Nahum can put his finger on.
The Gardners have not murdered authority, no more than has Ammi or the
narrator; but none of them is allowed either Macbeth's brave resistance or
Adam and Eve's brave acquiescence at the beginning of human history; they
are only allowed a "dusty death," disproportionate to any weakness. The retribution, then, must be for their very weakness, insofar as they represent our
weakness, the lassitude of our language that offers only so much knowledge,
a lassitude that we cannot overcome, and our inability to absorb the unknown that is a part of existence. In terms of our treatment in the last chapter of this work of the theme of life-in-death in Lovecraft's work, these
angels and Macbeth and the Gardners take their place in the living dead,
lost and aimless except in terms of their "deathwards progressing," to mis-
employ that wonderful phrase in Keats (*The Fall of Hyperion* 1.260), as
though entangled in a metaphysical heat-death; but the heart of this movement toward death lies in the two-sidedness of our words.

Lovecraft and Lawrence on the Hidden Gods

The occupation—or is it a vocation?—that emerges from our work in these pages is one of *recollecting the Gods* in all psychological activity. This is what archetypal psychology implies at its most fundamental level, and this is why archetypal psychology is necessarily nonagnostic and polytheistic. The images to which it turns and which give faith in psychic reality invoke the powers of religion just as images have always done. By entering the imagination we cross into numinous precincts. (Hillman 226)

Recent studies of "The Colour out of Space" have explored its dense literary quality. As a story that alludes to and plays with a variety of texts, it has slowly become to the minds of careful readers as iridescent a work as the stone it celebrates. First, it contains a network of allusions and parodies of various biblical moments: the destruction of Sodom and Gomorrah; the leading of the children of Israel out of Egypt; the incarnation, death, resurrection, and second coming of Christ; and the prophecies of the antichrist.[1] Most of these allusions parody the original texts as well as suggest an apocalyptic event. Also, as we have discussed, it layers allusions to *Macbeth* with allusions to *Paradise Lost*.[2] What we have not yet recognized is the possibility that some of the imagery of Lovecraft's story that we have so far ascribed to biblical material and some of its salient themes may have been suggested by Lovecraft's reading D. H. Lawrence's long novella *St. Mawr*, which appeared two years before Lovecraft's work. Once more, as Gayford and Mariconda have argued, we must consider the extent to which Lovecraft has connections with modernism

The evidence for this possibility is indirect. Lovecraft refers to Lawrence only twice in the letters, some three years after the writing of "The Colour out of Space." The second reference is appreciative, clearly the result of some thought. It begins by contrasting to writers who "violate people's inherited sensibilities for no adequate reason" other writers "whose affronts to conven-

---

1. Price ("A Biblical Precedent" 23–25), Burleson (*Lovecraft* 116), and Waugh ("Landscapes" 234–36) deal with these allusions in detail.
2. Burleson (*Lovecraft* 111–13) also discusses these particulars.

tion are merely incidents in a sincere and praiseworthy struggle to interpret or symbolize life as it is" (*SL* 3.264). Among these he would include Voltaire, Rabelais, Lawrence, and Fielding: "We would be simply foolish not to recognise the vigourously honest intent to see and depict life as a balanced whole, which everywhere animates their productions. When they commit a blunder in technique or proportioning, it is our place to excuse it—whether it concern a difficult or a common theme—and not to adopt a leering or sanctimoniously horrified attitude if the theme happens to be difficult" (*SL* 3.264–65). As for censorship, so often a question that arose with Lawrence's career, Lovecraft is not greatly concerned because "no censorship law ever kept any high-grade scholar from reading and owning all the books he needs—Bostonians read Dreiser and Lawrence, and Tennesseeans understand the principles of biology" (*SL* 3.265). As is so often his wont, Lovecraft draws back from the fray: "But life is a bore! And I don't know but that the frank expressers are about as damned a bore as the vacant-skull'd suppressors! That's why I light out for the fifth dimension" (*SL* 3.266). We must wonder, however, whether before he lit out "beyond the rim of Einsteinian space-time" (*SL* 3.266) Lovecraft had in fact like that Bostonian read Lawrence.

It is possible. The novella was published by Knopf in 1925 and from May through November reviewed in such places as the London *Saturday Review*, the *Nation and Athenaeum*, the *New York Times Book Review*, the *New Statesman*, the *New Republic*, the *Saturday Review of Literature*, and the *Dial* (Roberts 75–76). The publication of anything by Lawrence was not a minor event. And it is possible that Lawrence's repetitive, hypnotic style, exploring in close detail the atmosphere of a landscape, might have appealed to Lovecraft, whose aesthetic depends so much on atmosphere. Whether he had read that story, a passage in "Supernatural Horror in Literature" indicates that he had read Lawrence's ground-breaking *Studies in Classic American Literature* (D 402), which had been published in 1923. Apropos of Hawthorne's *The Marble Faun* Lovecraft writes that the romance "cannot help but being interesting despite the persistent incubus of moral allegory, anti-Popery propaganda, and a Puritan prudery which has caused the late D. H. Lawrence to express a longing to treat the author in a highly undignified manner" (D 402)—perhaps, his memory in this point not being too good, referring to Lawrence's image of Sinful Man in *The Blithedale Romance* dropping his pants for a flogging (111). Lawrence and Lovecraft are interested in different Hawthornes; the Englishman is fascinated by the duplicities of *The Scarlet Letter* and *The Blithedale Romance*, whereas the American is interested in *The Marble Faun* and *The House of the*

Seven Gables. Nevertheless, I think Lawrence did guide Lovecraft's reading of Hawthorne; and Lawrence's description of the American attempt to slough off European consciousness and to grow a new consciousness may also have attracted him. Most often, Lawrence writes, the laborious process plunges the American into a profound sickness:

> Out! Out! He cries, in all kinds of euphemisms.
> He's got to have his new skin on him before ever he can get out.
> And he's got to get out before his new skin can ever be his own skin.
> So there he is, a torn, divided monster.
> The true American, who writhes and writhes like a snake that is long in sloughing (62)

Wilbur Whateley in "The Dunwich Horror," trying to introduce an alien monster, his brother, through the means of the *Necronomicon*, a book of hidden wisdom from the old world, suffers this fate, a "torn, divided monster" on the floor of the Miskatonic Library, naked at last and revealing his nakedness that is such an affront to received wisdom. The story renders in narrative terms the analysis Lovecraft makes of the contradictions of Puritanism in the early paragraphs of "The Picture in the House." He and Lawrence are not far apart when they consider the dilemmas of being an American. By 1935, however, he considers Lawrence "overrated" ("Letters to Lee McBride White" 36).

With all these points in mind, let us consider Lawrence's novella. *St. Mawr* relates the story of a young woman who because of her encounter with a totemic Welsh horse decides to leave her husband and his shallow English society for the mountains and desert of Arizona. It is a conversion story that challenges basic assumptions of contemporary life, even the assumption that sexuality and intimacy can save the individual or that individual psychology has any significance whatever. Instead, the novella investigates the kerygma of the horse and of the western landscape. It is the description of that landscape, the climax of the novella, that most concerns our interest in Lovecraft; but the work has other moments that would have interested him, and we shall begin with them.

First we should note the story of the horse itself, staring out of the darkness as a challenging presence that is both solar with its sun-arched neck and chthonic with a neck that starts forth like a snake; he is a stallion, but does not "seem to fancy the mares, for some reason" (12), and his Welsh name means St. Mary. He is phallic, as his "lovely naked head" and his resemblance to a snake indicate, but he is also feminine; opposites coincide in him. When Lou Witt, the protagonist, looks at him that first time he stands there, "his ears back, his face averted, but attending as if he were some lightning-conductor" (12). The crisis of the novella occurs when the horse rears up and falls upon her husband who, not man enough to master it, pulls it back onto himself. One of the uncertainties of the work is whether the horse startles at a whistle or at the sight of a snake that children have stoned to death; but the text makes it most probable that it startles in sympathy with the death of an akin spirit. That image of the snake is to recur much more forcefully at the end of the novella.

Horses play a part in Lovecraft's story. Ammi's horse is sensitive to the transformation of the landscape (DH 61), breaks loose when the Colour in the well begins to move (71), and in the climax of the story screams and dies: "That was the last of Hero till they buried him next day" (77). The totemic name "Hero" indicates its chthonic aspect, the son of the Great Mother and the snake (Harrison, Themis 260–94). In addition, the name is androgynous if we keep in mind the Hero for whom Leander drowns or the Hero of Much Ado about Nothing. And St. Mawr no more endures to the end of Lawrence's novella than Lovecraft's Hero does; before Lou retires to her ranch where she has her climactic vision, her stallion deserts his heroic celibacy to chase after mares. No god is the ultimate god.

This description of the horses in Lovecraft's story, however, in no way testifies to the real presence of St. Mawr, for with his androgyny, his power, his hidden threat, and his character as a conductor of lightning, he much more suggests the role of the meteor, that messenger from another world. It is a phallic stone, but with hollows inside. It possesses "a torrid invulnerability" (DH 58) that renders it immune to chemical solvents. Most interestingly, the color of St. Mawr is difficult to fix. At first he is described simply as a bay, but three paragraphs later, when Saintsbury pats him, "Lou saw the brilliant skin of the horse crinkle a little in apprehensive anticipation, like the shadow of the descending hand on a bright red-gold liquid" (11). He emanates "a dark, invisible fire" that indicates his danger (12) and his kinship to the oxymoronic "darkness visible" of Milton's hell (1.63); he has already killed two men, Mr. Griffith Edwards's son who had "his skull smashed in" and a groom "crushed [. . .] against the side of the stall" (13). The influence from the meteor kills Gardner's sons, and the horse kills the young also, culminating in the injury he wreaks on Lou's husband.

Before Lou's vision on the ranch another god is introduced, the god Pan. The son of Hermes, himself an ambiguous figure in Greek mythology, Pan is both goat and human, an image that may have influenced the traditional Christian image of the devil with his sharp ears, tail, and cloven hoof. He feeds his flock of goats (Pan may in fact not mean "all" but "the feeder"), plays his pan-pipes, and sometimes at noon causes a panic in anyone who encounters him. Coleridge in a proto-Lawrentian mood read the figure as "intelligence blended with a darker power, deeper, mightier, and more universal than the conscious intellect of man" (2.93). Lawrence introduces a slightly different Pan, however, through a character that to some extent resembles an ironic self-image of the parody of Lawrence that was beginning to move through the popular press; this character, Cartwright, a man who dabbles in alchemy and the occult, is about thirty-eight years old (53), and Lawrence was almost forty when he began the novella.

Lawrence, however, may have had someone else in mind, whom Lovecraft would have recognized, Arthur Machen, a Welshman with a taste for the occult who in 1894 published a novella well known in its day, *The Great God Pan*. With his eyes "that twinkled and expanded like a goat's" (53), Cartwright is emblematic of the priapic god, but he argues that Pan is a force beyond the male and the female: "Pan was the hidden mystery—the hidden cause. That's how it was a Great God. Pan wasn't *he* at all" (54). This god transcends the misogyny inherent in Machen's story, at the conclusion of which a beautiful woman disintegrates into a loathsome jelly: "I saw the form waver from sex to sex, dividing itself from itself, and then again reunited. Then I saw the body descend to the beasts when it ascended, and that which was on the heights go down into the depths, even to the abyss of all being" (1.65). Finally a form appears that cannot be described, but "the symbol of this form may be seen in ancient sculptures [. . .] as a horrible and indescribable shape, neither man nor beast" (1.65). Helen Vaughan, however, through whom in Machen's story Pan is incarnated into the world of the *fin de siècle*, is not monstrous because of her descent to the original protoplasm, but because she engages in bisexual relations that transgress gender categories; though Pan is incarnate in a woman, the imagery attempts to suggest a biological force that lies beneath the male and female. And thus we return to Lawrence's vision.

A more classical Pan appears in E. M. Forster's 1902 tale, "The Story of a Panic," in which an "indescribably repellent" (1) young boy called Eustace becomes the apparent receptacle of the god when on a picnic with his relatives in the hills above Ravello, in a hollow that resembles "a many-fingered green hand, palm upwards, which was clutching convulsively to keep us in its grasp" (2). When everyone runs in a fit of inexplicable animal terror—

call it panic—Eustace remains behind and undergoes a transformation; goat-prints surround him at their return, evidence to his tutor that "the Evil One has been very near us in bodily form" (9). Worse than all this, however, is the sudden friendship that Eustace now feels for their Italian servant, who dies that night as Eustace escapes them in a pantheistic ecstasy:

> He spoke first of night and the stars and planets above his head, of the swarms of fireflies below him, of the invisible sea below the fireflies, of the great rocks covered with anemones and shells [. . .]. He spoke of the rivers and waterfalls, of the ripening bunches of grapes, of the smoking cone of Vesuvius and the hidden fire-channels that made the smoke, of the myriads of lizards who were lying curled up in the crannies of the sultry earth. (16)

Like Machen's Pan, this is a being whose sheer power is inimicable to human life. The lesbian imagery of Machen's story transforms itself here into gay imagery, but the point of sexual transgression and transformation is the same.

When Lawrence read Forster's story in 1915 he objected fiercely: "Don't you see Pan is the undifferentiated root and stem drawing out of unfathomable darkness, and my Angels and Devils are old-fashioned symbols for the flower into which we strive to burst? [. . .] But your Pan is a stumping back to the well head, a perverse pushing back the waters to their source, and saying, the source is everything" (*Letters* 2.275–76). The myth, in Lawrence's view, is always insufficient; he does not want to examine where Pan came from but where the force Pan symbolizes is going. Lawrence looks toward the difficult future. Pan needs to disappear into the landscape, become once more a hidden god, if he is to become potent. Given Forster's story it is not surprising that a poem by Aleister Crowley, "Hymn to Pan," written in 1929, makes something of the same point as Forster's story but in a much crasser mode. The second line, "O man! My man!" is a quasi-refrain in the poem. The frankly phallic imagery of "the token erect of thorny thigh" (l. 44) prepares the appeal, "I am a man: / Do as thou wilt, as a great god can" (ll. 48–49). This great god, however, is at least as much animal as human, so the voice of the lover cries:

> Io Pan! Io Pan Pan! I am awake
> In the grip of the snake.
> The eagle slashes with beak and claw;
> The gods withdraw. (ll. 51–54)

This language, its rhythms and its imagery, is closer to that of Lawrence than that of Forster. Though it is later than Lawrence's work and Lovecraft's, it is revelatory of the possibilities inherent in the demigod.

Much earlier in 1908 Kenneth Grahame in *The Wind in the Willows* had drawn Pan as a Christ-figure, the true Christ of the animals, following a tradition based upon a story that Plutarch related, one found in Elizabeth Barrett Browning's "The Dead Pan" and Friedrich Schiller's "Die Götter Griechenlands." A sailor, Thamus, hearing a command in the air "to proclaim that the great god Pan has died," does so and hears a loud lament (Plutarch 400–403). "As this story coincided with the birth (or crucifixion) of Christ it was thought to herald the end of the old world and the beginning of the new"; scholars today connect the story with the traditional lament for the fertility god Tammuz or Adonis ("Pan" 663). Something ambiguous resides, then, in the traditional interpretations of the story; either the voice announced the birth of Christ and the dispersal of the pagan gods, including Pan, or, more interestingly, it implied that Pan, the all who was the logos of the world, had died. In Grahame's novel Christ manifests himself as Pan, the god who cares for every lost creature but always allows the creature to forget its terror, "lest the awful remembrance should remain and grow, and overshadow mirth and pleasure, and the great haunting memory should spoil all the after-lives of little animals" (77; ch.7). But what if this terror of death were not removed? What kind of Pan would that indifference to death imply?

Lawrence and Lovecraft are aware of a Pan quite different from Grahame's, one much more ambiguous than we have observed so far, in Hawthorne's romance *The Marble Faun*. The work concerns four friends in Rome, one of whom, a young innocent named Donatello, bears an uncanny resemblance to the statue of a faun; so his friends believe, though only a few minutes later they doubt the resemblance because "faces change so much, from hour to hour, that the same set of features has often no keeping with itself" (9.20), any more than the stone out of space has any keeping with itself. Nevertheless, Donatello may more than resemble the faun, since he refuses to allow anyone to touch his ears, hidden by his thick hair. But though in the fancy of his friends he seems to incarnate the golden age and Eden, he suffers a fall, throwing a man over a cliff to his death, and Donatello's guilt infects the innocence of his friends. As one of them says, perhaps meaning more than she realizes, "If there be any such dreadful mixture of good and evil [. . .], then the good is turned to poison, not the evil to wholesomeness" (10.244–45). Hawthorne is in some perplexity about such an argument, and his perplexity extends throughout the ambiguous work, but Lovecraft would wholeheartedly agree, and "The Colour out of Space" may be read as a confirmation of that view. *The Marble Faun* concerns several mixtures, human and animal, natural and supernatural, innocence and guilt, real and fantastic, male and female, European and American, Puritan and Catholic, mixtures by which the characters are attracted and repulsed. However we understand these mixtures, we must take this language almost literally in the case of the innocent Puritan Hilda who witnessed Donatello's murder: "Poor well-spring of a virgin's heart, into which a murdered corpse has casually fallen, and when it could not be drawn forth again, but lay there [. . .] tainting its sweet atmosphere with the scent of crime and ugly death" (10.168–69). Machen, Forster, and Crowley suggest something much more sinister, Lawrence something much more powerful, and Lovecraft something much more aloof. For Lovecraft of course knows of Pan. By 1920 he had passed beyond his pretty classicizing and wrote of "dreaded Pan, whose queer companions are many" (D 30). Considering Machen, Crowley, Forster, Grahame, and Hawthorne, we now have a better idea who those queer companions would be. One year after Lovecraft wrote "The Colour out of Space" the figure of Pan clearly shaped the description of the goatish Wilbur Whateley, revealed as a powerful and alien sexual force in his death.

Several of Machen's and Lawrence's details recur in Lovecraft's story, the deliquescence, the death of god, the physical and the moral fall, the well, and the taint of innocence. Lovecraft is not surprised by the bisexuality, since he had found in Margaret Murray's account of the witch-cult a description of its god that contained bisexual elements. Originally, she wrote, "the god of this cult was incarnate in a man, a woman, or an animal; the animal form being apparently earlier than the human, for the god was often spoken of as wearing the skin or attributes of an animal" (12), not surprisingly of a goat or a horse (68–70). Murray does not suggest that Pan was this god but indicates the two-faced god Janus, Dianus, or Diana (12). So bisexual details find their place in "The Colour out of Space." The stone and its hollow globules are both male and female, testicles and womb. The lightning-bolt is a male fertility motif, but the iridescence of the Colour suggests Iris, the goddess of the rainbow. It lies in the water of the well, but it ascends to the constellation Cygnus, the swan into which Zeus transformed himself in order to seduce Leda. The Colour manifests itself as both male and female. In this regard it is significant that in St. Mawr two major characters, Lewis and Lou, bear the same name.

Lawrence hints in a number of ways that Pan, whatever Pan may be, presides over the crisis in which St. Mawr rears back. It is noon, the panic hour, and the whistle may indicate the sound of the Pan-pipe, a detail found in

Forster's story. When the horse rears, "his eyes were arched, his nostrils wide, his face ghastly in a sort of panic [. . .], his face in panic, almost like some terrible lizard" (67). The horse becomes the embodiment of the chthonic moment that in Pan appears as terror.

The figure of Pan recurs in Lawrence's novella when Lewis, the Welsh groom, speaking out of the darkness where Pan lives (95) reacts to a falling star by telling Lou's mother how it feels to live inside a mythology. For Lewis the trees are alive, watching the humans who move among them and eager to hurt them; the trees watch and listen and will kill the humans if possible (95–96). He reacts in this way because for him the sky is not the empty space suggested by Newtonian science, not like "an empty house with a slate falling from the roof"; instead, "many things twitch and twitter in the sky, and many things happen beyond us," and so when a meteor falls from the sky Lewis thinks, "They're throwing something to us from the distance, and we've got to have it, whether we want it or not" (97). Just as Lovecraft animates the universe of Einsteinian space with an indifference that seems malevolent and also describes trees thrashing in a windless night, Lawrence argues for a world where neutral space is filled with a vital life.

Closely connected with the figure of Pan is the myth of the horse that so much concerns the plot of the novel. When Lou first encounters the horse he already bears a totemic impact, his eyes arching out of the darkness with a challenge that Lou slowly responds to as the novella proceeds. He is demonic, like the classical daemons that encounter mortals in a personal fashion. Half snakelike, though with the sun in his neck, he represents an early version of the divinity that appears at the end of the novella. Lovecraft develops very little of this in connection with the horse itself, but it is possible that this imagery combines with the image of the oracular, cannibal horses in *Macbeth* to produce the horse that takes on an admonitory character in "The Colour out of Space."

The climax of Lawrence's novella occurs in an impassioned description of "the power and the slight horror of the pre-sexual primeval world" that Lou finds in the Arizona landscape. Lawrence's profound distrust of human individualism expresses itself as the individual vanishes in the animated divine landscape, a landscape where "pillars of cloud" appear in the desert that the mountain ranch that Lou has bought surveys. This is a divinity, however, that only slowly appears and that explicitly has nothing to do with the Christian god of love. It is a world "before and after the God of Love" (139), a repudiation of Grahame's Pan. First the "debasing" (133) and "invidious" malevolence of the landscape is once more insisted upon; it "unpiths" and eats the soul of anyone who attempts to live within it a life of trade and production (133–34). Especially, it reduces a New England woman who had moved there with her husband. No longer able to speak, she spends her days staring (137), unable to engage "the seething cauldron of lower life, seething on the very tissue of the higher life, seething the soul away, seething at the marrow" (141), a passage that recalls both the disintegration of Helen in Machen's story and the cauldron of the witches in *Macbeth*. The landscape, which is also to say the demonic divinity that is slowly becoming manifest within it, transforms her into a corpse that she tries to hide from, "the corpse of her New England belief in a world ultimately all for love" (141). And what happens to the New England woman happens to Lou's mother: "She sat like a pillar of salt, her face looking what the Indians call a False Face, meaning a mask. She seemed to have crystallized into neutrality" (142). Lot's wife, who looks back at the destruction of Sodom and Gomorrah, here freezes into a mask because she is unable to move into the new world of the Arizona landscape that her daughter finds so meaningful.

This section of the novella has an obvious relevance to the description of Mrs. Gardner, the New England woman traumatized and transformed by the Colour that has fallen as though it were a falling star. She becomes sure that "something was taken away—she was being drained of something. [. . .] By July she had ceased to speak and crawled on all four" (*DH* 65). All of these events become a religious challenge. The Gardners' god was never a god of love; Lovecraft knows his Puritans too well, better than Lawrence. For Nahum Gardner election has become preterition: "it must all be a judgment of some sort; though he could not fancy what for, since he had always walked uprightly in the Lord's ways so far as he knew" (*DH* 68). For Lovecraft the visitation of the meteor has meant an emptying of any metaphysical sanction, even that god of a greater life of which Lawrence was the prophet.

One of the most telling details of Lovecraft's story is the supernatural abundance that the landscape seems to manifest even as the people are destroyed within it: "The fruit was growing to phenomenal size and unwonted gloss, and in such abundance that extra barrels were ordered to handle the coming crop" (*DH* 60), though at last everything crumbles, "and it went from mouth to mouth that there was poison in Nahum's ground" (*DH* 62). The same abundance appears in Lawrence's landscape, filled with an intense, fiery, vegetative life: "The very flowers came up bristly, and many of them were fang-mouthed, like the dead-nettle; and none had any real scent"

(138). They do, however, possess colors that declare an inhuman savagery, "the curious columbines of the stream-beds, columbines scarlet outside and yellow in, like the red and yellow of a herald's uniform" (138), or the honey-suckle, "the purest, most perfect vermilion scarlet, cleanest fire-colour, hang-ing in long drops like a shower of fire-rain that is just going to strike the earth" (139), or "the rush of red sparks and Michaelmas daisies, and the tough wild sunflowers" (139). The landscape is overrun in "a battle, with banners of bright scarlet and yellow" (151). Even the roses, the traditional flower of love, are "set among spines the devil himself must have conceived in a moment of sheer ecstasy" (139).

This mention of the devil, like the earlier mention of those flowers that are "fang-mouthed" and the insistent imagery of fire, sparks, and lightning makes us consider what kind of divinity, what kind of "spirit of place" (141) inhabits this landscape. Certainly Pan has a part in it, for it had been a ranch of goats that the Mexicans called "fire-mouths, because everything they nib-ble die" (131–32), and as we noted Pan, half-goat, has been thought one of the sources of the traditional image of the devil.

The landscape, however, is animated by a deus loci that slowly becomes explicit. A part of that god can be seen in "the vast, eagle-like wheeling of the daylight, that turned as the eagles which lived in the near rocks turned overhead in the blue" (135). Beneath them "the vast strand of the desert would float with curious undulations and exhalations amid the blue fragility of mountains" (136–37). Against this, mortal life is as nothing: "The land-scape lived, and lived as the world of the gods, unsullied and unconcerned. The great circling landscape lived its own life, sumptuous and uncaring. Man did not exist for it" (137). Finally the god appears, "the animosity of the spirit of place: the crude, half-created spirit of place, like some serpent-bird for ever attacking man, in a hatred of man's onward-struggle towards further creation" (141). This is Quetzalcoatl, whom Lawrence will celebrate in his next novel, *The Plumed Serpent*.

The details of this description could have originated in many places. Though Lawrence had only arrived recently in the Southwest, he had already become fascinated by the mythic materials of the region. It may, however, have taken the shape that Tennyson's poem "The Eagle: A Fragment" could give it:

> He clasps the crag with crooked hands;
> Close to the sun in lonely lands,
> Ring'd with the azure world, he stands.

*   *   *

> The wrinkled sea beneath him crawls;
> He watches from his mountain walls,
> And like a thunderbolt he falls. (110)

Several of these details are to be found in both Lawrence and Lovecraft. In Lawrence the landscape seems a "seething cauldron" (141) where "sometimes the vast strand of the desert would float with curious undulations and exhalations" (147). In Lovecraft the narrator looks forward to the time when the reservoir "will mirror the sky and ripple in the sun. And the secrets of the strange days will be one with the deep's secrets; one with the hidden lore of old ocean" (*DH* 54). In Lawrence the lightning, a symbol of Zeus and fertility, has left a " perfect scar, white and long as lightning itself," upon a totemic pine (138); and we recall that St. Mawr is a "lightning-conductor" (12). In Lovecraft, the lightning strikes where the meteor has fallen and scarred the ground. The sense of the sun, though, is very different in these works; Lawrence shares with Tennyson a sense of its dominance in the high mountains, whereas Lovecraft mutes the sun as he represents the viewpoint of the Gardner family, slowly drowned in the effects of the miasmal Colour. A difference between Tennyson's and Lawrence's vision and Lovecraft's is the ring and circle of the horizon that obsesses the English imagination, the open space of the great world, and Lovecraft's narrow landscape of a claustrophobic New England valley. Tennyson's eagle appears in Lawrence as an actual creature and as part of the metaphoric landscape. Though no explicit eagle appears in Lovecraft, the lightning itself, as his classical mind would have recognized, belonged to Zeus, whose bird is the eagle. He would, in fact, have been aware of the portent in the *Iliad* when an eagle seizes a snake:

> *Jove*'s Bird on sounding Pinions beat the Skies;
> A bleeding Serpent of enormous Size,
> His Talons truss'd; alive, and curling round,
> He stung the Bird, whose Throat receiv'd the Wound.
> Mad with the Smart, he drops the fatal Prey,
> In airy Circles wings his painful way. (12.233–39)

Hector's brother warns that the eagle "Retards our host" (12.258); it warns humanity not to exceed its limit. More generally, the portent is an image of the antagonism between the sky and the earth; though it is the first plumed serpent that appears in European literature, before anyone in Europe had known or begun to interpret world mythology, it represents a failure at reconciling sky and earth, rather like what occurs in Lovecraft's story

Another way to understand Tennyson's lines presents itself, however, and thereby another way to understand *St. Mawr* and "The Colour out of Space." Given the traditional significance of the eagle as an emblem of contemplation (cf. Dante, *Purg.* 9.17–31), its domination of the earth may symbolize the poetic imagination, attempting in a lordly fashion to seize its subject, a seizure that is no more successful than is Coleridge's "Kubla Khan," if we keep in mind that each poem presents itself as a fragment, Coleridge's rather awkwardly so. Lawrence's novella is also a fragment; its failure of closure points beyond itself to the novel he was shortly to write, *The Plumed Serpent*, in which he would much more thoroughly investigate the cultural, sexual, and political meanings of that archetype. Like the eagle that circles and submerges itself in its landscape, Lawrence perceives himself as circling and submerging himself in every new landscape in which he attempts to find the new form of the gods that shall be.

This interpretation allows us to reconsider Lovecraft's story as an attempt to revision his own poetic imagination; that is to say, in James Hillman's sense of the word, he treats the Colour as a myth of his own power to create weird fiction. When the Colour returns to the sky it aims itself at Deneb in the constellation of the Swan, which is a traditional image of the poet. Socrates seems to put aside irony when he imagines himself as a swan, one that as a poet and a philosopher praises the good things it shall see after its death (Phaedo 85b). With more irony and more akin to Lovecraft's mode, at the end of the second book of the *Odes* Horace imagines himself as a half-human and half-swan, almost but not quite transformed into the great bard he believes and fears[3] that he shall be regarded as after his death. Lovecraft's Colour remains in this halfway state, bizarre and threatening while a small part of it remains in the well to infect Ammi, the narrator, and the reader. In this infection Lovecraft imagines his art as successful, but insofar as it cannot return to that great otherness in which it originates it is unsuccessful; and even the return aims at Deneb, the tail of the Swan, not its eyes or its wings. And just as the Swan in the constellation represents the swan into which Zeus transformed himself when he seduced Leda, with its own voice echoing internally, "Ipse deum Cycnus condit vocemque sub illo, / non totus volucer, secumque immumurat intus" [The swan itself conceals a god and his voice within him, / not completely a bird,

---

3. Horace was anxious that after his death his poetry would be good for nothing but teaching children their grammar (*Epis.* 1.20.17–18); and that is today too often our introduction to this poet.

and murmurs to itself within] (Manilius 5.381–82), just so the Colour, a messenger from the outside, retains its secret within itself; and Lovecraft, despite
his voluminous letters, retains the secret of his creativity in the dreams from
which so many of the stories originate. Tennyson's and Lawrence's imaginations glory in the day, Lovecraft's in the night. Tennyson's eagle, a contempla-
tive that stands "Close to the sun in lonely lands" and with great energy falls
upon its prey, performs an act of the apocalyptic imagination that informs the
sense of final things that we find in both Lawrence and Lovecraft.

These final things, the consummation of the world and its judgment, are
quite complex in both authors. In Lawrence it is a question of what gods shall
appear and what gods the protagonist Lou shall serve. She gives an indication
of this service early in her approach to her Arizona farm, as she turns to the
hidden gods and the hidden fire. Now it is no longer a question of Pan, but of
various mythological presences, which correspond to and argue with "the suc-
cessive inner sanctuaries of herself" (129). As she puts it, the chief god shall be
"my Apollo mystery of the inner fire," which is also "the hidden fire [. . .] alive
and burning in the sky" (129). It is as though she were about to become a Ves-
tal virgin, the oracle of Delphi, and St. Simon Stylites all at once, dedicated to
the gods that rule the zenith of the sky and the private hearth.

In contrast to this god, the goats of Pan that once roamed the mountain
are the spirits of inertia with their fire-mouths that kill everything and their
smell that "came up like some uncanny acid fire" (132), the creatures that
represent all the forces that slew the New England woman. These preside
over the poison-weed and the "curious disintegration working all the time, a
sort of malevolent breath, like a stupefying, irritant gas, coming out of the
unfathomed mountains" (133). This language is very like that language that
Lovecraft uses to describe the effect of the Colour that has left a scar on the
landscape "like a great spot eaten by acid" (DH 55), on occasion like a gas
that brushes past Ammi or the narrator and leaves them unable to react.
Above all, it is a venom and poison that cannot be leached out of the soil
(DH 65) and that in the climactic moment is revealed as an "undimensioned
rainbow of cryptic poison from the well" (DH 78). In both books the inimical
powers are fiery, impalpable, acidic, and poisonous, the destructive forces of
the snake that has not raised itself from the earth.

Nevertheless, despite this mythological mode we cannot help but admit
that Lovecraft's story contains little imagery that makes a direct connection
with either an eagle or with any other kind of bird except the poultry that
"turned greyish and died very quickly, their meat being found dry and noisome

upon cutting" (*DH* 66), a nasty death from which we can draw very little haruspical consequence. His serpent is not plumed. Mrs. Gardner seems to perceive things that "moved and changed and fluttered" (*DH* 65); the trees are "clawing at the grey November sky" (*DH* 69), at the crisis "twitching morbidly and spasmodiacally, clawing in convulsive and epileptic madness at the moonlit clouds; scratching impotently" (*DH* 76), but they are never able to escape the ground in the flight that they desire. This eagle tears from underneath the earth, not from above it. The plumed serpent does not appear. In this landscape Lovecraft can see no way how the things above and the things below can be reconciled; the *coincidentia oppositorum* does not take place. Though it comes from the sky and returns to it, a sign in the heavens and its messenger, this monster assumes a peloric form in the well; the reader perceives it for only a short time as a teratic portent.[4] It returns, explosively propelled from the center of the earth into the otherness from which it came, but a portion of it falls back; it tries to become one or the other but lags behind both. It is too, too American, "a torn, divided monster."

But whether the monster is peloric or "a hidden fire," what is the status of the monster and the fiction? Though the two stories work towards a revelation that is very similar, the differences are striking. Lovecraft's short story, to the mind of many critics his best,[5] is condensed and unveering and inevitable. Lawrence's novella is more diffuse, beginning as an analysis of a modern marriage, moving into a satire of modern culture, and only at the end revealing itself as a religious challenge. Also, something of a reversal of expectations takes place here. Lovecraft, the quondam disciple of Poe, deserts his fantastic pantheon and makes a number of decisive steps by which "The Colour out of Space" becomes a science fiction work rather than a weird tale, though not a science fiction work that remains content with the Newtonian laws of science. Lawrence, who began as a naturalist in the mode of Hardy, creates in the final pages of the novella, to use his own term, a fantasia of the unconscious that plays with a variety of mythological figures; he is as discontent as Lovecraft with the Newtonian universe.

Who would have expected that they could meet across such differences?

---

4. I have in mind here the contrast that Jane Harrison drew between teratic and peloric manifestations; the teratic is a sign in the sky, the peloric a monstrous growth in the earth (*Themis* 458–59).
5. Cf. Joshi, *A Subtler Magic* 134–39 and Cannon 86.

"The Rats in the Walls," The Rats in the Trenches

[. . .] Generations of toppled heads
have come to roost in my priory. (Ashbery 50)

Lovecraft wrote only a few stories that take place outside of New England, and most of them do not wear very well; a few of them are concerned with the Great War, but only in a rather peripheral way. "Dagon" and "The Temple" take as their settings the German naval warfare; both stories, however, have more to do with Jules Verne's *Twenty Thousand Leagues under the Sea* than with the actual war. The liberal discipline of the Germans in "Dagon," from which the mildly inept narrator escapes in a small boat, is reminiscent of Captain Nemo's regime; and the diving suit Karl Heinrich employs in "The Temple" probably depends upon the hatches and suits of the *Nautilus*. The closest these stories come to expressing any realistic reaction to the war is the phrase "war-exhausted humanity" in "Dagon" (*D* 19). Part five of "Herbert West—Reanimator," taking place behind the Allied lines in France, was written to prove that even an American for a bit of money could succeed in the Grand Guignol tradition; despite the various body parts scattered about the field-hospital, the story doesn't really concern the war. In none of these attempts can we say that the story is very successful. One exception we should mention, "Pickman's Model," in which we learn that the narrator Thurber had been in France where he was "not easily knocked out" (*DH* 20), but who nevertheless at a crucial moment when he hears an inexplicable noise in Pickman's cellar cannot but "[think] of huge rats and [shudder]" (23). In the North End as in the trenches rats are ghouls; but though these passages have more weight than those in the other stories, this story does not pretend to be about the Great War. The true exception is "The Rats in the Walls," although the reasons for its success are more difficult to fathom than may be at first apparent. It seems to be composed of two plots that do not fit very well together, one the story of the cannibalistic family and the other the story of the rats, stories that do not exist on the same level of reality. Startling as the story of the family is, Lovecraft's loving

53

historical details and his fascination with the relation of England to its ancient Roman and atavistic past assure its realism. The story of the rats is a
very different sort of tale. Based upon old fables, it remains uncanny and fantastic. The stories are only connected through the perception of the narrator, the last, insane, cannibalistic member of the family, who may or who
may not hear the rats in the walls, or, to put it another way, who hears what
is most probably not there. We might attempt to say that the family cult
through the ages is an attempt to propitiate the instinctual rats of human aggression; but such a formulation is not very satisfying, since it does not account for the different natures of the two stories.[1]

I propose another reading of this hybrid. Although it takes place in 1923,
I believe it is Lovecraft's World War I story, centering upon the narrator's
cry, "The war ate my boy, damn them all" (DH 44). But to understand it in
this way we need to recall the life of the trenches.

"Do you remember the rats; and the stench / Of corpses rotting in front
of the front-line trench[?]" Siegfried Sassoon asked (267). We have many
testimonies to the life of the trenches and the part the rats played in it, distinguished by "their hunger, vigor, intelligence, and courage" (Fussell 49).
Richard Aldington wrote they were "huge" (52). But a soldier could think of
them as his brothers. Consider these lines from Wilfrid Owen's "A Terre":

> Not worse than ours the existences rats lead—
> Nosing along at night down some safe rut,
> They find a shell-proof home before they rot. (65)

Something of the same perception occurs in David Jones's In Parenthesis, as
the platoon prepares to go over the top:

> Long side by side lie like friends lie
> on daisy-down on warm days
> cuddled close down kindly close with the mole
> in down and silky rodent [. . .] (157)

With more of an edge Rosenberg makes the same point in his poem "Break

---

1. This dual nature of the story may arise from the two legends Lovecraft made use of in Bar-
ing-Gould's Curious Myths of the Middle Ages, which Steven J. Mariconda has traced in detail.
One chapter recounts the legend of St. Patrick's Purgatory, the other the legend of the rats
that devour Bishop Hatto. The two legends are different in kind, the one a mythic geography
associated with a real place in Ireland, the other a narrative of a judgment executed upon a
cruel prelate by an army of rats.

of Day in the Trenches":

> Only a live thing leaps my hand,
> A queer sardonic rat,
> As I pull the parapet's poppy
> To stick behind my ear.
> Droll rat, they would shoot you if they knew
> Your cosmopolitan sympathies.
> Now you have touched this English hand
> You will do the same to a German. (103)

The passages are intimate because at a certain point in the trench experience anything creaturely alive becomes a soldier's brother. This is not Delapore's feeling at first, but we should keep it in mind. Shortly before the catastrophe he does consider "the hapless rats that stumbled into such traps [as the pits] amidst the blackness of their quest in this grisly Tartarus" (*DH* 44). By this point in the story he has become as hapless and as trapped as they. Rather different are the internal rhymes of E. W. Tennant:

> I can see them all asleep, three men deep,
> And they're nowhere near a fire—but our wire
> Has 'em fast as can be. Can't you see
> When the flare goes up? Ssh! boys; what's that noise?
> Do you know what these rats eat? Body-meat! (ctd. in Gilbert 287)

Our brothers are our enemies. At the conclusion of his poem "Trench Poets" Edgell Rickword writes of a corpse lying in no-man's-land, "He stank so badly, though we were great chums / I had to leave him; then rats ate his thumbs" (98). In the *English Review* in 1916 H. T. W. Bousfield sees them at work: "Where slain men rot [. . .] the young rats play / At their empty eyes" (313). Here, in no-man's-land, the place that was especially ill-fitted, both hunger and dissolution were satisfied. Considering this place that did not belong to humanity, David Jones wrote:

> You can hear the rat of no-man's-land
> rut-out intricacies,
> weasel out his patient workings,
> scrut, scrut, sscrut. (54)

No-man's-land was the special home of the rat. One of the voices in *The Waste Land* has this in mind: "I think we are in rats' alley / Where the dead men lost their bones" (40). Eliot of course was not in the war; he was merely picking up the language of the trenches that had become a part of the patois of the day, and the lines well express the difficulty of Delapore's position after the death of his son. We should keep in mind that Lovecraft read *The Waste Land* shortly before writing "The Rats in the Walls" (Joshi 314–16).

To the witness of these poets I would like to add another witness, an article in 1916 from the *Philadelphia Inquirer* that bears the title "Rats in the Battle Lines: Interesting Stories About the Ghouls of the Western Front." For anyone interested in Lovecraft's themes this title itself is sufficiently arresting. After describing the presence of the rats the article states:

> They have, however, increased in such great numbers that their ordinary food has become scarce, and they are now, it is said, eating the bodies in "no-man's land," the tragic stretch of ground lying between the opposing trenches.
>
> Their ghoulish feeding makes them all the greater peril to the health of our soldiers. The bite of a rat is at any time dangerous, but when the animal has indulged in carnivorous feeding, the risk of blood poisoning is immeasurably increased. (15)

Having reported with some ghoulish pleasure on the dangers the rats present in the trenches, the article proceeds to describe plagues of rats at other times, the most interesting of which calls on "an eye-witness" in Illinois in 1908, who "stated that as he was returning to his home in the moonlight he heard a great rustling in a field near by, and soon a vast army of rats was crossing the road in front of him" (15). The rats are an army of ghouls, a third army that indiscriminately combats and devours the other armies.

After we have read these testimonies, it is no wonder that Paul Fussell, the analyst of the language of the war, says that they were the "famous" rats of the war (49). Not only were they a part of the normal life in the trenches; they became one of the icons of the peculiarly bestial nature of the war upon which poets and others, such as Lovecraft, could draw. I am not here claiming that he was influenced by any of the works I have cited, but it is clear that this imagery was ubiquitous. When Delapore refers to "the scampering army" of the rats (DH 31), he is using a language common to many people writing about the war.

Besides the Great War and the War between the States, about which I will say more later, one other political event occurs in the story, so muted that we are liable not to notice it. This is the death of President Harding, which the narrator announces in solemn tones as he and his cohort of archeologists and scientists return to Exham Priory: "I felt myself poised on the brink of frightful revelations, a sensation symbolized by the air of mourning among the many Americans at the unexpected death of the President on the other side of the world" (*DH* 40). Harding, of course, had died in the middle of various investigations into the corruption of his administration, so after the initial shock his death came rather as a sense of relief to the nation. Lovecraft, both a Republican and a realist, dismisses the man in a letter as a "handsome bimbo" but adds, "I'm sure sorry he had the good luck to get clear of this beastly planet" (*SL* 1.253); cosmic indifferentism conflicts with human sympathy. In contrast, Lovecraft had no truck with Woodrow Wilson, whose project of the League of Nations he described in 1931 as "Woody Wilson's monumental asininity" (3.272). Lovecraft had written an article against the League and argued against it in several letters. The good thing about Harding, in his view, was that he had albeit with some qualms successfully opposed the entrance of the United States into the League. America was to have nothing to do with old Europe—unlike the narrator of "The Rats in the Walls" who cannot help himself from plunging into the truth of Europe and into the truth of his own material, genealogical, and psychic inheritance. One theme of the story would seem to be that whatever the consequences may be it is not so easy to dismiss Europe.

Harding represents a complex of themes for Lovecraft. He could not have been ignorant of the charge, much bandied about during the campaign for the White House, that Harding's ancestry had black blood in it, that as Harding had rather engagingly put it to a friend his people had perhaps "jumped the fence" (Russell 40). With that detail in mind the function of Nigger-Man in the story becomes all the more significant. Only someone or something connected with the fearful other, be it the cult of death in Egypt or the voodoo cult in Mexico, could for this narrator further suggest hidden meaning, place him "on the brink" of revelation. The death of Harding and the mourning for him makes him a psychopompos like Nigger-Man, guiding the mind of the narrator downward to hidden meanings.

Needless to say, Lovecraft like many other people of his generation had fierce feelings about the war that had brought them to the confusing world of the 1920s, which seemed to have so little in common with the world before the war. At first he felt that England and Germany were committing racial suicide, since both shared an Aryan heritage; as he put it in his 1915 article, "The Crime of the Century," they were "blood brothers" (*CE* 5.14).

As the war continued, however, and his Anglophilia took hold, he reacted to the German strategies violently. The German blood brother becomes the Hun, whose "savage lust of combat" is something the politer nations have need of if they are to win the war (SL 1.53). In the poem "Germania—1918" he is a "rav'ning beast" (AT 418); when America enters the war "The Goth, unheeding, plans continued wrong, / And ruthless drags his brutish horde along" (AT 420). What has happened to our brother? In galloping anapests Lovecraft answers that question in the slightly earlier poem, "Ad Britannos—1918": "'Tis the blood of the past that is raging within him, / The hot blood of pillagers ruthless and bold" (AT 414). The German nation has experienced a mass regression; it is destroyed in the same way as Delapore is destroyed. As much as any other man Lovecraft suffered the effects of Allied propaganda, which he was later to condemn; but the propaganda has fruitful consequences in the story.

The problem with this language of Lovecraft's poems is its abstraction. In his letters, essays, and poems he shows little awareness of the actual nature of trench warfare, of barbed wire and machine guns, to say nothing of rats. The Somme and Gallipoli do not move him. What does move him is the submarine warfare that sinks the Lusitania, an event that lies behind "Dagon" and "The Temple," stories, however, that do not finally appeal to the details of such warfare but to the element of the ocean in which something more monstrous than the submarine resides. Herbert West, a monster in his own right, stays far behind the lines when he volunteers as a doctor during the war for the sake of the fresh body parts it provides. None of these characters understands the experience of the men in the trenches that Valentine Fleming describes, who are "unable to reply to the everlasting run of shells hurled at them from three, four, five or more miles away and positively welcoming an infantry attack [. . .] as a chance of meeting and matching themselves against human assailants and not against invisible, irresistible machines [. . .]" (ctd. in Gilbert 112). The war remains for Lovecraft what he called it early on, "this stupendous fray" (CE 5.14); on the one hand it is gratifyingly large, an expression of sublimity, but on the other hand it is a mere brawl. Though "fray" is cognate to fear as Doctor Johnson noted, who also mentioned its archaic significance of "a battle; a fight," ("Fray"), it now signifies little more than "a noisy quarrel; a brawl" (OED "Fray"). Some contradictory feelings about the Great War hamper Lovecraft's comprehension of it, but we should admit that it was difficult for many people to comprehend.

Now we return to that cry, "The war ate my boy." But it is not the war that ate the narrator's son. He did, he and his forbears. The violence of the family regresses to prehistoric times, as though Darwin and Freud had opened up the door on the animalistic instincts of the race, absolving humans of their violence; but evidence of violence in America lies much closer to hand in the Revolution and in the War between the States,[2] a violence institutionalized in West Point, and rampant up and down the frontier as the new Americans removed the Native Americans from their lands. The narrator describes the burning of the Delapore plantation as though the family had nothing to do with the acts of the Confederacy; yet the father of the narrator was at the time "in the army, defending Richmond" (DH 27). More specifically, it became a commonplace among the Lost Generation after the War to End All Wars that the older generation through acts of fatuous arrogance was guilty of initiating the war, of sending its sons off to the war, and of bullheadedly continuing the war when the nature of life in the trenches, brothers to the rats, had become evident. Wilfred Owen expresses this in the last two lines of his poem, "The Parable of the Old Man and the Young," in which he retells the story of Abraham and Isaac. Once more an angel offers the old man a ram to sacrifice instead of his son: "But the old man would not so, but slew his son, / And half the seed of Europe, one by one" (42). One of Kipling's "Epitaphs of the War" says bluntly, "If any question why we died, / Tell them, because our fathers lied" (443). In *Mourning Becomes Electra*, in which the Civil War works as a metaphor of World War I, O'Neill has Orin, the son of the dead General Ezra Mannon, under whose command he serves, report: "I had a queer feeling that the war meant murdering the same man over and over, and that in the end I would discover the man was myself! Their faces keep coming back in dreams—and they change to Father's face—or to mine—" (2.95). Delapore is as guilty of these acts as are the other fathers. Because of these lies the sons were happy to deploy for the war; but the fathers know that their sons, those that survive, after the war feel like Orin. Finally the son must kill either his father or himself.

There is another aspect to this story of a father eating his son that we cannot ignore. It is the story of old Saturn, to which Lovecraft was to allude

---

2. The narrator, incidentally, never says "The War between the States" or "The War of Northern Aggression," though he was born in the South of a proud Southern heritage. Instead he uses the Northern phrase, the "Civil War" (DH 27); he has purposefully turned his back on the South, just as his ancestor had turned his back on England. For reasons that shall be clear later, I believe that for his personality, being of both the South and the North, the more contumacious "War between the States" would better express his true feelings.

in 1926 in "Pickman's Model," when Pickman paints a Goya subject to life: "The monster was there—it glared and gnawed and gnawed and glared" (*DH* 23). The two stories must have some knot in common, the one from the father's point of view and the other from the son's—let us recall that Pickman is most likely a changeling who meets an ill end. The family that eats together—well, it puts a whole new twist on the German proverb, "Man ist was er ißt" [You are what you eat]. The two stories record Oedipal aggressions from the oral stage. Chronological time, that is to say adult, senile time, devours the eternity of the child; and the story of the rats, like so many of Lovecraft's stories, records a span of very specific years that conclude in the apocalypse of the Great War.

But should we accuse Delapore, the narrator of the story, of such acts as incestuous cannibalism? In making such an accusation we need to look at his words more carefully. His narrative is double-layered. On the one hand it presents a story in the past tense that nevertheless presents events that surprise him in a lived now; on the other hand, as a true past tense, this is a story told by a madman, whose words are not to be taken as raw evidence of factual events. For instance, early in his account the narrator describes Norrys as "a plump, amiable young man" (*DH* 28). Later he comments that Norrys was "stouter" (38); and later, immediately before the climax, he again marks Norrys as "plump" (44). The swinish creatures that he sees in his dreams have "flabby features" (37); and he denies too intensely in his final madness that "it was not Edward Norrys' fat face on that flabby, fungous thing!" (44). Now whether Norrys was plump and stout, fat and flabby or not is beside the point when we discover that the narrator, who is oppressed by visions of hunger, has attempted to eat him in his madness. His insistence that Norrys is plump becomes a rhetorical defense that Norrys causes his own death because of his tempting fat—who could resist him? Quite simply, then, since his narration is colored by his madness, we must read it carefully.

For instance, when he and Norrys first investigate the sub-cellar, he finds on its walls the word Atys and comments, "The reference [. . .] made me shiver, for I had read Catullus and knew something of the hideous rites of the Eastern god" (*DH* 37). Leaving aside the question why this allusion to self-castration should make an elderly man who has lost his only son shiver, for the answer to that question is too obvious—the construction "and knew" is less than precise, for it either means "and therefore knew" or "and also knew." If as a child learning Latin this businessman read the Catullus poem in which Atys is a character, he would not necessarily have learned anything further about the god Atys—but why should the businessman have learned such information unless led to it by the propensities of the family? Is not his "shiver" akin to the "tickle" (122) the old man in "The Picture in the House" feels when he pours over the cannibals' abattoir? The phrase, then, makes us ask more questions than we had expected about the old man who narrates the story.[3]

Another sign of the problems in this man's narrative is his use of the word "doubtless" and "must." He is extremely insistent that the reader read the text as he intends it should be read and see the things that he believes he has seen. His first use of this language is so low-key we are liable to miss it: "What I afterward remembered is merely this—that my old black cat, whose moods I know so well, was undoubtedly alert and anxious to an extent wholly out of keeping with his natural character" (DH 33). The next morning, to explain to a servant Nigger-man's scratching at the new panels "I told the man that there must be some singular odour or emanation from the old stonework" (33), though he believes no rats or mice "could hardly be found" there for some three hundred years (33). The climax of the story brings this language to a crescendo. When Nigger-Man seems to leap into the gulf, "I was not far behind, for there was no doubt after another second. It was the eldritch scurrying of those fiend-born rats" (44). When he bumps into "something soft and plump," presumptively Norrys, he argues in retrospect, "It must have been the rats" (44). In the last paragraph, speaking of his guards, he says, "They must know that I did not do it. They must know it was the rats" (45). The final effect of this language is double. On the one hand we are convinced that he is insane and that we must doubt very much that any substantial rats infest the Priory; but on the other hand we are convinced that the rats represent some kind of inner reality that we must accept for the sake of our own sanity. If we deny the rats we deny something compulsively real in ourselves.

What do we actually know about this narrator? First, let us be careful about his age. Seven years old when the plantation was burned, apparently during the siege of Richmond in 1865, he was probably born in 1858. After the war the family came north, where he became over the years "a stolid

---

3. Given the prudery of the English-speaking world that Byron excoriates in Don Juan 1.41–45, we may wonder how the narrator, a simple businessman, learned of this poem. For what it is worth, my fourth-year Latin text from high-school, dating from 1933, does not have the poem in its selections from Catullus (Carlisle and Richardson 373–89).

Yankee" (*DH* 27), so stolid a Yankee that he exhibits Republican sympathies at the death of Harding. When his son was ten years old in 1904, he was 46. He was 59 when his son went to war and 60 at the war's conclusion, when his son returned "a maimed invalid" (*DH* 28) and he bought Exham Priory. He began the rebuilding of the Priory when he was 63 years old and 65 at its completion when he moved in and the events of the story overwhelmed him. Since it is possible that he was born earlier than we have supposed, we can be certain, considering the normal life spans of the time, that this is indeed the narration of an old man who shall soon die, believing himself the last of his line. Is there not, then, already a touch of dementia in his stubborn determination to rebuild and refurbish the Priory, attacking the problem as he says with "an elderly obstinacy" (*DH* 31), attempting to transcend the injuries of the Great War, the War between the States, the American Revolution, and the English Civil War? Is this not a bizarre decision? He says that it was the "legendry" of the Priory, recounted in his son's letters, "which definitely turned my attention to my transatlantic heritage, and made me resolve to purchase and restore the family seat" (*DH* 28), a resolve for which Norrys bears some of the blame, since it was he who recounted that "peasant superstition" to the young Delapore in the first place.

How did the father regard this "legendry"?

In a variety of ways. Once he arrives he finds himself "ostracised" and "disliked" by most of the villagers, for little reason he thinks except that he is a member of this ancient, "abhorrent" family, though he is well received by Norrys (*DH* 29). This dislike he believes comes from the legendry; English tradition has a long memory, although that memory may be distorted. The architecture of the Priory—what remains of it—indicates a Roman, druidic, and predruidic past, associated with the worship of the Magna Mater. The antiquarian aspects of these remains disinfect them of any terror. More charged for the narrator are the tales and ballads that surround his family in the medieval period, especially those from the Welsh border: "These myths and ballads, typical as they were of crude superstition, repelled me greatly," he writes, perhaps because they were "unpleasantly reminiscent" of his cousin "who went among the negroes and became a voodoo priest after he returned from the Mexican War" (*DH* 30–31). Clearly there is more to this family that has nobly upheld the traditions of the antebellum South than he would allow. His disgust for a cousin who "went among the negroes" is palpable.

The narrator is less disturbed, he assures us, by "tales of wails and howlings" or of "graveyard stenches after the spring rains" or of "the squealing white thing"—all of these tales are "hackneyed spectral lore" that a man of taste, a confirmed skeptic, cannot be moved by (*DH* 31), although these are just the kind of thing that prove factual later. He admits that "accounts of vanished peasants" might have some truth, "though not especially signifi-cant" given medieval habits, for after all "prying curiosity meant death" (*DH* 31)—which is to say that he condones any murder that his ancestors com-mitted in the past. He has no sympathy for the peasants or any curiosity they may have exhibited. As Paul Montelone suggests, "If anything took place at the site it would be for him conventionally evil, uncivilized surely, offensive, ungentlemanly, decadent, a stain on his family tree, but not innately or abso-lutely evil. His moral reading of the legendry would be [. . .] wholly com-monsensical. He is after all a businessman" (19)—an American business-man, I would add, so determined to be an Englishman that he is willing to accept the ethics of an aristocracy that displayed the heads of their murdered peasants on the battlements of the Priory, heads that give some point to his later dream of "a Roman feast like that of Trimalchio, with a horror in a covered platter" (*DH* 40). Is it any wonder that he finds himself disliked by the villagers?

Finally there are those "extremely picturesque" tales of witches' sabbaths and "most vivid of all" the story of the rats, "that unforgettable rodent army," pouring out of the Priory to devour everything in its path, "for it scat-tered among the village homes and brought curses and horrors in its train" (*DH* 31). This is a demonic version of Browning's "The Pied Piper of Hamelin," in which the rats, to a jolly patter of anapests and recherché rhymes, live side-by-side with the townspeople. The rats, according to his account at this moment, are a spectacle, distanced by the observing eye; but when he experiences them in the Priory he only hears them, and the ear de-livers a much more immediate experience.

What, then, are we to say of the narrator according to his account of the "legendry"? He is a racist American who has assumed, rather easily, a benign view of the values practiced by his aristocratic ancestors. A head on the bas-tion does not disturb him. In addition, unmoved by the story of the rats, he does not accept the possibility of instinctual motivations. Though he is at-tracted and repelled by the legendry, he does not admit that the sins of old England have anything to do with him; he is another version of the Ameri-can Adam, returning to England in all innocence to recapitulate a story by Henry James. The villagers therefore may have personal reasons to dislike him, not simply, as he assumes, because he is a member of an ancient family of bad barons. A victim of the typical American discontinuity, dramatized by the letter burned by the Federal troops, he attempts to overcome it; but it cannot be overcome through mere imitation and a rationalized modernity, his aesthetic Gothicism and electric lights.

He needs his Nigger-Man. As much as Longrifle needs Chinkachook, Ishmael needs Queequeg, and Huckleberry Finn needs Jim, this white-as-white narrator needs the dispossessed and the other; and if Leslie Fiedler's analysis in *Love and Death in the American Novel* is persuasive, then Lovecraft is as American an author as Cooper, Melville, and Clemens. Delapore could know nothing if it were not for his familiar and intimate connection to American racism.

Three elements combine here. One is his love of the cat, his only connection now with his former life in America when he was an innocent business man. The next is the racism implied in the cat's name, a detail prepared earlier in his account of the negroes "howling and praying" as the plantation of the family burned to the earth, as though those slaves were that concerned with the destruction of the plantation house emblematic of their oppression (DH 27); this element is connected with the cousin who "went among the negroes" (DH 31). The third is the cat as cat, a symbol of intuitive knowledge that Lovecraft inherited from Baudelaire's poems in *Les Fleurs du mal* (but more of that in a later chapter). His cat, the beloved pet and symbol of the oppressed that return possessed with dark knowledge, allows him to hear what the cat hears, the rustling of the rats in the draperies, the sense that although he had rebuilt the Priory as a modern, Gothic imitation of the Priory as it had been, this Priory now, a symbol of his own will and a substitute for his family and for his son, was now infested with creatures of animalistic instinct that shall lead him to the truth of himself and of his family.

The other cats, cats as cats, also attest to the existence of the rats, but for the narrator and for his Nigger-Man they exist fearfully. And Nigger-Man and the other cats agree that the direction the rats are taking is downward. Their going down, a word repeated several times in the father's narration, brings him and the men with him, including Norrys, to the twilit grotto of the climax.

At the same time, however, as Nigger-Man and the other cats are disturbed, the narrator has begun to have the dreams that attest to the grotto. He knows of it before Sir Arthur Brinton, an authority on the Troad and presumptively on Atys and Cybele, opens the door of the altar. A number of elements are at work here. First is Lovecraft's insistence that dreams connect with a reality that otherwise the dreamer would not know (Burleson, "On Lovecraft's Themes" 140). Second is the major Lovecraftian theme, in which several scientific thoughts intersect, that humanity has evolved from earlier life forms to which an individual might once more devolve, usually with most unpleasant consequences. Third, however, is the devolution implied in the trench experience. The soldier either goes mad, or he learns to turn off the sensory impact of the bombs, machine-guns, mortars, and screams of the wounded. It may be objected that every protagonist in a Lovecraft story suffers from such traits as alienation and a living death; my point is that in this story these traits and others find their accurate historical context in the war. According to Eric Leed's analysis of the character of a man in combat during World War I, the soldier finds himself alienated from civilian experience but possessed of a secret no one in civilian life could discover, buried in the trenches and invisible, a person who only lives when dead and buried, polluted and sacred, dead but reborn into a new comradeship that cuts across class lines and national affiliations, imprisoned by the new impersonal technology, no longer human, living a life that only a mythological language could account for, homeless and compelled to relive his homelessness. He becomes a brother to the rat. Everyone, whether German, French, American, or English, is a brother to the rat. That is to say, the father dons the character of the son, his son who had become a rat, because he has already suffered these traits from the time he was driven out of Carfax and forced, presumptively by the authority of his mother, to assume the invisibility of the Yankee businessman; but that disguise is as ill-fitting as the clothes that Macbeth wears. Then, having lived with his maimed son for two years after the war, he suffers from the same liminality that his son the soldier had internalized, and attempts to find his home in the Priory to which his son had pointed him. By coming to the Priory he attempts to be prior to every father and every son in his family's history; despite his cultured pretense, he must acknowledge that he is the archetypal swineherd in the grotto, who is prior to all this borderline existence except for the rats that in the narrator's dream overwhelm the scene.

But though the cats and the dreams attest to the presence of the rats, neither the narrator nor the reader ever see one, not the barest tip or flip of a tail. According to the narrator's account of the legendry, the "epic of the rats" is the "most vivid of all" (DH 31), yet he sees nothing. Nevertheless, they are a "scampering army of obscene vermin," a "lean, filthy, ravenous army" (DH 31). The first night he hears the rats it is a mere "low, distinct scurrying" (DH 34), but the next night "the walls were alive with a nauseous sound—the verminous slithering of ravenous, gigantic rats," which make the tapestry perform "a singular dance of death" (DH 35). These rats, "in numbers apparently inexhaustible, were engaged in one stupendous migration from inconceivable heights to some depth conceivably, or inconceivably, below" (DH 36). These rats have something of the lemming about them, devoted to Thanatos. The next night he hears "the same babel of scurrying rats" and becomes convinced, given their downward plunge, that the entire cliff on which the Priory rests is "riddled with questing rats" (DH 38). Now he associates the rats with pride and the confusion of tongues and with tunnels that, punningly, challenge him with a puzzle—and the reader too. At the climax in the grotto he is beset by "the eldritch scurrying of those fiend-born rats, always questing for new horrors and determined to lead me on" to the realms of Nyarlathotep, "the mad faceless god" (DH 44). At this point we realize that Nigger-Man has a double nature; he is a mythic manifestation of Nyarlathotep, and he is simply one of the several naturalistic cats that attest that something wrong riddles the Priory, while in a remarkable transformation the rats also become a mass psychopompos that leads the narrator to the realm of a meaningless death that he feels compelled to explore despite his fear and repulsion. Cat and rat are conflated; but at this point neither cat nor rat need guide him any further, for it is not "the viscous, gelatinous, ravenous army that feast on the dead and the living" (DH 44), specifically on Norrys, but he that feasts. He is the rat. That is the significance of the degeneration of tongues he experiences, his personal babel, that concludes "chchch . . ." (DH 45). He becomes the rat that he always was; and thus his task force finds Nigger-Man, no longer plunging downward into "the illimitable gulf of the unknown" but "leaping and tearing" at the throat of the narrator who is "crouching in the blackness over the plump, half-eaten body of Capt. Norrys" (DH 45), Note that word "half-eaten." Only a very large rat or a swarm of rats could have devoured that amount.

But if we leave aside the young man's plumpness, why should the narrator want to eat Capt. Norrys? First, it was the Norryses that received the Priory after Walter de la Peur slaughtered his family and fled to the banks of the James River, probably late in the reign of James I if a plantation on the banks of the James River seems plausible. A small mystery surrounds this receival, whether it was the Stuarts or the Protectorate that gave the Norryses the land. I think there can be little doubt that the de la Poers would have been loyalists during the English Civil War. Some time passed before the

land was allotted to the Norrys family, so it is quite possible that their for-
tunes rose with that of the Parliament and Cromwell. The de la Poers were
Barons, whereas the Norryses were never anything more than gentlemen.
"Shall a Norrys hold the lands of a de la Poer?" the narrator pointedly asks
(DH 44).[4] And if all this is true, then by a pun it makes an insane sense that
Norrys, the mere name, plays an evil part in the War of *Northern* Aggression.
In addition, Capt. Norrys symbolically takes the place of the maimed Alfred,
and the narrator may unconsciously hold that easy-going young man responsible for Alfred's death; he can certainly hold him responsible for the narrator's purchase of the fatal Priory. Shortly before he attacks Norrys the young
man's posture in the abattoir, "used as he was to the trenches" (DH 43), reminds him of Norrys's part in the war. In any case, in an act of unconscious
filicide he may be killing his own son Alfred when he kills Norrys, his son's
good friend. After all, the Oedipal fear that Laios wants to kill his son is sub-
stantiated first in the exposure of the child and then later in his attempt to
run the young stranger off the road; and thus we are reminded of the older
generation's responsibility for the war.

Lovecraft achieves a remarkable transformation of the rats through the
course of the story. At first associated with the "rav'ning" German army, the
war that killed the narrator's son, the rats become something more, a "gigantic" creature that performs a "dance of death," a medieval emblem of death's
ubiquity. The narrator cannot answer the riddling "babel" because he is the
thing itself; he cannot answer himself because the letter from his fathers has
been lost, but also because no one can answer the riddle that he himself is
without dire results. Oedipus once more comes to mind, who answers the
riddle of the sphinx, man, and the riddle of himself, the man that kills his
father and marries his mother, at the cost of stabbing his eyes out. It is important that the founder of the Delapores in Virginia commits patricide, that
the narrator regains his heritage through the death of his maimed son, and
that the narrator feels fear at the death of the highly questionable father of
the nation, President Harding. At the conclusion, however, the rats transcend personal psychology; they represent a mass psychology in which every
war is inevitable and devouring. Not only did the war eat the narrator's son,
the War between the States ate Carfax "and burnt Grandsire Delapore and
the secret" (DH 44); and in Lovecraft's judgment the American rebellion

---

4. John Hitz goes so far as to argue, I think with some exaggeration, that the Norrys family
were usurpers of the de la Poers' land (32).

renounced the colonies' connection to the fatherland of England. Thus human discontinuity is not simply a fact of the migration that every American suffers; it arises from the human participation in an animal aggression that always seems greater than the individual, sweeping the individual along because aggression is built into the human psyche, which then insists upon building it into its institutions, even if they are institutions of peace like the League of Nations. This "wave of hunger" (Montelone 21) is actuated by every priority; and thus the rats plunge downward in the walls of a Priory.

The psychosis of the narrator, then, is not personal. When he eats his son, we eat ours.

Epilogue

It is gratifying to recognize that "The Rats in the Walls" found one of its first posthumous publications in *The Dunwich Horror and Other Weird Tales*, which appeared in the Editions for the Armed Services that S. T. Joshi writes "introduced Lovecraft to large numbers of servicemen still stationed in Europe after the war" (637–38). One can only speculate that this story appealed to them for the very reasons we have outlined in this essay and that its popularity rides on the crest of that publication.

The Hounds of Hell, the Hounds of Heaven, and the Hounds of Earth

"But what be bones that lie in a hole?" (Tolkien 1.12; 253)

A troll gnawing upon a hobbit bone in a comic verse that Sam recites has no respect for the bone but as food. What be bones indeed! A more serious version of the question occurs in Ugo Foscolo's great poem *I sepolcri*: "Qual fia ristoro a' dì perduti un sasso / Che distingua le mie dalle infinite / Ossa che in terra e in mar semina morte?" [What restoration to our lost days does a stone make / That distinguishes my bones from the infinite number / That death sows in earth and sea?] (ll. 13–15). Foscolo's question is more difficult than it seems. The dignity of our funeral customs has an ancient origin, but the reasons for such dignity, the dignity that we accord a corpse, are hard to express. Lovecraft's story "The Hound" does not answer the question, but it does raise it; and a close examination of the story forces the reader to face the question from new angles.

This assertion may seem to claim too much for the story, which has always excited a wide variety of responses, from disgust to laughter. It seems so extreme, so hyperbolically conceived and executed. To me it has always seemed an early example of the figure at the center of Lovecraft's narrative program, the ghoul, but I have never examined the story closely, being perhaps warned away by its detractors. Now I wish to return to it, both to ask more about the ghoul and to ask why the story is so extreme.

First, let us note how much the story is about ghouls. It is not simply that the young protagonist and his friend rob graves, "that hideous extremity of human outrage" (D 172), and decorate their secret museum with the skulls and cerements and rotting flesh they discover. Although they do not eat the corpses they exhume, all their activity is described with oral imagery. They do it because the world is "stale" (171). They work "with the satanic taste of neurotic virtuosi" in order to excite their "jaded sensibilities" (172), in a room where decorative daemons "vomited" light and pipes emitted "the

69

odours our moods most craved," such as "the frightful, soul-upheaving stenches of the uncovered grave" (172). They have "nauseous musical instruments" to play (172). They were, the narrator assures the reader, "no vulgar ghouls" (173): because the "ecstatic titillation" they sought could be destroyed in a moment by a false aesthetic effect, their "quest for novel scenes and piquant conditions was feverish and insatiate" (173). The mythic allusion to "the corpse-eating cult of inaccessible Leng" from which the amulet the two men steal descends (174) confirms and objectifies this language, which culminates at the conclusion to the first part of the story when the two young men think that the bats fly to the grave of the ghoul to seek "for some cursed and unholy nourishment" (175). The language is not peculiar to this story; in "The Picture in the House," though the narrator at the conclusion has received a severe shock from an actual cannibal, at the beginning of the story he describes the reader for whom he is writing as an "epicure in the terrible" (DH 116). Although this list may help us understand why commentators like Joshi (A Subtler Magic 90) are determined to regard the story as a parody, not as a serious attempt in the genre, we must admit that the language may very well tell us something important about Lovecraft's program.

This language does not occur throughout the story, only in the preliminary description of the two men's activities, but it exists to gesture toward a variety of attitudes toward death. The two men display the contents of the grave in order to control them for an aesthetic effect, so the narrator assures us, always employing "a fastidious technical care" (D 173), but the material of this art is not indifferent. A "technical care" attempts to overlook the material, but it fails. The eating of death (possibly the eating of shit symbolized in these dead bodies) aims at a transcendence of death. The ghoul is very different from the cannibal, who eats in order to absorb the strength and virtues of his enemy, and the action takes place within a sacred context. Pickman, perhaps Lovecraft's most exemplary ghoul, means to desecrate the past, and Joseph Curwen means to exploit it. The two characters of this story seem to have purer motives.

Nevertheless, a problem does exist. True, a distinction does seem to exist between the aesthetic ghoul and the actual ghoul; one contemplates the corpse, the other eats it. The one maintains a proper distance between the self and the object; the other assimilates the object. But given the insistent oral imagery of this story, Lovecraft would seem to assert that despite the aesthete's claim that "we were no vulgar ghouls" (D 173) they cannot help but act out, albeit symbolically, the perversion of the ghoul. From a moral standpoint the two ghouls are finally the same. Despite their devotion to a decorative effect, they do intend to trespass the moral decorums upon which their activities depend.

From one point of view there is a great divide between the young men and the ghoul; for the ghoul is what he is simply because of what he is. His nature is his fate, so he has nothing to be proud of. The two young men are doing their best to become something they cannot be and to control something, death, they cannot control. The ghoul is not an epicure, for there is nothing sophisticated in the preparation of his vittles; he eats what he must. Pickman, whom we have treated as a ghoul, is one only in Dreamland, that is, only in his dreams (or at the most in our collective dream of him). Despite his technical mastery he is yet a failure, as inauthentic as St. John and his friend the narrator.

The decor they construct is an aspect of their self-dramatization and self-admiration; they are much too knowing. "We thrilled at the picture of ourselves," the narrator says as they exhumed a body when every detail of the scene was right (D 174). Even when they realize that something is pursuing them, "it pleased us more to dramatise ourselves as the victims" (D 176). But despite the theatricalities of playing at being dead, they discover that they very much want to live. This of course was Lovecraft's discovery when he recovered from the various breakdowns that had led to his self-immurement in his mother's house after high school, a discovery accentuated by his mother's death. From this point of view the parodistic language of the story has a therapeutic effect.

There is a language, however, that the narrator does not use. Though he uses the word "mummy," a properly distanced word as far as the West is concerned, a word redolent of the East (D 172), he does not use the forthright words "corpse" or "cadaver," the one a good flat Anglo-Saxon word, the other a flat Latinate word. Neither word has any romance about it. "Corpse," however, flat as it is, means simply body but once meant simply a body, whether living or dead. "Cadaver" derives from the Latin "cadere" (*Webster*) so it means "that which has fallen, that which has become heavy, helplessly and hopelessly heavy, and at last died." Both words point at more than the prosaic body, the thing at our feet. If these are taboo words for the narrator, the words that he must avoid, then the bodies that the two men dig up, "our unmentionable treasures" (D 173), are in fact objects they regard as sacred before they ever arrange those objects, more than objects, in their underground sanctum.

What does this story, parodistic as it may be, a mockery of itself, add to the theme of the ghoul? The answer lies in its insistent references to *The Hound of the Baskervilles*, a novel that Lovecraft had certainly read.[1] The chief reference is to the heart-stopping, memorable line that Dr. Mortimer, a collector of skulls, utters at the end of the second chapter, "Mr. Holmes, they were the footprints of a gigantic hound!" (794). In Lovecraft's story the phrase "gigantic hound" occurs six times, beginning with the story's first sentence, "In my tortured ears there sounds unceasingly a nightmare whirring and flapping, and a faint, distant baying as of some gigantic hound" (*D* 171). That baying is also significant, for it occurs ten times, eleven times if we include "a faint, deep, insistent note as of a gigantic hound" (*D* 177). These references are not to be ignored in a story only eight pages long.

That baying is important in Doyle's novel because the hound does not appear until the climax. Before that moment the animal is only present through its howl; Watson hears it first when standing with Stapleton: "A long, low moan, indescribably sad, swept over the moor. It filled the whole air, and yet it was impossible to say whence it came. From a dull murmur it swelled into a deep roar and then sank back into a melancholy, throbbing murmur once again" (828–29). At night he hears it again, "a long deep mutter, then a rising howl, and then the sad moan in which it died away. Again and again it sounded, the whole air throbbing with it, strident, wild, and menacing" (848). Then he and Holmes hear it at night, "a deep muttered rumble, musical and yet menacing, rising and falling like the low, constant murmur of the sea" (871). A difference between the two hounds is immediately evident; Lovecraft's supernatural creature bays, but Doyle's creature, which as we realize at the end of the story is not supernatural, suffers. Its sound is sad, melancholy, and musical. Though it becomes a symbol of the moor and of the Grimpen Mire, it is in fact half-starved, being kept by the human villain who incites it. The dog gains its magnitude from the legend of the hound that rips the throat out of Hugo Baskerville and then turns "its blazing eyes and dripping jaws" (790) upon the three men who have followed Hugo and from the description of the valley in which that death took place according to the legend: "In the middle of it rose two great stones, worn and sharpened at the upper end, until they looked like the huge, corroding fangs

---

1. In 1918 Lovecraft wrote to Alfred Galpin, "I used to be infatuated with [Holmes]," adding that he had read every Holmes story, though that was a bit of an exaggeration (*Letters to Alfred Galpin* 19, 24n9). S. T. Joshi has pointed out the relevance of Doyle's novel to Lovecraft's story, but he does not pursue the details of their connection ("Explanatory Notes" 91).

of some monstrous beast" (835). If we consider how often, in contrast, the word "bay" occurs in Lovecraft's story, we realize how important that sound is. It is half-heard, distant, directionless, daemoniac, insistent, and faint, very faint as the narrator approaches the grave of the ghoul from whom he has stolen the amulet. The death that bays, that which devours the devourer, is very far away until it reveals itself as the beast in the grave.

Much more develops from Lovecraft's use of the word "bay." When the hound of the Baskervilles howls it is reacting to its pain. But baying is a purposive act. Dr. Johnson declares that to bay is "to bark as a dog at a thief, or at the game which he pursues" ("To Bay").[2] I think that it is easy enough to see that the two young men become the game of the ancient ghoul; it is more interesting to note that the hound pursues them because they are thieves; and to compound this imagery of theft, thieves in Rotterdam steal the amulet from the narrator, only to be destroyed themselves "in a squalid thieves' den" (D 177). The two young men, however, are not simply thieves of the amulet that the ancient ghoul had stolen in his own time (D 173) but of death itself. A parallel to their story is that of the three young men who blasphemously mean to kill death in Chaucer's "Pardoner's Tale": "Deeth shall be deed if that they may him hente" (l. 422). But how shall one capture death, much less slay him? A mortal cannot slay death, much less steal death because death does not belong to a person who shall die, despite the claims of an aesthete like Rilke who makes it a moral imperative that one's death should be one's "eigen," one's own, in order to escape the anonymity of contemporary life. Death, as he insistently says in the "Requiem: Für eine Freundin," should be "deiner, / dein eigner Tod zu deinem eignen Leben" [yours, / your own death for your own life] (407)—an insistence that at the least speaks to the difficulty of the imperative.

Doubtless the corpse has its own dignity—at least that is what our culture assumes. That dignity may proceed from the primitive taboo that attaches to the corpse, which in part is placated by the gifts presented to it and by the communal feast that is often celebrated; what we most often identify as the Irish wake takes also the form of the foods we bring to the homes of the bereaved ("Funeral Rites"). That dignity needs to maintained in the

---

2. Lovecraft used this language of baying and howling a year earlier in "The Music of Erich Zann," in which Erich Zann continues to play with his "night-baying viol" (DH 90), giving forth a "ghoulish howling" (91) even after his death. The trespass of death cries out in its own language, very like the tongue of the hound.

most extreme circumstances. Bones that were dug up in graveyards because room had to be made for the newly dead were placed in ossuaries, not thrown into dust heaps. Aquinas, in discussing whether burial is one of the seven acts of corporal mercy, argues that we can do neither good nor ill to a corpse but that it is nevertheless necessary that we pay attention to it in so far as it lives in the memory of the living. The "honor [mortui] dehonestatur si insepultus remaneat" (2-2 q. 32, a.2); the honor that we owe the corpse would be lost if the corpse remained unburied. It is in this light that Spenser prays, "Ah dearest God me graunt, I dead be not defould" (*Faërie Queene* 1.10.42)—and with great pomp, after the Irish had burned him out of his castle, he was buried in Westminster Abbey.

In the European tradition the dignity owed a corpse was once the pious hope that it should be buried in sanctified ground (and thus the church possessed the threat not to bury a corpse in sanctified ground as a sign of the second death of the soul). With the advent of Protestantism this dignity and power were diminished; now it is sufficient that a body be buried in a cemetery sanctified by this or that denomination, and nowhere was this development more immediately evident than in the pluralism of the Netherlands, as Lovecraft probably knew. The British formula that "A corpse is not the subject of property, nor capable of holding property" has the effect of handing the corpse over to the jurisdiction of the ecclesiastical and secular courts for the sake of its primordial dignity ("Burial"). In order to protect this dignity laws have long existed against the disinterment of the dead for any purpose other than the exemptions granted under the power of the ecclesiastical or secular courts; the point of these exemptions nevertheless grants the dignity of the corpse. Only a judge can allow a disinterment for carefully stated reasons. The most interesting exemption is that granted for the criminal, who thereby has lost his dignity and his rights. Anyone who views Rembrandt's painting *The Anatomy Lesson of Dr. Deyman* should know that the corpse in this scene is that of a criminal, Joris Fonteijn, also known as Zwarte Jan, which the court granted to the Anatomy theater after his execution and which they buried three days later in the Zuiderkerkhof "met een redelijcke statie" [with reasonable ceremony] (Middelkoop 5). Even the criminal, after he has been disrobed and disassembled, more naked than naked, is granted some final tokens of respect.

In Lovecraft's own day Rhode Island law was quite explicit: "Every person who shall, without proper authorization, disinter, dig up, remove, or carry away any human body from its place of sepulture, or who shall knowingly conceal any such body so disinterred or carried away, shall be imprisoned not exceeding ten (10) years or fined not exceeding on thousand dollars ($1,000)" ("Rhode Island General Laws §11–20–1"). Broader laws, much more detailed, obtain for the desecration of the grave that set a fine of $3,000 ("Rhode Island General Laws §11–20–2). The law does its best to be as precise as possible; we should note, however, that the law of Rhode Island still employs the language of desecration, a language that Lovecraft would have had no truck with—and yet as far as the narrator is concerned this story does seem to depend upon the notion of supernatural dignity. The possibility within our contemporary laws that the individual can sign over his or her corpse and its organs for medical purposes protects the corpse by suggesting that it lies within the possession of that individual even if death has occurred; thus a legal dignity is assigned the corpse. But though the corpse has its own dignity, whether it is buried whole or whether it is distributed to further use, it still suffers the ultimate indignity that it does not belong to itself; it belongs to death, and it is a moral trespass to steal from death its own.

Robert Louis Stevenson's story "The Body-Snatcher," which Lovecraft mentioned with favor in "Supernatural Horror in Literature" (D 388), is enlightening in these matters. The story concerns the illegal and sometimes murderous connections between graverobbers and the anatomical theater. A part of the story, however, is first concerned with the insult to the grave: "The Resurrection Man—to use a by-name of the period—was not to be deterred by any of the sanctities of customary piety. It was part of his trade to despise and desecrate the scrolls and trumpets of old tombs" (8.424). Still the language of desecration! More peculiar is the language one of the doctors uses to another when they decide not to acknowledge that the men bringing them the bodies are in fact murders, no better than Burke and Hare: "You can't begin and then stop. If you begin, you must keep on beginning" (8.422). It is as though graverobbing, which at first seems merely simple theft, actually constitutes a second murder that lies in a beginning that ceaselessly repeats itself. The work of the ghoul is obsessional, lying beyond mere cupidity and the thirst for knowledge. In the supernatural climax the doctors are confronted by the presence of the man that one of them had earlier killed. A body reoccupies its corpse; the vicious body they have murdered takes the place of the sainted old woman they had meant to steal and accuses them of their crime, just as the narrator of "The Hound" finds a very different body in the grave than he had expected. The two doctors react in very different ways to this accusation. One becomes a stolid drunken sot; the other becomes a well-known physician but ever after secretly bears the slang name Toddy. The obsessional trespass is no better than intoxication.

We need to consider this trespass further. Existentialism insists that no individual achieves the meaning of his or her life until death, since before that moment the life is still open; having not achieved a conclusion its meaning is at best inconclusive. Undoubtedly that meaning is then rubbed away through the years just as the statement on the funeral stone blurs in the rain, but this meaning is still, at least in theory, capable of retrieval. The ghoul disrupts this meaning. The two young men co-opt it so that the various bodies become objects in the aesthetic spectacle they are arranging in their underground room. The trespass, then, is a trespass upon the meaning of the individual whose body they objectify, in precisely the same fashion that one sex may objectify the other and therefore deny any other meaning than the sexual. We should note not coincidentally that the narrator in fact accepts this dignity of the corpse when he buries St. John, mumbling over the grave "one of the devilish rituals he had love in his life" (D 176); his trespass, then, crosses the external boundary of law and the internal boundary of his own moral sense.

Besides these important details, several others in Lovecraft's story are reminiscent of Doyle's. Both hounds carry with them the whiff of the supernatural, only in Doyle's novel to be evaporated by Holmes's rationality. The main action takes place on a moor and in a swamp; the protagonists of Lovecraft's tale live "in a few rooms of an ancient manor-house on a bleak and unfrequented moor" (D 175), along a path some distance from a railroad station where St. John, "walking home after dark" (D 176) is torn to pieces. Sir Henry in Doyle's novel, under Holmes's instructions, walks home at night to be attacked by the hound; he is not torn to pieces, but his composure is sufficiently shattered that only a long trip around the world will allow him to regain his well-being. The first sentence of Doyle's novel establishes that Holmes, like the young men, is a night-creature. The young men collect corpses, and Stapleton, the villain of the novel, collects butterflies. The main action in both stories takes place in the autumn.

Only one detail is surprising, one which seems to have no place in Doyle's novel, the fact that the main crime of Lovecraft's story takes place in the Netherlands and returns to the Netherlands at the story's climax. To understand that detail, and thereby much else in the story, we need to listen to its genesis. At the end of September Lovecraft described to his aunt Lillian a recent episode of his life in New York City:

That evening Kleiner and I investigated the principal antiquity of this section—the old Dutch Reformed Church—and were well repaid for our quest. . . . Around the oil pile is a hoary churchyard, with interments dating from about 1730 to the middle of the nineteenth century. Nearly all the stones bear inscriptions and epitaphs in the Dutch language—beginning with the characteristic "Hier lygen", which analogy makes quite recognizable to the devotee of English graveyards. Up to about 1815 or 1820 the Dutch tongue predominates. . . . From one of the crumbling gravestones—dated 1747—I chipped a small piece to carry away. It lies before me as I write—and ought to suggest some sort of a horror-story. I must some night place it beneath my pillow as I sleep . . . who can say what *thing* might not come out of the centuried earth to exact vengeance for his desecrated tomb? And should it come, who can say what it might not resemble? (SL 1.198)

We do not know whether Lovecraft did dream upon his stolen talisman, but most of the story is present here: the season, the two men who rob a grave, the Dutch churchyard and the Dutch language, and the notion that the creature, whatever kind of creature might be in the grave, would exact revenge. An earlier visit to the Dutch Reformed cemetery added another detail, the vulture descending from the sky in the penultimate scene to peck "frantically at the grave-earth" until the narrator kills the bird with his spade (D 178; cf. Joshi, "Explanatory Notes" 381). Most interestingly, Lovecraft visits the tomb with Rheinhart Kleiner, whom he had christened Randolph St. John, as though he were a relative of the English lord Henry St. John, Viscount Bolingbroke, who had been the patron of Pope and Swift but who went into exile with the ascendancy of the Whigs under George I. I do not know why Lovecraft had christened his friend so, but St. John who, according to the story, "was always the leader, [. . .] who led the way at last to that mocking, that accursed spot which brought us our hideous and inevitable doom" (D 173), is the only character in the story to bear a name. If the story is a parody, then, it is originally a parody of Lovecraft and his friend, their pleasure in visiting graveyards and their belief by so doing that in some fashion they have come into a meaningful relationship with the past.

One further point should be made here, the resemblance that this story bears to one of Lovecraft's earlier stories, "The Statement of Randolph Carter," in which the weird explorations of two men culminate when the leader descends into a sepulcher that proves to be deeper than anyone could have expected, reporting his discoveries over a wire until he is lost and a different voice, "deep; hollow; gelatinous; remote; unearthly; inhuman; disembodied," reports the man's death (MM 305). That story had originated as a dream in which Lovecraft's friend Samuel Loveman makes the descent; and Loveman is not far from "The Hound," since the collection that its two characters gather resembles the collection of weird objects that Loveman had gathered and that Lovecraft saw in his visit to Cleveland in September, 1922, a month before he wrote the story (Joshi, "Explanatory Notes" 378). The discovery that this narrator makes, then, in which the "bleached and cavern-eyed face" of the ghoul is transformed into the face of a supernatural hound, "covered with caked blood and shreds of alien flesh and hair, and leering sentiently at me with phosphorescent sockets and sharp ensanguined fangs yawning twistedly in mockery of my inevitable doom" (D 178), is a discovery that parallels that made by Lovecraft/Loveman in the earlier story and foretells the discovery made by the narrator of "The Outsider" at the conclusion of that story, having emerged from a sepulcher much deeper than anyone might expect. The other and the self, refracted through the lens of homoeroticism and decay, are the same.

As a story about friends, of course, "The Hound" is also a parody of the relationship between the aesthete Holmes and the doctor Watson. It is not simply a question of the seven-percent solution with which *The Sign of Four* opens; more to our interest in "The Hound" is the Holmes in *A Study in Scarlet* who is given to battering corpses in order to study the bruises that his assault causes. This bizarre scene foretells the interests that the later work indulges in. A part of this parody must rest upon our reconstruction of Lovecraft's attitude toward Doyle's study of the Baskervilles, which so strikingly uses the materials of horror, the supernatural hound, the labyrinth of the moors, the problem of mistaking the regressive, instinct-driven convict for the actual villain who disguises himself as a harmless butterfly collector, but who is himself a throwback to the Hugo Baskerville of the legend, only to disinfect this horror at the end with Holmesian rationality. What a chance, Lovecraft must have felt, was lost here when Holmes wipes the phosphorescence from the hound's muzzle! The insistent "gigantic hound" of Lovecraft's story redresses the balance.

Beyond this point, however, the threads between the two works are less obvious. It is striking that *The Hound of the Baskervilles* contains three collections, the "anthropological museum" (787) that Dr. Mortimer hopes will someday be graced by Holmes's skull, the numerous collections that Holmes keeps on Baker Street, and the collection of butterflies that Stapleton has formed. The collection that the two men in Lovecraft's story have made is not a matter of indifference to the meaning of the story: "Niches here and there contained skulls of all shapes, and heads preserved in various stages of dissolution. There one might find the rotting, bald pates of famous noblemen, and the fresh and radiantly golden heads of new-buried children" (*D* 172). It forms an anthropological museum; its subject is human variety, the old and the young, the famous and the unknown, the guilty and the innocent, and the common fate that awaits us. Unlike Joseph Curwen, they have no need to question the essential salts of their collection; it speaks for itself when artistically arranged. The art is all-important, for without its intuitive force the collection would be speechless. If the couplet that appears in "The Call of Cthulhu" speaks to us—

> That is not dead which can eternal lie,
> And with strange aeons even death may die. (*DH* 141)

—it speaks through being a couplet, perhaps Lovecraft's best poem in a career of poetic pastiche. It is his best poem because of its complex allusion to the epistles (I Cor. 15:55 inter alia), to Donne's sonnet that concludes, "Death, thou shalt die" (284), and to the paradox that death may die (though not as the three drunkards think in "The Pardoner's Tale") because of the paradox explicit in the first line, and because of the pun in the word "lie." The couplet is much stranger than Lovecraft ever wrote.

The differences between the young men's collection and those in *The Hound of the Baskervilles* are important. Dr. Mortimer's collection is scientific, objective, though he is passionate about his subject. Holmes's collection serves the purpose of pursuit; it is scientific, but an applied science, and Holmes is not passionate about it, only about the hunt. Stapleton's collection of butterflies is the most interesting of our comparisons. It is scientific, but much more a question of art; and like Holmes he enjoys the pursuit, though his beautiful victims are innocent. A long tradition of disapproval emanating from the humane studies trails the activity of the amateur scientists who captured butterflies. Addison and Pope, no great friends, both agreed that butterfly collecting was a perverse act, an attitude still present in John Fowles's novel *The Collector*. Addison attacked the naturalists who "amuse themselves with the stifling of Cats in an Air Pump, cutting up Dogs alive, or impaling of Insects upon the point of a Needle for Microscopic Observations; besides those that are employed in the gathering of Weeds, and the Chase of Butterflies" (1.91; #21). In *The Dunciad* Pope satirized the butterfly collector who sins against God's holistic act of creation (4.421–36).

But in this regard all these collections, Dr. Mortimer's, Holmes's, Stapleton's, and the young men's, are alike: the objects of the collections are dead. Dr. Mortimer does not kill, Holmes does not; Stapleton kills his butterflies but he murders through the agency of his hound; and the young men do not kill; but death is the point of the collections. On the other hand, the butterfly is a symbol of the resurrected soul. Death and resurrection are very much the problem in Lovecraft's story; the art of the ghoul offers one means of controlling death through the careful manipulation of its inert materials, but this careful manipulation the story condemns

There is no butterfly in Lovecraft's story, but the butterfly has been transformed. On the first page the narrator hears "a nightmare whirring and flapping" (D 171) that earlier in chronological time though later in narrative time had seemed "a whirring or flapping sound not far off" (175). The amulet they steal bears the carving of "a crouching winged hound, or sphinx with a semi-canine face" (174). When St. John is killed the narrator hears "a whir of wings" and sees "a vague black cloudy thing silhouetted against the rising moon" (176); and in the last sentence of the story "the stealthy whirring and flapping of those accursed web-wings circles closer and closer" (178). *Stealth* and *steal* are of course related.

That whiff of the supernatural that we have mentioned earlier, an integral part of Doyle's story that Lovecraft, given the kind of story he is writing, must make literal, is also influenced by another work, Francis Thompson's once famous poem "The Hound of Heaven."[3] Just as the first sentence of the first paragraph points at Doyle, the conclusion of the first paragraph points at Thompson: "Down unlit and illimitable corridors of eldritch phantasy sweeps the black, shapeless Nemesis that drives me to self-annihilation" (D 171). This influence is not except in certain minor ways verbal. There is certainly no stealth here. Putting aside the subject, God's pursuit of the soul, which Thompson treats in something of the same way that Donne or Crashaw treated the metaphysical conceit, the poem is most remarkable for the way that its long and short lines and its broken syntax create an onomatopoeic effect of the rapid, exhausting pursuit. The four long stanzas,

---

3. I say "once famous" because this poem, once to be found in all major literary anthologies, has now vanished from them, though Thompson certainly exemplifies several characteristics to be found in writers as different as Hopkins and Swinburne. Though he was influenced by Shelley, as were Browning and Swinburne, he is still his own poet. Lovecraft knew his work well enough to comment with approval in a 1929 letter that his poems avoid inversions. In Lovecraft this is no damnation with faint praise (SL 3.12).

which might otherwise be shapeless, receive their form from the varied refrain that describes the rhythm of the divine Feet:

> But with unhurrying chase,
> And unexpected pace,
> Deliberate speed, majestic instancy,
> They beat—and a Voice beat
> More instant than the Feet—
> 'All things betray thee, who betrayest Me.' (ll. 10–15)

At the conclusion of the poem the refrain takes this form:

> Now of that long pursuit
> Comes on at hand the bruit;
> That Voice is round me like a bursting sea. (ll. 155–57)

There is simply no escape from this gigantic presence. The first-person protagonist, for all his attempts to appeal to his contemporaries or to his knowledge of the natural world, finds every metaphoric casement of escape
impossible, for "The gust of His approach would clash it to" (l. 23). The inexorable rhythm of the poem as it alternates imagery of an enormous beast,
both Feet and Voice, in pursuit of a protagonist reduced at last to the earth
of which he is made, may well have provided Lovecraft with encouragement
for his story, in which there is no escape from a supernatural being that is
both of the earth and of the air, of the earth and of the sea. The trespass that
the two men have committed is sufficiently profound to break apart everything that has seemed natural in our world.

Two other aspects of the poem need comment. First there is the rhetoric
of the first lines, continued in the rest of the poem, by which the external
world and the internal world provide similes to each other, so that the internal world seems enormous and the external world claustrophobic:

> I fled Him, down the nights and down the days;
> I fled Him, down the arches of the years;
> I fled Him, down the labyrinthine ways
> Of my own mind [. . .] (ll. 1–4)

In "The Hound" the story seems to exist externally, as happens in most
weird tales, but the terror of the protagonist arises actually from his own oral
exhaustion, that can find no satisfaction in the exterior world.

This terror is corroborated in "The Hound of Heaven" by the extensive passage in the third stanza in which the speaker tries to ingratiate himself with the children of Nature, to remain with the phenomena of the natural world and to find in them a "delicate fellowship" (l. 62). He hopes that he can overcome the natural fallacy and insists, repeating that earlier lovely phrase, "I in their delicate fellowship was one— / Drew the bolt of Nature's secrecies" (ll. 74–75). The sexual language, however, will not allow him the inwardness he craves. He admits the severe disjunction between the human and the natural world:

> For ah! we know not what each other says,
>   These things and I; in sound I speak—
> *Their* sound is but their stir, they speak by silences.
> Nature, poor stepdame, cannot slake my drouth. (ll. 96–99)

Next to these lines consider the odd language of the protagonist of "The Hound": after they had run through the attempts of the symbolists and the Pre-Raphaelites to approach and interpret nature, "Only the sombre philosophy of the Decadents could hold us, and this we found potent only by increasing gradually the depth and diabolism / of our penetrations" (D 171–72). Whether the individual courts nature or rapes nature, the result is the same, the discovery that nature is composed of nothing but human excretion. In the last stanza the protagonist of "The Hound of Heaven" asks with dismay, "[M]ust Thy harvest-fields / Be dunged with rotten death?" (ll. 153–54), to learn that he is indeed no more than "Of all man's clotted clay the dingiest clot" (l. 166). The resemblance of "dunged" and "dingiest" is a pointedly painful piece of rhetoric, especially when we read it in the context of the oral fixations of "The Hound."

In Lovecraft's story, of course, it is this deep penetration of nature that excites the retribution of the ghoul in the form of the hound, that as it were brings the hound into the upper world. It is not, then, a great leap to suggest that lying behind his story is the myth of Hercules' descent to the underworld to bring back the guardian of the underworld, the three-headed dog Cerberus. Traditionally this is the last and most dangerous of Hercules' labors; he has dealt with monster after monster, but this is the monster that most emphatically symbolizes the aggression and isolation of death. The reason for the connection between the dog and death is quite natural. At the climax of "The Body-Snatcher," as the two doctors carry their ghoulish burden through the countryside, "the farm dogs accompanied their passage with tragic ululations; and it grew and grew upon [the one doctor's] mind that some unnatural miracle had been accomplished, that some nameless change had befallen the dead body, and that it was in fear of their unholy burden that the dogs were howling" (8.429). It may not, however, be simply that the dogs recognize the doctors' crime and cry out against it. In the opening lines of the *Iliad* the singer assures us that the bodies of the heroes "Devouring dogs and hungry vultures tore" (Pope 1.6). Dante's Cerberus behaves as violently in the *Inferno*: "He tears the spirits, flays them, and their limbs / Piecemeal disparts" (6.17–18). Cerberus is the dog that is most obviously a ghoul, and in "The Hound" it seems only proper that ghoul should eat ghoul. The hound of heaven pursuing us to our salvation may well be the hound of hell pursuing us to our damnation; or perhaps it is only the hound of earth that wants nothing more than to eat us, and this dog, since it is only a dog, commits no trespass and no desecration. For the truth of the matter is, as far as the materialist Lovecraft is concerned, the Lovecraft of the letters, that no desecration is possible in a world that has no purpose.

This story like "The Rats in the Walls" concerns a supernatural, bestial destroyer, but the origin of that destroyer in "The Hound" is more difficult to discover given the scope of the story's allusions; there is no doubt, however, that we are implicated in that origin, whether we are ghouls, aesthetes, positivist detectives, or radical Christians, yearning for the hound of heaven to devour us before we are displayed in a new hell. That is the point of the two stories; as devourers ourselves, we wait in great expectation for our own devourers.

The Ecstasies of "The Thing on the Doorstep," "Medusa's Coil," and Other Erotic Studies

This is the very ecstasy of love,
Whose violent property fordoes itself
And leads the will to desperate undertakings
As oft as any passion under heaven.
[...]
That unmatched form and feature of blown youth
Blasted with ecstasy. (*Hamlet* 2.1.102–5, 3.1.160–61)

"The Thing on the Doorstep" is a remarkably unsatisfying yet compelling story. When we read it with any attention the questions it raises, lacking any convincing answer, seem without end caught as they are in the flickering light of countless gender transformations. With some dismay we face their increasingly perverse implications and call out with Macbeth as the phantom descendants of Banquo parade before him, "What, will the line stretch out to th' crack of doom?" (*Macbeth* 4.1.133). In this story the line is a matter of ancestors. It stretches out until we realize that both Edward Derby and Asenath Waite are dead, and it is with a great finality that her name, in the possessive form, is the last word in the story. With some hesitation, then, I wish to offer another reading, one that may seem highly unlikely, examining it as though it were Lovecraft's study of erotic love. True, Edward Derby seems a pallid figure to imagine as an erotic lover. I think, however, that in this story we meet in some distortion and repression a work that deals with Eros, with erotic love and erotic obsession, as Plato and the theologian Josef Pieper understood it. Yes, we can learn something about the hermit of Providence from Platonism and Neo-Aquinian thought. In part we are involved in another palinodia, very like the one that Plato and Pieper describe; we confess to Helen of Troy that we have insulted her, that she, the goddess, if she was a goddess, was never the cause of that endless war that caused the deaths of so many men. No, she, the handmaid of Eros, was always guiltless;

84

and like her Asenath and Marceline were also guiltless; not only guiltless, they were spiritual lights that led the men who fell in love with them into a higher realm of being (Pieper, *Begeisterung* 78–80).

So we cannot read "The Thing on the Doorstep" in this light without reading "Medusa's Coil" in this light also. A great difference seems to exist between the narrators; in the first story the narrator is a friend of the tragic lover, in the second story the central narrator is the father of the lover and the peripheral narrator a traveler who knows none of the main actors. Their levels of concern, responsibility, and personal engagement are quite different, as is the mere difference in the generations. Granted these differences, we shall see that several of their details are comparable and that the parabola of love, its dream of ascent and its destruction, a destruction that neither Plato nor Pieper envisage, follows a roughly similar trajectory. Having determined the different stages of this trajectory we shall find that it is also possible to read "The Dreams in the Witch House" and "The Whisperer in Darkness" in the light of their erotic ecstasis.

I

> Set me as a seal upon thine heart, as a seal upon thine arm: for love is strong as death; jealousy is cruel as the grave: the coals thereof are coals of fire, which have a most vehement flame. (Song of Solomon 8:6)

In a few superficial ways "The Thing on the Doorstep" and "Medusa's Coil" are not that incomparable. Different as the narrators are, they certainly seem to be narrators on the margin of the story, not at its center, so that the true subject of the plot remains impenetrable. These two stories seem to be the only ones in which the overt concern of the plot is the erotic connection between a man and a woman; though Lovecraft may seem uncomfortable with such a subject, it is remarkable that given such a discomfort he does deal with the subject twice. At the center of the horror in both stories lies the body buried in the cellar that will not stay dead; and that body represents a connection between this world and an archaic world that lies beyond our accepted histories and our accepted dimensions. In both stories a rather weak young man consummates a marriage with a daemonic figure that leads him beyond the world we know; and in both stories the narration insists that an old, honorable family, represented in both stories by a father, is destroyed; we might recall that this is the final point of *Romeo and Juliet*. Finally, almost as an afterthought, the narrator assures the reader that the true horror lies in an act of miscegenation, in the first story with a fishlike creature, in the second story with a black; which of these acts from our contemporary perspective is less horrific or less embarrassing we must leave to our individual sensibilities, but surely something is imbalanced in such narratives.

These comparisons, however, must yield to the theme of erotic, ecstatic love, as Plato outlines it in his description of Eros in the *Phaedrus*. First, he places it within the context of a divine mania, a characteristic it shares with prophecy, healing, and poetry (244a–245a). Properly understood, these are gifts from the gods; they do not depend upon the intellectual, technical skill of the prophet, doctor, or poet. Before Socrates proceeds to Eros, however, he finds it necessary to establish the immortality of the soul (a consistently important tenet of the Platonic system). In this dialogue the immortality is established by the argument that the soul depends upon a first principle that, as it were, exists as the basis of the soul by which, through the soul's own nature, it moves of itself (245c–246a); the activity of the soul is its first principle. It is at this point that Socrates compares the soul to a charioteer who must control two very different sorts of horses. Founded upon its autokinesis, the soul does not perish because it does not come into existence. Consider this principle within the context of "The Thing on the Doorstep" in which the reader is persuaded to believe that Asenath is controlled by her father's soul, which itself is controlled by an entity that has nothing to do with humanity; this "it" is the true basis of the soul, to speak as Derby and Upton speak, that animates Asenath and that strikes Derby out of himself. In "Medusa's Coil" Marceline, whatever the details of her biography, whether she did or did not come from Martinique, actually incarnates something older than anything that can be located within human prehistory; the Great Zimbabwe is as true and mythological a place as the Marse Clooloo to which Sophonisba appeals, presumptively Cthulhu as we turn the name. Soul meets soul outside of time. Thus the erotic event begins in an ecstasis in which the soul stands outside itself, an ecstasis caused by the sudden recognition of a very concrete, physical beauty. In this ecstasis one feels winged, ready to take part in the procession and banquet of the gods, overcome by a memory of one's origin and a promise of return (246d–247b, 249d–e).

Because of this memory and its promise of a return to an authentic self, Socrates insists that erotic mania is superior to the three other divine manias he has passed over so swiftly, though Pieper claims that those three, the prophetic, the cathartic, and the creative, are in some fashion summed up by the erotic. Love is prophetic, cathartic, and poetic. To consider it as a catharsis is especially interesting, since Pieper argues that Plato does not have in mind here the diseases of the body but the diseases of the soul, call them fate, call them the anger of the gods, call them a family curse "from the third and fourth generation of them that hate me; and shewing mercy unto thousands of them that love me, and keep my commandments" (Ex. 20:5–6). Doubtless the main thrust of this commandment offers mercy, but that was not how the Puritans read it, and it renders tersely the sense of such Greek works as the *Oresteia*. From depth psychology we are dreadfully aware of the inertia of our flaws within the family. Suicide, addiction, abuse, and incest, their effects are carried out through the innocents who thereby inherit and act out guilt. We must be healed, but that can only happen at a severe psychic price. Whether this price shall be in the hands of divine powers or in the hands of the unconscious is difficult to say; the *theia mania* always feels external, like a gift, not something that the self has accomplished (Pieper, *Begeisterung* 98–105). The structure of Eros, then, implies that the god must make a person mad, stricken outside of the self, in order to heal the self. The personality must be destroyed before it can be reconstructed on a higher plane of existence.

How can that be so? Pieper's commentary upon divine mania, especially the divine mania of the erotic, offers us a number of details that will enrich our description of Lovecraft's story. First, let us note that the prophet suffers a raptus or an ecstasis; the words are roughly equivalent, but a raptus implies that the self is stolen, whereas as the ecstasis implies simply that the self, for whatever reason, is stricken outside the self. Aquinas uses the word raptus for the suffering of the prophet, that he describes as *contra naturam*. It is a spiritual act but it is also an act that the prophet suffers. (*Ver.* 13, 1 obj. 1 and *Sum. Theol.* 2, 2. 171 prolog.; ctd. in Pieper, *Begeisterung* 96–97); and in the same manner the lover suffers his ecstasis, his being put outside of himself. He does not, however, merely stand outside himself as the word ecstasis suggests. In fact the state is described in two ways. Either the person is possessed (245a), so that it seems as though someone or something else were speaking through him; or he is violently torn away from himself, no longer living the daily life to which we are all accustomed—too accustomed Plato insists—but living elsewhere, transposed to the life of the gods as they circle the universe. It is no surprise then that Edward Derby suffers his encounter with Asenath or that Denis de Russy suffers his encounter with Marceline. Pieper emphasizes that the comparison of the soul to a winged chariot pulled by horses with contrary goals in mind is simply that, a comparison that because it treats of such things as soul and god is insufficient; but no comparison can exhaust such subjects or reduce them to objects of the pure understanding: "Es ist uns nicht gegeben, von Gegenständen wie Seele, Geist, Gottheit mit dem Anspruch der direkten Kennzeichnung zu reden" [It is not granted us to speak of such objects as soul, spirit, divinity with the pretension of direct signs] (*Begeisterung*127). In a similar way I do not think it was granted Lovecraft to speak in such a manner; instead he employs narrative, one narrative after another, none of them sufficient to the subject at hand, the terrors and elations of the spirit.

This problem of language is one reason that Plato is so often driven to a variety of different myths that outline his basic doctrines; thus, for instance, he develops two different myths of the after-life, one at the conclusion of the *Republic* and another at the conclusion of the *Phaedo*. So we find in the *Symposium* a variety of different speeches in praise of Eros, some of them quite interesting and others clearly wide of the mark; only the last speech, reported by Socrates as the words of the priestess, seems to be valid. In this speech she reveals that love is a spirit, neither mortal nor immortal but between the divine and the human. It is like all the other spirits,

> the envoys and interpreters that ply between heaven and earth, flying upward with our worship and our prayers, and descending with the heavenly answers and commandments, and since they are between the two estates they weld both sides together and merge them into one great whole. They form the medium of the prophetic arts, of the priestly rites of sacrifice, initiation, and incantation, of divination and of sorcery, for the divine will not mingle directly with the human, and it is only through the mediation of the spirit world that man can have any intercourse, whether waking or sleeping, with the gods. [. . .] There are many spirits, and many kinds of spirits [δαίμονες], too, and Love is one of them. (202e–203a)

In this passage we see that Eros is an important messenger and translator between the divine and the human; he fulfills something of the role that is so often given to Hermes, whose name is embedded in the hermetic art; but we also see that Eros, a messenger of the gods, is not a god himself but a daemon. In the Platonic world this is not unimportant, for he makes much of the daemon that shaped Socrates' life.

This passage had a great deal of influence over Goethe, who habitually referred to the daemonic in human affairs. It was for him incommensurable, active in the political world, in poetry, and in love. In all these matters the irrational was at play, compelling unaccountable actions as though it were a personality: "Das Dämonische [. . .] ist dasjenige, was durch Verstand und Vernunft nicht aufzulösen ist. In meiner Natur liegt es nicht, aber ich bin ihm unterworfen" [The daemonic . . . is that which cannot be resolved by the reason or understanding] (Eckermann 438). We already noted this point in Pieper's commentary; it is not possible to reduce love to a rational account. As Goethe says, it does not lie in my nature, but I am subject to it. Furthermore, to continue in this mythic mode, it is not simply a matter of the lover and the beloved: "Und dann, was nicht zu vergessen, kommt als ein mächtiges Drittes noch das Dämonisches hinzu, das jede Leidenschaft zu begleiten pflegt und das in der Liebe sein eigentliches Element findet" [And then we must not forget that the daemonic appears as a mighty third that is accustomed to accompany every passion and that finds in love its very own element] (Eckermann 671). Doubtless Goethe is speaking in a mythic fashion, a mode that may not have much to do with facts but very much to do with truth. Something happens in this ecstatic relation that seems to introduce an alien power that overcomes it, taking the lovers into a new space that neither had expected.

The transformation of the personality through love, which as we have seen must feel like a sickness, feels at last like a sickness unto death; but it also feels beyond all hope like a sickness that shall transcend death. Christianity says very clearly that the individual that truly loves Christ must be buried in Christ to share his resurrection (Rom. 6:4). Edward Derby is resurrected after he is buried in the decaying body of his wife, and the resurrection does bring him to his triumphant last meeting with his friend and to a revenge on the other side of the grave upon the woman and the spirit behind her that has taken him outside himself. For love is suffering.

To step back for a moment, we need to ask what is erotic about Asenath, what in her awakens desire in Derby, who is something of a cold fish? We only have the words of the narrator Daniel Upton, which might or might not reflect Derby's words, as well as the various words, hers included, that describe Sonia Greene. Lovecraft himself was very careful to refrain from such language. Let us then consider Daniel Upton's words. She "was dark, smallish, and very good looking" (*DH* 280), words that might account for Derby's attraction. With some distaste Upton calls her eyes "overprotuberant" (280), adverting then to her background in Innsmouth and recounting as rumor and legend the story that Lovecraft's readers might well remember from the earlier novella "The Shadow over Innsmouth"; but some might call her eyes spiritual or sensitive, for we are accustomed to say that the soul looks out of the eyes; in some accounts the hypnotist works through the eyes, and Upton grudgingly allows that she is "a genuine hypnotist" (281), so her blazing eyes, which Upton suggests are actually the eyes of her father, become a recurrent and compelling phrase in the story.

This beauty, perhaps because of its unconventional nature, has an apparently immediate effect upon Derby; "wildly taken with her appearance" he suffers an upheaval from merely looking at her (*DH* 281). To Upton this is a mere infatuation. This word, however, may be understood in other ways than Upton means it. Though Dr. Johnson glosses it pejoratively, "to strike with folly; to deprive of understanding" ("Infatuate"), the root of the Latin word "fatuus," foolish, is "fatigo," to make weary or to exhaust (Tucker). An infatuated man is rendered quite other than he is; and in the crisis of his infatuation Derby vacillates between a great vigor and a severe exhaustion. What is happening to him is not what happens to a teenager despite Upton's opinion that Derby is a "perennial child" (*DH* 282); this is not a hormonal but a spiritual eruption.

This judgment that Daniel gives upon Derby's love may be the reason for the immense insult Derby presents when he appears on the doorstep and the smell of his body, the body that is actually Asenath's that he has with great pain clawed out of the grave in which he had thrust it, rocks Daniel back on his heels. That "insufferably foetid wind" that "almost flung [him] prostrate" (*DH* 301) represents an act of aggression that I think we can only account for if we realize how belittling Upton's language is. He really cannot sympathize with the ecstatic aspect of Derby's love. How can he? Though he is married, he says almost nothing of his own wife, who must have taken some kind of part in the drama that is now unfolding; but since he says nothing about her, we must assume that his own marriage is not in any way excited by the ecstasis that Derby experiences. But there is more to this aggression than simply Upton's sheer misunderstanding, and we shall examine it further in a later chapter.

II

One cannot maintain that the world was very grateful to psychoanalytic research for its discovery of the Oedipus-complex. (Freud, *General Introduction* 174)

A further comment Upton makes upon the affair as he understands it brings us into another region: "The perennial child had transferred his dependence from the parental image to a new and stronger image, and nothing could be done about it" (*DH* 282). From this point of view the marriage may not be such a bad thing, he believes, for "the *change* of dependence" might at last lead "to responsible independence" (*DH* 283). This language that Lovecraft is using rather loosely he learned from Freud, whom he had begun to read by 1921 though he said at that time he preferred Adler's thinking (*SL* 1.134); despite this preference, however, he refers to Freud three times as often in the *Selected Letters* as he refers to Adler. Thereafter he refers to Freud most often in conjunction with other thinkers, but it is difficult to establish what he has actually read; rather, his knowledge of Freud seems to be at second or third hand. Nevertheless, he had time in which to learn the basic Freudian concepts. In *The Interpretation of Dreams*, which first appeared in English translation in 1913, Freud had discussed infant sexuality and treated the myth of Oedipus at length as a model of infantile male desires and fears (294–97). Perhaps more useful for Lovecraft was Freud's *General Introduction to Psychoanalysis*, which lays out the basic concepts of Freudian theory at that time: the theory of the unconscious as revealed in slips of the tongue; the doctrines of the manifest and latent structure of dreams and of the operation of the wish-fulfillment in dreams; and the doctrine of the polymorphous perverse in children that gives rise to normal sexuality and abnormal, perverse sexuality. Most interesting is Freud's insistence to his audience of the original lectures that "the trouble is that you believe in the illusion of psychic freedom and will not give it up" (31); or, as he puts it later in the book, "In each one of you there is a deep-rooted belief in psychic freedom and volition, a belief which is absolutely unscientific, and which must capitulate before the claims of a determinism that controls even the psychic life" (84). This is the claim that Lovecraft cannot accept.

Or rather, better put, he does accept it intellectually but he cannot accept it artistically—and what artist truly could? I have little doubt that Lovecraft could have accepted the theory of infantile sexuality if only Freud had not expressed it in so deterministic a fashion. This is one of the points at which Adler becomes more *sympathique* to Lovecraft because the unconscious for Adler, the seat of the self, is not deterministically formed; it is not the past that matters for it, but the future that it imagines for itself. The self is creative, aimed toward a goal that Adler expresses in a variety of fashions but is nevertheless a viable fiction that shapes the self at the same moment that the self creates it.[1] The unconscious for Freud is as mechanistic as it was

---

1. Heinz and Rowena Ansbacher point out how strongly Adler was influenced by the *Als-ob* phi-

for Locke, for both of them insist upon the associative process, which in Freud becomes the associative technique employed in the psychoanalytic treatment. What Lovecraft did not realize, fortunately so as far as his creative process was concerned, was the ease a reader has in reading his fictions as though the unconscious were indeed operative. Charles Dexter Ward, for instance, so heavily dependent upon his family, becomes so fascinated by the figure of his powerful ancestor Joseph Curwen that he at last acts as though he were that figure; the story plays out the wish-fulfillment of a dream.

The central problem about Freud for Lovecraft is the theory of dreams in which the theory of the unconscious is realized. In March 1926 he wrote to his aunt Lillian, "I don't believe you'll find much sound science in Freud's 'Dream Psychology', since his theory of dreams is perhaps the weakest link in his whole chain. Many of his hypotheses can be punctured quite readily by careful evidence, & it is one of Mortonius' many ambitions to refute Freud in a ponderous treatise on dreams" (ms., JHL). Lovecraft is content to leave the scut work to his friend James F. Morton. The point here is that the dream is radically important to Lovecraft as an emblem of his own creative power and his own authentic privacy. The dream belongs to him and he belongs to the dream; it happens outside his ken, but it is his dream and no other's. The various Freudian interpretations, especially any that proceed out of the darkness of childhood, have no power upon it.

How, then, if Freud and Adler were presented with the Platonic myth of the winged chariot as though it were a dream, would each man interpret it? For Freud the answer is simple: every dream of flying is a sexual dream, a means of sublimating the desire for orgasm and preventing a wet dream (*General Introduction* 127). For Adler the answer is more difficult, since he insists that the psychic life of every individual is peculiar to the individual and not to be interpreted by a normative scheme like Freud's collection of symbolic equivalences. "We need to warn ourselves," Adler insists, "that we cannot explain a dream without knowing its relationship to the other parts of the personality. Neither can we lay down any fixed and rigid rules of dream interpretation" (362). He would certainly argue that the dream is aimed into a future that it imagines as a feast of the gods and a parade around the universe; the individual imagines a coherent, social future through the creation of a work within the cultural sphere. Perhaps, then, neither psychoanalyst is as dis-

---

losophy of Hans Vaihinger (76–87), which makes much of the Zweckmäßigkeit, expediency of purposiveness, of the useful fictions that form the core of his thought (cf. 1–13, 135–36, 174).

tant from Plato as we might imagine; Freud emphasizes the erotic significance of the dream, Adler the preparative and prophetic.

One aspect of Plato's description of the erotic ecstasis, the flight through the universe that the lover experiences, would seem to be lacking in Lovecraft's description. Though the Lovecraftian weird tale aims at the breakthrough of natural law, its basic mode is naturalistic; the breakthrough will not be convincing if natural law is not well established throughout most of the narrative. So it is simply not possible for Derby to sprout wings and ascend into the stratosphere. Instead, when Derby is in his ecstatic state he climbs into Asenath's "powerful Packard" and drives it with a dash that he had never exhibited before, "handling it like a master, and meeting traffic entanglements with a skill and determination utterly alien to his accustomed nature" (*DH* 284). He is like the charioteer in Socrates' account, driving a winged chariot by which he confronts every nook and cranny of the universe. Derby drives to northern Maine where he descends the secret steps and finds his way outside the universe as we know it. This detail is all the more impressive when we consider how seldom cars play a major role in Lovecraft's stories that are more often peripatetic than motorized.

In its flight through the universe the soul participates in the parade of the gods, though one goddess does not take part, Hestia, who "abides alone in the gods' dwelling place" (247a). Plato may be playing here on a pun, for the word ἑστία means the banquet that is associated with the hearth, the center of the house. While the gods and the soul circle the universe the banquet that is the intimate identity of the self remains at the center. This imagery is akin to the medieval statement that god is the center that is everywhere upon the circumference; in Plato's language the lover who pursues the track of the gods there feasts upon true being (247e). For Lovecraft this feast takes place in the Walpurgis Night that takes place outside the world we know; but if we keep in mind the Platonic pun, that extra-physical banquet has an identity in the ecstatic lover; but we have much more to say about the Walpurgis Night in a later chapter.

In his extreme state Derby battles against his attraction to Asenath, talking about the need to save his identity (*DH* 284); but that is specifically what the lover ought not to do. The identity needs to be sacrificed in the name of the larger world that the lover enters. The great moment of the love is expressed in the words, "I'll kill that entity . . . her, him, it . . . I'll kill it!" (287). At this point the life of the self, the self that the person thought was authentic but was not, is in a life and death struggle for itself; and in this struggle it utters the great secret as it admits the shape-changing it experiences. "Her, him, it." Eros is transsexual and impersonal, erasing the categories by which we are accustomed to identify ourselves. This is the point at which Eros and Thanatos exchange identities, the point at which they melt into each other.

In this extreme state he exhibits strange objects to his friend, "elusively coloured and bafflingly textured objects like nothing ever heard of on earth, whose insane curves and surfaces answered no conceivable purpose and followed no conceivable geometry. These things, he said, came 'from outside'; and his wife knew how to get them" (*DH* 286). If we think of them, however, as his own works and of him as the Platonic artist who does not know the meaning of his own work, we understand once more that the divine mania is at work. It is a favorite theme for Plato that none of the Homeric rhapsodes can account for their work. It is a favorite and thoroughly understandable theme in Lovecraft that strange objects, as in "The Shadow over Innsmouth," need to be explained away as objects from elsewhere, never from the hands of a mere mortal; the exception to this pattern of denial is Henry Anthony Wilcox, who admits that he woke up to find himself working on the bas-relief that is the first premonition of the rise of Cthulhu (*DH* 128–29).

The story concludes in the identification of the thing on the doorstep as Asenath, her dental work and her crushed skull. Before this moment, however, the reader of the story performs an act of recollection and regression in attempting to sort out what has happened in the soul of the story. Derby is possessed by Asenath, who is actually Ephraim who had years earlier possessed his daughter; but Ephraim is actually an alien being, "some monstrous intrusion" (*DH* 290) that is unimaginably in excess of humanity. So in erotic ecstasis the male and female being is fused into the macrocosmic hermaphrodite from which all human appearances have descended; this hermaphroditic nature appears both in Aristophanes' comic fable in the *Symposium* (189d–e), which was taken so seriously in the Renaissance, and in the Kaballistic doctrine of the Sephiroth, whether in terms of the triads that emanate from the Ên Sôph or in terms of the human soul that is male and female before creation ("Kaballah"). We have long argued over the status of this being in Lovecraft's story, but I think it is best that we finally accept that whatever it is it is at least two or that as two or as something else it transcends the divisions of human gender.

In turning to "Medusa's Coil," which we shall also be discussing in later chapters, the question again arises about the nature of the attraction that Marceline exerts. A part of that answer again lies in her eyes, "large and very dark" like the eyes of Asenath (*HM* 172), but the title suggests more profoundly that it is the coil of hair, "that dense, exotic, overnourished growth of black inkiness" (173). The word "coil" of course is very striking. According to Johnson the verb is defined as "to gather into a narrow compass; as to coil a rope, to wind in a ring" ("Coil"), and this meaning suggests the way that she binds men to her; but the word has a secondary meaning as noun that is now more archaic than in Johnson's day, "tumult; turmoil; bustle; stir; hurry; confusion"; and his three citations from Shakespeare are arresting. There is "this mortal coil" that Hamlet contemplates shuffling off (3.1.66); but there is also Prospero's question to Ariel, his own daemon, about the magical storm the spirit has created, "Who was so firm, so constant, that this coil / Would not infect his reason?" (1.2.208–9), as well as Hermia's accusation of Helena, "You, mistress, all this coil is 'long of you" (3.2.340). Her words suggest the irrational sexuality that gives rise to a coil out of which a man cannot escape, very pertinent to this story.

The coil of hair of course is the snake, several of them, braid by braid, or the one within which all the other hairs exist. This description is justified by the myth of Medusa that the story alludes to and meditates upon, which I do not mean to say much about, except later when we consider how the face and hair of the goddess turns people to stone. There is another myth, however, that the story lightly alludes to, the dance of the virgin and the snake, most thoroughly realized in Flaubert's novel *Salammbô*, in which the Carthagenian priestess of Tanit has a most remarkable relationship to her black python: "Sa démarche rappelait les ondulations des fleuves, sa température les antiques ténèbres visqueuses pleines de fécondité, et l'orbe qu'il décrit en se mordant la queu l'ensemble des planètes, l'intelligence d'Eschmoûn" [Its motion recalled the waves of rivers, its temperature the antique darkness, viscous and full of fecundity, and the circle it formed in biting its tail the order of the planets, the intelligence of Eschmoun] (187; ch. 10). The serpent symbolizes (though not to the weary eye of the author Flaubert) the totality of the world, the water, the fecund, primitive heat, and the circle of the world. One detail in this description is not present in the De Russy plantation as the narrator encounters it; it is no longer wet or fecond, but dry and sterile, waiting for the apocalypse that any stray flame shall bring it.

Due to a good classical education the grandfather suggests a further understanding of the hair when he alludes to "the later Ptolemaic myth of Berenice, who offered up her hair to save her husband/brother, and had it set in the sky as the constellation Coma Berenices" (*HM* 170). Our immediate familiarity with this story comes from Catullus' translation of a Greek original. Once more we owe so much to Catullus, just as we owe the story of Atys to him that appears in "The Rats in the Walls." So we should not ignore this short allusion here. It is possible that Denis has not gone to France to find his other in Marceline but his sister, confirmed as she is in the last paragraph of the story that reveals that he has married the black woman with whom, as such things go, he was raised. I have in mind here, I must confess, such novels of incest and miscegenation as Faulkner's *Absolom, Absolom!* Lovecraft, the innocent Northerner, would like nothing better than to believe the best of the South, but instead he stumbles in horror upon its most comfortable secret. Marceline is a black, just as Asenath is a fish.

I suggested earlier that the car of the narrator stands in the place of the flight, but much more interesting in this regard is the painting that Marsh creates. Despite the time that he spends with her he emphatically denies that he loves Marceline or could ever be in love with her, but then admits something more subtle: "The case simply is, that one phase of her half hypnotizes me in a certain way—a very strange, fantastic, and dimly terrible way—just as another phase half hypnotises you in a much more normal way. I can see something in her—or to be psychologically exact, something through her or beyond her—that you don't see at all" (*HM* 178). In the language of the Renaissance his love is heroic[2]; uninterested in physical attractions, with a certain unconscious snobbery at Denis's merely physical love, it passes through appearances to the Platonic idea. De Russy is rather skeptical, but finally agrees that Marsh's claim must be true.

The remarkable aspect of the painting is the sense of a complex space that it creates within which all seems possible. This is, if you will, a virtual flight in which the poetic mania, led by the erotic, has constructed a representation of "the ultimate fountainhead of all horror" that is R'lyeh. Marsh has created much better than he knows. Besides the nude, inviting portrait of Marceline a Witches' Sabbat is taking place in which she is the high-priestess, accompanied by "the black shaggy entities that are not quite goats—the crocodile-headed beast with three legs and a dorsal row of tentacles—and the flat-nosed aegipans dancing in a pattern that Egypt's priests know and called accursed!" (*HM* 193). This is not the banquet of the gods as Plato understood in his myth, but it is a banquet that celebrates its own understanding of the world.

---

2. Cf. Marvell's poem "The Definition of Love" and Bruno's poems in *Gli eroici furori*.

Having come this far, let us consider what follows if we extend this discussion by considering the breakthroughs experienced in "The Whisperer in Darkness," and "The Dreams in the Witch House," arguing that those stories are also erotic in their underpinnings. This extension seems possible because both Henry Akeley and Walter Gilman suffer an ecstasis, being taken out of themselves, and a raptus, a flight through the universe. More difficult for us to understand is the nature of the erotic encounters that they suffer, for the only encounter that Gilman seems to have is with the hateful crone Keziah and Akeley is a widower.

In "The Dreams in the Witch House" the beloved is a demonic version of the beloved, for she is Keziah (a perfectly fine Biblical word that means cassia, one of the daughters of Job after his great afflictions [Job 42:14]). There is nothing spicy, though, about the witch. From the beginning of the story Gilman desires her, for he took his apartment for no other reason than the fact that she had lived there more than two hundred years earlier and offered him the possibilities of "lines and curves," a repeated phrase, through which he could "delve deeper" than anyone had before; the sexual aspect of the language is patent. His study in geometry at Miskatonic University has another aspect that would have interested both Freud and Adler. She fascinates him with hypnotic eyes, an "unmotivated stare" (MM 268) that almost makes him shiver, and through her he enjoys and suffers a series of rapt ecstasies across the universe. The dream becomes the means of joining the procession of the gods. Before the narrator can exposit the dreams, however, he has to describe this room in great precision, one of the first moments in the story where a geometrical language is required; and though the narrator does not say so, I think that with some confidence we can say that it is the same shape as the object in "The Haunter of the Dark"—it is a trapezohedron. Only an asymmetrical, irrational shape can be the proper springboard into a non-Euclidean universe.

This outline of his situation is of course troubled by her age and by the presence of Brown Jenkin. We cannot but suspect that the actual beloved is the mother and that Brown Jenkin is a double of Gilman, since it "was nursed on the witch's blood" (MM 266). The difficulty with this analysis is the creature's beard. Gilman is young but the ratlike creature is old, so it is possible that it represents the father. We suspect this all the more because of his ratlike appearance and our analysis of the rat in an earlier chapter, for we have here a similar imagery to that of the vermin army pouring downward. When Gilman hears the sounds of rats in the ceiling he braces himself "as if expecting some horror which only bided its time before descending to engulf him utterly" (MM 266). At the conclusion of the story one of these rats, presumptively Brown Jenkin, kills Gilman by eating through his heart after the young man kills Keziah. In the Oedipal conflict the father almost always wins, even if the son kills him.

The title of this story, "The Dreams in the Witch House," implies that the important thing as far as the plot is concerned is not Keziah or Brown Jenkin but the dream that the narrator describes in great detail. The first paragraph devoted to the dreams says that although Gilman "plunges through limitless abysses" it is difficult to employ a physical language for his experience since "he did not walk or climb, fly or swim, crawl or wriggle" (MM 267). Though the language is negative, properly so, it resembles the language that Milton employs to describe the journey of Satan through the uncreated world to the throne of Chaos:

> [. . .] So eagerly the fiend
> O'er bog or steep, through strait, rough, dense, or rare,
> With head, hands, wings, or feet pursues his way,
> And swims or sinks, or wades, or creeps, or flies. (*Par. Lost* 2.947–50)

Like Love, Satan is always, not matter what he does, an ἄγγελος and daemon, fallen and reduced, but thereby a messenger between the spirit world and the human world; he is, however, Love's opposite, the spirit of hatred and fear and opposition, not the spirit of connection, though the one may be mistaken for the other. Gilman hates Keziah fiercely, but we should suspect the roots of that hatred; and he fears that in the middle of the raptures that constitute his dreams he shall be carried to the throne of Azathoth, Lovecraft's central incarnation of the principle of chaos.

In order to render Gilman's experience the narrator turns to geometric terminology, a language that Lovecraft uses often in his last stories as a part of his program to move the stories into the mode of science fiction. This terminology has other purposes, however. First, it is a language that distances the narrator and the reader from the language of the suffering subject and his somatic condition. It is enlightening that immediately after the passage we have just examined of Gilman's progress through the higher dimensions "of his own condition he could not well judge, for sight of his arms, legs, and torso seemed always cut off by some odd disarrangement of perspective" (MM 267). At the beginning of these dreams the body vanishes, perhaps because of a bodily *pudeur*.

The dreams are of two kinds as far as Gilman is concerned, though the reader soon understands more about them than he does. There are the dreams that recount raptures through space and time, perhaps to a state where time does not exist (MM 285), and the dreams that often encapsulate those raptures, dreams characterized by a violet light and by the presence of Keziah, Brown Jenkin, and the imposing figure of the tall black man. The former dreams take place within a state of multiple dimensions or upon alien worlds, so the language of these dreams is necessarily metaphoric. The latter dreams take place within the witch house and within the environs of Arkham; they are real, immediate, and inescapable until Gilman at last takes his fate into his own hands and attacks the figures of the phantasmagoria.

Gilman has many dreams, dreams beyond count, but only six are recorded in the story. I think it is useful to read them backwards, beginning with the last and moving toward the first, to unpack the meaning and the emotion that they contain. I do this for two reasons: first I have in mind Gadamer's suggestion that this procedure may be enlightening in certain poetic cases, and second I have in mind Freud's suggestion in *The Interpretation of Dreams* that dreams can be read backwards. I confess, thereby, that I mean to read these dreams precisely as Lovecraft would not have wished them read, in a manner consistent with Freudian thought. We find Lovecraft here in some difficulty. As Burleson has shown, Lovecraft liked to write as though "the world of deep dream may be as real as, or more real than, the waking world" ("On Lovecraft's Themes" 136), rather in the same way as Tolkien liked to speak in his letters as though Elves really existed. Both write and speak in this way because they assert something rather important by such language. In Lovecraft's case, he asserts the way that dreams seem to come from sources quite other than our personal daytime concerns and that they give us insights that would otherwise be quite impossible. He has to deny the reductionism that he found in Freud's theory of dreams. With such a caveat then, reading these dreams with the admission that they certainly mean more than a Freudian reading, let us proceed crabwise.

In the last dream Keziah tries to force Gilman to take part in the Sabbat and kill the child that she has kidnapped. This is a matter of course. Arkham knows that at the time of the Sabbat children will be kidnapped and killed; it does not approve but it seems incapable of preventing the murders despite the threat. It is perhaps to that extent complicitous in the murders; no matter what polite Arkham believes, the university and the common people know what happens at the Sabbat. Gilman, however, refuses to agree and kills Keziah. His last words, rendered in indirect discourse, are ecstatic: "Iä! Shub-Niggurath! The Goat with a Thousand Young. . . ." (MM 293). His last words are ejaculations toward the gods of fertility, words we should keep in mind in our further reading. Though he himself is rendered deaf, cast out from any immediate human communication, he has conquered; the woman who has plagued him and attempted to seduce him is dead. Yet Brown Jenkin, her simulacrum, lives to drill through Gilman's breast and eat "his heart out" (MM 295). His heart is at the root of the matter. He has conquered, but he has not because he is too concerned in these matters. For "each man kills the thing he loves" (Wilde 726). Though Lovecraft has transcended his decadent period it still exerts its own peculiar power. Though this dream is victorious, it is also fearful.

Not only are the dreams fearful, they are increasingly infantile. In the fifth dream the next morning after the one in which Keziah attempts to drag him through a deep mud to the tall black man, he finds "that his feet and pajama-bottoms were brown with caked mud" (MM 287). The dream continues as she drags him into "a dark open doorway," up "evil-smelling staircases" (286) and presents him with a baby that she thrusts into his arms. In shock "he plunged recklessly down the noisome staircase and into the mud outside" (287). This repetition of the word "mud" is significant. No doubt the word "pajama-bottoms" refers to the cuffs of the pants, but one cannot but hear the pun that suggests he has shat in his pants out of fear. Despite the geometric terminology the somatic pathos of the story grows as it approaches its climax.

The wide-awake world the next day explains the dream. "The two-year-old child of a clod-like laundry worker" has been kidnapped (MM 288). The ugly word "clod-like" begs the question of what this woman does. She has no husband that is ever mentioned, "and her friend Pete Stowacki would not help because he wanted the child out of the way anyhow" (288–89). I believe this is the closest that Lovecraft ever comes to suggesting that one of his characters is a prostitute, and the actions of Keziah during that night seem in retrospect the actions of a madam, first trying to bring Gilman into the seductive allure of the violet light and then breaking off to rid the brothel of an unwanted child.

The fourth dream is relatively short, but in it the "tall, lean man of dead black colouration but without the slightest sign of negroid features" first appears (MM 281). The denial of negroid features attempts to place Nyarlathotep outside of American prejudices at the same time as touching on those prejudices; from his first appearance in Lovecraft's imagination Nyarlathotep came from Egypt with a dark complexion. In *The Dream-Quest of Unknown Kadath* he is swart, so this description "dead black" places him in a thoroughly different condition, but Lovecraft here asserts the negritude of the god and denies it. The newspapers of Arkham have no difficulty in identifying the figure as negroid, and we need to admit this appearance as one more to the various transformations that Nyarlathotep assumes in the stories in which he takes part. But if we ask why this description is made, I think the answer lies in the miscegenation of "Medusa's Coil." It seems that the beloved must have something that is strongly other.

But something significant happens in this dream. Keziah thrusts into Gilman's right hand "a huge grey quill" with which to sign his name to the devil's book and to provide the necessary blood. Brown Jenkin races across his body, up to his shoulders and down his right arm, to bite him in the wrist, causing a "spurt" of blood at which Gilman faints (*DH* 281). The next morning "his cuff was brown with dried blood" (281). The stories of the devil's book are, let us admit, rather unimaginative, but they conceal a masturbatory fantasy that seems actually at work here. Gilman faints away because he cannot accept the wet dream. More generally, like the mud the blood dirties him, but that is another part of the attraction Keziah exerts.

The third dream begins with the approach of Keziah and Brown Jenkin, but Gilman escapes them, "glad to sink into the vaguely roaring twilight abysses," though he finds the pursuit of their shapes projected into the geometries of an "iridescent bubble-congeries" and a "kaleidoscopic little polyhedron" rather "irritating" (*MM* 276). If it were not for the distancing effect of the geometric language and the brilliance of the words "iridescent" and "kaleidoscopic," the word "irritating" would seem understated. He then finds himself on a sunset terrace looking out giddily across an enormous city two thousand feet below him. Peter Cannon has analyzed this image that appears throughout Lovecraft's work, magnifying his favorite view of Providence; both parts of the dream admit that they come from Gilman's own concerns. The end of the dream, however, denies this, for when he wakes up he finds in his hand an alien object that testifies to the reality of the dream, an object of "exotic delicacy" that his right hand falling upon had steadied him until he broke it off (278). At that crisis Keziah and Brown Jenkin appear once more, in the company of three aliens so terrifying that he wakes. Once more the masturbatory imagery and his anxiety are patent.

The second dream begins with Keziah now much more clear than she was in the first, for it is as though she and her familiar are in fact materializing slowly out of his own consciousness; he wishes to see her and she slowly responds to that wish. In this moment "the expression on her face was one of hideous malevolence and exultation" (MM 272). The exultation is understandable; because of his interest in her she is gaining more substance. The malevolence, however, is hard to understand; either she is simply evil, bearing an evil will when she lived in Arkham and bearing that evil will with her when she unaccountably escaped from prison, or she has reason to hate him and he will have to discover that reason in himself. She does, however, promise to introduce him to the Black Man and to Azathoth. As we have seen, though, such a promise is not necessarily fearful, for he is being invited to the center of the universe and the center of its meaning. He escapes into the deeper abyss, where flight is wonderful, but suddenly the next night, in a dream that seems a continuation of that previous flight, finds himself in an alien landscape from which Keziah and Brown Jenkin show him the way back. He owes them more than he seems to admit.

There is no first dream. The narrative simply speaks of the dreams that he begins to have in the witch house, so often at first simply the dreams of flight through geometries of "prisms, labyrinths, clusters of cubes and planes, and Cyclopean buildings" (MM 267). The dreams begin in the vaguest abstractions and only gradually concretize into the visions of Keziah and Brown Jenkin; the most clear language we have already noted, the way that the language compares him to Satan as he flies through "intricate Arabesques roused into a kind of ophidian animation" (267). The dreams begin in the turmoils of an unspecified desire that must rehearse itself through the many dreams before it begins to find its object in Keziah, whom he must kill. Something, however, is shocking in that conclusion when we consider her in the light of Fritz Leiber's suggestion that she represents the hag aspect of the triple goddess (*The Second Book* 192).

This unsatisfying beginning is mirrored by an unsatisfying conclusion. I do not have in mind here the death of the protagonist; it is a given that in Lovecraft's fiction the protagonist shall die, and this death seems particularly suitable given our analysis. What disturbs me is that no banquet of the gods is available. The Walpurgis Night occurs as expected, but it is a relatively minor affair in which Gilman does not take part, except in attempting futilely to save the child whose life is offered up in the traditional parody of the Eucharist.

"The Whisperer in Darkness" may appear as one of the more aseptic of Lovecraft's stories. Here is a widower bereft of his head. This plot would seem to be as distant from erotic matters as one could imagine. Still, like

Gilman he is offered an extreme raptus, and certain other details suggest that the erotic may be at work in the story. Let us at least assume that as a possibility and see how far it takes us in our reading.

The most striking aspect about the story from the beginning is the landscape, those "wild domed hills" and "endless trickles of brooks" that we are told upon the first page Henry Akeley "mortally feared" for no immediately evident reason (*DH* 208). Only later does the narrator, referring to Akeley's second letter, speak of "the pits of primal life, and of the streams that trickled down therefrom" (223), responding to the question that is left hanging earlier of "the streams [that] trickle from unknown sources" (210). Through the next pages the narration refers often to the hills and the brooks, the "crowded green precipices and muttering forest streams" (215), as though they had something to say that remains impossible to utter. Much later when Wilmarth is trying to sleep in Akeley's house after his conversation with the whisperer, the only exception to the great silence is "the sinister trickle of distant unseen waters" (262). Probably these trickling streams, so fearful and yet so difficult to understand, are the correlative in the landscape of the whispering that becomes fearful; this significance, however, lies within the context of the total landscape. Once we are sensitized to this imagery it begins to assume a meaning that lies beyond the merely topographical; it feels like the imagery of a dream before one has begun to dream that dream, and we realize how sexual this language is. The sexuality of the language is all the more evident when the narration begins to describe the floods that bring down "swollen, organic shapes" (209) that bear "superficial resemblances" to the human (210), "pinkish things" (210), a phrase that is varied as "monstrous pinkish forms" (223). This language does not make sense unless either the narrator or Henry Akeley, with whom the narrator comes to sympathize profoundly, have problems in facing the female body that, as a misogynist would put it, bears only a superficial resemblance to the human, i.e. male, body. The story, then, is sexualized from its earliest pages.

After much periphrasis and indirect description the story comes to the imperfect transcript, recalled only in memory, that Akeley has sent the narrator Wilmarth. The striking aspect of this transcript, after we have pondered "The Dreams in the Witch House," is that we find once more the names of Shub-Niggurath, the figure of fertility, and of Nyarlathotep, designated here a Mighty Messenger and a Great Messenger (*DH* 226).

For several pages after this transcript Wilmarth copies the various letters he receives from Akeley, and little here is of interest to our reading except

the sense that though Akeley is truly terrified he expresses a good deal of
ambivalence about leaving his farm, so long in his family, to join his son in
California. For a New Englander that might as well be across the universe.
Twice Wilmarth says that Akeley is a recluse "with very little worldly sophis-
tication" (*DH* 215), "a man of much simplicity and "with little worldly experience" (*DH* 249). Despite being a widower he rather resembles the young
Derby. Then a remarkable letter arrives that records an utter transformation
in him; anxiety and repulsion are suddenly transformed to desire. He casually announces that he shall now be the interpreter of the aliens upon earth
and that though he will not be called upon to undertake "any trip *outside* just
yet" he seems confident that he "shall probably *wish* to do so later on" (*DH*
239). If we had read this letter within any other context would we not have
said that the speaker had fallen in love? Before these words Akeley had realized that the creatures, whatever they might be, possess "undoubted tele-
pathic and hypnotic powers" (*DH* 231), powers such as we saw Asenath and
Marceline possessed, and thus it seems clear that they as an aggregate are
the beloved. As it turns out these words about the journey, the great journey
outside, are not Akeley's words at all, or probably not, for he has quite literally lost his head. The words of the lover, in the state of ecstasis, are not his
words but those provided by the daemon Eros. But if this were Akeley what
a bumptious, confident Akeley he is: "With such an exchange of knowledge
all perils will pass, and a satisfactory *modus vivendi* be established. The very
idea of any attempt to *enslave* or *degrade* mankind is ridiculous" (*DH* 239).
These words remind us of the easy optimism of a newlywed who ignores all
the emotions that lie in the past of every couple, not so easily dealt with
through a superficial rationalism, and who ignores all the possibilities of a patriarchal society versed in ancient feelings of sadomasochism.

Wilmarth reacts to the letter with complex feelings but finally comes to an
erotic agreement with the Akeley that he thinks has written the letter. What
that man had loved he shall love, "the same old passion for infinity" (*DH* 242):
"to shake off the maddening and wearying limitations of time and space and
natural law—to be linked with the vast *outside*—to come close to the nighted
and abysmal secrets of the infinite and the ultimate" (*DH* 243). This desire for
knowledge is thoroughly tinged with an erotic imagery that we are familiar with
from the Romantic period. Wilmarth's reaction is to leave for Akeley's home in
Vermont, though he takes care not to arrive at night; and leaving when he
does he realizes on the train that he "was entering an altogether older-
fashioned, ancestral New England without the foreigners and factory-smoke,

billboards and concrete roads" (*DH* 244). What a relief! He is regressing to a prior state and remembering things that had not bothered him for many years. As the mysterious Noyes drives him to Akeley's farm Wilmarth comments on "the hypnotic landscape" in which "time had lost itself"; and after comparing the landscape to the backgrounds of paintings by Leonardo da Vinci he concludes "we were now burrowing bodily through the midst of the picture, and I seemed to find in its necromancy a thing I had innately known or inherited, and for which I had always been vainly searching" (*DH* 248). This ecstatic experience stands in the place of the raptus we had expected when either he or Akeley were escorted through the universe by the Outer Ones. The closest we approach that ecstasis in the narrative comes in a paragraph in which a series of variations on the phrase "I was told" bears the reader along in a rhetorical increase in the tempo of the whisperer's words (*DH* 256).

The following page declares the conditions of such an ecstasis, the "harmless" extraction of the brain and immersion in the metal cylinder. The whisperer insists that the brain would enjoy "a full sensory and articulate life—albeit a bodiless and mechanical one," though there is some contradiction between that "full sensory [. . .] life" and that "bodiless" life; the process was "as simple as carrying a phonographic record about" (*DH* 257). For this ecstasis one need only lose one's head. To Wilmarth, however, the details come down to a mere "mechanical mummery" (*DH* 259), an experience that has nothing to do with the strenuous philosophic path outlined in the *Phaedrus*. When Wilmarth fully realizes this in his confrontation with the wax mask and hands, he escapes in Akeley's old Ford—the man clearly has no need of it again.

This Ford was mentioned at the beginning of the story when he referred to it as "a commandeered motor" (*DH* 208), and Akeley offhandedly referred to it in his account of his daily life (229) and later suggested that someone would meet Wilmarth with his car (241). Sensitized as we are to this imagery in "The Thing on the Doorstep" we must wonder whether once more it represents the Platonic chariot; but in fact the old Ford is good for nothing but escape. Much more significant a vehicle is the new model that Mr. Noyes drives, "bearing Massachusetts licence plates with the amusing 'sacred codfish' device of the year" (246). There is nothing amusing, however, about this drive through the landscape that is the actual ecstasis of the story.

In this story, however, the protagonist, neither Akeley nor Wilmarth, does not ascend to the parade of the gods nor to their banquet. If Akeley ever does ascend to the realm of Yuggoth and the worlds beyond he does so probably without his consent. We are fairly certain, despite the language he uses in that remarkable conversion letter, that he is now at the conclusion of the story either dead, a dead letter, or merely a head in a metal cylinder. He leads now only a mechanized life that has been made possible through a symbolic castration. This story, then, is the bleakest of Lovecraft's accounts of the erotic life.

My description so far of the erotic in these stories may be accurate, but we must confess that it still misses something basic to the whole tenor of the stories. Nothing is pretty here, and nothing saves us; but the erotic mania as Plato and Aquinas understood it offers at least an insight into the construction of the world and sets the manic lover into the center of that world at the banquet of Hestia; erotic love reconstitutes the Ptolemaic universe. This kind of moment allows us to see that Lovecraft searches for other moments in his world view than the destruction implicit in materialism; but there is no doubt that for Lovecraft this divine mania is demonic. Given the very existence of these stories as weird tales, we have either not addressed or only glancingly so their demonic nature. "The Thing on the Doorstep," "Medusa's Coil," "The Whisperer in Darkness," and "The Dreams in the Witch House" demonize the erotic narrative into tales of murder, suicide, castration, and mutilation. I do not, however, see this as a great problem. In the *Symposium* Socrates had argued that Eros is not a god, certainly not one of the major gods, but a daemon, a rather eerie and untrustworthy being that moves as a messenger between the gods and humanity. Eros is a being that communicates our need and lack and purveys mere opinion that may or may not be true. He is rather similar to the muses that meet the poet Hesiod and announce that often they tell falsehoods and also, if they wish, sometimes gossip the truth (*Theogony* 25–27); and they are goddesses! As Socrates had argued, the poets may tell the truth, but they may not know when they do; as humans, however, because we have little else than opinion, we deeply need poetry and even more Eros.

Now I do not mean to argue that the relation of the words daemon and demon is definitive or convincing. However, as far as humans in their daily lives are concerned, the daemon Eros stands as a judgment and accusation: we do not live as we ought, we do not pay heed to what we ought, and we do not prize beauty, truth, or goodness as we ought. Since we do none of these things, unless we are lovers or philosophers, that is to say unless we seem to others demented, since we have no experience to bring to bear from our daily lives, we are clumsy and inept; we seem to ourselves erratic, and lost in that error as though we were lost in a labyrinth we stagger through the corridors of our lives until we meet the Minotaur. *Quel dommage.*

Free Range

Bloch and Leiber: the Siblings at War with Lovecraft, the Compound Ghost

Let me disclose the gifts reserved for age
>To set a crown upon your lifetime's effort.
First, the cold friction of expiring sense
Without enchantment, offering no promise
>But bitter tastelessness of shadow fruit
>As body and soul begin to fall asunder. (Eliot 54)

Once upon a time, before old age had overcome the world, the eighteen-year-old Robert Bloch politely asked his grandfather Lovecraft if he could kill him off in a story; and when Lovecraft readily agreed the young man published "The Shambler from the Stars," which accomplished the deed soundly. Lovecraft, however, may not have been as generous as he seemed, for in short order he responded with the considerably weightier story, "The Haunter of the Dark," in which he killed off Bloch under the easily deciphered name Robert Blake (Joshi, *HPL: A Life* 601). As though to put Lovecraft in the grave once more, Bloch wrote a further murderous narrative, "The Dark Demon," and then, not to leave well enough alone, in 1950 wrote a sequel to Lovecraft's story, "The Shadow from the Steeple." All in good fun among friends. Some fifty years later Fritz Leiber, a bit older than Bloch but also an epistolary disciple of Lovecraft during the 1930s, responded with a novel, *Our Lady of Darkness*, that strikingly resembles several details in Lovecraft's story and in which Lovecraft reappears as a compound ghost. These texts offer telling instances of literary influence, both its anxieties and its playful pleasures.

I

"Little Bloch's story is an earlier effort than the one previously printed. He is struggling hard with his juvenile tendency toward more gruesomeness & overcolouring, & the next few years will reveal how much genuine literary ability he has." (*Letters to Richard F. Searight* 58)

"Yes—little Bho-Blôk, the Daemon Lama of Leng, is certainly quite a boy, & and his pictures display a surprisingly natural talent." (*SL* 4.258)

Some people still remember at the convention celebrating Lovecraft's centenary the display of the drawings the young Robert Bloch sent Lovecraft. He always possessed a strong visual sense that stood him in good stead in the visualization of his stories; but we cannot emphasize how young Bloch was when he wrote his first fan letter to Lovecraft, all of sixteen years old (Bloch, "A Man of Letters" 5). He had just graduated from high school in the midst of the depression, full of the confidence of the young that he could do anything (Bloch, *Mysteries of the Worm* 329–30). After writing a few early stories, some of which he sent to Lovecraft who responded with stylistic advice and long lists of weird fiction that the young man might read, Bloch conceived of the idea of killing off his friend in a story. Is this the first indication that he was wisely beginning to feel some discomfort in the face of the older man's formidable personality and learning? For there can be no doubt that Lovecraft was behaving as an amiable teacher; the autodidact was giving his young protégé a first-class introduction to the complex world of the weird tale. Lovecraft responded to Bloch's proposal with a short note, authorizing him "to portray, murder, annihilate, disintegrate, transfigure, metamorphose, or otherwise manhandle the undersigned" (*Letters to Robert Bloch* 67). Shortly thereafter the story appeared in *Weird Tales*, whose readers could appreciate its several allusions to Lovecraft and to the material in his stories. The story accomplishes its goals.

Still, is it really so good a story? In 1981 Bloch was happy to republish his early Mythos stories, but with some embarrassment at their gaucheries, of which this story has a good number. Having admitted that, we still have much to admire. The title for instance. Yes, the monster does shamble, moving about the room in the climax of the story with a clumsy violence; he makes a shambles of it as he sucks the blood from the broken body of the mystic of Providence. But we cannot but feel that the title hints that the

story we are about to read is a sham. Although it is inventive, it conscientiously dresses itself in the style and materials provided by Lovecraft's earlier
stories. It is a tribute in an uneasy balance with shameless imitation.

It begins with the rather awkward admission that the man who writes is
very young, an author of weird tales that are written as much for the pitiful
remuneration available from the pulps. "The depression complicated matters
to an almost intolerable degree," he writes artlessly, "and for a time I was
close to utter economic disaster. It was then that I decided to write" (36).
After composing several stories he begins to feel confident that he has mas-
tered "the more obvious tricks of the trade" (37). Forthright as these passages are, they also suggest that the young narrator, in many ways a
projection of Bloch himself, is already the kind of writer that Lovecraft never
quite achieved; he is a professional.

His downfall happens when he decides not to be a professional but an
artist. "I wanted to write a real story, [. . .] a real work of art" (37). With
Hans Christian Andersen's story "The Princess and the Pea" in mind, in
which the narrator presses the word "rigtig" several times (1.49–51), we realize that there is something problematic about the word "real." Rather than
constructing a story, the narrator is driven to discover material from such
books as the *Necronomicon,* the *Book of Eibon,* or *Cultes des Goules,* works
familiar to the readers from stories by Lovecraft, Clark Ashton Smith, and
August Derleth. Bloch is indicating that he is about to join the *Weird Tales*
authors as "one of the family" (*Letters to Robert Bloch* 67), with Lovecraft's
permission making use of the books and creatures in the master's stories.

His actual initiation takes place in his description of the book that the narrator finds in a used book store, *De Vermis Mysteriis*—Lovecraft helped him
with the Latin title—in translation, *The Mysteries of the Worm* by a Flemish
magician with the unlikely name of Ludvig Prinn. Bloch expends some three
pages describing the book and its author, perhaps calling too abrupt a halt to
the pace of the story; but with this material he indicates how much a story of
this sort within the context of the other stories by Lovecraft, Smith, Howard,
and Derleth is logocentric. A library could be created out of the list of these
imaginary books. Lovecraft, however, no matter how important the *Necronomicon* is to the action of a story and no matter how measured the pace of
his stories is, never halts the action in this fashion; and when he was more experienced Bloch would never do so either. Nevertheless, something of the
later Bloch is present in this sentence: "There were fresh blood-stains on the
alars, and fresh blood-stains on the rack, too, before the questioning of Prinn

was finished" (41). Bloch has a sometimes grim, sometimes fey sense of humor that came to salt his style; Leiber in this regard is his equal, but Lovecraft never achieves the deftness of his two disciples in comedy.

One small detail in this passage is striking, the reference to Prinn as an "archimage" (42). This is a rather rare word. The only use of it with any emphatic effect is to be found in the first book of Spenser's *The Faerie Queene* in which Archimago, the figure of hypocrisy, causes great harm through his ability to change his shape; and given that ability no one can capture him or reveal his true identity. Now I do not believe that we should identify Prinn as hypocrisy, but it is possible that this word in conjunction with our reading of "shambles" warns us of the peculiar nature of this story. Despite its logocentric insistence something is not quite real here.

Since the book is in Latin the narrator despairs of reading it, but his friend, the "mystic dreamer" in New England, promises his help if the young man will visit him; and thus begins the main body of the action. This section begins with the rather sterile report that "Providence is a lovely town" (43). The young Bloch, living in distant Milwaukee, had only seen the city through Lovecraft's eyes, so this description is quite perfunctory. The narration quickly moves to the New England mystic, in a series of descriptions remarkable owing to the fact that Bloch had not met Lovecraft. The man has a "lean profile" and a "waxen face" (43). Two pages later the profile is "cadaverous," his eyes are "feral," and when he reads from the *De Vermis Mysteriis* his voice "became as soft as a viper's hiss" (45). This man is on another side of human life. In his letters Lovecraft liked to present himself as an elderly man, but this description is quite extreme for a man who in 1933 was in fact only forty-three. Since we are concerned in this essay with how Lovecraft became a compound ghost in his friends' fictions, this is the first step in the process.

The salient feature of the mystic's house is the "enormous window" of the workroom and library in which the climatic action takes place. This window surveys "the azure sea" that is soon hidden by a moonless night and fog (43). Either Bloch does not know that the window of Lovecraft's room looked west, as Lovecraft shall pointedly remind him in his story, or Bloch chooses that the fictional window should look out over an ill-defined immensity. This window as he imagines it is rather like the all-important window in Lovecraft's "The Music of Erich Zann," through which the wind rushes to destroy all evidence of what happens in that luckless musician's room.

The climax of Bloch's story again admits its debt to Lovecraft's works, especially to the invisible monster of "The Dunwich Horror." Bloch, however, realizes that he cannot simply steal this monster without doing something inventive with him, so he gives the monster the power to suck blood, which coursing through his system makes him visible, "a bloody glow" in which the narrator can distinguish "tentacular trunks that waved and waved. There were suckers on the tips of the appendages, and these were opening and closing with ghoulish lust" (48). The details of the tentacles and suckers come straight from Lovecraft's description of Wilbur Whateley, but Bloch felt compelled to make the possibilities of the details obvious in the phrase "ghoulish lust" and pushed the material too far.

At the conclusion the narrator congratulates himself on his cleverness in setting fire to the apartment and escaping Providence, but despite this rather bumptious confidence he adds that he shall not truly escape. The Shambler, he is convinced, shall return for him, and "then I too shall learn, once and for all, the *Mysteries of the Worm*" (49). Strong last sentence.

What are we to make of this story? It is at the same time pat and suggestive. Though the conclusion despite Bloch's inventive twist is too stale, that word "shambler" remains striking. It is possible that the shambler is "mon semblable," my like, as Baudelaire insisted in the last line of the introduction to *Les Fleurs du mal*. After all, the shambler simply acts for the author; Bloch wished to kill off his spiritual father, with permission, and the shambler, the sham that was his *semblable*, performed the act for him. This is an act for which he himself now must die, and Lovecraft will take that revenge upon himself. The first great difference between the two stories is Lovecraft's clever decision to name the narrator of Bloch's story Robert Blake and to quickly sketch the events of that story in his second paragraph. This opening, however, reaches back to Bloch's story in a more subtle way, as this anonymous narrator hints that Blake had died in the middle of an act of "charlatanry" or "hoax" aimed at advancing his literary career (*DH* 92–93); perhaps, the narrator speculates, Blake "pretended" to see what he claimed to have seen (93). As the climax of the story nears he repeats that "the factor of conscious charlatanry can by no means be excluded" (112). Lovecraft carries over the theme of the sham into his story.

The plot of the story, however, is radically different from Bloch's. Robert Blake, living now on the crest of the hill that defines East Side and Brown University, in an apartment that clearly belongs to the actual Lovecraft, down to the "huge, friendly cats, [sunning] themselves atop a convenient shed" (*DH* 94), becomes fascinated by "the spectral hump of Federal Hill"

(94), its mazes and labyrinths now occupied by "a vast Italian quarter" (94), and by "the great tower and tapering steeple" of a large church that seems to be deserted. One day in April he decides to visit the church. It is the same opposition we find in "Pickman's Model" between Beacon Hill where the Brahmins of Boston live and Copp's Hill where the Italian immigrants live.

Blake's walk to the church is accompanied by an interesting shift in imagery. He has entered a scene in which the Italian signs tell him nothing, and all is muted by "brown, decade-weathered buildings" and "bewildering mazes of brooding brown alleys" (*DH* 96). At last the spire of the church appears "above the tiers of brown roofs" (96). The church is surrounded by "brown, neglected weeds and grasses" (97); and it strikes Blake as "odd that the green of spring had not touched the brown, withered growths" (98). After these few pages the brown imagery vanishes, but it is frequent enough to make its own statement of age and desolation; and it is an imagery that Leiber will return to, giving his novel in serialization the title *The Pale Brown Thing*.

The church itself is rather peculiar given Lovecraft's interest in architectural matters. Here is a Free Will Baptist church, a church nestled in a firm Protestant tradition, built in 1810 or 1815; yet the narrator insists that its style is "that earliest experimental form of Gothic revival" (*DH* 95). The Gothic revival, however, as far as churches were concerned, began later in England, where at first the nobility were only interested in the construction of fanciful castles and follies (Davenport-Hines 59–150), and later still in America where the first Gothic churches were built by Catholics and Episcopalians, mere examples of the follies of Popery as far as the Protestant churches were concerned; only in the 1840s and 1850s did Baptists, Methodists, Congregationalists, and Presbyterians begin to construct churches in the Gothic mode (Smith 84–92). Nevertheless Robert Blake notes as he circles the church "high stone buttresses [. . .] and several delicate finials" (*DH* 97). It is as though a Roman Catholic ruin, quite proper to the Gothic landscape of England, had unaccountably sprouted in New England. More precisely and more accurately, it is as though an area of Providence that Irish and then Italian immigrants have inhabited now provided a proper soil in which a Roman Catholic church could grow, despite the fact that it is, though no longer in spirit, a sober Baptist edifice. Though the narrator speaks of the Italians with some respect, for he recognizes that they know the danger of the entity in the church and they know how to constrain it, the church represents that landscape so basic to the English Gothic in which the ruins of the Roman Catholic church symbolize that ancient irrationality repressed by the Age of

Enlightenment that the Romantic Age now yearns for.[1]

In the vestry Blake finds a library composed of such books as we expect, the *Necronomicon,* the *Liber Ivonis,* the *Cultes des Goules,* the *Unaussprechlichen Kulten,* and now, accepted into the canon, Bloch's addition, the *De Vermis Mysteriis.* For a story such as this, you know at this point that all is as it should be.

More peculiar details arise that point at Egypt as the source of the mystery. On the altar the cross is not at all usual in design "but resembled the primordial ankh or crux ansata of shadowy Egypt" (*DH* 100). From a reporter's notebook we learn that the church was founded by a Prof. Enoch Bowen in 1844 after he had returned from archeological work in Egypt (103). Later Blake believes that the cult has a much older history, reaching back to Yuggoth, before the Pharaoh Nephren-Ka built a temple and crypt for the jewel that is the cult's liturgical object. Nephren-Ka does not appear in the chronicles of Egypt, only in Lovecraft's stories; and here we learn that he is unknown because for some unspecified crime his name had been erased from all Egyptian records (106). In the last notes that Blake scribbles before he dies he writes this rhetorical question about the Haunter: "Is it not an avatar of Nyarlathotep, who in antique and shadowy Khem even took the form of a man?" (114). This is obviously a nod Lovecraft makes toward that very early dream he had in which Nyarlathotep had appeared for the first time: "Nyarlathotep came out of Egypt. Who he was none could tell, but he was of the old native blood and looked like a Pharaoh. [. . .] He said he had risen up out of the blackness of twenty-seven centuries, and that he had heard messages from places not on this planet" (*MW* 32). This is a remarkable conclusion. Nyarlathotep, the crawling chaos, takes so many forms in Lovecraft's opus that it is not strange to learn that one of his forms is this creature that avoids all light.

One last problem needs consideration, the mysteries of the Shining Trapezohedron and of the three-lobed burning eye. Actually, I do not think the latter problem any problem at all. A traditional emblem of God in trinitarian denominations is three circles woven into each other in the center of which an eye looks out. In the final vision at the end of the *Paradiso* Dante sees "Three orbs of triple hue, clipped in one bound" (1.109), out of which our

---

1. Lovecraft identifies the model of the Free-Will church as the St. John's Roman Catholic Church, "a red-brick edifice of the 1870's," and admits that his description is idealized (*Letters to Richard F. Searight* 70).

human visage looks. This is the imagery that lies at the root of the emblem on the American dollar of a pyramid with an eye at the top, circled by the Latin tags "Annuit coeptis" and "Novus ordo saeclorum," both of them insisting upon a new order of things. But this eye is burning—God is angry. We do not know at what the anger is directed, but we should remember here some of the contexts that we have explored in the nightmare theodicy of the blasted heath and the embittered space over which Pan rules. Robert Blake has done nothing wrong except to will the death of his father, as was to be expected, so the father, a semi-divine creator, exacts his revenge.

The Shining Trapezohedron is slightly different, but its nature being akin to the pyramid on the dollar suggests that its shining is also akin to that burning eye. The striking aspect of a trapezohedron is that it is a crystal whose trapezium sides are congruent with one another; but since none of the sides of a trapezium are equal, the crystal is utterly asymmetrical. It gives rise to that fear of the irrational that so benighted the late stages of Greek geometry; and that, I think, is the point for Lovecraft. As the imagery of his stories became increasingly geometric, it is rather specialized in expressing its fears and anxieties through an increasingly irrational imagery. So the Haunter of the Dark, that which fears the light and a rational treatment, must be Nyarlathotep.

The story of course is grossly unfair, in that a master pays back the presumption of a novice. So it was only right that in the following year Bloch should have killed off Lovecraft once more in "The Dark Demon," though as S. T. Joshi has pointed out he does so in the most deferential manner (*The Evolution of the Weird Tale* 111–12), embedding in the story his great gratitude to Lovecraft for all his help. Still, kill him off once more he does, this time through the dreams that were so important to Lovecraft's methods. This is the great point, that Bloch understands and accepts Lovecraft's fiction that dreams are revelations of the essence of things and he makes that fiction the center of the story; in a truly religious sense, though the character that stands in for Lovecraft tries to deny it, the dream is prophetic (100).

Some fifteen years later Bloch wrote his sequel to Lovecraft's "The Haunter of the Dark," an economical story called aptly "The Shadow from the Steeple." This is a genre at which he became quite adept, a sequel that cleverly deconstructs and rewrites an earlier story. He did this with his different stories on Jack the Ripper, and he did it with his various sequels to *Psycho*. A special skill is required for this sort of work, for the writer must respect the older work, but must also find those gaps and uncertainties that allow a reinterpretation of the material. This story shows his early mastery of the form.

The doubling of characters in this story is profound. First there is Lovecraft who takes some part in Bloch's sketch of the events in Lovecraft's story; here we are told that Lovecraft had offered his apartment to Robert Blake, counseled the young man, and tried to save him from the fate that Lovecraft felt confident was threatening him. In addition, Lovecraft would have helped in a further investigation of Blake's death if he had not himself died two years after the action of the story. We have to keep in mind this distinction between the actual Lovecraft and the fictional Lovecraft.

Then there is the protagonist of the story, Edmund Fiske, a good friend of Blake and himself an author of weird fiction, who lives in Chicago; all these details suggest that he is another mask for Bloch who had originally lived in Chicago before his parents moved to Milwaukee; and he wrote a number of stories under the pseudonym of Tarleton Fiske. The mention of Nephren-Ka in the sketch leads the narrator to mention that the name was familiar to him because another author of weird fiction, hailing from Milwaukee, had made the name known in his story "Fane of the Black Pharaoh," which in fact is a story Bloch had published in 1937. We are dealing then with four Blochs, the actual man, the fictional author of "Fane of the Black Pharaoh," Edmund Fiske, and Robert Blake. Bloch seems to have had a reputation as a fairly self-effacing, humorous man, but this density of self-reference indicates an intense preoccupation with self-identity under the guise of so much play. Once the game is begun, who would not play it to the hilt? He thus offers Fritz Leiber an occasion for his own autobiographical self-reference in *Our Lady of Darkness*.

Fiske is in pursuit of the truth of the death of his friend, but he is at first disappointed to discover that practically all the people associated with that death and with the existence of the church have died. The only person still alive is Dr. Dexter, the man who according to Lovecraft's story had dropped the Trapezohedron "into the deepest channel of Narragansett Bay" (*DH* 114). Bloch gives this mysterious doctor a complex history, turning from medical science to physics and becoming involved in the Manhattan Project. After fifteen years of several futile attempts to meet the doctor, Fiske at last confronts him, believing now that Dr. Dexter has in fact been possessed by the Haunter who is the avatar of Nyarlathotep. As some proof of this he cites, slightly inaccurately, a few lines from Lovecraft's poem "Nyarlathotep" from the *Fungi from Yuggoth* sequence. Rather casually the doctor points out that no wild beasts lick his hands, but it is his connection with the Manhattan project that forms the contemporary point of Bloch's story—only an alien to the human race could have invented the atomic bomb. This truth is too deadly for Dr. Dexter to allow the rather presumptuous Fiske to live. When he dies of a heart attack, as Robert Blake had died, the doctor goes out to the back yard where two black panthers, recently escaped from a circus, lick his hands.

Since "Fane of the Black Pharaoh" is mentioned, we mustn't ignore it. It does have a number of interesting details. In it the pharaoh is said to have seen the entire future of Egyptian history and painted it upon the wall of his enormous tomb. An English archaeologist believes such stories are "bogus balderdash," "sheer drivel," and "rubbish" (167)—note that Bloch is beginning to escape Lovecraft's vocabulary—but out of "curiosity, cupidity, the lust for concealed knowledge" (174), and the desire for fame he follows a man at midnight through the streets of Cairo to find the lost tomb.

He is convinced of the truth of the legend when he looks at the painted wall and discovers that "Nephren-Ka was a realist" (177). His style has an "unerring consistency" 178) in which "the features of all the men were almost photographically exact" (180). He is a painter that Richard Pickman would have been proud to meet. At the conclusion the archaeologist sees his own face on the wall as though in "a miniature mirror" (182) as his guide stabs him in the back, adding him to the Elizabethan gentleman and the French scientists who in the past have come too close to the truth of Nephren-Ka's masterpiece.

Shortly after the story was published Bloch heard of Lovecraft's death, and the news so took the fun out of the game that he did not publish another Mythos story until he wrote the very different "Shadow from the Steeple" thirteen years later.

II

In the *Haunter* I think I also tried to suggest some reason for the victim's passiveness—implying that the experience almost paralysed his will and that the Entity was exchanging personalities with him, but I know I did it badly and listlessly. I surely must pay more attention to this point. (Lovecraft, *SL* 5.358)

In this late letter to Fritz Leiber lamenting his own weakness in handling character Lovecraft may have unwittingly provided his acolyte with a spur and challenge in his own late novel *Our Lady of Darkness*, but Leiber had an explanation ready to hand for his character's own problems, for this novel is

both a profoundly autobiographical and profoundly literary work. The epigraph and title refer to De Quincey, and the implications of the title form
the subjects of several meditations of its characters. Clark Ashton Smith
functions within its action, as do more tangentially such San Francisco figures as Jack London, George Sterling, Ambrose Bierce, Nora May French,
and Gertrude Atherton. M. R. James is mentioned several times, so often
that we must consider his presence one of the fundamental poles of the
novel. Edgar Allan Poe, Arthur Machen, Dashiell Hammett, Sax Rohmer,
W. B. Yeats, Céline, Colette, Henry Miller, Edgar Rice Burroughs, William
S. Burroughs, Jacob Wassermann, Robert Graves, John Keats, S. T. Coleridge, Herman Melville, Aleister Crowley (one of the models for the wizard
de Castries), Peter Viereck, Baron Munchausen, the Marquis de Sade, Sa-
cher-Masoch, Diana Vaughan (a hoax figure), Lewis Carroll, and Arthur
Conan Doyle appear briefly. Two quotations from *Macbeth* glide past (88,
137), not surprisingly since Leiber had memorized the play by the time he
was four years old (Byfield 8), and slight references to *Julius Caesar* and
Othello; and those two literary triumphs of the French cinema, *Les Enfants du
paradis* and *L'Année dernière à Marienbad* (written by Jacques Prévert and
Alain-Robbe Grillet, respectively) form a part of the imagery of the work
(105, 164). The democracy of the list is breathtaking; some of the authors
are canonic, some are cult figures, and some are almost forgotten. One of the
major themes of the book is the impact and persistence of the written word,
whether for good or ill, despite the death of its author.

The name most frequently mentioned, however, forms the purloined letter of the novel, for it is an open secret that the novel is a loving and conten-
tious debate that Leiber is conducting with H. P. Lovecraft. Thus Leiber in
his old age returns with a new degree of awareness to the author who had
stimulated him since the beginning of his career (Clements 23–24; Byfield
11–25). The main situation, in which a man explores a hill that his window
faces, only to have a spirit from it attack him in his apartment, is quite like
that in "The Haunter of the Dark," as Leiber tacitly admits when his protagonist Franz Westen recalls a passage from it (63). Further references to
Lovecraft stud the text. L. Sprague de Camp, the early biographer of Lovecraft, merits a slight mention (14). "The Thing on the Doorstep" and "The
Colour out of Space" are mentioned; Franz notes the resemblance between
de Castries and Nyarlathotep (101), and the reference to "the essential dusts
(salts?)" (128) recalls the terminology of *The Case of Charles Dexter Ward*.
Among the several possible interpretations of the reference to Rhodes (Mon-

tague Rhodes James, the island of Rhodes where Tiberius lived in exile, and the connection of that island to the Knights Templar), is the existence—the fortunate existence, for San Francisco seems to possess every detail that Leiber needs—of Rhode Island Street (40). An oblique reference to "The Rats in the Walls" occurs when Fernando says, "Hechereria ocultado en murallas" (161), a witchcraft that seems eight pages later to be "a very faint scuffing in the wall, like that of a very large rat trying very hard to be quiet" (169). When at the climax of the novel the supernatural attack is composed from a variety of imaginary works, such as the scholarly *Sex, Death, and Supernatural Dread*, *The Subliminal Occult*, and *The Spider Glyph in Time*, the pornographic *Ames et Fantômes de Douleur* and *Knochenmädchen in Pelze (Mit Peitsche)*, we recognize the nod to Lovecraft's *Necronomicon* as well as the jest upon typical motifs in Leiber's career.[2]

Is the novel Lovecraftian, however, as John Howard believes? This is a point we must doubt, if to be Lovecraftian a work must embody Lovecraft's views on a universe indifferent to humanity that works to crush most of his protagonists. It is not a small matter that Franz escapes at the end of the novel, thanks to his lover. As Howard writes, "Only reacting in the right way to this information [the indifference of the universe], plus luck, can enable [Leiber's characters] to survive"; but this outcome is not available in Lovecraft's stories, those that most embody his views, such as "The Colour out of Space," which Franz remembers "had depressed him when he'd read it in his teens" (166). Is Leiber's universe indifferent to humanity? His interest in Jungian archetypes suggests a universe riddled by forces that circle the potent human psyche; undoubtedly they proceed from the psyche, but once in the world they behave as objective entities. The complex entity that attacks Franz is a compound ghost, composed of male and female archetypes, of the forces that seem unleashed in the modern city that humanity has built to house its culture, and of the literary tradition that fascinates Leiber, not least potent of which is the presence of that spiritual father, H. P. Lovecraft.

Thibaut de Castries, the wizard who influences the action of the novel though he is dead, may be the most Lovecraftian figure within it. The name de Castries is very like the name of Adolphe De Castro, for whom Lovecraft ghost-wrote, as Franz almost remembers: "Hadn't Lovecraft done some ghost-writing for a man with a name like Castries? Caster? Carswell?" (66). Indeed

---

2. For much of this information I am indebted to Pardoe and Howard's annotations to Leiber's novel.

he had, though the name Carswell is also a nod to M. R. James's magician in "Casting the Runes" (Pardoe, "*Our Lady of Darkness*: A Jamesian Classic"). Later Jaime Donaldus Byers recalls De Castro also, only to deny that he and de Castries might have been the same man (101–02). Yet these questions are delicate. De Castries is not amiable, but he may be a charlatan; he is seldom unctuous, yet he is certainly an old hypocrite (102)—these phrases from Lovecraft's letters both distance the two figures and bring them closer. Lovecraft was not a hypocrite, but the figure of the charlatan hangs about his protagonists. Such denials as Byers makes suggest all the more powerfully that De Castro and the man for whom he ghostwrites may function as doubles for de Castries. By referring to himself as the author of the short story "A Bit of the Dark World," Leiber at once asserts that Franz is not his double and confesses that he is. It does not seem fortuitous, then, as far as the spectrum drawn by de Castries, De Castro, and Lovecraft is concerned, that Castro Street is casually mentioned (88). Another Castro of perhaps as great importance for de Castries' presence is the character Castro in "The Call of Cthulhu," "an immensely aged mestizo [. . .] who claimed to have sailed to strange ports and talked with undying leaders of the [Cthulhu] cult in the mountains of China" and who "remembered bits of hideous legend that paled the speculations of theosophists and made man and the world seem recent and transient indeed" (*DH* 140). Among the names that Clark Ashton Smith bestows on de Castries are such as Tiberius, the decadent Roman emperor; Tybalt (perhaps a glance at Juliet's thought of the tomb "Where bloody Tybalt, yet but green in earth, / Lies fest'ring in his shroud"? [4.3.41–42], as de Castries lies festering in his pale brown robe); Thrasyllus, the sorcerer of Tiberius; Theudebaldo and Dietbold; and another version of these names, Theobald, which was one of Lovecraft's playful nicknames for himself. One of Lovecraft's late letters to Leiber confounds this mask when he ascribes his own eldritch verses to a translation by the historical Lewis Theobald (*Letters* 5.386–87).[3] A further reference to Lovecraft occurs when Leiber's character Clark Ashton Smith refers to him in his diary: "I should write Howard about it, he'd be astounded and—yes!—transfigured, it so agrees with and *illuminates* the decadent and putrescent hor-

---

3. De Castries's actual name, Thibaut, may be a nod to Theobald I, also known as Thibaud le chansonnier, a count of Champagne and Brie and king of Navarre, a troubadour who took part in the crusades against the Albigenses and the Saracens; or the name may be a nod to the violinist Jacques Thibaud. In addition, Jacques Thibault was the real name of the French author Anatole France (*The New Encyclopædia Britannica*).

ror he finds in New York City and Boston and even Providence (not Levan-
tines and Mediterraneans, but half-sensed paramentals!). But I'm not sure he
could take it" (65). Franz recognizes that Smith is quite accurate about "Lovecraft's horror of the swarming towers of New York" (68) and later recalls "his
fascinated dread of vast rooms with ceilings that were indoor skies and far
walls that were horizons, in buildings vaster still" (139). The peculiar character
of the metropolis did preoccupy Lovecraft, who in this regard much more seriously than in his early decadence followed the lead of Baudelaire, the first author to imagine the potential of the city to generate paramentals in his poem
"Les Sept Vieillards": "Fourmillante cité, cité pleine de rêves, / Où le spectre
en plein jour raccroche le passant!" [Ant-hill city, city full of dreams, / Where
the specter in full day solicits the passer-by] (97). Leiber would have found
passages substantiating Smith's description of Lovecraft's views in stories like
"The Horror of Red Hook," which meditates on "old brick slums and seas of
dark, subtle faces [. . .], this blatant, evasive welter of outward greed and inward blasphemy" (D 247). Though Leiber renounces Lovecraft's racism, he
also shares this nostalgia for cities long ago vanished, in this novel the San
Francisco that sank in the great earthquake.

No doubt one reason for these frequent references to Lovecraft is the personal impact that his work made upon Leiber, an impact to which Leiber
paid tribute in his autobiographical and critical essays. And autobiography is
important in this novel, as Byfield has demonstrated. The novel records and
shapes Leiber's loss of his wife, his alcoholism, his move to San Francisco,
and his love affair with that city; it also records his Jungian interpretation of
these events, an aspect of the work that should not be ignored and that Byfield deals with thoroughly. Besides that aspect, however, the novel looks
backward, with a critical eye, at Leiber's literary career and attempts to come
to grips with what it means to write weird fiction.

One of the signals that the novel confronts and recapitulates that career
is the appearance of Fafhrd and the Gray Mouser as Gunnar and Saul, the
one "a tall, slim man, ashen blond, a fined-down Viking" (19), the other a
Jew "with dark hair shoulder-length and dark-circled eyes" (34), the one interested in exterior reality, his computers, the other a worker in a psychiatric
ward. Though Franz at one point speculates about the degree of homosexu-
ality in their friendship (19), at the conclusion of the novel they celebrate
the principle of heterosexual union with Franz and Cal, as Fafhrd and the
Mouser do in "Rime Isle": "Gunnar's Ingrid was tall and blonde as he, and
worked in the Environmental Protection Agency [. . .]. While Saul's Joey

was a red-haired little dietitian deep into community theater" (181). Hardly participating in the action, Gunnar and Saul represent two perspectives upon Franz's experience as he attempts to uncover the history of the moun-tebank de Castries.

Another moment that recalls an earlier novel is Cal's rebuke and disper-sal of the paramental that rises out of Franz's scholar's mistress. Earlier Saul remembers how she had calmed the psychotics in his ward with music "as if she were some sort of witch making black magic with music" (58). Her magic, however, if we are to call it that, is a white magic that liberates rather than binds. In her own words, which Franz recalls, music has the power "to release [. . .] things and make them fly and swirl" (59). This possibility, that magic might unbind the tormented and obsessive characters, is something that Lovecraft never considers. At the climax she releases Franz through go-ing "down on her haunches, like a witch doctor" and banishing the spirit in the name of music and number (175). This description picks up that of the white witch Tansy in *Conjure Wife*, who labors for the sake of her husband, though Cal is clearly an Enlightenment witch; Tansy uses the same shaman-istic materials as her opponents. Most remarkable, however, is the difference in time: Tansy labors for her young husband to rescue him from the wives of his colleagues, whereas Cal labors for her older lover to rescue him from his obsession with his dead wife Daisy.

Just as Fafhrd and the Mouser came to represent for Leiber two aspects of the self and as Cal and Daisy represent different aspects of the Anima (By-field 64–65), so a variety of self-reflections appear in this novel. This is the significance of Byers, who prefaces his long account of de Castries in the cen-ter of the novel with the argument that Leiber might well have advanced for his own more baroque works: "I'll probably tell the story—at least in spots—in a somewhat poetic style. Don't let that put you off. It merely helps me or-ganize my thoughts and select the significant items. I won't be straying in the least from the strict truth as I've discovered it" (97). Such a style may indeed be an instrument toward truth, hence the extravagance of Leiber's metaphors that shape Franz's meditations upon his problem. Byers is also a double of Franz/Fritz when he imbibes brandy rather copiously during his account and at its conclusion urges the bottle upon Franz, who recognizes that the style may shape our approach to truth but that the bottle certainly does not.

The short story "A Bit of the Dark World" that Leiber casually mentions in the novel (82), following Bloch's lead when he mentioned "Fane of the Black Pharaoh," points at a profound way in which the novel recapitulates

his career, thus making him a part of the literary world that the novel meditates upon. The story like *Our Lady of Darkness* opens with "rocky pinnacles
that looked like primeval monoliths or robed and hooded stone monsters"
(69), objects that owe much to Lovecraft's hills in "The Dunwich Horror" or
"The Whisperer in Darkness." Thinking of Lovecraft, one character denies
that there are "any lost worlds in darkest Africa or Mountains of Madness
near the South Pole" (72). More profoundly, Leiber provides a double for
himself, the science-fantasy writer Franz Kinzman, whom the monster,
whether a bit of the dark world, a giant spider, a black empress, or a black
tiger, "burning bright" (77), devours on the last page (the reference to Blake
reminds us that Leiber had already alluded to that poem in *The Wanderer*).
But a further double appears in the narrator Glenn Seabury, who works on
cheap monster movies and who has a relationship with his colleague Viki
Quinn; the allusion to Seabury Quinn, one of the most popular authors associated with *Weird Tales* during the 1920s and '30s, far outshining the work
of Lovecraft, Smith, and Howard, is an open secret of Leiber's story. In this
typically oblique fashion he looks with some irony upon his own role as the
author of a fiction that must be received with some skepticism in the contemporary world. The great difference in emphasis between this story and
the novel is the story's assertion that the experience of the weird can only
take place far from the "Hive," where "our ears are so full of the clack of the
mass media that it's practically impossible to think or sense or feel anything
deeply, anything that's beyond humanity" (71). In the novel the weird arises
directly out of the city, its massive construction and its bureaucratic structures. Leiber's city is horrifying[4] because it is massive, Lovecraft's because it
is filled with immigrants and mixed marriages, whence the half-breeds and
mongrels that threaten the Anglo-Saxon purity of the Yankee settlers. It is
this very mix, however, that renders Leiber's city delightful, as well as the
opportunities it offers for a sophisticated culture; Gunnar and Saul, Fernando and Dorotea, and Calpurnia embody those aspects of the city that
Leiber loves and Lovecraft abhors.

The problem of the modern city occupied Leiber throughout his career. In
The Sinful Ones the modern city, Chicago in that case, reveals the automatism
of modern life. In *The Wanderer* the modern city is writ large in space, where a
planet of interstellar police pursues a planet of stylish outlaws. In "Smoke
Ghost" and "The Hound," which Leiber had written early in his career, odd

---

4. Ro Pardoe and John Howard make this point in their annotations to page 18 of their edition.

entities walk the streets of the city, rather like the paramentals that de Castries invokes (Byfield 14, 63). *Our Lady of Darkness* simply picks up this persistent apprehension that something has changed in human consciousness.

The most persistent double of the novel is Theobald de Castries, whom we must consider as a weird fantasy writer, one who inspires other writers such as Clark Ashton Smith. Note the modest malice expressed in his paro-distic curse: "Go out, my little book, and break some necks!" (122). Intent upon manipulating the paramentals against whom he warns and with whom he connives, De Castries cannot bear the presumption of the wizards of fic-tion, Smith, London, Franz, Lovecraft and Leiber, who manipulate the fic-tional world for an aesthetic effect, though their aims are utterly serious. Hence his attempt to "break some necks." In effect he writes two books, *Megapolisomancy*—such an impossible title!—which collects some cult read-ers at first but which then loses its attraction, and the Grand Cipher, which works very well years after his death but which is composed of "that mathe-matical will-o'-the-wisp—a set of completely random numbers" (180). He possesses a powerful intellect that comes to nothing. That is the personal nightmare of any author who takes the work seriously.[5]

To return now to Lovecraft, who died at forty-six with little in print, let us reconsider "The Haunter in the Dark." A man upon one hill becomes fas-cinated by a place upon another hill across the city and in going there wakes a threat that pursues him to his apartment (which Lovecraft had modeled upon his own and which Leiber modeled upon his own) where it kills him. The Italians and Irish around the church in Providence make the sign of the cross, but they also make "a curious sign" with their right hand (*DH* 96). Leiber's sinister children echo Lovecraft's innocent children "who shouted and played in the mud of the shadowy lanes" (97). Lovecraft's protagonist comes upon a veritable library of the infamous books that Lovecraft, Smith, Howard, and Derleth had invented before he finds "a small leather-bound record-book filled with entries in some odd cryptographic medium" (*DH* 100), composed of astronomical, alchemical, and astrological symbols "massed in solid pages of text" (*DH* 101), rather like de Castries's Grand Ci-pher, its pages "covered from top to bottom [. . .] with unbroken lines of neatly yet crabbedly inked black astronomical and astrological signs and other cryptic symbols" (179). After Blake cracks the code, the entity in the

---

5. Recently John Langan has treated de Castries and his nephew Rudolph as characters in his novel *The House of Windows*. The echo-chamber does not cease.

church begins to exert a power that forces him in his sleep to return to the church, just as Franz returns to the top of Corona Hill to confront the monster that has returned to his apartment. The great change is that the threat in Lovecraft's tale lies in a Free Will Baptist Church that looks like an ancient Roman Catholic church; Leiber, uninterested in Lovecraft's anti-Catholic racism, secularizes the scene, but it is still significant that, taking a page from Poe, he sets the ashes of the wizard beneath the Bishop's seat.

The early history of de Castries makes Byers think, as he pours himself more brandy, "of Lovecraft's Nyarlathotep, who came out of Egypt to deliver pseudoscientific lectures heralding the crumbling away of the world" (101). Indeed, at the end of Lovecraft's early sketch a demonized Providence is split in two, opening a pit into which the narrator falls. A further reference to Nyarlathotep in the novel may lie in the name of Nicola Tesla, "America's other electrical wizard" (109), who Will Murray believes provided Lovecraft the model of Nyarlathotep.[6] These references to Nyarlathotep and Tesla suggest both the mountebank quality of de Castries and the demonic quality, a further aspect of which lies in our not being able to establish where he was born, whether Paris, in Egypt, or in Vermont. We, of course, are not surprised that Nyarlathotep should be under discussion here, given the allusions to him in the Bloch/Lovecraft/Bloch cycle we have examined.

More needs, however, to be said on the subject of Tesla. In Leiber's unpublished early novel *The Dealings of Daniel Kesserich* the scientist is "a sardonic mystifier" (57) whose work bears a resemblance to that of Tesla (Clements 24). He uses "quite a bit of electrical stuff" (74) in experiments that dim the lights throughout the town (75) and that finally lead to "a sort of mass feeling, an epidemic of guilty faces and fearful eyes" (48). "Nyarlathotep" opens upon a distressed populace: "To a season of political and social upheaval was added a strange and brooding apprehension of hideous physical danger [. . .]. The people went about with pale and worried faces, and whispered warnings and prophecies which no one dared consciously repeat or acknowledge to himself that he had heard. A sense of monstrous guilt was upon the land" (MW 32). In this pre-apocalyptic climate of existential guilt Nyarlathotep appears to present exhibits of electrical experiments in which sparks play across the heads of the audience, denounced by the narrator as mere static electricity before he and everyone else are driven

6. As a portent of the underground myth of America Tesla is a character in Thomas Pynchon's novel *Against the Day*.

mad. De Castries, though he has a "morbid fear of electricity" (123), calculates the electricity in the thousands of miles of wire looping the city (12–13); and he has a chair in his apartment rigged to give an electric shock to "salesmen and salesladies, children, and other stray visitors," including a young woman who did not appreciate this "genuine sadomasochistic touch" (123). To conclude this odd knot of Tesla, Nyarlathotep, and de Castries, we should consider that, as a youth in Croatia, Tesla had a black cat whose fur introduced him to electrical phenomena. "Is nature a gigantic cat?" he asked. "If so, who strokes its back? It can only be God, I concluded" (Murray 29). This passage not only reminds us of Lovecraft's love of cats and the association of cats with Nyarlathotep in such stories as "The Rats in the Walls"; in the present context it reminds us of the black panther that accompanies de Castries and his mistress. Kesserich, that demonic manipulator of dimensions, explains his work to the narrator in the bar The Black Cat (with a nod to Poe). In *Our Lady of Darkness* Leiber seems to be picking up material that he had handled in his earliest novel, written under the impact of his letters with Lovecraft.

Late in the novel Franz thinks of "The Colour out of Space" that had so much depressed him as an adolescent: "Yet at the same time it had been so fascinating. What was the whole literature of supernatural horror but an essay to make death itself exciting." This story about a family "rotting away alive, poisoned by radioactives from the ends of the universe" (166), now provides him a model for what is happening to the earth, "blackly cancerous," and to the universe, "terminally diseased" (168). All this language, however, magniloquent as it strives to be, is nothing but a blind to his true anxiety that arises from his wife's cancerous death; and à propos of her death is that of the wife Nabby in Lovecraft's story, rotting away in the attic. The only thing that can redeem this bleak vision is the iridescent color that plays across the decay, making death not simply exciting. Death is sexy.

It is also late in the novel that Franz thinks of "The Thing in the Doorstep." Bemused by his late night consciousness, he murmurs to his scholar's mistress, "Don't deliquesce now, dear, like poor Asenath Waite" (164). The problem with that story is, however, the very question of identity, the question of who it is that deliquesces at the story's climax, Edward, his wife Asenath, her wizard father, or the entity that might stand behind him. This is the question Franz explicitly asks when the creature embodied in all those books attacks him, "whether it was just such an intense look that the witch Asenath (Waite) Derby would have turned upon her husband Edward Derby when they were in bed, with old Ephraim Waite (Thibaut de Castries?) peering with her from her hypnotic eyes" (172). The entity is compound, layered in archetypes that flicker through one another. Whose is that look? This is the question that a reader faces in considering whether that creature in the bed is de Castries or his mistress, male or female. This question also arises if we consider the problem of the novel's title, which in its original appearance in *Fantasy and Science Fiction* had been *The Pale Brown Thing*, a title that emphasizes the male threat, the presence of de Castries's spirit as a mocking, jejune phallus. At first the phrase relates to Corona Heights, "humped and pale brown," (3) "pale brown in the morning sunlight" (4). The paramental resembles a pale brown rock, as though "in a long raincoat or drab robe" (7); later Franz learns that de Castries was buried there in "a pale old brown" robe (127). When the creature appears in his window it is "pale brown, like old bones" (29–30) and leaves "clumps of brownish paper" (34). That this creature is his double comes clear not only from its exchange with him but from his colliding with "a pallid drunk in a shapeless, dirty pale grey shirt"— "There but for the grace of God," he thinks (80). The death of Daisy not only threatens that Franz will die; it implies the impotence of the pale brown thing, driving him from his tentative relation with Cal to the arms of the scholar's mistress, whose cranium is pale brown (170). Perhaps most threatening to a writer is this imagery of brown paper, the suggestion that every writer's effort comes down to no more than brown paper, pulp paper, that shall crumble away faster than an author's flesh and bones. Many authors, I think, have the experience of inspecting the books in a used book store and wondering whether his or her book shall be a part of that general rot.

The present title emphasizes the female aspect of the threat, the scholar's mistress that Franz keeps in his bed, "a very secret / playmate, a dashing but studious call girl, a slim, incestuous sister, eternal comrade" (4–5), and the mistress who accompanies de Castries. The description of that woman derives from several sources, fetishistic and literary; the possibility of connecting her with the black panther that de Castries may have possessed—shades of Dr. Dexter as Nyarlathotep in "The Shadow from the Steeple"!—returns us for a moment to Tigerishka in *The Wanderer*; she is "a tigress," says de Castries, an "all merciless night animal [. . .], my Queen of Night, Our Lady of Darkness" (104). Contracting the image, Byers's two mistresses are cat-like, with cat-masks that give them a "nasty triangular snouty appearance," reminiscent of the features Franz saw in the stairwell, a "foreshortened, ghostly, featureless oval of a small face" (18). She is akin to the murderous

Invisible Nurse who generates such appellations as "our fairy snooze mother, our dark goddess of oblivion" (46), and "our queen of dreams" (47). At the concert a woman wears "a beige turban and pale brown flowing gown"; she seems to wear a veil also, but in fact she is African American (142). Earlier Byers had mentioned that veil "with its array of black polka dots" (105), a description that returns as Franz caresses his scholar's mistress before she attacks him, "those very odd black beauty marks, a whole page of them" (164), suggestive of the veil that Arletty wears in the second part of *Les Enfants du paradis*. Our Lady of Darkness incarnates the most radical form of obsessive love. When she attacks her face is "mottled pale brown and yellowish with age," her limbs braided in "pale brown paper" (174). From this survey it is clear that these two images, the adjectival phrase of the male pale brown thing occurring most often in the first part of the novel and most of the nouns referring to the female Lady of Darkness occurring most often in the last part, are finally not to be distinguished. The archetype of the impotent father, whose impotence is itself a matter of aggressive accusation, and the archetype of the powerful mother, she who has taught us our mother tongue, fuse in the final scene.

This double form of the creature confronts us with an unanswerable difficulty. Throughout this essay I have had in mind that moment in "Little Gidding" when the poet meets on the streets of London, during the Blitz, "the eyes of a familiar compound ghost / Both intimate and unidentifiable" (53). That ghost, a spiritual father, is undoubtedly a particular poet, probably Yeats, but Swift, Mallarmé, Pound, Dante, and Virgil are also present. In *Our Lady of Darkness* Leiber confronts his deep heritage, his debate with Lovecraft throughout his career (and with Jung, and James, and Smith, and his own younger self), his sense that something has changed through the consciousness of the modern city (call it a paramental), and his debt to the word that has allowed him to be this writer who now stands near death. In terms of the novel, what is it that attacks Franz? Is it de Castries or de Castries's mistress? Is it a paramental? Is it the Anima? Is it the word? Or is it "the solitary, steep hill called Corona Heights" with which the novel opens (1)? Whatever attacks Franz, it is also made up of his vision of Daisy, the cancer in her "pushing insidiously and insistently, like grass from sidewalk crack, out of her *pale brown* cranium, bursting apart the squamous, sagittal, and *coronal* sutures" (170; my italics). And then in terms of debt, the debt that can never be repaid, there is the compound ghost of Asenath Waite, her father behind her, and the putative entity behind him; but we have no idea how far that line extends. The terrifying point of the novel is that we cannot offer any definitive answer to our question, and perhaps on that level it is most Lovecraftian.

To speak with the voice of Lovecraft in "The Colour out of Space," it was only a pale brown thing, perhaps analogous to the thing on the doorstep. A death with no sublimity awaits us, though nevertheless it seems to attract us with all the power and mystery of sex. Leiber's novel certainly concerns the angst of an author under the burden of his predecessors and the further angst, as he nears his death, whether his word shall persist. No clear answer can relieve such an angst. Bloch tried twice over to relieve himself of this angst early in his career when he felt he had discovered the game of litera-ture; later he was not so sure, and the several sequels he wrote, albeit under professional pressure, were also written to forestall that end. When he was untrue to himself Lovecraft knew the answer to these anxieties, that each of his protagonists would recognize a life-shattering truth about himself and his place in an indifferent universe and that this truth would destroy him. This is quite pat. When Lovecraft was true to himself, as he so often was in his fiction, he didn't know, and this was the great gift he presented to Bloch and Leiber; so for Leiber above all, no matter how dense the specter that may at-tack, survival and integrity are possible, albeit in the last word of the novel "chancy" (183).

The Weird Historical Novel: *Jonathan Strange & Mr Norrell*, *The Case of Charles Dexter Ward*, and Other Historical Ventures

Reading Susanna Clarke's extraordinarily popular *Jonathan Strange & Mr Norrell* I was suddenly struck by a number of points at which it seemed to share an affinity with Lovecraft's work; and not simply because both show a jocular though nonetheless real affection for King George III. Lovecraft, as we know, was fond on occasion of signing his letters "God save King George!" In his own fashion he entertained the possibility of an alternate history in which the American colonies were still loyal subjects of the British Empire. When the mad king appears in chapters of Clarke's novel, his madness is not so bad that he cannot see the realities of Faerie that are hidden from his warders; more seriously, the English novelist and the grandfather of the modern weird tale from Providence are not alien to each other, though let me hasten to add that she is not adding another work to the Cthulhu Mythos.

I do not know whether she has read Lovecraft; it is possible that their affinities are natural to anyone entering the field with some acquaintance with its state of the art. Two passages in her book, only a page apart, suggest that she may well have read "The Colour out of Space." In order to demonstrate his assertion that "English magic was shaped by England—just as England herself was shaped by magic" (608), Jonathan Strange tells a story of how a town on the coast of Yorkshire had been ruined by magic:

> First a wind came out of the north and blew through the town. As the wind touched the beasts of the town they grew old and died—cows, pigs, fowls and sheep—even the cats and dogs. As the wind touched the town itself houses became ruins before the very eyes of the unhappy householders. Tools broke, pots shattered, wood warped and split, brick and stone crumbled into

131

dust. [. . .] The townspeople, very wisely, began to run from the town and when they reached the higher ground they looked back and were just in time to see the remains of the town slip slowly under the cold, grey waves. (609)

The passage is very like several passages in Lovecraft's story in which the disintegration of the Gardner farm is described: "By September all the vegetation was fast crumbling to a greyish powder. [. . .] Poultry turned greyish and died very quickly, their meat being found dry and noisome upon cutting. Hogs grew inordinately fat, then suddenly began to undergo loathsome changes which no one could explain" (DH 66–67).[1] Lovecraft's description is more extensive than Strange's anecdote, but the effect is the same; the only real difference is that Lovecraft lets the cats escape. Immediately after Strange's story the box containing Lady Pole's finger arrives: "It was a beautiful shade of blue, but then not exactly blue, it was more like lilac. But then again, not exactly lilac either, since it had a tinge of grey in it. To be more precise, it was the colour of heartache" (610). In this book it is not remarkable that the box should have a "colour," but the topos of a magical color that cannot be identified surely comes directly from Lovecraft. But whether Clarke has read Lovecraft or not, these affinities lead us to think not only about her work but to approach Lovecraft from an angle we have not used before.

I

All I saw farther, in the last confusion,
    Was, that King George slipp'd into heaven for one;
And when the tumult dwindled to a calm,
I left him practising the hundredth psalm.
               (Byron, The Vision of Judgment ll. 845–48)

Anyone who has read the first chapters of Jonathan Strange & Mr Norrell becomes aware that it deals with England during the Napoleonic Wars and their aftermath and that various historical figures appear in its pages, such as the Duke of Wellington and Lord Castlereagh. This alternate England, however, believes in magic, or rather it has come to believe in magic once more, and some people have been moved to perform it after the period of Enlightenment in which all magic fled, and this magic works; great magicians are a part of its history, and adjacent as it were to this England lie the other lands

---

1. It is possible that Clarke may be aware of the English Dunwich that did sink into the sea, since Swinburne later apostrophized that coastal town (Waugh, Monster 25–26).

where fairies live and Hell and on the other side of Hell "the Bitter Lands" (212). It is difficult to say how the other place exists, whether as another universe where different physical laws and different geometries exist as we might describe it in the pages of the *Scientific American,* as a non-Euclidean space as Lovecraft likes to express it, the place outside, or as Faerieland as we find in the pages of Clarke's novel. It is the fact of that existence that matters, not its how. In that other place there is a different apprehension of space and time. In Lovecraft and Clarke it is described in similar images such as canals and bridges; and in order to make that other space apprehensible both writers allude with some irony to the *Carceri* of Piranesi. Jonathan Strange describes these spaces in this language:

> There were canals of still water in stone embankments. The water appeared black in the gloomy light. I saw staircases that rose up so high I could not see the top of them, and others that descended into utter blackness. Then suddenly I passed under an arch and found myself upon a stone bridge that crossed a dark, empty landscape. [. . .] I saw a shadow moving along a white road that crossed the dark moor. You must understand that I was upon the bridge at the time and it was much higher than any bridge I have ever seen in this world. (395)

In comparison to this language consider this passage from "The Whisperer in Darkness," "The black rivers of pitch that flow under those mysterious Cyclopean bridges," (DH 254); or this passage from *At the Mountains of Madness,* the experience of the explorers "traversing rooms and corridors in every stage of ruin or preservation, clambering up ramps, crossing upper floors and bridges and clambering down again, encountering choked doorways and piles of debris, hastening now and then along finely preserved and uncannily immaculate stretches" (MM 79).

There is no doubt that Lovecraft means to present this other place as terrifying, yet it frequently does have an abstract beauty. There is something of this abstract beauty in the descriptions we find in "The Dreams in the Witch House." In Clarke's novel the other place is frankly seductive, especially as it is revealed in its king, the man with the thistledown hair. Slowly, however, we realize that this seduction is alienating and deadly.

Insofar as both authors posit a complex history, they both make use of invented books. We cannot point to anything in Clarke as central as the *Necronomicon,* but we have a large number of magic books authored by characters who slowly become important in the alternate history to England that Clarke is sketching, especially in the footnotes. I do not know another author who makes such use of footnotes, though Clarke's footnotes do seem to be a part of the postmodern condition under which she is working. An aspect of this characteristic is her use of documents, especially letters that are riddled with lacunae and doubtful readings. I have noted elsewhere that Lovecraft is fond of the document upon occasion, but he seldom presents documents that have holes in them.

Certain real people connected with literature also appear in her work, such as Henry Lintot (166), a publisher with whom Pope had difficulties; and John Murray, Byron's publisher, plays a fairly major role in the conclusion of the novel. Perhaps most amusing is the reference to Doctor Johnson's definition of *thaumatomane* in his dictionary (282), whereas the word of course is not to be found there. The most interesting figure that Clarke has included in the narrative at length is Lord Byron, but we shall discuss his presence later. On a more circumscribed stage Lovecraft's fiction mentions historical figures from Providence and New England history.

A further characteristic Lovecraft and Clarke share is a taste for an antique style, one that Clarke invents very carefully, with certain words such as "shew" or "chuse" spelled according to the conventions of the day. Lovecraft does not have to invent or elaborate this style because he learned it as a young boy in the eighteenth-century library of his grandfather, but he consciously insists upon it, paying attention to such aspects of it as the British conventions of spelling. It is not, as far as he is concerned, a matter of decoration, for he passionately believes that English culture has been truly harmed by the simplifications of Webster. In each author this attention to the spelling of a foredone day leads to an arch and distanced style; we are often not sure of the extent to which we must take the narrative seriously, since the style seems so often to assure us that this is really a literary matter, a mere literary matter, not a matter of deep personal or historical concern. In both authors it does become a very serious matter indeed, but the narrative moves at that moment obliquely.

If we look aside from Lovecraft for a moment, is there anything that Clarke's novel resembles? It is very like John Barth's *The Sot-Weed Factor* and Thomas Pychon's *Mason and Dixon*; using the alienating forms of the language of the period, it is attempting to investigate the modern world under the garb of the world that was and, so their argument goes, still is. That the world that interests her is England forms one of the major differences between her and the American authors, though both of their novels begin in

England and return to it; but that it is England forms one of the reasons that Clarke's work and Lovecraft's are so similar, because his England, the England that he cherishes, is essentially an alternate England in which the American Revolution does not occur.

One aspect of their plots is the possibility that the oppressed and the marginal shall be lifted up. In Lovecraft this theme leads to both an anxiety and a repressed exaltation; this is to say that although he is deeply anti-Semitic and racist, railing against all the immigrants flooding into the United States and often choosing to ignore how thoroughly the Italians have already permeated the life of Rhode Island, he seems to participate in the rites of the dispossessed with great energy and glee. The expectations of the mongrel cultists in "The Call of Cthulhu" is an example of this movement; they shall be "free and wild and beyond good and evil, with laws and morals thrown aside and all men shouting and killing and revelling in joy [. . .], and all the earth would flame with a holocaust of ecstasy and freedom" (*DH* 141). In Clarke the theme leads to the possibility that Stephen Black, a black man from Jamaica who serves as the excellent butler and factotum of a Cabinet Minister, may become the next king of England through the offices of the highly ambiguous king of the fairies. Slowly the novel builds to the supposition that he is, or he is not, the nameless slave, one of the names by which the once and future king of the north of England, known throughout the novel as the Raven King, called himself; and at the end of the novel he receives an ambiguous coronation. I believe that another aspect of the oppressed and the marginal, as far as the novel is concerned, is the tension between the south of Britain and the north, especially the often deprecated county of Yorkshire, a tension that has only lifted itself once more into historical and political consciousness within the last thirty years with the political empowerment that has fallen into Scotland's hands from the North Sea oil.

This political and historical concern, then, assures us that Clarke's novel is an historical novel, as is Lovecraft's novella *The Case of Charles Dexter Ward*, which is the aspect of the two works that I would like to study at some length. In order to do so it will be useful to review various points that Georg Lukacs, the Hungarian philosopher and literary critic, made about the historical novel. Though he surveys the genre through the nineteenth and first part of the twentieth century, I plan to consider mainly his remarks about Sir Walter Scott, the inventor of the genre, and Tolstoy, its perfecter. First, Lukacs makes the point several times that the historical novel as Scott and Tolstoy create it is infused by a popular appeal that is based upon a broad, popular life (86); long before it leads the reader to a familiar historical figure, one who is truly world-historical (to use the language of Hegel as Lukacs does), it treats of the lives of the peasants, the middle class, and the aristocrats at length. The historical novel is about the day-to-day lives of people in the midst of an inchoate historical crisis.

Further, if we conceive of this crisis as a civil war, the novelist is concerned with a broad continuum of experience that comprehends and sympathizes with both sides of the issue (37); though Scott was a conservative Tory who believed in the ultimate good of the established world, he sympathized deeply with the fate of the Highland clan structure that in the course of two centuries was destroyed: "Victrix causa diis placuit, sed victa Catoni" [the victorious cause pleased the gods, but the vanquished pleased Cato] (Lucan, ctd. in Lukacs 54). To accomplish this breadth of concern Scott always chose a rather neutral protagonist, "a more or less mediocre, average English gentleman" (33) who is much more of a seeing eye than an eccentric, deeply involving individual. This is in part to say, as Lukacs does at some length, that the successful historical novel as Scott practiced it is not a Romantic work; it has no place for the Byronic hero who flourishes in the Gothic world (33–34). Instead, Scott practices a "middle way" that results in the Glorious Revolution, that Whiggish invention of compromise (32). This political maneuver, however, is patently founded upon the Anglican doctrine of the *via media*; its sanction derives from a theological perception that is attempting to find its way among the Lutheran, Calvinist, and Roman Catholic understandings. Through these various complexities the protagonist at last meets the world-historical figure through whom, for all his own detailed complexity, the compromise among these different factions is effected (38). This is not necessarily a happy ending for all concerned—far from it; but at least a solution has occurred that moves the mass of the body politic forward, and the protagonist, our neutral hero, survives and prospers as happens in the best of comedies.

None of this is accomplished, however, unless through the style and language the author makes it clear that we, author and reader, are involved in this past action: "Without a felt relationship to the present, a portrayal of history is impossible" (Lukacs 53). No author of an historical novel should strive for a detailed, archeological accuracy; Lukacs makes clear that anachronisms in language, morals, and manners are not only inescapable, they are necessary to the aesthetic success of the enterprise. As Scott argues, "It is necessary for exciting interest of any kind that the subject assumed should be, as it were, translated into the manners, as well as the language, of the age we live in" (ctd. in Lukacs 62). In reading historical novels we are never released from the present but bound to it all the more securely; everything else is romance.

In confronting the historical novel we should keep other points in mind. Since it is concerned with the action of a rather average individual in this historical moment, it is not concerned with any theoretical pattern of history, not even the Marxist that Lukacs brings to it. Let us think of the triumphalist tone of Herodotus, the tragic of Thucydides, the laborious of Livy—as far as the historical novel is concerned they do not matter, and neither does the progressive model of Saint Augustine. Vico, Spengler, and Toynbee matter. Several critics have felt that the theoretical sections of *War and Peace* do not work well with the actual narrative; so though those sections were useful in the construction of the novel and do matter as far as the character of General Kutzov is concerned, they do not matter either. These are metahistorical constructions that do not interest us in the fate of an average person. That is why I am not interested here in the well-named "The Shadow out of Time." Any utopian fiction is a mere shadow with none of the substance we find in a narrative; it is metahistorical, not historical.

What, then, are we able to say of history once we have given up our metahistorical pretensions? I take Joseph Pieper once more as my guide in a few useful suggestions. First, history is something that humans are involved in, not ordered by nature or fate; it is our freedom, choice, responsibility, and guilt that we see at work (*Hoffnung* 38–39). Then, more contentiously, we worry over the question whether history is a mere chaos, a jungle, or whether with more restraint we confess that it remains for each of us a fragment and mystery that we cannot disentangle though we still believe that some sense lies within it (50–51). Whether or not we believe in a supernatural world that obtrudes into our world, we know "daß menschliches Dasein sich ganz und gar im Kraftfeld einer unendlichen, übergeschichtlichen, kreatorischen Wirklichkeit zutrage; daß niemals das erfahrbar Hiesige identisch sein könne mit dem Ganzen der Existenz" [that human existence conducts itself totally within a field of infinite, over-historical, creational reality; that the experiential presence can never be identical with the whole of existence"; and that neither the end nor the beginning of our existence, whether historical or individual, is available to our understanding (103–4). We know enough to realize how little we can know. We also know that we can prophesy little of what shall become of the world because from experience we have learned how discontinuous history is (109). Revolutions befall us, remarkable leaders, whether good or bad, befall us, technologies befall us, and thus history takes a turn we could have had no notion of at all.

As we look , then, at *Jonathan Strange & Mr Norrell,* "The Picture in the House," *The Case of Charles Dexter Ward,* and "The Shadow over Innsmouth" we are interested in these various matters, their popular basis, their breadth of sympathy, their protagonist and the world-historical figure who appears, the nature of the solution to the crisis, and the extent to which we feel that our present, Lovecraft's in 1926 and Clarke's in 2004, is involved in that past. We are interested in the accidents of history; but we are also interested in the extent to which all this is changed by the presence of magic. To rephrase the matter, Clarke's book presents a history but an alternate history, close to a reality we believe that we recognize, especially the reality of the Napoleonic wars. It puts thereby a special spin on our common understanding of the historical novel. According to Lucacs an historical novel investigates the ambiguous process by which the past has led to the present, though of course our present is only involved tacitly. In Clarke the question frames the tension between Enlightenment England, represented by the elderly Mr Norrell, Romantic England, represented by Jonathan Strange, a rather frivolous young man in the beginning of his narrative, and the implicit ironies of England today. In Lovecraft, in such works as "The Picture in the House," *The Case of Charles Dexter Ward,* and "The Shadow over Innsmouth," the question frames the tension between pre-Revolutionary America and the decadence of America in the 1920s, again through employing an alternate history in which the alien universe, the other place, has inserted itself into our world at particular points; thus the past demands a continual, subversive reinterpretation that casts a baleful light upon the world that we think we know.

Clarke's novel is so massive that it will be most profitable to deal with only a few moments in its plot. Nevertheless, since we need to have an understanding of that plot I will summarize it briefly. After years of being only a matter of study, the performance of magic is taken up once more by Mr Norrell in order to aid Britain in its ongoing war with Napoleon; he does this out of personal reasons as well as patriotic reasons, though he seems a rather dry, pedantic, and withdrawing personality, an Enlightenment antiquarian lost in the Romantic age. Jonathan Strange is a young man who takes up magic mainly because, without anything else to do, he wishes to impress a young lady called Arabella. The relationship of the two men, at first a master and an apprentice, becomes slowly more adversarial because they are so different in nature and have such different conceptions of how magic should be pursued; and the relationship is further complicated by the fact that Norrell has secretly applied to a fairy, the man with the thistle-down hair, to resurrect the wife of a cabinet minister, and this figure, now free of the world, enchants Arabella to her apparent death. To save her, Strange finds himself forced to become mad because that is the only way to deal with the fairy. The action spans some ten years, from the autumn of 1806 to the spring of 1817.

One element of Strange's alienation from Norrell is Strange's determination to aid Wellington in the Peninsular War by going to Spain; despite Norrell's cautious warnings the young man believes that he must work magic on the spot if he is to be of any true help. Wellington, in Lukacs's phrase the world-historical figure of the novel, is at first less than interested in the help Strange can provide, so he must prove himself by coming to know the situation in a truly direct fashion that means living with the soldiers who are he discovers, as Wellington would have it, "the scum of the earth" and "the best fellows in the world" (298). Being unlike Norrell a gregarious chap, Strange succeeds in his life with them and shortly begins to aid Wellington by his magical transformation of the landscape, wonderful for the men though a bit bewildering to the Portuguese. We see here at work the popular basis of the novel that Lukacs had praised in Scott.

The most remarkable magic Strange performs in the Peninsular War is actually in the service of a small matter, the retrieval of cannon that Neapolitan deserters from the French army have captured. To discover where the cannon are Strange employs necromantic arts to resurrect seventeen corpses from the battlefield who have that information. It is difficult, however, to extract that information from these men who come alive screaming in the language of Hell. Once they begin to speak in their native Neapolitan they are happy to surrender the information, but when Wellington has no use for them they become a nuisance; they smell and are liable to leave pieces of themselves in the shackles the English try to contain them with. They want a full, real life, but Strange does not know how to do that—the novel frequently plays with the motif of the magician's apprentice who does not know how to contain a magic once he has performed it; it gets out of hand. The Neapolitans do not want to die again, for "they had seen Hell and were not anxious to return there" (333). It is at this time that Goya makes his disquieting sketch of the corpses pleading in a circle around the helpless magician. As a last resort at Wellington's order that the men should be de-

stroyed the English throw the unobliging dead men onto a bonfire. The narrator comments:

> The raising of the seventeen dead Neapolitans was a good example of the
> sort of problem faced by Strange in the latter half of the war. Like the Minis-
> ters before him, Lord Wellington was becoming more accustomed to using
> magic to achieve his ends and he demanded increasingly elaborate spells
> from his magician. However, unlike the Ministers, Wellington had very little
> time or inclination for listening to long explanations of why a thing was not
> possible. After all, he regularly demanded the impossible of his engineers, his
> generals and his officers and he saw no reason to make an exception of his
> magician. (334).

Clarke has done careful research in the matter of Wellington and renders him
nicely, but we might wonder whether he really functions as Lukacs argues
ought to be done. This Wellington fights the Peninsular War successfully, like
the brutal and arrogant man he really was, a classic example of the Regency
aristocrat. But in this alternate history magic changes little in the war.

This scene casts a special light on Joseph Curwen's behavior with the
men he raises from their essential salts. Strange is a sympathetic character
who does what he has to do for the patriotic sake of England, but he does
not like it at all, whereas Wellington is much more like Curwen in that he
has no moral sense. In both narratives we resurrect the dead for the sake of
particular information; it is as though they examine with some remorse the
work of the historical novelist who must treat the historical record with
some distance. Clarke's style is permeated by a wit and irony that make clear
the difference between the world of the Regency and our world, but slowly
that style moves into lament as Strange struggles with the redemption of his
wife; Lovecraft's style affectionately renders Colonial America as it moves
toward the Revolution

A few years after Strange's return to England the Duke of York presents
him a new task, an attempt to cure King George of his madness. This important scene is very near the center of the novel and is most peculiar, for the
king was certainly a world-historical figure once, but he is one no longer, reduced to incoherence because of the death of his daughter; since the narration
is from the view of the period, nothing is said of the porphyria the king seems
to have suffered. To deal with him directly Strange bewitches his doctors, an
act he would not have done earlier but the narrator comments that "like many
other gentlemen who had been in Spain with the Duke of Wellington, he had

begun unconsciously to imitate his Grace, part of whose character it was always to act in the most direct way possible" (344); this transformation in Strange is to help him immensely in the climax of the novel.

The king is in a pitiable state because "the misery of madness was compounded by the misery of blindness," and Clarke draws the immediate conclusion that he resembles a tragic figure from Shakespeare, a tragedy heightened because "in his madness and his blindness he was Lear and Gloucester combined" (350). At this point the assumptions of the nineteenth century are superseded by the assumptions of the sixteenth century as the narrator suggests that the madness of the king affects the health of the nation (359). The symbol of this general malaise lies in the man with the thistledown hair, who is present throughout this scene but only visible to the king because the mad though blind have secret sight.

Only slowly does Strange realize that someone else is present, a magician of great power who is other than Mr Norrell. The reader may understand then that the man with the thistledown hair is the other world-historical figure in the novel. In thinking this we are clearly broadening Lukacs's understanding of the term, for the fairy is, to say something perhaps too obvious, an imaginary character, one that we do not find in our historical annals, just as John Uskglass, the Raven King who during the Middle Ages ruled a kingdom that lay between England and Scotland and that extended into the fairy lands also, is an imaginary character. This, then, is the point at which we realize that the weird historical novel is different from the classic historical novel. It is not simply that magic is important in this narrative; the novel characterizes certain periods through the presence of world-historical figures that never existed. John Uskglass's kingdom never existed, but the Barons' War, the wars of the Edwards against Scotland, the Hundred Years War, and the Wars of the Roses did; this is the historical tension that John Uskglass represents, who from 1100 (495) to 1434 (419) ruled from his capital in Newcastle (35), a kingdom composed of "Cumberland, Northumberland, Durham, Yorkshire, Lancashire, Derbeyshire, and a part of Nottinghamshire (212), roughly the area of the Danelaw, as well as a kingdom in Faerie and a kingdom on the other side of Hell (122). Clarke projects a background history of England, ruled by a man who like Arthur shall surely come again (211). Enlightenment figures, rather like us, believe that the Raven King never existed but was an invention of the northern English to keep themselves from the tyranny of the south (7). As for that name "the Raven King" within the context of our present thinking about monarchy, it may refer to the ravens kept religiously in the Tower upon whose presence the monarchy depends. Magical thinking lies on the outskirts of the English tradition, but especially belongs to the Celts. In this context we recall that the English of Shakespeare's day apprehensively believed in the magical powers of the Welsh and the Scots. Glendower boasts in Shakespeare's *1 Henry IV*, "I can call spirits from the vasty deep" (3.1.53). The man with the thistledown hair represents the incommensurable element in the shift from the rational violence of the eighteenth century to the irrational violence of the nineteenth century; and though he dies at the end of the novel, the consequences of his interference in English history continue.

A year after he meets the king Strange assists Wellington at the battle of Waterloo. Before the battle Wellington makes an odd pronouncement about General Blücher: "Excellent old fellow. Loves a fight. [. . .] Unfortunately, he is also mad. He believes he is pregnant. [. . .] With a baby elephant"; and indeed, at the conclusion of the battle Blücher pats his stomach significantly (432). His madness does not affect his performance in the battle; Wellington is not concerned about that possibility at all. The point of this small detail would seem to be that in this novel madness is a major theme. The king is mad, Blücher is mad, the man with the thistledown hair is mad, since all fairies "by human standards [. . .] are barely sane" (235), and Strange makes himself mad in the climax of the novel. Human history is deeply involved in madness, some of it quite frivolous and some much more profound. Wellington is sane, but maddeningly so as he casts about for men that he uses as tools to achieve rather narrowly defined goals.

Much of the battle of Waterloo is as we have learned from Byron, who is to play a major role in the conclusion of the novel, and Thackeray; Clarke is perhaps at her most literary as she plays with popular materials from *Childe Harold's Pilgrimage* and *Vanity Fair*. Again Strange shifts the landscape about, and this time I believe we realize that this particular magic renders the difficulty that any army has in war as it tries to cope with what is either an alien landscape or a familiar landscape transformed by the violence. He brings on a torrential rain that slows down the French army—only the English, the veterans of the Peninsular War insist, find the mud friendly (442)—and brings up gigantic hands from the soil to snatch to the earth the French cavalry. At the end of the battle the hands "seemed frozen in gestures of outrage and horror as if the land itself despaired" (449). Though the magic does not change the course of history, it accentuates the horror of the event; even Wellington appears sobered at what he has wrought.

Finally, let us say something about Clarke's treatment of Byron. Here we have another world-historical figure in the way that his impact was to be felt throughout the rest of the century in the Byronic hero, an unstable compound of the man himself and of the characters that appear in his poetry, an instability that Clarke plays upon. Strange meets him first in Switzerland in 1816, but his middle-class morals cannot abide the chaos of the people around Byron; and Byron finds the magician rather tame for his taste and turns to rectify that in writing *Manfred* (554). Later in Venice they make up their quarrel when Byron takes affront at Mr Norrell's attempt to censor Strange's work and when they discover that they can be quite amiable over a game of billiards (570–71). When Strange goes mad Byron enthusiastically supports his condition because he believes that all individuals, if they only thought through their state, would go mad also. The reason for Strange's madness, he argues, is "purely metaphysical. They lie in the vast chasm between what one is, and that which one desires to become, between the soul and the flesh" (639). His argument is quite self-centered of course, for Strange is only mad in order to deal with the man with the thistledown hair and rescue his wife, yet Byron does realize that Strange's state is desperate. Clarke may portray Byron as more foppish than he was and she misses the man's considerable humor and self-irony, but she uses him in order to highlight the motives of Strange.

II

Some man of powerful character to command a person, morally subjected to him, to perform some act. The commanding person to suddenly die; and, for all the rest of his life, the subjected one continues to perform that act. (Hawthorne, *American Notebooks* 226)

In comparison to Scott's opus or to Clarke's, "The Picture in the House" is a small work; but already in its third paragraph it offers a theory of Puritan history that simply as a theoretical act might remind us of Tolstoy's explicit appeal to a theory of history in *War and Peace*. The narrator then introduces himself on his bicycle in 1896, about the time that the young Lovecraft began to move about Providence on his bicycle, and introduces the place of the story, Western Massachusetts in a storm; time and place are important. When he enters the house that offers him shelter he is quick to note the four books of the library, the eccentric Pigafetta and its illustrations, the Bible, a *Pilgrim's Progress* that he scorns because of its "grotesque woodcuts," and

Cotton Mather's *Magnalia* (DH 119)—books that delineate the character of
the owner of the house, an old-time Puritan with a taste for the bizarre. "Di-
vorced from the enlightenment of civilization," as the beginning of the story
announced, he has turned "into singular channels" (117). We may at this
point admit that the consequences to be drawn from the radical contradictions and the books offer a close comment upon religious history in the
United States, whether in 1896, 1920, or 2011.

The story proper and the shape of its historical concerns begin with the
talk of the old man and his mutterings about Captain Ebenezer Holt and the
death of Parson Clark; but let us admit at once that the story does not contain any historical meditation with the scope of Scott or Clarke. On the other
hand, it certainly has a basis in popular life, one assured by the dialect in
which the old man speaks. Captain Holt represents the outward thrust of the
Bay Colony once its merchant class became established; and Parson Clark
represents the inward, centripetal thrust of the old Puritan culture, one that
rants on a Sunday. Since the parson drowned in the pond, or so they say, we
suspect that the old man felt himself attacked by the parson and took action;
the murderous undertow of his language is palpable. He can never escape his
condition, living in the woods of Western Massachusetts, so his only escape is
through the material he has bought from the obliging captain and the imaginative energy he brings to that material. It is a solution to the crisis of the Puritan mentality, but it is of course a ghastly solution from which the young
man only escapes fortuitously through his marriage to the lightning. We do
not feel, however, that this is the happy ending of a comedy.

This conclusion, incidentally, may owe something to the book *Sunlight and
Shadow* to which Lovecraft felt that he owed his teetotaler stance, which we
will discuss in more detail in a later chapter. The author recounts this story:

> Some years since, in a hotel not far from Boston, a poor fellow who had been
> gambling nearly all night cut his throat in the room over the bar on the Sun-
> day morning. The group round the bar were startled by a heavy drop of blood
> falling on the counter, and, looking up, discovered a large red stain on the
> ceiling, from the centre of which the drops of blood were gathering and fal-
> ling on the counter, faster and faster, till they splashed on the floor. It was
> known that before the blood was cleaned from the bar and floor men were
> drinking and the trade went on, though it was the Sabbath-day. (252–53)

The last sentence delivers the moral of the story, but the imagery of the story
itself, the spot of blood on the counter and the growing spot of blood on the

ceiling, has its own force. The subtext of the story, then, might be an equa-
tion drawn between cannibalism and drunkenness.

With this possibility in mind, let us consider the story from a different
angle. First, the Puritans are described in the opening paragraphs by a number of qualities that the old man incorporates, as though he were a test case
for the theory that the narrator propounds; these qualities are strength, isolation, grotesqueness, and superstition, while the individual is driven by the
desire for freedom that is betrayed by a slavery to sexual instincts. And indeed the old man is strong, though some details contrast his strength to his
apparent weakness, strong enough to capture men, kill them, and butcher
them. He is isolated, as the description of the houses in the backwoods of
western Massachusetts suggests; and his own house is just such a house as
those. He is grotesque; he is picturesque, as the derivation of the word "grotesque" shows, but also, in the more recent connotation of the word, he is
shocking. Like Quasimodo, the hunchback of Notre Dame who can be taken
as the model of the modern grotesque, as Hugo argues in his introduction to
the novel, his distorted body at first appears weak but in fact is strong. He is
superstitious; he believes, perhaps with good reason as the story attempts to
persuade us, that if he eats men that he has butchered their bodies will
lengthen his life. And finally he is free, utterly free in the isolation of his
house to kill anyone he likes, but he commits these crimes driven by a sadomasochistic perversion powered by the picture in the book and by the crimes
themselves; the young narrator attests to the sadomasochistic aspect of these
crimes when he is himself attracted to the picture.

So far, so good. The second point, however, depends upon whether we
can believe the narrator's implicit interpretation of these events. Has the old
man actually succeeded in lengthening his life through this remarkable
means that would, as Lovecraft puts it in his description of the purpose and
means of the weird, lift the boundaries of natural law? Or is the old man
simply mistaken, a madman who believes in this superstition because he has
so brilliantly succeeded in imitating the forms of such a superannuated existence? He has learned to speak in this arcane dialect perhaps as a child and
learned the secrets of such historical figures as Captain Ebenezer Holt. This
dialectical and historical knowledge is one of the reasons that the narrator
comes to believe that the old man is ancient, but surely a student of genealogy should know that such knowledge, albeit with some effort, can be come
by. Does a spatter of blood assure the truth of the story, as many readers
think? We never learn, however, what is really in that upstairs room. It

could be an abattoir of human flesh, or merely sheep (unlikely, I grant, as that must seem in an upstairs room). We have no detail that allows us to decide whether the old man is the monster that he intimates he is or merely a clever or perverse imitation of a monster.

Why then do readers believe he is a monster? The basic reason, I believe, is that we concur with Lovecraft that the point of such a story should be the lifting of natural law. We desire in such a story as this, if it is such a story, a freedom of the imagination, but this freedom that we desire may become an enslavement because we are determined to surrender our imaginations to the genre.

The Case of Charles Dexter Ward is a more massive historical meditation than "The Picture in the House"; but to gain a measure of the shape of history in that story it helps to rehearse the early history of Rhode Island. It begins in 1635 with the archetypal flight of Roger Williams from Salem because of his various liberal conflicts with the Puritan authorities to found Providence in 1636—a flight that Joseph Curwen was to imitate in 1688 "at the beginning of the great witchcraft panic" (MM 117).[2] In Rhode Island Williams helped to establish the Baptist movement in America, but he himself remained outside of all denominations, a religious force unto himself (Gaer 39), which might as well be said of Curwen. The 1663 charter that protected Rhode Island "from partition by powerful neighbors" (Morison 94) unsympathetic to its principle of religious tolerance enshrined that principle as long as the citizens were "behaving themselves peaceably and quietly, and not using this libertie to lycentiousnesse and profaneness, nor to the civil injurye or outward disturbance of others" (Gaer 39). This tolerance did have certain limits; but because of this tolerance and because of the tolerance that the Providence Plantations extended to smugglers and privateers (Gaer 43), it became known as New England's Dumping Ground and Rogue's Island (Barck and Lefler 105).

Despite this scabrous reputation, perhaps because of it, Rhode Island prospered, and the names of prosperous citizens, privateers, shipbuilders, architects, educators, and politicians fill the pages of Lovecraft's novella, which alludes casually to the Willetts, Slocumbs, Crawfords, Carters, Fen-

---

2. There was some reason for this connection of name and place, since in 1638 a certain Captain George Curwen live in Salem (Beckwith 45). But the name is also apt, since its Latin form "Corvinus" (MM 220) is probably related to "corvus," raven. Joseph Curwen is not related to John Uskglass, the Raven King, but each man has the power to insert himself into different periods of history.

ners, and Tillinghasts. The four Brown brothers involved in the attack on the Pawtuxet farm were worthy figures in the colony's commercial and cultural history. John Brown was a leading figure in Rhode Island commerce, the first Rhode Island merchant to trade with the Orient; Joseph Brown became a professor at Brown University and an architect, designing the Old Market House, the John Brown House for his brother, and the First Baptist Church in which Lovecraft was raised; Nicholas Brown, a substantial merchant, contributed funds to the establishment of Brown University, named after him; and Moses Brown presided over some of the first textile mills in New England (Gaer 67–69, 264) and donated land for the Moses Brown School that Charles Dexter Ward attended (Gaer 289).[3] With the privateer Captain Abraham Whipple, a cousin of the grandfather of the enterprising Dr. Elihu Whipple in "The Shunned House" (MM 239) and the Reverend James Manning, the first head of Brown University, the group gathered to destroy Joseph Curwen represents the cream of Providence society in the years leading to the Revolution.

After many years of commercial success, being one of the apexes of the trade powered by "the infinite rum, slave, and molasses sloops" (MM 122), Rhode Island joined the other colonies in the drift toward the Revolution. In 1765 a mob seized a boat from the Maidstone that "had been impressing sailors in Newport Harbor, and dragged it through Queen Street to the Common, where it was burned" (Gaer 43). Following this example in 1769 citizens of Newport cut the cable of a ship called Liberty and burned it when it drifted ashore, prompting a number of British ships to occupy the harbor until in 1776 sharpshooters drove them out (Gaer 207). The true flashpoint was the clash with a revenue cutter, the Gaspée, which was authorized to enforce the customs laws in Rhode Island, "that home of notorious smugglers" (Barck and Lefler 545); but on June 9, 1772, a year after the attack on Curwen, when the ship ran aground near Providence some one hundred and fifty citizens, including John Brown and Samuel Whipple (Gaer 257), burned it, upon which a commission delegated to investigate the matter and arrest those responsible came to no judgment because of the general refusal of the city to testify. Because the affair strengthened the hand of radicals throughout the colonies it was an important step toward the Revolution (Barck and Lefler 545–46). On May 4, 1776, the Rhode Island Assembly in effect de-

---

3. Lovecraft expatiates at great length about the virtues of the Browns in a late letter to Richard F. Searight (80).

clared its independence and its governor instructed the colony's delegates to the Congress in Philadelphia that they were free to vote for independence, rather bold measures since "many Rhode Islanders [were] strongly attached to the crown and perfectly satisfied with their own form of liberal government" (Barck and Lefler 593). At the end of the Revolution Rhode Island at first refused to endorse the Constitution and by the slimmest of margins was the last to do so (Barck and Lefler 728–30).

From this sketch of early Rhode Island history certain analyses of the figure of Joseph Curwen stand out. The first point is that, try as he will to ingratiate himself with the society of Providence, he is an outsider like Roger Williams, always in flight and never condescending to align himself with any denomination. At the end of his life in Providence—at the end of his first life—he decides to marry in order to cement his position within the increasingly suspicious Providence society, and this marriage forthrightly takes place in the First Baptist Church; but in order to compromise with his wife's Congregational ties they together become members of King's Church in which his child is baptised, and thus he declares himself, though he was baptised within the First Baptist Church, a High Church Anglican at the precise moment that the coming Revolution renders that an unwise identity. Yet he has as a precurser followed precisely the trajectory that Lovecraft follows, raised as a Baptist and married in an Episcopal Church. Lovecraft projects himself onto both protagonist and antagonist; he is Charles Dexter Ward, the impassioned searcher-out of genealogical records, and he is the young man's ancestor who does not give a rap for genealogy.

The second point, more interesting for our investigation into the nature of the historical fantasy novel, is that magic, the magic that Joseph Curwen possesses and there is no other, is absolutely blasphemous to the society of Rhode Island. Despite the principle of religious tolerance, the colony cannot accept what Joseph Curwen is doing. Somehow he stands at the boundary of their imagination; by implication, not even Roger Williams, despite his troubled acceptance of the Quakers, could have ever accepted Joseph Curwen. What, then, is the crime of this mild-mannered albeit unaged commercial gentleman? He accepts every social constraint that lies below the religious tolerance that the society parades before itself with such complacence, yet the society knows that he has trespassed something quite basic; he wants a knowledge that lies beyond its normal discourse. Though he accepts every word of its society, he has reservations that are represented by the farm at Pawtuxet, maintained by Indians, half-breeds, and blacks, everyone marginal to this society; and he won't die. So they have to kill him.

The third point is implicit in the first two; we simply need to make it explicit. The man is a Tory. In the political radicalization of the society as it moves toward the Revolution, his interests and manners lie on the side of the Crown. Even in Salem, almost a hundred years earlier than the events of the *Maidstone,* the *Liberty,* and the *Gaspée,* he spoke with the accent and manners of an Englishman, the pitch of Lovecraft's father: "His speech, when he deigned to use it, was that of a learned and cultivated Englishman" (MM 120). Lovecraft's manipulation of the chronology so that the attack on the Pawtuxet farm occurs one year before that on the *Gaspée,* with the same significant citizens involved in both attacks, assures a reader that the colonial animus against the British is one of the major motives in the attack on the farm that seems to be an important contributor to Curwen's wealth. These several politicians who have a stake in the black market from which much of Rhode Island's wealth flows have no compunction in attacking their commercial rival for both political and commercial reasons.

Given Lovecraft's explicit though doubtless tongue-in-cheek allegiances to King George and the colonial world, this description of the antagonist as an Anglican Tory is quite interesting; though born in Salem he returned to it "with the speech, dress, and manners of a native Englishman" (MM 149). These insistent passages remind us of that late dream Lovecraft had, later transcribed as the fragment "The Evil Clergyman," in which a disquieting, smooth clergyman, an obvious Episcopalian, is revealed to be an image of the self, as though stepping out of a mirror or a picture. The remarkable part of this description, as far as Lovecraft is concerned, is the apparently Nietzschean revaluation of all values. Something has happened to Lovecraft's idealization of his Anglican father and to his idealization of himself as an English gentleman; in Curwen and the evil clergyman the English gentleman is demonized, as if that English heritage, as the Revolutionary forces had insisted, were not to be accepted. The image in the mirror or the picture, the self as the father, the much more intelligent or authoritative father, must be rejected if at all possible; but most often it is not.

Who is the world-historical figure of this plot, which is to ask who actually solves the problem that Joseph Curwen's existence presents Providence? Lovecraft describes him thus in a letter to Frank Belknap Long shortly before he wrote the novella: "That damn'd prophane ruffian Capt. Abraham Whipple, ringleader in the lawless burning of His Majesty's arm'd schooner Gaspee" (SL 2.88). Lovecraft is related to Whipple of course, as he admits immediately before this comic tirade, but its comedy neither disguises the animus of the outburst nor, on the other hand, the relish that Lovecraft takes in the reprobate privateer, a relish that he extends in several stories to the long history of the New England smuggler. In the novella the captain leads the attack upon the Pawtuxet farm, suffers in the attack, and in later years confesses that the attack might have been a failure. "Pox on that ——— —, but he had no business to laugh while he screamed. 'Twas as though the damn'd ——— had some'at up his sleeve. For half a crown I'd burn his ——— — house" (MM 148). A possible translation, bringing this down to our present day, might run, "Damn the British monarchy! It goes on serenely as though the American experiment meant nothing to its perpetual reconstruction of itself—and how we still do seem to hanker for it. Can we never end this dependence on the father?"

This dependence is symbolized in the novella by the descent into the earth, for historical research and speculation are performed in the novella in various ways; but however they are performed we must at last have the archetypal scene of descent. Charles Dexter Ward is obsessed by historical investigations that he pursues through documents, and Joseph Curwen by the more direct research of interrogating the dead he has raised to life—many historians would like very much to undertake such interrogations, though most would probably pause before using the whip or the rack. To discover the facts of the matter, the citizens under Captain Whipple's command, who in their proto-Revolutionary fervor have no interest in historical investigations, descend into Curwen's basements and 150 years later Dr. Willett repeats the descent, in which he learns of the spell of the ascending node and the spell of the descending node that are in a palindromic relation to each other. The chiasmic structure of the narrative, beginning and ending in Dr. Waite's asylum, comments on this history that only exists through repeating itself. The structure suggests that in order to survive we must always be in descent. On the other hand, the novella does not insist upon a cyclic pattern of history; the first descent would never have occurred if it were not for the accident of Ezra Weeden's erotic passion, and the second would never have occurred if it were not for Dr. Willet's affection for Charles Ward, his spiritual son.

More broadly we need to consider the function of magic in this history. Since the historical novel has history as its subject in all its complex processes, expectations, and longueurs, recorded by documents that demand an interpretative and skeptical eye attempting as far as possible to understand its own prejudices and desires, history is a dense, conflated, and fissured object. At the end of constructing a history that is more than a mere chronology, the historian remains baffled by a mass of materials as mysterious as ever. Our traditional appeals to fate and chance and our appeals to various sociological theories go only so far to lighten this mystery. As far as Goethe was concerned, the historical experience was one more stratum of our lives in which the daemonic was at work; and he also knew that when we call up spirits, as happens in his ballad "Der Zauberlehrling," things may go drastically wrong: "Die ich rief, die Geister, / Werd' ich nun nicht los" [The spirits I have summoned / I never shall escape] (1.279). So perhaps magic, in the hands of a man as reckless as Joseph Curwen or Jonathan Strange, becomes a new way of understanding the process; and in a metahistorical fashion Curwen, a man caught up in an historical process that is moving toward the Revolution, is himself an historian determined to torture the truth from the primary sources resurrected from their essential salts. But we must not take Curwen at his own estimation, for his language translated to the 1920s does make him sound rather ridiculous, and essential salts are no help; in our encounters with the past, the past always speaks in its own language.

Does he realize that we use the word "salt" in a great variety of ways? Salt is itself an element in the medieval tradition. Salt preserves foods, and its taste is a symbol of a pungent wit. We are worth our salt if we are the salt of the earth, and we hope that we shall never lose our savor; salt is primal. An old, experienced sailor is an old salt, so Curwen makes use of those salts to bring him knowledge from afar. Consider "the seasoned salts" who managed the sloops of the Browns, Crawfords, and Tillinghasts (MM 122); this is a passage that accuses every merchant of Providence who dealt in essential salts. But as far as any news is concerned, we should take it with a grain of salt. If it proves useful we should salt it away; but we may salt a mine to inflate its worth. This language gives us all sorts of problems.

Some readers might question my decision to regard "The Shadow over Innsmouth" as an historical novel, since the narrative proper only deals with the history of Innsmouth in a retrospective fashion, mainly through the account of Zadok Allen. But the events of the visit that this rather colorless narrator makes to Innsmouth, a visit that lasts barely a day and a night, make no sense unless we see them as the result of an historical process.

These events begin and end in Captain Obed Marsh, although the narrative nods to a vague past in which the Old Ones, "whoever they was" (DH 310), had laid down their signs to contain the creatures in the ocean (DH 333). This part of the account assumes a vague plasticity of times past in which "a man ud often be a-talkin' to his own five-times-great-grandfather" (*DH* 332), just as the transformed narrator will find himself doing at the conclusion of the story.

Nevertheless, the history proper begins with Captain Marsh, though the time is still rather vague; it is after the War of 1812, in "them days" (*DH* 329) when Obed makes contact with the Kanakas and strikes his Faustian bargain, but no firm date is given until 1838 when the nearby islanders exterminate their diabolic neighbors at the same time that "the fishin' was peterin' aout an' the mills wa'n't doin' none too well" (*DH* 333); but he would not have made the bargain he does in the far East if the situation at home immediately after the War of 1812 had not become so dire: "Trade fallin' off, mills losin' business—even the new ones—an' the best of our menfolks kilt a-privateerin' in the War of 1812 or lost with the Elizy brig" (*DH* 329). These events, especially the slow deterioration of several mills as did happen in the fluctuations of the dollar that followed the war, are representative of the broad history of New England; several panics did occur thereafter, especially that from 1837 to 1842, dates significant for the history of Innsmouth, but most of the time "growth of demand kept pace with growth of capacity, so that profit depressions were of short duration" (McGouldrick 210); nothing as disastrous befell the region as happened to the mills in New England in the 1920s (Beard and Beard 174–75, 203). What happens in Innsmouth is much more exemplary of the events that came to pass in Lovecraft's own day than of the events in the first half of the nineteenth century.

Shortly after 1838 the tempo of the action accelerates in Innsmouth when the Masonic hall agrees to its takeover by the Esoteric Order of Dagon over the protests of Matt Eliot, a persistent opponent of Captain Marsh; and not long thereafter Eliot vanishes (*DH* 336). This event mirrors a broad historical process, for in 1826 a former Mason, William Morgan, who had threatened to reveal the mysteries of the fraternal order, disappeared in Western New York, sparking for ten years a series of antimasonic actions, both cultural and political, that threatened not only the Lodge but the various political understandings of the day and the integrity of the two-party system (cf. Goodman 3–19). One irony of the story is that the Esoteric Order of Dagon does seem to ape the regalia of the Masons, the robes and outré headpieces, and the rising orders of commitment and secrecy, into which Zadok Allen is drawn (*DH* 337), though he insists that he would never have taken the third oath of the third degree, "I'd a died ruthr'n take that—" (*DH* 338).

This paranoia was all the more remarkable given the blandness of the Masonic movement in America, which had begun to lose the pointedly Enlightenment flavor of Europe during the eighteenth century. The Lodge offered a refuge for middle-class and upper-middle-class men to gather and make the business and cultural connections necessary in a society that was now changing; but more than a refuge, it offered a certification of acceptance, in part based on the dues that the Lodge demanded. The Lodge was therefore an urban phenomenon, which paid allegiance only to a nonsectarian God; though it insisted that it was a Christian society, with no atheists allowed within its walls, that was as far as it defined its religious commitments. Episcopalians and Unitarians, Congregationalists and Baptists, priests and parsons were all accepted as members. Most of them were members of the liberal protestant churches, though several Calvinist clergy also joined (Goodman 11–13, 34–53). The antimasonic movement was led by men suspicious of those qualities; to them the Masons seemed secretive, atheistic, hierarchical and thereby anti-democratic, anti-American in fact. The regalia of the order resembled a bit too much that of their archenemies, the Roman Catholics. It is not surprising that a rural protest, centered round a conservative understanding of Christianity and focused by the concerns of the proletariat, led to a rebellion against the Lodge and its members. These people had no sympathy with the England from which they had torn away, emotions enflamed by the War of 1812, so it was time to rebel against a Lodge that seemed to be allied with cosmopolitan feelings. Sarastro's hymn to Isis and Osiris did not appeal to antimasonic feelings.

What did the order some seventy or more years later have to say for itself? It had very little to say about the antimasonic people, nothing more than the ambiguous claim that "to them its present popularity is due, the cheapening of its Degrees, the invasion of its Lodges, that are no longer Sanctuaries, by the multitude; its pomp and pageantry and overdone display" (Supreme Council 814). It had much to say about its highly syncretistic philosophy, appealing insistently and prolixly to Pythagorean, Kabbalistic, Gnostic, Hermetic, and Alchemical texts, a rich ragout in which the symbolic import of the imagery is foregrounded. It insisted upon a belief in one God, but did not insist upon the nature of that God, though its frequent use of trinitarian language belied its suggestion that there could be Jewish or Mohammedan lodges (524, 548–68). Perhaps because of this syncretistic, Protestant nature the order felt at some enmity with the Roman Catholic church (3, 27, 74). Most striking in the language of the order is its persistent optimism about the nature of human life, asserting "there is no Savage, Re-vengeful, and Evil God: but there is an Infinite God [. . .], with perfect power, wisdom, justice, holiness, and love" (716). In fact the order very little imagined the depravity of the human being; it was too much absorbed in the nineteenth-century myth of human progress. Thus, though the order did have something to say of Dagon, in connection with its treatment of the great dragons, the passage occupies a half page in a volume of more than 800 pages. "Ophioneus," who warred against Kronos, was cast into the sea, where "he is installed as the Sea-God Oannes or Dagon, the Leviathan of the watery half of creation, the dragon who vomited a flood of water after the persecuted woman of the Apocalypse" (498). The passage is so slight it is hardly to our purpose.

What might Lovecraft have made of all this? His beloved grandfather, Whipple Van Buren Phillips, who educated him in his immense library, was a Freemason (S. T. Joshi, "Introduction and Notes" 412n22), but in the *Selected Letters* Lovecraft never mentions the order. Given its sturdy optimism we are hardly surprised. The Masons never personalize evil, but Lovecraft does. His Dagon is great threat in the early stories and then assumes a new form in the Esoteric Order of Dagon that overthrows the Masons in Innsmouth; and this new Lodge, which offers a refuge for the creatures of the sea when they wish to come on land, is so potently anti-American that the narrator urges the reader to agree to the secret Federal raids and the es-tablishment of the concentration camps (*DH* 303–4).

When we consider the relation of Masonry to the story, which is close but in no way precise, we realize that it does no good to find an actual series of mill closures and depletions in the fishery to match the events in "The Shadow over Innsmouth" that occur over an imaginary time bracketed by actual events (e. g., the War of 1812 and the Civil War), just as Innsmouth is an imaginary space inserted into the Massachusetts coastline north of Bos-ton. Yes, a depression did occur after the war of 1812, but during the nine-teenth century New England suffered several painful bubbles and busts in the mill industries that provide the background to Innsmouth's agony. These financial cycles represent abstract powers against which the community is helpless, though in fact various labor groups did strive against them with an increasing effect that Lovecraft chooses to ignore; more to the point, as Obed argued, none of the religions provided any defense against these capi-talist structures. His attempt to provide a religion with real power and a physical immortality is therefore a peculiar blasphemy. It is difficult to say whether his creation of the Esoteric Order of Dagon stems from an authentic religious impulse or a fraud. The myth of Mother Hydra and Father Dagon, the narration suggests, is based upon the truth of evolution, of human evolution as well as the evolution of all life from the sea (*DH* 337); and this story also refers a part of its truth to the witnesses of those earlier stories, "Dagon" and "The Temple." The irony of Obed's new religion, however, is that it fails as much as normative religion has, for after the Civil War the mills and shops were shut down, the shipping stopped, the harbor choked up, and the railroad failed (*DH* 338). Only the fish abounded, but they now belonged to the creatures in the abyss beyond the reef. This failure, however, occurs in the midst of the Gilded Age when the fortunes of entrepreneurs in the North escalated, upon which the decadence of Innsmouth casts a dark shadow. All that remains is a hope for eternal life in the abyss.

We need to return to the events of 1846, when the creatures effectively took control of Innsmouth in a coup d'état. That, however, is the secret history. The public history is that recounted by the ticket agent in Newburyport, who speaks of a putative epidemic, "probably some foreign kind of disease from China" (*DH* 307). This is the same kind of language that Miss Tilton uses to describe the Esoteric Order of Dagon as "a debased, quasi-pagan thing imported from the East" (312). And this is the same language that a delegate to the 1831 Massachusetts Antimasonic convention used to describe their enemies as the "willing vassals of this worse than Asiatic dominion of masonry" (Goodman 20). Several other of Lovecraft's stories make a conventional nod to the yellow peril, but here that paranoia is contextualized within Captain Marsh's expeditions to the South Seas and within another aspect of the Antimasonic paranoia.

An historical novel does not change history. Though these several narratives inject magic into the historical process, the Peninsular War, the Battle of Waterloo, and the post-Napoleonic period proceed much as they did; and the politics and personalities of Providence in the pre-Revolutionary period and the fate of New England as the prosperity of the mills waxed and waned proceed as they did. History is illuminated but it does not change. This general principle, however, only holds for the recent, well-documented past, but does not hold for the distant past when the scale of the narration is vastly different, whether that lies in the past when the Raven King ruled in the north of Britain or when the Great Race created a utopian world across the surface of the prehistoric earth; but the history unrolled in "The Shadow out of Time" and *At the Mountains of Madness* so clearly concerns the politics of the 1930s that these works pass from historical fiction into allegory and thus reveal that a truly historical fiction, based firmly upon normative and world-historical characters, whether weird or not, is always speculative at the same time that it is respectful of the world as it is. Authors like Lovecraft and Clarke are too fond of history to fiddle with it.

"Hey, Yew, Why Don't Ye Say Somethin'?" Lovecraft's Dramatic Monologues

> Now, don't sir! Don't expose me! Just this once!
> This was the first and only time, I'll swear—
> Look at me,—see, I kneel,—the only time,
> I swear, I ever cheated,—yes, by the soul
> Of Her who hears—(your sainted mother, sir!)
> All, except this last accident, was truth—
> (Browning, Mr. Sludge, "The Medium" ll. 1–6)

The dramatic monologue is a shifty genre. Browning needs to assure the reader through the quotations marks that surround "The Medium" that Sludge is no such thing, though the man's impassioned speech insists that there is something of truth in what he has to say; and it may be more important for criticism to sift this elusive truth than to pin the man down to what is obviously false in him. I do not mean to do that here, but we should keep these difficulties in mind when we consider Lovecraft's use of the genre. For though Lovecraft deprecated his ability to create character (cf. *SL* 4.114 and 5.310), several of his stories are first-person narratives or, more remarkably, dramatic monologues, a form peculiarly apt for the display of character. Though Lovecraft did not appreciate the poetry of Browning or Tennyson (cf. *SL* 2.276, 3.104, or 4.109), the masters of the dramatic monologue in the nineteenth century, he did exploit the form for a number of literary effects. Sometimes he used it in order to avoid the necessity of writing dialogue, for which he felt he had no ear (*SL* 4.72); but he also used it to relate a narrative or, much more typically, to recall a narrative (Faas 157), to concentrate material, or to give a character the opportunity for argument, meditation, and confession. In cases where the materials are in excess of these purposes Lovecraft is attempting something more than character, what he often called atmosphere. To understand something of what he meant by atmosphere Linda K. Hughes's distinction between personality and consciousness is useful: personality is the outward orientation of the self toward the world and others; consciousness is the inward orientation of the self toward a subjective, amorphous experience in which sensations, volitions, desires, and thoughts are liable to be indistinguishable (14–15). Personality is public, consciousness private. In Lovecraft consciousness colors the narrative so thoroughly that it is liable to seem a collective, public matter. From this point of view Lovecraft's weakness becomes a strength, for the dramatic monologue is not only economical and a mask for his deficiencies; it serves an expressive purpose that controls the shape and rhythm of the story.

In its pure form the dramatic monologue presents the uninterrupted words of a single speaker, something that Lovecraft does very seldom. I propose, however, to include moments when he allows a single speaker to proceed at a much greater length than is realistic, at the same time that he suppresses the responses of an auditor, as well as to include those moments when he presents the words of a single speaker at great length in indirect discourse while again suppressing the words of an auditor; most dramatic monologues are presented *verba ipsa*. In both cases Lovecraft is obviously striving for a concentration unusual in dialogue.

Given such considerations, let us consider the normative form of the dramatic monologue. It does not present itself as a first-person narrative that has been composed but as an oral record, a conversation between two people with one of them suppressed; thus it maintains a tension between the appearance of spontaneity and the fact of a great selectivity and artifice, its tone constrained by the invisible, inaudible auditor and by the event that precipitates the confrontation and self-revelation that constitute the heart of the work. The suppression of the auditor leaves a gap in the story that is more or less significant and that the reader bridges in some cases unconsciously as though the gap were not noticed, in other cases very consciously. Elisabeth Howe summarizes current thinking about the form in this way: it is objective, presenting a specific voice rather than a generalized lyric voice, though in Lovecraft's case that specific voice sometimes assumes the quality of a chorus or of a collective voice; it creates a distance between the author and the speaker as well as between the speaker and the reader, to which we must add that given an auditor a distance usually exists along the several axes that create a multiple voice within the voice of the speaker and thus an ironic tension; the narrative element often involves internal as well as external conflict; finally, in a very crucial way, especially in Browning's poems, the form often raises questions about personality, since language seems insufficient to render personality and since the character's point of view and self-interest often renders the personality indeterminate, something that the form is in search of (2–16).[1] We know on several counts that Mr. Sludge is a liar but cannot but search for some truth in his passionate farrago to the man who has just caught him out.

One of Lovecraft's earliest stories, "The Tomb," might be considered a dramatic monologue, spoken as it is by a man in a madhouse attempting to justify himself. "The Statement of Randolph Carter" has something of the same nature, as Carter tries to convince the police that he had nothing to do with a friend's disappearance. "The Rats in the Walls" is also a story spoken by a madman; this story, however, does not reveal the situation of the speaker until its remarkable last page, which reveals his words as they regress through the languages of his forebears—and ours. Here the reader receives a true sense of crisis, repugnant but with the distance rendered perilously narrow. But in these stories the auditor is nothing but a disembodied ear, not a surprise given their debt to Poe's "The Tell-Tale Heart." "Cool Air," opens, "You ask me to explain why I am afraid of a draught of cool air" (*DH* 199)—rather similar to the opening of "Pickman's Model" in the same year—but the reader never learns the identity of that "you" nor the place where the conversation takes place. The story is more important than the speaker, and no moral distance exists between the speaker and the reader. The same effect occurs in Lovecraft's ghostwritten stories, "The Curse of Yig" and "Medusa's Coil." Most of the first story is rendered in indirect discourse, without the doctor or the narrator to whom he tells the story being greatly characterized; and most of the second story, though delivered in a long direct monologue by the father, exists for the sake of the story rather than for the sake of the father, who is overwhelmed by the story he tells. In both cases Robert Browning's late poems come to mind, in which both the speaker and the auditor are overwhelmed by the complexities of the materials and the drama of confrontation is absent. None of these stories is a dramatic monologue.

Other stories use the dramatic monologue in a minor fashion. In "The Other Gods" the final words of Barzai exist for the sake of a vision that Atal cannot see, an effect rather like what happens at the conclusion of "The Statement of Randolph Carter"; no conversation occurs. The short jeu

---

1. For this last point Howe refers to the work of E. Warrick Slinn, *Browning and the Fictions of Identity*; Lee Erikson, *Robert Browning: His Poetry and His Audiences*; and Clyde de L. Ryals, "Browning's Irony" in *The Victorian Experience: The Poets*, ed. Richard A. Levine.

d'esprit "In the Vault" concludes with Dr. Davis's attack on Birch; as the narrator makes a breach in "all the rules of his calling" (*DH* 10), his three paragraphs give a nice snap of fury and disgust to the tale. "He" is composed in part of the strange man's monologue, but the effect is diluted by the conversation that follows. This survey leaves eleven stories, some of Lovecraft's most famous and typical, from "The Picture in the House" in 1920 to "The Haunter in the Dark" in 1935, in which he employed the dramatic monologue, sometimes by itself, sometimes subtly mixed with indirect discourse and dialogue.

It is the dramatic monologue of the old man in "The Picture in the House" that makes that story remarkable, with its wheedling and confidential tone, as though the old man were attempting to assuage the loneliness of his fate: "New faces is scurce araount here, an' I han't got much ta cheer me up these days" (*DH* 121). His monologue is a history lesson, but no less significant is his language, Lovecraft's first extended attempt at rendering the dialect that he thought had been "formerly prevalent throughout the United States" but was now to be found only in "backwoods Northern New England" (*SL* 3.421); it is a relic of a homogenous nation. From the point of view of history, of course, the old man's monologue is not so much a lesson as a document, both of what happened and of what tongue expressed and experienced it. In addition the monologue contains an exposure as well as an exposition; the old man is confessing something shameful that the narrator has already confessed, his "susceptibility to so slight a thing, but the drawing nevertheless disturbed [him]" (*DH* 119). And this shame extends to the reader.

The old man's monologue bulks all the larger in the story because it occupies ten of the story's twenty-three paragraphs. After alluding to the plight of the narrator in the first paragraph he turns to himself, just waking up: "I need a paowerful sight o' naps naowdays" (*DH* 120). Very seldom does he thereafter refer to the young man, so self-absorbed he is. In the second paragraph he refers to a private joke, one that only in retrospect reveals that he has probably murdered and eaten the schoolmaster. The attention of the narrator wanders at this point so that he does not record the old man's ramblings, leaving a gap in the narrative.

Only with the young man's question about the Pigafetta volume does he record the old man's speech again. The short third, fourth, and fifth paragraphs tell how the old man obtained the book from Ebenezer Holt—a name that almost alerts the narrator to the supernatural age of the old man. More interesting is the old man's confession that he cannot read Latin; it is the pictures, not the text, that he "relished" (*DH* 121). The young man translates some of the text at the old man's request, but none for the reader's benefit. Another gap opens in the narrative, one unimportant to the old man, however, who responds in his sixth paragraph, "Queer haow picters kin set a body thinkin'" (*DH* 122). It is fantasy, not self-interest, that seems to have drawn him into the book originally, the pictures of trees "with big leaves a-floppin' over an' daown" (*DH* 122), the people who look like Native Americans rather than Africans, the creatures that look like monkeys, "or half monkeys an' half men" (*DH* 122), and the patently fabulous creature, half dragon and half alligator. Though the question remains whether his description of the book is meant to draw the narrator into the climactic revelation of the butchery plate, which the narrator has already examined before the old man appears, a continuity of imagination is established; the relish that the two men take in the pictures is revealed to be alike, both in the hybrid art of fantasy and in the possibilities of taste and new life that such an art reveals. This picture is, as the old man mutters in his short seventh paragraph, "the best un" (*DH* 122).

Twice in the next paragraph he confesses that this is a picture that will "stir ye up an' make yer blood tickle!" (*DH* 122). The repetitions of his speech become more evident as we near the climax of his monologue and of the story; senility and obsession turn his speech upon itself. This is a perversion that finds its materials everywhere, even in the Bible—a detail that confirms the narrator's meditation upon the nature of Puritanism at the beginning of the story. It is not surprising that the old man is "right sot" on the picture of butchery, a confession that startles the narrator and for a moment arrests the monologue, though now it is unstoppable as the voice sinks down and for a short time becomes inaudible, again a rambling that the narrator drops from his narrative. Both gaps represent aspects of the old man's experience that remain opaque to the reader; personality, the persona that he attempts to erect between himself and the narrator, keeps turning into consciousness.

The last paragraph is the most disjointed; five dashes indicate a sudden swerve in the old man's attention before the drop of blood that interrupts his final sentence. Killing sheep is fun—but not satisfying. A craving takes a person—don't tell anyone—don't be afraid—these thoughts are purely hypothetical, purely fictional—but meat and blood and flesh, the same flesh, might make a person live forever (*DH* 123). This final paragraph circles from fantasy and fiction to the innermost desire of flesh to preserve itself, a desire that the rhetoric of the telling reveals as a solipsism when the narrator repeats the old man's last words, with the old man's emphasis, *"more the same"* (DH 123). The use of the dramatic monologue makes clear that it is not what the old man does that renders him horrible; murderers and cannibals abound. The horror is his existential plight, what he is and what he merely is, a lonely gray old man trapped in his relish to continue as this old gray lonely man, fixated upon a few inept pictures; what had begun as an adventure of the imagination stagnates in these pictures and a shambles.

"The Call of Cthulhu," in 1926, has no dramatic monologue as such, but it does have a fascinating passage divided into two sections in which the account of the Cthulhu worshippers in the Louisiana bayous is rendered in indirect discourse that allows a certain breadth in diction. The first is a summary in two paragraphs of the cross-examination to which the police submit "men of a very low, mixed-blooded, and mentally aberrant type" (DH 139). The first paragraph concerns their worship of the Great Old Ones and of Cthulhu, in a language that resembles the ornate syntax of the narrative. The second paragraph uses short sentences: "Meanwhile no more must be told. There was a secret which even torture could not extract. [. . .] But these were not the Great Old Ones. No man had ever seen the Old Ones" (DH 139). This passage is closer to the style of the men, though it also approaches a biblical style: "No man hath seen God at any time" (John 1:18). The second part of the cross-examination centers upon the mestizo Castro, whose account in four paragraphs is more coherent than that of the chorus. Because he is old and far-traveled he can describe the cult in global terms, first alluding to China and the Pacific, then in second paragraph attempting to account for the age and odd nature of the Old Ones; the style of both paragraphs resembles the style of the main narrative. In the third paragraph the style loosens into a paratactic vision of apocalypse:

> The time would be easy to know, for then mankind would have become as the Great Old Ones; free and wild and beyond good and evil, with laws and morals thrown aside and all men shouting and killing and revelling in joy. Then the liberated Old Ones would teach them new ways to shout and kill and revel and enjoy themselves, and all the earth would flame with a holocaust of ecstasy and freedom. (DH 141)

The two sentences act out the freedom to which the repetitions point, with an allusion unlikely in Castro's mouth to Nietzsche (though this passage is in indirect discourse), indicating the threat to conventional morality. His final paragraph returns to the style of the first two paragraphs and another mention of "the deathless Chinamen" (*DH* 141), as well as alluding to a secret that cannot be told—both Castro and the half-breeds are reticent—and concluding on the couplet of Abdul Alhazred, already important in the narrative. This passage, then, parallels the shape of the first passage, moving from a rationalized style toward one that more closely renders the heart of the cultists and their hopes. This treatment condenses the material, preserving the proportions of the three-part story; otherwise this section would have been quite long and suffered the danger of an anticlimax.

Next to "The Call of Cthulhu," "Pickman's Model," written in the same year, seems a minor work, but in its short span it works out a number of intricate procedures, not least being the fact that it contains two dramatic monologues, the one, Pickman's speech to Thurber, embedded in Thurber's to a friend called Eliot. That auditor surely represents the reader, but it is a reader already devoted to weird art. To that devotion, however, Thurber's monologue presents certain problems, for once more the shame evident in "The Picture in the House" arises.

Thurber's monologue begins haltingly, in an abrupt rejection of a question that Eliot has just asked, and the next three paragraphs also respond to Eliot before Thurber at last agrees to tell the story. These opening paragraphs also set the scene, "up the hill from Park Street" (*DH* 12), on Beacon Hill, the center of Bostonian gentility. Pickman's monologue sets the other scenes of this story: his public studio on Newbury Street, a polite commercial district with no history, and the North End epitomized by Copp's Hill where his secret studio lies in the middle of Italian slums that mask an immense history. Neither Newbury Street nor the North End is acceptable to the sense of style, civility, and public service that finds its bastion on Beacon Hill. Thurber himself belongs on Beacon Hill. He believes in style and scholarship, but his civility is not strong, as he scoffs at those "fussy old women Dr. Reid or Joe Minot or Bosworth" (*DH* 13) who cannot bear the consequences of a thoroughly logical style or genius, no matter what the subject. Four paragraphs are devoted to Thurber's theory of morbid art, a justification of Pickman's subjects and treatments, though one of these paragraphs is interrupted by a pause for a drink, the first of three drinks before he keeps the decanter to himself; Thurber no longer aligns himself with the sobriety of Beacon Hill.

Pickman's monologue, his "harangue" as Thurber calls it (*DH* 17), rages under high pressure through eight paragraphs. The first begins with an at-

tack on Newbury Street, to which the second paragraph contrasts the North
End, a place that "actually *grew*," a place where "people weren't afraid to live
and feel and die." "What do moderns know," he asks rhetorically, "of life
and the forces behind it?" Pickman is a vitalist historian; the past is alive for
him, as we can see in his diatribe on Cotton Mather, "looking sanctimoniously on, [. . .] damn him" when Pickman's four-times-great-grandmother
was hanged (15). This animus powers the third paragraph when Pickman
rails against Mather's "stupid *Magnalia* or that puerile *Wonders of the Invisible
World*" (18); Pickman has the same feelings for Mather, dead these many
years, as he has for Reid and others in the Art Society, his contemporaries.
But half this paragraph concerns what Mather did not know, the tunnels of
the North End "that kept certain people in touch with each other's houses,
and the burying ground, and the sea" (18). A communal life rooted in death
is at work beneath the separate houses. The fourth paragraph continues this
theme; in the past witches, pirates, smugglers, and privateers, people accustomed to crossing a variety of borders, lived in the North End, "people who
knew how to live, and how to enlarge the bounds of life" (18). Such promis-
cuous transgressions, symbolized by the ghoul, are the center of Pickman's
concerns, though we may wonder whether some contradiction does not exist
in the notion that besides representing trespass the ghoul, who feeds upon
death, also represents more life. No wonder these transgressions make the
"pale-pink brains" of Beacon Hill, very delicious we may be sure, shudder
(18)! Unlike Thurber, Pickman never emphasizes technique; he is totally
committed to the ideology of his scenes, to the revolt against moral convention.

The fifth paragraph turns toward the present, for if Beacon Hill refuses to
recognize the opportunities that Copp's Hill offers, the contemporary inhabitants of Copp's Hill are not able to recognize them either. "What do those
Dagoes know of their meaning?" Pickman asks, a bit of racism that the
reader recognizes as a part of Pickman's exclusivist nature (*DH* 16). The
immigrants can not see that "these ancient places are dreaming gorgeously
and overflowing with wonder and terror and escapes from the commonplace" (16); they are "kicking free of this accursed cage of monotony" (16).
In the next paragraph Pickman offers to take Thurber to his North End studio, a place that "those cursed old maids at the club," such men as Reid,
cannot bear, who believes that Pickman is "a sort of monster bound down
the toboggan of reverse evolution" (17). Reid, of course, has a reason to
think so, as the beginning of the next paragraph may suggest when Pickman

claims that no one but "three living Nordic men besides myself have ever seen" his studio (17). Leaving aside the unanswerable question who those three Nordic men might be—is Herbert West one of them, or Randolph Carter?—the reader in retrospect realizes that Pickman's claim to the purity of the Nordic race is probably false and that his need to make such a claim reveals a secret shame in the changeling. He quickly begins to describe the secret studio that he rents under the name of Peters and that, in the last paragraph of the monologue, he offers to show to Thurber. Pickman's monologue concludes on a rather jaunty note, but beneath that arrogance he offers to initiate Thurber into an experience of art that has for reasons of history and class been closed off to others.

As Thurber's monologue begins once more this invitation to go slumming opens one of the most fascinating themes of this story, its sense of place. North Station, Battery Street, Constitution Wharf, and Greenough Lane give some notion of where the studio lies in the North End, as do Charter Street and Hanover Street when they leave it; this setting, which Lovecraft has imagined thoroughly, takes on a solid life in the assured tone of Thurber, the perfect Bostonian, though when the two men leave Newbury Street for the North End he quickly becomes lost in the crosslanes of the place. As they climb Copp's Hill they also seem to be going backward in time, for Thurber believes that he sees "a peaked roof-line of the almost forgotten pre-gambrel type, though antiquarians tell us there are none left in Boston" (*DH* 18) and the paneling of the hallway to the studio reminds him of "the times of Andros and Phipps" (18), evidence of Pickman's claim that in the North End the past seems to persist.

In the first room Thurber gives Eliot his first, sketchy impressions of Pickman's private art. It does not resemble the work of Sime or of Smith, contemporary artists whom Eliot, the representative of all that is Boston, would have probably despised if he had ever heard of them, nor does it resemble the works of Angarola or Roerich, other contemporary artists to whom Lovecraft refers on occasion—and artists whom Eliot might very well have despised also. Instead, the motifs that Thurber describes, the tunnels and vaults, the creatures squatting upon the chests of sleepers, and the hanged witches, are more suggestive of such classic artists as Piranesi, Fuseli, and Rosa. Pickman's work looks backward. As Thurber describes it in more detail and as he appeals more frequently to Eliot, the drama of the monologue increases: "But don't get the idea. . . ," he begins, then asserts, "It was the *faces*, Eliot, those accursed *faces*," exclaims, "By God, man . . .!" and concludes, "Give me that decanter, Eliot!"

(*DH* 19). The turmoil of this passage works more through the syntactic imperatives than through the artistic details.

As for the paintings themselves, two are described, one called "The Lesson," of ghouls in a churchyard teaching a child how to feed, and the other, untitled, of a Puritan interior in which a child in the cradle resembles Pickman himself, a combination of historical painting and self-portrait. The real point of these two paintings, however, is that they seem to confirm the opinion of Pickman's enemy Reid that Pickman is someone living between the human and the other, but even more broadly they suggest that there is "a linkage and evolution" (*DH* 19) that connects the human and the other independently of Pickman. No matter how we interpret these paintings, however, the suspicion grows that Pickman is no pure man, Nordic or otherwise, despite his father in Salem. What of the mother, the reader may ask, remembering the genealogical horrors of the early story "Facts concerning the Late Arthur Jermyn and His Family" or the later novella "The Shadow over Innsmouth"; and what of the real father?

The next room contains the "modern studies," in which Pickman "brought the horror right into our own life" (*DH* 20). Again Thurber appeals to Eliot that he is no "mollycoddle," that he is "middle-aged and decently sophisticated," that he has met action in France (20); by this time such appeals function as attempts to reassure himself that he is the man he had always assumed himself to be, an objective person who is not moved by the matter of the artwork, only by the technique, a person who does not raise questions of morality as far as art is concerned. These paintings, "Subway Accident," a dance on Copp's Hill in the graveyard, cellar views, a cross-section of Beacon Hill (another moment suggestive of Piranesi), and the comic "Holmes, Lowell, and Longfellow Lie Buried at Mount Auburn," convince Thurber at last that Pickman is "a relentless enemy of all mankind," a person gleeful at "the torture of brain and flesh and the degradation of the mortal tenement" (21). Why, we must ask again, has Pickman chosen to show these pictures to Thurber? Is it an act of aggression against Thurber, or does he believe Thurber shares in his aggression, not a bad assumption when we remember how often Thurber curses other members of the art club, but an assumption qualified by his friendship with Eliot, unless his appeal to Eliot is an attempt to dissociate himself from the shameful connection that he as much admits. It is at this point that Thurber claims that in his technique Pickman is "a thorough, painstaking, and almost scientific realist" (21); but such realism is at odds with the intensity of hatred that the paintings also display.

The two men now go "down cellar," an idiom common to Boston (Eckhardt). In the first room there is a well, a "solid work of the seventeenth century" that suggests that their experience in this studio extends into the past (*DH* 21). They pass it to enter another room where unfinished paintings demonstrate the pains that Pickman takes, the guide-lines on the paintings showing his old-fashioned adherence to perspective, even though cubism and other modernist schools have been active for over ten years; the camera shows that he has not been affected by the anxiety that photography caused among the Impressionists, and Thurber, the "decently sophisticated" Thurber who has been to France, does not feel that anxiety either. The remarkable point about Pickman's art, then, does not seem to be its technical innovation—though Thurber insists, "It was the technique, Eliot, . . . the unnatural technique" (23)—but the fact that he applies a realism comparable to that of painters like de la Tour or Hopper to a content that is often blurred. This point seems confirmed in the painting of "a colossal and nameless blasphemy" holding something "that had been a man, gnawing at the head as a child nibbles at a stick of candy" (22). The painting, as Donald R. Burleson remarks (*Lovecraft* 92), resembles Goya's painting of Saturn devouring his children, a resemblance so strong that Pickman may well have ordered his model to take a pose that alludes to the Goya work, which is to say that the painting as far as the pose is concerned departs from reality; on the other hand, a comparison of Pickman's painting with Goya's would show how vague the Spaniard's is and point up the realism upon which Thurber insists, although the size of Pickman's creature must seem a departure from realism. These various considerations complicate attempts to regard Pickman as Lovecraft's self-portrait, suggesting that his scientific realism might be as suspect as Pickman's. Moreover, if as Thurber claims the triumph of Pickman's art is portraiture, his portraits are often composed within larger works that are constrained by a variety of genres, the historical piece, the morality, or the fantasy; and thus it is with Lovecraft, whose dramatic monologues are often encased in larger structures that refer to a variety of genres.

The problem of the colossal ghoul is broken, however, when Pickman rushes to the outer room, speaks in gibberish and fires his gun, and returns to deprecate what has just happened; the two men then leave, proceeding by Tremont up Beacon and parting at the corner of Joy; if any of the events in the studio have been dreamlike, a series of disjointed images as the narrator passes from painting to painting, Lovecraft, the other voice of the monologue, constructs the frame of the dream conscientiously.

The last four paragraphs, each shorter than the one before, provide another frame. Once more the dramatic aspect of the monologue is emphasized as Thurber rings for coffee and tells Eliot to take it black rather than with the milk and sugar most Bostonians use to doss their coffee. Thurber then exclaims that Pickman was "the foulest being that ever leaped the bounds of life into the pits of myth and madness" (*DH* 24), language reminiscent of Pickman's language. But Thurber now believes that Reid, despised when the story opened, was correct in thinking that Pickman is a person descending the evolutionary ladder. Thurber's words, "Here, let's have the chandelier going" (25), note the approach of night, of the end of the story, and of the growing fear, at the same time that the colloquialism again asserts his and Eliot's presence against the absence and inhumanity of Pickman. "Don't ask me," he says twice (25), reminiscent of the questions with which his narrative began, as the narrative arrives at its terminal climax and the revelation that the piece of paper he had inadvertently taken from the studio was a photograph of the model for the imitation of Goya. More frightful than the ghoul, however, has been the arrogance of Pickman and Thurber, the assumption that art is indifferent to morality, which the conclusion of the story shatters.

To which painters, then, does Pickman belong? Rosa and Piranesi seem closest to his aesthetic, a meticulous rendering of a daemonic subculture, as in Rosa's painting of the Witches' Gathering, located within a cavernous space that dwarfs humanity. This affinity is interesting, since Richard Davenport-Hines argues that the Gothic originates in Rosa's images (17–23). We can never escape the suspicion that Pickman is a fake, someone who pretends to paint from his imagination that which he relies upon a photograph to render. He has surrendered to that realism that drove Western artists to Impressionism. These comparisons, however, are offered only in order to indicate how much of a *sui generis* artist Lovecraft actually considers Pickman to be, a complex creator whom Thurber, for all his admiration, cannot understand.

The Dream-Quest of Unknown Kadath, written between 1926 and 1927, has no dramatic monologue except at its conclusion—a remarkable moment, since Nyarlathotep's address to Randolph Carter represents one of the few times when one of Lovecraft's alien entities condescends to human speech, the other moment occurring in "The Whisperer in Darkness." But why should such a being condescend at all? The *Dream-Quest* is remarkable in many ways, but this confrontation is not the least. Nyarlathotep, "whose proud carriage and swart features had in them the fascination of a dark god or fallen archangel" (MM 398), is a mesmeric personality who sends the somnambulist Carter upon an extraordinary flight.

The address to Carter is in seventeen paragraphs. The first three consider Carter's quest and the problem that Nyarlathotep suggests that Carter represents. It is a quest that has disturbed the Great Ones and the Other Gods; it causes an imbalance in the material constitution of the universe, at the least an imbalance in the valueless world, forcing it to the distress of the Other Gods to assume value. Others have tried to find Kadath, but only Carter has tried to find the city beyond it, his city he says, as though it were his natural right; and it is this presumption of ownership that has caused the imbalance and seduced the gods of earth to possess the city and dispossess him, so that he wakes up every time he almost walks into the city; his ambivalence toward his city is patent. These three paragraphs, with their blend of scorn and respect on Nyarlathotep's part, outline the ambivalence that other parts of the novella present and personalize Carter's predicament.

The next three paragraphs develop this theme of the gods' desire for his city. Especially interesting, after several sentences of ornate description, is the suggestion that the departure of the gods of earth from Kadath has led the Other Gods to take possession of that city and thus caused a breach of the outside, that part of the universe removed from human concerns, into the far edge of the universe we know. Paradoxically, Carter's creation of his personal values has caused the universe of indifferent values to come nearer.

The next five paragraphs are the heart of the monologue, as Nyarlathotep both orders Carter to find his city—his original purpose—and describes the city and its sources in Carter's memory of the great cities and landscapes of New England. At this point the rhetorical aspect of the monologue increases:

> Not hard to find is that roseal fever of the gods, that fanfare of supernal trumpets and clash of cymbals, that mystery whose place and meaning have haunted you through the halls of waking and the gulfs of dreaming, and tormented you with hints of vanished memory and the pain of lost things awesome and momentous. Not hard to find is that symbol and relic of your days of wonder, for truly, it is but the stable and eternal gem wherein all that wonder sparkles crystallised to light your evening path. (MM 400)

The intricate parallelisms and repetitions of this passage, the awkward "cymbals" and "symbol," are the epitome of such tendencies within the style of the entire *Dream-Quest*; fond of this rhetoric in his early work, Lovecraft al-

lows it to become almost the center of attention at this point, more so perhaps than the city itself and the catalogue of its sources by which Nyarlathotep overwhelms Carter and the reader. The allusions to Antares and
Tremont Street, juxtaposing the indifferent stars that must be avoided and
the intimate details that Carter must embrace, conclude this section.

The next four paragraphs descend from this flourish to the directions that
Carter must follow; the shantak returns to the grotesque materials of the
Dream-Quest. The last two paragraphs, however, the peroration, return to
the marvels of the city, set within the cosmic perspective of Vega, and Nyarlathotep's revelation that he is the Crawling Chaos that Lovecraft has already invoked so fearfully in other works.

How dramatic is this monologue? If we are to agree with Gestalt psychology, every character in a dream represents some voice of the self, so in the
Dream-Quest nothing happens, or so much happens, as one part of the self
speaks to the other, the superior self to the inferior self that slowly realizes its
own power in the silent monologue. In one sense, the monologue for a short
time forestalls reaction on the part of Carter, who obeys only to discover that
Nyarlathotep has attempted to trick him, albeit in vain, since on the last
page of the *Dream-Quest* he does enter his city and wake up triumphant, safe
in Boston; he is in command of his own dream. But if Carter does not inter-
rupt Nyarlathotep—and that acquiescent silence may be the weakest aspect
of these paragraphs—his voice does accompany the god's, since this work is
the record of Carter's dream, a dream within which Nyarlathotep exists.
And of course Lovecraft's voice accompanies their voices also, since Nyarlathotep alludes to Lovecraft's stories in his oration. Shaped by Carter's
memories and affections, Nyarlathotep's words devoted to New England had
to be self-defeating insofar as the section makes Carter aware of his own
creative power. Whose is this section, then? Does it not belong more to
Carter than to Nyarlathotep? And is this figure then indeed Nyarlathotep, or
is this figure, among his thousand forms, one of the least? This manifestation, immediate as it seems, may be one of the most mediated of the Nyar-
lathoteps in Lovecraft's works. It is this aspect that makes this dramatic
monologue one of the least dramatic, because the personality of the figure
dissolves into a variety of mediations that leave it impotent. The personality
of Nyarlathotep dissolves into the consciousness of Carter.

Written shortly after the *Dream-Quest*, *The Case of Charles Dexter Ward*
does not employ the dramatic monologue extensively. Something resembling
the form occurs when Dr. Willett visits Ward, or rather Joseph Curwen, and

hears him speak in a style that recalls "the spirit and occasionally the language [. . .] of the past" (MM 186). His vocabulary is indeed of the past. "I am grown phthisical" (186) he complains, but his language soon becomes more contemporary though still simple: "Any man might be frighted of what I have found, but I am not to be put off for long. I was a dunce to have that guard and stick at home" (187). This is a language that demonstrates at least an infection from the past, as well as a rooted paranoia; yet it also renders an affection for that past. Dr. Willett asks another question, in a sharply condensed indirect discourse, with Ward's answer also condensed, alluding to "the fat sheriff's wig," the Histrionick Academy in King Street, Steele's *Conscious Lovers*, "the Baptist-ridden legislature," and other details that place a reader very close to Curwen's actual voice, as even the spelling suggests (188). The same treatment reappears in another confrontation when Ward answers Willett's indirect discourse directly: "Damn 'em, they *do* eat, but they *don't need to!* That's the rare part! A month, you say, without food? Lud, Sir, you be modest! D'ye know, that was the joke on poor old Whipple with his virtuous bluster!" (121). Short as the passage is, it is remarkable for its swift shifts: exclamations, emphases, questions, anachronisms, irony. Curwen appears in all his triumph as well as in his foolhardy energy; the indirect discourse of Willett makes him pale beside Curwen.

"The Colour out of Space" in 1927 has only one passage that might be considered a dramatic monologue, though rather short, the moment when Nahum speaks before his collapse, using a dialect not at all as extreme as we find in "The Picture in the House" or "The Shadow over Innsmouth," though the syntax is disrupted by his experience: "suckin' the life out of everything . . . in that stone . . . it must a' come in that stone . . . pizened the whole place . . ." (*DH* 71). The short phrases mimic Nahum's fragmentary experience of the Colour, as well as registering its oxymoronic quality: "it burns . . . cold an' wet, but it burns" (71). Just enough of Nahum exists to witness his collapse, but on the whole this passage is not personal; it expresses what anyone would suffer exposed to the Colour. On the other hand, the entire story is being narrated by Ammi, in indirect discourse, to the actual narrator who at the end of the story feels strongly implicated in it. Only at the end of the story, however, do we receive any sense of Ammi's life, so that the story does not work as a dramatic monologue but as a meditation.

"The Dunwich Horror," written the next year, is composed of a series of passages that may be considered dramatic monologues, in an alternation with dialogue that creates a story with its own peculiar narrative rhythm. It is this rhythm that redeems the story from the disfavor into which it has fallen among recent commentators. In the first chapter we have a paragraph of Reverend Hoadley's sermon on "Matters of too common Knowledge to be deny'd," sounds that have been heard "by above a Score of credible Witnesses" including himself (*DH* 158). Despite the written form of this sermon, as a reader can see in the free use of capital letters, the sermon obviously relies upon the assent of the congregation for its power and thus displays a rhetoric that is often employed in the story, a variety of utterances from the individual to the choral; for this story as much as any other of Lovecraft's relies upon the community for its effect. The second chapter contains Wizard Whateley's comment upon Wilbur's paternity and the prophecy fulfilled at the conclusion: "*Some day yew folks'll hear a child o' Lavinny's a-callin' its father's name on the top o' Sentinel Hill!*" This short paragraph establishes the indifference—"I dun't keer what folks think" (160)—and aggression that the Whateley men feel toward the community, an indifference that is one cause of the Dunwich Horror; the Whateleys do not simply give birth to the Horror, they nourish it and prepare for its entrance upon the world stage.

The third, fourth, and fifth chapters of the story exemplify one pattern, a short dramatic monologue by either Wizard Whateley or Wilbur followed by a very short commentary by another person—a peddler talking to the community in one case, given as indirect discourse, Lavinia's anxiety about Wilbur, and Armitage's anxiety about Wilbur. Wizard Whateley's first monologue is a recurring comment about his library: "'I made some use of 'em,' he would say as he tried to mend a torn black-letter page with paste prepared on the rusty kitchen stove, 'but the boy's fitten to make better use of 'em'" (*DH* 161). One of the interesting points of this short passage is his abnegation in the face of his growing son; the sense that Wilbur shall be greater than he prepares for the pathos of first his death and then his grandson's; thus horrifying as Wizard Whateley is, he is not an Oedipal father. His second monologue runs through his death, a paragraph about the whippoorwills spoken to the loungers at the country store, "Yew'll know, boys, arter I'm gone, whether they git me or not" (166), and then two paragraphs of anxious orders to Wilbur about how to take care of his horrific brother, because Whateley does fear for the success of his project after he dies. The fifth chapter contains Wilbur's futile attempt to obtain the *Necronomicon* from the Miskatonic library. First he confronts Armitage in as bumptious and aggressive a manner as his grandfather had displayed, "I calc'late I've got to take that book home. They's things in it I've got to try under sarten conditions that I can't git here, an' it 'ud be a mortal sin to let a red-tape rule hold me up," only to snarl as he leaves, "Maybe Harvard wun't be so fussy as yew be" (171). The reader might not feel so sympathetic with the callow Wilbur if these lines did not reveal his naïveté. The climax of the first section of the story, the death of Wilbur in the library, has neither dialogue nor monologue; its effect is purely visual.

The seventh chapter contains the most extensive use of dramatic monologues in the story, monologues that belong to various people as the Horror wreaks havoc upon Dunwich. The first speaker is Luther Brown, telling Mrs. Corey about the track of the Horror: "It smells like thunder, an' all the bushes an' little trees is pushed back from the run like they'd a haouse been moved along of it" (*DH* 177). Both his dialect and his grammar are more extreme than the Whateleys'. Mrs. Corey telephones Sally Sawyer, the second speaker of this chapter, though much of her five paragraphs is a second-hand report from her son Chauncey, "just come back a-postin', an' couldn't half talk fer bein' scairt!" He says that cows in the fields have been sucked dry of their blood, with marks resembling those the Whateleys' cows suffered through the years. At this point Sally Sawyer sagely claims that the Whateleys "must a raised suthin'" as inhuman as Wilbur She adds that in the morning Chauncey went to the Whateleys' house where "he see enough, I tell ye, Mis' Corey!" (178). In the last paragraph Sally warns Mrs. Corey that whatever is in motion must have arrived now at Cold Spring Glen: "The whippoorwills an' fireflies there never did act like they was creaters o' Gawd, an' they's them as says ye kin hear strange things a-rushin' an' a-talkin' in the air daown that ef ye stand in the right place" (179). The mixture of hearsay, superstition, and shrewdness in Sally's monologue, along with her pride and fear for her son, makes this passage very effective. It is followed by an indirect discourse that describes the experience of the Fryes, who agree that they heard "a sort of muffled swishing or lapping sound" (179), a passage closer to their language than to the sedate language of the narrator. When the community gathers at the Fryes' that morning and finds the tracks, Zebulon Whateley "made darkly wild suggestions about rites that ought to be practiced on the hill-tops," though the reader can be sure that this member of a branch of the family "that hovered about half way between soundness and decadence" (180) did not use that vocabulary or that syntax. This chapter concludes the next night with a plea for help on the phone as this choral round of the natives of Dunwich closes; its economy rests upon skillful variations of the dramatic monologue, as the reader is brought very close to their experience and then distanced from it. Lovecraft prevents the reader from feeling that any expectation of dialogue propriety will be met. In contrast the short eighth chapter has neither dialogue nor monologue, as Dr. Armitage suffers his fever; though Lovecraft seems to present a variety of voices in Dunwich, this community does not rank high in his global concerns.

Chapter nine returns to the choral experience of Dunwich, now much of it anonymous as the people hunt for the Horror. One man is shocked that the Horror walks by day. Another man repeats what Zebulon Whateley had heard on the phone from Mrs. Corey, who again reports what her hired boy Luther had seen; these two paragraphs concern happenings at fourth hand. But before he can finish his story the first speaker returns to Sally and her son Cauncey, but her story is cut off as the house collapses and the phone goes dead. This speaker concludes that they have all gathered to see what can be done, "Not but what I think," he adds, "it's the Lord's jedgment fer our iniquities, that no mortal kin ever set aside" (DH 191). After Armitage meets this touch of Puritan fatalism with a short speech of encouragement, the crowd follows him on the next stage of the tale.

The last chapter observes the final confrontation of Armitage and his friends with the Horror from a distance; what happens the reader learns through elliptic phrases uttered by Curtis Whateley, who sees too much through a telescope. After Armitage performs the exorcism, Curtis attempts once more to describe the sight, "a octopus, centipede, spider kind o' thing, but they was a haff-shaped man's face on top of it, an' it looked like Wizard Whateley's, only it was yards an' yards acrost. . . ." (DH 197). This is a very specific language. Armitage's speech at the end of the story is abstract and moralizing: "We have no business calling in such things from outside, and only very wicked people and very wicked cults ever try to" (197). It is a speech that simply does not account for the pathos of the Whateleys nor for the terror of the townspeople and the collective experience suggested by their monologues.

Lovecraft's most extensive use of the dramatic monologue occurs in his 1931 masterpiece "The Shadow over Innsmouth." A fair amount of that narration is composed of four dramatic monologues: the first is the exposition of the train agent in Newburyport in direct discourse; the second is a short exposition by Mrs. Tilton, the curator of the Newburyport Historical Society, in indirect discourse; the third is by the grocery-boy in Innsmouth, also in indirect discourse; and the fourth is by Zadok Allen, the town drunk, in a rich direct discourse. The variety is striking.

The train agent speaks in a contemporary voice, shrewd but detached, a man who seems as distant from Innsmouth as the narrator; but though the agent pretends to disbelieve most of what he says, he clearly hates the Innsmouthers and is ready to believe the worst of them. His monologue in seventeen paragraphs, therefore, often contradicts itself. The first four paragraphs describe how to travel by bus to Innsmouth—geography is very important to this story—with a quick sketch of the town as it degenerated from its mills, a traditional factory in New England, to its solitary, odd gold refinery. This section concludes in a description, from at least second-hand, of the grandson of Obed Marsh, his supposed sickness, and the possibility that the degeneration of Innsmouth has come about through miscegenation with foreign blood from halfway around the world. All these details are quite vague; and though they seem shrewd, they also miss the point.

Here, in response to a question from the narrator, the agent expatiates upon Innsmouth's degeneration, recounting a history that Zadok Allen shall repeat with great variations. In seven paragraphs the agent first disclaims any belief in the story he is about to tell: "I come from Panton, Vermont, and that kind of story doesn't go down with me" (DH 306). Nevertheless he proceeds with one of the stories told by some old-timers, such as Zadok Allen, of Devil Reef, like the tale of the pirate gold that Obed Marsh had discovered there. Then he recounts the epidemic of 1846, brought from China perhaps, that might have caused the town's decay, adding that the animus that people feel against Innsmouth comes from race prejudice, a feeling in which he concurs because Innsmouth had traded among many foreign peoples who undoubtedly contaminated the town. At this point he adds that the narrator probably has no notion of such things, since, given his voice, it is clear that he comes from the West rather than from New England. Simply to look at a person from Innsmouth, however, is to dislike that person; not only is Innsmouth physically cut off from others, it is cut off by the Innsmouth look, a theme that the rest of the story develops at great length. People in Innsmouth are "offish," he concludes, though no one is off fish; they are off-ish when outsiders "fish" in their waters (308); the unconscious off-rhyme leaves the section inconclusive.

The last six paragraphs of the agent's monologue respond to the narrator's question whether there is a hotel in Innsmouth. Indeed there is, but no one would wish to overnight in it. A factory man heard odd sounds when he stayed there—Casey his name was, the agent adds, making clear that Casey is his source for information about the refinery, a subject that leads him to its jewelry and the people that wear it, "gotten to be as about as bad as South Sea cannibals and Guinea savages" (DH 309); though his information is second- and third-hand, his opinions are strong. Talk of the people returns him to the 1846 epidemic and the degeneration of the town to four hundred people, "as I told you" (309), aware of his increasingly aimless garrulity. In the last two paragraphs he returns to the nub of the narrator's question: though no one can keep track of the townspeople, neither school officials, census-takers, or government men, and though people have disappeared there and one man, they say, gone crazy, Innsmouth is probably safe for a day trip. It is just the place for someone like the narrator "looking for old-time stuff" (309). The agent makes Innsmouth a temptation that the auditor/narrator and the reader cannot resist.

One of the details of the agent's story brings the narrator to visit the Historical Society in order to view a tiara from the Innsmouth refinery. The curator Miss Tilton, who like the agent has never visited Innsmouth, comments on the piece in a monologue of four paragraphs rendered in indirect dialogue. First she tells something of its history, how the Society obtained it from a pawn shop after its owner, a drunken man from Innsmouth—the theme of intoxication shall return later—was killed in a brawl; the piece only left Innsmouth through violence. As for its origin, she tentatively regards its attribution as East-Indian or Indo-Chinese, but supports the notion that it came from the reputed pirate treasure discovered by Obed Marsh, all the more so since the Marshes had offered a good deal of money for its return, although she adds that the treasure was only a popular notion. She belies her objectivity, however, when she admits that she hates the Innsmouthers because of the Esoteric Order of Dagon, a secret cult that had "engulfed all the orthodox churches, [. . .] undoubtedly a debased, quasi-pagan thing imported from the East" (DH 312), doubtless more Masonic than the Masons. Though most of Miss Tilton's language is indistinguishable from the narrator's, a studied language that lends itself to the condensations of indirect discourse, this passage with its absence of qualifications and frank repugnance may bring a reader much closer to her actual viewpoint, that of the conservative New Englander shocked by the outlandish. Miss Tilton fears Innsmouth because it threatens cultural miscegenation.

Upon arriving in Innsmouth the narrator asks directions from a grocery-boy, a teenager from Arkham who lives with an Ipswich couple. His dramatic monologue in fourteen paragraphs of indirect discourse centers upon Zadok Allen, ninety-six years old, probably senile, certainly a drunkard, who is the source of the more outré stories; Zadok is the subject of the seventh and eighth paragraphs. The sixth and ninth paragraphs talk about what is unseen in the town, the people hidden in the hovels north of the river and the fact that the town is totally unsafe at night. The third, fourth, and fifth paragraphs and the tenth, eleventh, and twelfth talk about the people of Innsmouth, their drinking, their festivals on April 30 and October 31, their swimming, the absence of old people, their sickness—the danger and Zadok Allen then arise—and on the other side of that core he talks about the fish and refinery and the Marsh family, concluding with the Marsh daughters and the jewelry. The first two paragraphs and the last two concern the practical purpose of the monologue, how the narrator is to find his way about, including warnings about the refinery, Dagon Hall, and Washington Street where the Marshes live; but since the street signs are down and Innsmouth is a labyrinth, difficult to enter and difficult to leave, the young man draws the narrator a map.

The chiasmic shape of this monologue demonstrates how carefully Lovecraft shapes his material. It is also a monologue of some tension insofar as much of its style, unlike the style of Miss Tilton's monologue, is extremely different from the style of a young man of seventeen; when he describes the Innsmouth look, for instance, he discusses "osseous factors as basic as the shape of the skull" (*DH* 321). In its own fashion this monologue is as discordant as the monologue that follows, that of Zadok Allen. His monologue is one of Lovecraft's most remarkable, as he once more varies that dialect that he had developed in "The Picture in the House," not quite as distorted as that old man's voice, since Allen is not that old, and "The Dunwich Horror." This is a voice that as much marks Lovecraft's fiction as the Renaissance voices in Browning's poems mark his work. Despite arguments about the correctness of this dialect, we cannot deny its effect—an effect that arises from the contrast between its apparent immediacy and lack of rhetorical intricacies and the studied, rhetorical quality of most of Lovecraft's narrative prose. The effect of these passages would not be so strong if the prose surrounding them were not so consciously and conspicuously wrought.

The drunkard's monologue is in forty paragraphs with very few narrative interruptions, a monologue considerably more ordered than a reader might expect; yet it does give the appearance of disorder. Broadly speaking, the first paragraph is an introduction, the next fifteen paragraphs the story of what Obed Marsh discovered in the Pacific, concluding in a paragraph that picks up a motif from the beginning of the section and in a long pause as

Zadok empties the quart of whiskey; like Thurber's monologue in "Pickman's Model," this speech is powered by liquor. The next fifteen paragraphs tell the story of Obed Marsh in Innsmouth after the islanders in the Pacific have been destroyed, down to Obed's death in 1878; since it is a story that Zadok Allen witnessed as a young boy, he is much more involved in its telling and the prose is much more disrupted than the prose of the first part. The seven paragraphs of the last section are considerably shorter than the earlier para-graphs; this is Zadok's deeply intoxicated peroration, his challenge to the narrator to respond to the story, until he breaks off in a scream and runs away. He has told all the truth he is capable of, thanks to the quart of Prohi-bition hooch.

A few details in this monologue require comment. He begins by staring at Devil's Reef, "whar it all begun" (DH 329), and it is a glance at the reef that makes him flee at the end of his babblings. The story proper begins in "them days" (329), back in 1812 and 1825; the story of Innsmouth's decay begins long before Obed meets the islanders. But the story also begins in Obed's confrontation with his first mate Matt Eliot, as Obed begins to yearn for "better gods like some o' the folks in the Injies—gods as ud bring 'em good fishin' in return for their sacrifices, an' ud reely answer folks's prayers" (329), unlike the increasingly distant god of the Protestant establishment, Miss Tilton's god; this confrontation parallels that between Ahab and Starbuck in Moby-Dick, though Obed's motives are not at first as titanic as those of Ahab. In the sixth paragraph Zadok sees in the eyes of the narrator the same ability that Obed possessed of reading people, a theme he returns to later when much more drunk. Like the grocery-boy he mentions the calendar of the islanders, the festivals of May-Eve and Hallowe'en and the end of Octo-ber, in the ninth paragraph connected with the themes of miscegenation and the Old Ones, a slight glance at Lovecraft's loose mythography. In the tenth paragraph the theme of evolution from the ocean is introduced, the possibil-ity of returning immortal to origins and "a-talkin' to his own five-times-great-grandfather" (332), passages that prepare the narrator's meeting with his grandmother at the end of the narrative. At the end of this section in a casual remark Zadok reveals that he was born in 1831, a detail that reminds the reader that his knowledge of the Pacific story is at least second-hand, quite probably more removed than that. The Pacific story is the kind of tale a seven-year-old boy might hear around the hearth at night, a warning to avoid Old Man Marsh. The extermination of the islanders leads to a sudden depression in Innsmouth that most people are inclined to bear "kind o' sheeplike and resigned" (333) until Obed rouses them with words that round the section off: "he'd knowed of folks as prayed to gods that give somethin' ye reely need" (333), belaboring the Innsmouthers until they ask him "to set 'em on the way to the faith as ud bring 'em results" (333). This is the moment of the Faustian pact for Innsmouth.

After Zadok empties the bottle he tells how Obed ovecame Eliot's fears, in a language very different from the first section's, and the eighteenth paragraph contains mythic material typical of this section, as are the dashes: "Wrath o' Jehovy . . .—Dagon an' Ashtoreth—Belial an' Beelzebub— Golden Calf an' the idols o' Canaan an' the Philistines—Babylonish abominations—*Mene, mene, tekel, upharsin*—" (DH 334). Only this wretched prophetic language can render Zadok Allen's deep sense of the radical wrong in Innsmouth. The nineteenth paragraph is a string of rhetorical questions, while the twenty-fifth and twenty-sixth are composed of frequent ellipses. These sudden shifts in tempo make this section more intimate, since much of it is dependent upon Zadok's eyewitness; as a fifteen-year-old he watched events with "my pa's ship's glass" (335), and the final catastrophe of 1846, when his father died, occurred to some extent because "I done a bit by tellin' Selectman Mowry what I see from that cupalo" (336). Oedipal pressure is at work in his monologue, perhaps not surprisingly in a story devoted to the generations. As it is, he is not safe in Innsmouth: "They'd a kilt me long ago fer what I know, only I'd took the first an' secon' Oaths o' Dagon offen Obed, so was pertected unlessen a jury of 'em proved I told things knowin' an' delib'rit . . . but I wudn't take the third Oath—I'd a died ruther'n take that—" (338). Oedipal and religious pressures combine to make him a drunkard, for as long as he only talks when drunk he can claim that he has said nothing "delib'rit."

After he concludes the story with Obed's death he begins the last section of the monologue with a challenge addressed to the narrator and to the reader: "Hey, yew, why don't ye say somethin'? Haow'd ye like to be livin' in a taown like this, with everything a-rottin' an' a-dyin', an' boarded-up monsters crawlin' an' bleatin' an' barkin' an' hoppin' araoun' black cellars . . ." (DH 339). But this challenge is unexpectedly broken off: "Curse ye, dun't set thar a-starin' at me with them eyes—I tell Obed Marsh he's in hell, an' he got to stay thar!" (339). One of the ironies of the narrative is that Obed and the fish creatures he has married have returned in the form of the reader as well as in the form of the narrator. It is this truth, as Zadok turns to the reef and its creatures, that sends him screaming out of the story.

Of the sixty-six pages that make up "The Shadow over Innsmouth" in the Arkham edition, more than twenty pages, approximately a third, are made up of these four monologues, but their effect is disproportionate to their size because of their variety. Four different voices are turned on Innsmouth, modulated in quite different ways, so that Innsmouth takes on an immense solidity in the mind of the reader as the work proceeds; this is one of Lovecraft's triumphs, to make a place come alive through the words of characters who have such different investments in their hatred of the place and of the fascination it arouses in them.

I will conclude this survey with "The Whisperer in Darkness," written in 1930, "The Thing on the Doorstep," written in 1933, and "The Haunter in the Dark," written in 1935, because in them we see Lovecraft near the end of his creative career using the dramatic monologue in a much freer manner than earlier, for the sake of a more realistic narrative, and thereby dissipating its effect.

The three monologues in "The Whisperer in Darkness," although interrupted by a number of passages of narrative by the protagonist, nevertheless contain a certain energy insofar as the speaker purports to be Henry Akeley but in fact is one of the creatures from Yuggoth and insofar as his speech develops into a seductive attempt to convince the narrator that his surrender to the aliens, volunteering his brain to travel to the outer edges of the solar system in a metal cylinder, would gain him an ecstatic knowledge; Lovecraft works a number of variations upon the Satanic offer of knowledge and immortality. The monologues are presaged by Akeley's letters, informative and fearful before they break off into a new tone, confident and potentially ecstatic.

The first monologue, in seven paragraphs, occurs when Wilmarth meets his host for the first time. The first paragraph is full of civilities, polite nothings, although the real purpose of the meeting, the creature's eagerness to possess Wilmarth's information, arises immediately; though in the second paragraph the creature invites Wilmarth to make himself at home, he adds that Wilmarth can leave the material before he goes to his bedroom. In the third paragraph, after the counterfeit Akeley denies any need for help he turns to "the utterly stupendous nature of the matter before us" (DH 253), a passage suggesting that the creature really does wish to convert Wilmarth to its own point of view, that its possession of the materials is secondary to a plea for its cosmic vision; this passage and that which follows, the main body of this monologue, certainly contradict the polite nothings and the creature's pretense that it is sick. The fourth, fifth, and sixth paragraphs expand on the vision of the creatures from Yuggoth, their ability to transcend time and space, the beauty of their planet at the edge of the solar system, and their knowledge that transcends that of Cthulhu and K'n-yan, even that of "the Atlantean high priest Klarkash-Ton" (254). This last paragraph works climactically insofar as the reader is familiar with Lovecraft's published and ghostwritten works; but it also seems something of a hoax or a joke, when the reader is aware that Klarkash-Ton refers to Lovecraft's friend Clark Ashton Smith; the creature from Yuggoth is cardboard as well as wax. The last paragraph, therefore, is quite short; the creature recovers itself with the perfunctory words, "But we will talk of all this later on" (254), and dismisses Wilmarth.

A few pages later the second meeting takes place. The creature's monologue takes two forms, at first in indirect discourse for five paragraphs and then in direct discourse for three paragraphs as it describes the process of extracting brains and placing them in metal cylinders. This section concludes with a monologue in five paragraphs as the brain in one of the cylinders speaks. At first the creature speaks in the same mood as that of the afternoon, describing "the frightful position of our known cosmos of space and time in the unending chain of linked cosmos-atoms" (*DH* 256) and referring once more to the materials of Lovecraft's and others' works, Cthulhu, the Hounds of Tindalos, Yig, Azathoth, and the Black Stone; it's a fine farrago. Given this playfulness, the reader is entitled to ask how Wilmarth, a mere instructor of literature, is expected to make sense of a science that renders Einstein obsolete. In any case he makes clear that much that "that raucous voice" told him he "[could not] even hint" at (255); this passage is in indirect discourse because of the strong resistance that its auditor felt to the actual words. The creature's speech takes a new direction, however, when it proposes that not only shall it—the false Akeley—traverse the void to Yuggoth but that Wilmarth can also. His speech is interrupted at this point: "He must have been amused by the start of horror I gave at hearing a cosmic voyage on my part proposed. . . . Subsequently he spoke very gently of how human beings might accomplish—and several times had accomplished—the seemingly impossible flight" (257). The creature is not totally self-absorbed. It concludes its proposal by describing how the brain is extracted from the body to be placed in a cylinder, a process "as simple as carrying a phonograph record about and playing it" (257). Personality, the complex experience created between individuals, is exchanged for a material consciousness.

The possibility of the cylinders occupies the direct discourse that follows, especially the information that the cylinders contain a variety of races, "three humans, six fungoid beings, . . . two beings from Neptune, [. . .] and the rest entities from the central caverns of an especially interesting dark star beyond the galaxy" (*DH* 258), for "Round Hill [. . .] is a very cosmopolitan place!" (258). The next two paragraphs specify how Wilmarth is to hook up one of the cylinders and to hear its own witness.

The monologue of the cylinder in five paragraphs, meant to be seductive, is chilling instead. Rather oddly, since we never learn the name of the man whose brain is there, the voice asserts that it knows Wilmarth by sight and reputation but dismisses details as it reminisces about the thirty-seven celestial bodies that it has visited and claims that it is potentially immortal. It then formally invites Wilmarth to join him, Akeley, and Noyes in the journey, revealing now that it is Noyes whose voice was recorded on the disc that Wilmarth had received from Akeley. This information interrupts the monologue for a moment, as far as Wilmarth is concerned, for it is that voice and Noyes's that have seemed most antipathetical to him through this entire experience, not surprisingly since Noyes may very well be another incarnation of Nyarlathotep. Perhaps the most suspect claim of all, the cylinder blandly claims that "all transitions are painless" (*DH* 260). With all this said, a speech to support the claims of Akeley, the machine asks Wilmarth to turn off its switches—any order will do.

These monologues blend two styles, the rational and the ecstatic, but both styles are inhibited by the bland tone that predominates. To the creature from Yuggoth and the voice in the cylinder all difficulties have been overcome, all pain abolished, all the conditions of space and time made obsolete. It is the tone of arrogant common sense that warns Wilmarth that all is not well in the cosmopolitan order the creature proposes. And this tone of bland arrogance lessens the tension of the story that exists instead in its narrative; these monologues impede the narrative rather than support it.

"The Thing on the Doorstep," the last story that makes use of the dramatic monologue, does so at three points: when Daniel Upton goes to retrieve Edward Derby from the jail in Chesuncook, when Edward announces that Asenath has gone for a trip—after he has murdered her—, and when Edward feels the consciousness of the dead Asenath reaching out to possess him again. His voice in the Chesuncook episode takes two forms. At first it is quite disconnected; he appeals directly to Upton for help and belief, but much more he is reeling off disjointed details of what he has seen, much of it material from other Lovecraft stories. After this paragraph filled with ellipses Upton summarizes Derby's talk in the car, an indirect discourse that begins in a rational syntax but that becomes increasingly disjointed: "Yes, he knew about the Innsmouth blood now. There had been traffick with things from the sea—it was horrible. . . . And old Ephraim—he had known the secret, and when he grew old did a hideous thing to keep alive . . . he wanted to live forever" (*DH* 288). It is the subject of Ephraim, then, that Upton renders on the next page as a direct dramatic monologue, again as an appeal to understand what Ephraim has done but in the form of several rhetorical questions that are as much questions to himself: "Asenath . . . *is there such a person?*" (289). The jumble of rationality, desperate appeal, and sudden swerves of thought, along with the frequent use of italics, reveals the crumbling of Derby's intellect. This speech, however, is suddenly broken off, and when Derby resumes a very different voice is at work: "I hope you'll forget my attack back there, Upton. [. . .] You know what my nerves are, and I guess you can excuse such things. [. . .] The trip was a bit queer, but it's really very simple" (291). This common-sense, self-deprecating, straightforward voice marks a great difference between itself and the voice that it interrupts. Lovecraft makes palpable in these two voices the immense difference between Derby and Asenath/Ephraim.

The next monologue comes when Derby announces his separation. In order to tell his story, however, Edward has to resort to drink, just as Thurber and Zadok Allen had done. It is not only that these characters need to loosen their inhibitions in order to tell their stories; Lovecraft needs the pretense of drink in order to achieve the apparently free forms that their monologues take. Edward announces the separation in a reasonable syntax, but his second paragraph begins to introduce his paranoid fear that she was stealing his body and to suggest his actual strength, her belief that he is weaker than he really is. Barely begun, however, he takes another drink, and the main body of his monologue follows. The first paragraph is calm as he tells how he dismissed her Innsmouth servants, though they laughed as they left. In the next paragraph he alludes to his sudden change of manner in the car and appeals to Upton, "You know, it was she you must have ridden home with . . . that preying wolf in my body. . . . You ought to have known the difference!" (*DH* 294).[2] In the fifth paragraph, as the syntax becomes more disjointed, he changes direction, insisting that he had to save himself: "I suppose she'd have put me out of the way—killed her own ex-body with me in it, damn

---

2. The image of the wolf may come from the story Plutarch tells of the Spartan boy who stole a fox and hid it under his shirt, but would not speak though the fox gnawed at his vitals until he died (*Lives* 64). The childish Derby speaks but not very well.

her, *just as she did before*—just as she, he, or it did before . . ." (294). This is the point, incidentally, that most directly suggests that whoever Asenath or Ephraim may have been it might not have been human at all, that it might transcend the gender wars that much of the story seems to provoke; this point, however, reignites the gender wars, since it seems to imply that women are simply not human at all. In the next paragraph Edward finishes his account of what had happened in the car and directly asserts that Asenath is Ephraim. Having said that, he speaks more calmly in the last two paragraphs, again pleading for understanding and again fretting about the possibility that the Innsmouth servants might attack him. Thus, if we ignore the first two sentences as an introduction framed by the whiskey, as so often in his monologues Lovecraft shapes the speech into a ring-structure.

This is the main dramatic monologue of the story. The last one, as Edward realizes that the mind of the dead Asenath is reaching after his, is composed of four short paragraphs, so much separated by other matter that the cumulative impact is small. The mythological language of Chesuncook returns. After a gulp of wine Edward inadvertently reveals that he has murdered Asenath: "Nothing can stop that force; not distance, nor magic, nor death . . ." (*DH* 297). His last words, after they place him in the Arkham Sanitarium, are pitiable: "I had to do it—I had to do it . . . it'll get me . . . it'll get me . . . down there . . . down there in the dark . . . . Mother, mother! Dan! Save me . . . save me . . ." (297). Before the famous words that conclude the story, "*Glub . . . glub . . .*" (301), he is reduced to the pleas and repetitions that have formed so much of his utterance.

"Through the Gates of the Silver Key" also makes use of the dramatic monologue, though here the effect is muted by a variety of means, and we do wonder whether this occurred because of Lovecraft's discontent with the idea that E. Hoffmann Price proposed to him. The problem lies in how the adventures of Randolph Carter in the extravagant universe were to be related. The Swami Chandraputra—actually, as we discover at the end, Randolph Carter himself imprisoned in an alien body—recounts the story on various syntactic levels; yet that alien body is in truth one aspect of the essence of Randolph Carter. He is in battle with himself as he speaks.

His first account in the second chapter reads as though it were in direct discourse, but at the beginning of the third chapter a description of his words suggests we are actually reading an account in indirect discourse. The description, "As the Hindoo continued his tale, he had difficulty in avoiding what seemed [. . .] an air of trivial, puerile extravagance. Mr. Aspinwall, in disgust, gave an apoplectic snort and virtually stopped listening" (MM 429). We are assured that the Swami's style is quite New England, as though that were as sure a sign of authenticity as that of the hand as we have discussed elsewhere (Waugh, *Monster* 17–20), but the material is too abstract for that assurance to be realized. His language is never so dialectical as to refer to Hahvahd yahd.

Despite the various moments in which Mr. Aspinwall's disgust punctuates the indirect discourse, with a few exclamations of wonder from M. de Marigny and Mr. Phillips, the account proceeds through the next five chapters until Mr. Aspinwall attacks the Swami and dies of shock at seeing what the man, the creature, actually looks like. The difficulty is that the style is neither sufficiently New England nor sufficiently alien; here Lovecraft does not meet the challenge of the dramatic monologue.

Finally, let us consider an interesting although short use of the dramatic monologue in the late story "The Haunter of the Dark." When Robert Blake climbs Federal Hill for the first time he meets a policeman, "a great wholesome Irishman" (DH 97), whom he questions about the history of the former Baptist church. This stock character launches into a garrulous account, rendered in an indirect discourse that incorporates certain turns of phrase from the man's own tongue: "There had been a bad sect there in the ould days. [. . .] It had taken a good priest to exorcise what had come, though there did be those who said that merely the light could do it. If Father O'Malley were alive there would be many the thing he could tell" (DH 97–98). This indirect monologue allows Lovecraft certain advantages: he can take advantage of a certain color in the Irish brogue without doing it to the hilt. The indirect discourse makes possible a rapprochement between a local dialect and Lovecraft's own careful style.

A number of characteristics stand out in these monologues. Though we find it only used in "The Call of Cthulhu" and "The Dunwich Horror," Lovecraft's use of the dramatic monologue as an expression of group experience extends the effects of such naturalistic works as Zola's *Germinal* and Verga's *I Malavoglia*. Connected to this treatment is the fact that Lovecraft finds the dramatic monologue useful for exploring his major theme of regional life, one aspect of which is his use of dialect, especially in "The Picture in the House," "The Colour out of Space," "The Dunwich Horror," "The Shadow over Innsmouth," and "The Haunter of the Dark." Lovecraft conceives of regional life, however, vertically as well as horizontally, not simply as an expression of geography and culture by also as an expression of time, so that the dramatic monologue becomes an excellent tool for exploring the complexities of historical experience, as we see in "The Picture on the House," "Pickman's Model," *The Case of Charles Dexter Ward,* and "The Shadow over Innsmouth." The Yankee cannibal, the ghoul Pickman, Curwen, and Zadok Allen become spokesmen for an alternate history in which the marginal people, those left behind when the unity of American history began to break up, achieve a voice for one last moment; and that historical complexity is frequently paralleled by Lovecraft's use of the dramatic monologue to display the disintegration of character in "The Picture on the House," "The Colour out of Space," "The Whisperer in Darkness," and "The Thing on the Doorstep." Through that disintegration more truth is told by the language of madness than by the language of common sense. These characters can tell a hawk from a handsaw.

Finally we should note that several of these stories, "The Picture in the House," "The Call of Cthulhu," "Pickman's Model," "The Shadow over Innsmouth," and "The Thing on the Doorstep," are energized by the problem of shame, a problem for which the dramatic monologue is peculiarly suited, given its tension between reticence and logorrhea. Such a shame probes close to the personality that hesitates at exposing the secrets that render desire so vulnerable, and in this hesitation personality turns inward to become consciousness diffused into atmosphere. A problem with "Through the Gates of the Silver Key" is that the shame appropriate to the story is overwhelmed by the awe the story wants to express.

Lovecraft may not probe character very deeply, but he is excellent at creating the impression that he is doing so through the variety of voices in his stories. Very important to these works as narratives is the virtuosity he displays in shaping these voices through direct and indirect discourse; and often it is these dramatic monologues that offer Lovecraft a flexibility by which he can shape his stories and control their tempo, effects so ably created in "Pickman's Model," "The Dunwich Horror," and "The Shadow over Innsmouth." The center of these stories is often inexpressible, but these different voices and their flexible modes, sometimes more colloquial and sometimes less depending upon his use of direct and indirect discourse, and the peculiarity of consciousness that the voices display allow the reader to feel that the quest for the center is not in vain. The variety of means that Lovecraft possessed for handling his dramatic monologues demonstrates what an excellent storyteller he was.

The Surreal and the Organic Imaginations: Lewis, Tolkien, and Lovecraft

What does Lovecraft truly think the work of art ought to do? And toward what work of art does his imagination compel him? These two questions, moving in very different directions from each other, are not so far afield from our study of erotic ecstasis in his stories, for in the *Phaedrus* one of the manias that Plato treats is the mania of the artist; and though Plato does not go so far as to claim that the erotic is an aspect of the artwork, several latter-day thinkers do suggest this. We do not have to invoke Freudian thought to be aware of this direction in aesthetics.

Several times as critics we have investigated the question of Lovecraft's aesthetics, what he consciously intended to make as a maker of art and what he actually achieved. Another way to approach this question is by looking in some detail at the function of art in the narrative of his stories; for a good number of the stories do deal with the work of art. "The Picture in the House," "The Music of Erich Zann," and "Pickman's Model" announce this theme directly in their titles; *The Strange Case of Charles Dexter Ward* and "Medusa's Coil" have at the center of their plots portraits with very remarkable properties. What do these stories have to say about Lovecraft's concept of the artwork?

Before addressing these stories, however, I would like to suggest something about the nature of Lovecraft's imagination by looking at it within the context of a problem in the history of fantasy, the conflict between C. S. Lewis and J. R. R. Tolkien that erupted in their mutual misunderstandings of each other's works.

I

"I don't know where he came from, nor who or what he was. He was Gollum [. . .] (Tolkien, *H* 82)

For two gentlemen who agreed upon so much, Lewis and Tolkien had much to disagree about. Some of this disagreement was religious, some of it temperamental. More to our purpose, I wish to focus upon the disagreements between their imaginations, to analyze one way in which their imaginations began in very different inspirations and proceeded upon very different tracks. Once we have arrived at some clarity in these matters we can turn to Lovecraft.

This disagreement is highlighted in the way that their two children's books originated. As far as Lewis is concerned, we have various stories of the origin of *The Lion, the Witch and the Wardrobe*. According to one account it began in a series of dreams, perhaps some of them threatening, that he had about lions (Carpenter, *The Inklings* 223). According to another account, it seems to have begun simply in an image from childhood of a faun walking through a forest with an umbrella in his hand (Green and Hooper 237–38), an image we shall discuss shortly. Other images also appeared, such as a queen in a sledge (239). This was a normal process for Lewis when he worked on fiction—to begin with images, to lay himself open to them and see where they would lead. For the purposes of this essay we shall concentrate upon another image that, as we shall see, could have begun in the same hypnagogic condition, of a lamp-post in the forest. In Tolkien's case, *The Hobbit* originated in a sentence that he wrote on the back of an examination he was correcting (*Letters* 215): "In a hole in the ground there lived a hobbit" (*H* 9). Each man found himself gripped by the question of discovering the meaning of his donnée, what that image of the lamp-post in the forest and what that word *hobbit* meant. Each man was upon a quest, a literary parallel to the quests that gradually manifested themselves within the novels, to search out the meaning of something that seemed given. These two quests, however, were of a very different nature, given the difference in their origins, the one in an image and the other in a word; and this difference, I believe, dictated the tropes of the two works and also dictated the two men's responses to each other's works. To put not too fine a point upon the matter, in their most secret hearts their imaginations were antithetical.

Let us consider first Lewis's image. The lamp-post looks like a tree; it is straight and vertical. Yet it is artificial, made of metal rather than of wood, and it gives forth a light such as no tree is capable of. A lamp-post does not belong in a wood; it belongs next to a street in a city where a number of people live in order to guide them when their congestion makes them rub upon one another; it turns the night of the city into day. A lamp-post in the middle of a wood is absurd, for in a wood there is presumptively no one who needs its light, though a lamp-post upon a street is not absurd and neither is a wood in the country-side. A wood in a fairy-tale exists so that an individual protagonist or a pair such as Hansel and Gretel can become lost and find no one to help them except a witch; in Lewis's story this happens to Edmund when he leaves the lamp-post. One of the tasks that Lewis finds himself involved in, then, is to rationalize the image, to explain why this lamp-post finds itself in the wood. But he does not undertake that task until the penultimate novel, *The Magician's Nephew*. In *The Lion, the Witch and the Wardrobe* the image remains surreal, followed immediately by an image at least as surreal, a faun trotting through the wood with Christmas parcels in one hand and an umbrella in the other, across which his tail is draped. Lucy, who is seeing all this and whose act of seeing emphasizes that these are images, does not say curiouser and curiouser, as Alice would have; she simply accepts the images for their own sake and, rather excited, follows where they shall lead her.

A digression is in order here, though its purpose will only come clear later. It is beside the concern of this essay to investigate the literary origins of this image. Green and Hooper believe that it lies in Kipling's poem "The Brushwood Boy," in which these lines occur: "Over the edge of the purple down / Where the single lamplight gleams" (Green and Hooper 242). According to this reading, the lamp-post lies at the edge of the world of dreams, not a bad reading in the light of what we shall shortly argue. It is also possible, in something of an odd turnabout of expectations, that the image originated in Tolkien's image of the two trees that illumine Valinor in the early *Silmarillion* material; and if so, that may explain the way in which Lewis later rationalized the image of his artificial tree. Another possible source, however, is very much to the point, the argument early in Chesterton's *The Man Who Was Thursday* between Syme and Gregory about order and anarchy as Gregory hits a lamp-post: "There is your precious order," he says, "that lean, iron lamp, ugly and barren; and there is anarchy, rich, living, reproducing itself—there is anarchy, splendid in green and gold" (10). Coleridge's description of an organic form has found its spokesman here in a moment of late decadence. Syme's answer is that of a neo-Aquinean: "All the same

[. . .], just at present you only see the tree by the light of the lamp. I wonder when you would ever see the lamp by the light of the tree" (10). Only in the light of the *logos* does the created world become apparent and only in its light is discourse possible. The contrast between the lamp-post and the forest is clearly drawn, but I do not mean to say that Lewis means anything allegorical in the way that he develops these two images.

Let us consider the actual passages in which the lamp-post appears. Lucy steps into the wardrobe, and finding her way deeper and deeper into it (the first scene in which the motif of *further in*, so important in the last pages of the Narnia saga, takes place), "instead of feeling the hard, smooth wood of the floor of the wardrobe, she felt something soft and powdery and extremely cold." Her reaction is not cool; she does say, "This is very queer" (6), and presses further in, interested in the nature of a light that she sees ahead of her. In the next two paragraphs she realizes that she is pushing through branches of trees rather than fur coats and that the cold, powdery material is snow. Having assured herself that the door of the wardrobe is still visible, for unlike Alice who fell down the rabbit hole Lucy remains in control of her journey as though she were dreaming wide awake, she follows the other light that is still visible. Lewis writes: "In about ten minutes she reached it and found that it was a lamp-post. As she stood looking at it, wondering why there was a lamp-post in the middle of a wood and wondering what to do next, she heard a pitter patter of feet coming towards her" (7). So Mr. Tumnus appears with his umbrella, at which Lucy and the reader set aside that interesting question about the presence of the lamp-post. His presence, however, might answer our anxiety about the purpose of a lamp-post in a wood. It is there to give light to fauns and such creatures as intelligent beavers; symbolically it might represent the eye of God that perceives even the fall of a tree in the wood.

A number of points arise with this passage. First, as Bachelard asks, "Does there exist a single dreamer of words who does not respond to the word wardrobe?" (78). It offers Lucy an intimate privacy in which she can hide, and it is warm; but that warmth is immediately qualified by the flakes of snow falling on her, out of a sky that should not exist in a wardrobe. Next, we notice the passage's facticity. It is much more important that the central facts be presented with as little fuss as possible than that the objects be described. The phrase "soft and powdery and extremely cold" is important because Lucy does not yet know that she is about to enter a winter landscape, but after that moment Lewis feels no necessity to describe the snow. And there is no necessity to describe the lamp-post either; every child in a city knows what a lamp-post looks like. Lucy notes that one may need to account for the presence of the lamp-post in the wood, but it is more important for her to consider what she shall do next, a problem that the appearance of Mr. Tumnus resolves. The lamp-post does not appear within an artful verbal context; the style is transparent for the sake of the action. Only at the end of the novel, when age and experience has transformed the children into kings and queens of Narnia whose style is quite different from their childhood style, do they perceive the lamp-post as anything strange in itself. It is first "a tree of iron" (182); then it seems, to Edmund, "a pillar of iron with a lantern set on the top thereof" (183); and he shortly adds, "This lamp on the post worketh on me strangely. It runs in my mind that I have seen the like before, as it were a dream, or in the dream of a dream" (183). In the first scene the lamp-post had struck Lucy in no such way; but for that very reason, because it did not seem to present any great problem for the character, narrator, or reader, the lamp-post should strike us in retrospect as all the more dreamlike, a perception realized in the final pages of the book when the children as adults work themselves back to the word "lamp-post" and back to themselves as children, tumbling out of the wardrobe. The lamp-post in the wood is a surreal image.

I do not use the word *surreal* lightly. It is the program of surrealism[1] to allow itself to remain open to images composed of discordant elements, images that fuse materials from the unconscious which would otherwise seem to have no connection with one another, images composed from realities more or less distant from one another (Reverdy, ctd. in Breton 31). The language of surrealism, according to Breton, may very well be incomprehensible to the poet himself, though it will later seem to the poet that he or she has relearnt its meaning (37):

> Force est donc bien d'admettre que les deux termes de l'image ne sont pas déduits l'un de l'autre par l'esprit *en vue* de l'étincelle à produire, qu'ils sont les produits simultanès de l'activité que j'appelle surréaliste. [So it is neces-

---

1. I have in mind here only the surrealism promulgated by Breton in his first manifesto, which expresses several sentiments which Lewis might have found congenial: the exaltation of child-like experience, the exaltation of dream, and the declaration with which the manifesto concludes that "l'existence est ailleurs" (64). He would not have approved of the second manifesto with its frontal attack on family, country, and religion (82). Lewis would, I think, have admired Breton's lines, "L'armoire est pleine de linge / Il y a même des rayons de lune que je peux déplier" [The wardrobe is full of linen / There are even moonbeams that I can unfold] (ctd. in Bachelard 80). Even French surrealists find Narnia in a wardrobe.

sary to admit that the two terms of the image are not deduced the one from the other by the spirit that *considers* the spark of creation but that they are the simultaneous productions of that activity that I call surrealist.] (51)

This toying with the language of Platonism is a trace within the surrealist movement that is quite congruent with a direction within Lewis's thought (Smith 14). It may very well be argued that both Lewis and Tolkien are open to images from the unconscious, "la toute-puissance du rêve" [the omnipotence of the dream] (Breton 37)—consider for instance Tolkien's dream of the flood pouring across green fields, which has nothing surreal about it—floods are floods—but Tolkien much more than Lewis is concerned with the rationalizing of such material, fitting it very carefully into the evolving structure of his entire history and finding himself very disappointed if such a fit proves difficult. In *The Lord of the Rings* he remakes the bizarre but potent image of the hobbit with wooden shoes (*RS* 137) into the heroic figure of Aragorn with his broken sword, a sword that has an intricate history important for the history of the Ring; Tolkien reshapes the surreal possibilities of the original image into an image adapted to the nature of the story he is writing.

It is possible to think of Lewis's images in another fashion, as metaphors, for in them two elements quite dissimilar are joined; his images are composed of juxtapositions, lamp-post and wood, faun and umbrella, warm wardrobe and snow. In a metaphor, of course, one thing is asserted to be another; but metonymies work through congruity. The crown rules because the king wears a crown, though we should also note that the king rules because he has been anointed to wear the crown. In Lewis's images we see metaphors at their point of origin, two things with no relationship being cast into a relationship through the power of the hypnagogic imagination. Considering the images from this angle, the peculiar thing is that although Lewis believed that metaphor revealed meaning rather than creating it (Smith 14), we would be hard pressed to say what meaning is revealed by these images. It seems, instead, that these images create meaning and thus take a short cut through Lewis's lucid argument.

Lewis's unpacking of the image is interesting in regard to the problem of meaning. Only in *The Magician's Nephew* did he decide that the lamp-post originated as an import from the world of London, the world of Sherlock Holmes as the first page of *The Magician's Nephew* announces, a generation earlier than Lucy and her brothers and sister. The witch Jadis tears a crossbar off a lamp-post, "lightly, easily, as if it were the most ordinary thing in the world" (92), later to cast it at Aslan outside of time as the lion sings Narnia into being; taking root, it grows into a complete lamp-post, "thickening in proportion, as they watched it; in fact growing just as the trees had grown" (110). The phenomenon moves Uncle Andrew to dream of growing "brand new railway engines, battleships, anything you please" (111), but his dream is as futile as it is foolish. In this account the lamp-post represents a weapon that has been converted through the magic of Narnia into an organic object of enlightenment.

At the same time as Lewis clarified the rationale of the lamp-post, he decided that the wardrobe should also have a pedigree: the tree that in the world of Narnia functions analogously to the tree of life in Genesis provides Digory with an apple to cure the illness of his mother; from the seed of that apple grew a tree that was considerably later to provide the wood from which the wardrobe was made. Lewis connects lamp-post and wardrobe to images that flow from Eden and Calvary, a rational decision in the light of Pauline imagery (cf. I Cor. 15:45–49). His quest to read the lamp-post is successful because he follows it backward in sacred time. The wardrobe and the lamp-post are intimately connected in their origin and thereby in their function, for the lamp-post draws anyone in the wardrobe from this world into Narnia and indicates to anyone in Narnia the proximity of the wardrobe and this world. To consider the lamp-post more speculatively, its light comes, I believe, from the treatment of the cross in "The Dream of the Rood," in which it is called a "bêacan," a beacon, signal, or portent (l. 6), a metaphor that may have stemmed from the story of Constantine's making the cross a banner for his troops, in response to the dream in which he heard the words "In hoc signo vinces." In "The Dream of the Rood" the cross is made of wood, yet to the dreamer it seems artificial, "begoten mid golde" and studded with gems (l. 7).

I am not sure, however, how many readers might be content with this reading based upon sacred origins. I feel confident that many might be interested in a Freudian account of the lamp-post, regarding its phallic appearance as a primary image that allows Lucy without thought to pursue her faun (though Lewis disapproved of Freudian approaches). And many might be more persuaded by a further biblical reading, arguing that the lamp-post in the wood alludes to those lines early in the gospel of John, "The light shineth in darkness; and the darkness comprehendeth it not" (1:5). I am personally more persuaded by the suggestion that the lamp-post and the wood form an amalgam of two nostalgias, one for the fairy-tale world of the wood and the other for the childhood of the late Victorian world in which Lewis grew up. I offer these three very different readings only to suggest that we are in the position of that darkness, still scratching our heads over the problematic nature of the lamp-post.

But however Lewis unpacked the meaning of the lamp-post, it simply would "not do" for Tolkien, who felt that Lewis had sinned against his understanding of the consistency demanded by a story: "I mean to say: "Nymphs and their Ways: The Love-Life of a Faun!" (Carpenter, *Tolkien* 201).[2] In considering Tolkien's response we need to remember that he and Lewis enjoyed talking bawdy at the Eastgate Hotel or, perhaps, at the Bird and Baby where the Inklings sometimes met, a perfectly suitable place to talk bawdy given its dedication to the amours of Jove and Ganymede (Carpenter, *The Inklings* 54–55).[3] He did not object to the erotica as such but to its presence in the kind of story that he imagined Lewis was telling; the habits of the contemporary pub are not consistent with the other world, a sub-creation that ought to proceed from deeper aspects of reality at the same time that it employs traditional figures. Lewis sinned against the warning that one should be careful in describing a green face or a blue moon (*Monsters* 157). We doubt that Tolkien would have approved of Breton's peroration: "Cet été les roses sont bleues; le bois c'est du verre" (64). The first clause is a bit too reminiscent of Oscar Wilde's boutonniere; but the second clause seems, in retrospect to us, prophetic, looking ahead to Lewis's lamp-post. Tolkien would have objected to surrealism that it indulged in "the fantastical complication of shapes to the point of silliness and on towards delirium" (*Monsters* 146); and it is true that several of the French surrealists saw many advantages in delirium.

This pretty piece of faunish erotica is not the only moment at which Lewis sins in this way. Tolkien objected to the presence of Father Christmas, but he might as well have objected to so much else in the story, such as Fenris Ulf from Norse mythology. Narnia has many more direct albeit diverse

---

2. Either Tolkien or Roger Lancelyn Green, who reported this remark, misremembered the more innocent title that Lewis had actually invented, *Nymphs and Their Ways* (12).

3. In this connection we should consider what Lewis meant by Mr. Tumnus's name, which appears to be Latin but is not. The two words that most resemble it are *tum* and *tumere*. The first word means "then, of past time"; Mr. Faunus leads Lucy past the nineteenth-century nostalgia of the lamp-post into an alternate world compounded of medieval and classical materials. The second word means "to swell" and leads to such derivations and cognates as tumult, tumulus, tump, or tomb; but he is a most bland faun for one whose name suggests the swellings of anger, pride, sexual excitement, or burial. Perhaps most fittingly for such a name, his home is in a cave under a hill.

connections to this world than has Middle-earth, which purportedly lies in the far past of this world and looks ahead to it. Lewis has no compunction against importing mythic materials from a great variety of sources. The principle of the lamp-post in the wood is manifested in several ways.

Tolkien's quest takes a very different direction from Lewis's careful rationalization of the image. First, let us note that Tolkien's sentence, "In a hole in the ground there lived a hobbit," is constructed from verbal means, not imagistic. No one is there to see the hobbit; the reader learns of the creature through a very present narrator, whose hapax legomenon *hobbit* is embedded in a sentence introduced by two parallel prepositions, *in a hole* and *in the ground;* and further the word is anticipated by the alliteration *h.* Thus *hobbit* is one of a piece with its surrounding verbal materials, as we might expect given the way in which the sentence seems to have appeared whole in Tolkien's imagination. And the quest proceeds through a series of identifiable rhetorical tropes, a series of recusations and intricate parallelisms that seem generated by that first sentence, which as we have seen is not simple despite the simplicity of its vocabulary: "Not a nasty, dirty, wet hole, filled with the ends of worms and an oozy smell, nor yet a dry, bare, sandy hole, with nothing in it to sit down on or to eat: it was a hobbit-hole, and that means comfort" (H 9). The word *comfort* with which this series concludes shall become a key to what it means to be a hobbit, so overwhelming a part of the characterization that Bilbo's own quest, once it is introduced, shall be the problem of how to escape that comfort and what place that comfort should assume within the ethical questions of the book, concluding in Thorin's words on his death bed: "If more of us valued food and cheer and song above hoarded gold, it would be a merrier world" (H 301). Although his words are not an absolute endorsement of comfort, they do indicate something of the distance Bilbo has traveled in his moral journey, providing comfort to the dwarves where in the beginning of the book they least expected to find it.[4]

It is also important, in regard to this hole in which a hobbit lives, that it shall as it were generate most of the narrative: Bilbo shall be entering and escaping holes throughout the story, of which the goblin caves, Mirkwood, the palace of the Woodland King, and the mountain of Smaug are the most undeniable examples. Thereby the work is of a piece, the several parts corresponding to one another; and we can only read the work properly when we allow

---

4. I owe this last point to my former colleague, Professor Ernelle Fife.

ourselves to understand these relations. *The Hobbit* and Tolkien's other works
have this in common with Coleridge's water-insect, one of the poet's images
for how the mind operates when involved in a work of the imagination; it
"*wins* its way up against the stream, by alternate pulses of active and passive
motion, now resisting the current, and now yielding to it" (1.86). This passage
describes very nicely the rhythm of Tolkien's narrative, the image of the hole
marking the beat. It is a rhythm that may owe something to his habits of composition, writing in pencil and later tracing the words in pen, often to introduce a new plot twist in the process. Nothing of this kind of structure appears
in Lewis's narratives, nor need it. Lewis writes, as we have said, to render
transparent the image that he sees; Tolkien writes in order to discover his image through a process that is often very pains-taking.

These several comments indicate something of what Tolkien meant by
consistency. *The Hobbit* is notable among his books by the gradual transformation of its style, from the faux simplicity of an adult talking down to a child to
the more complex style of its final chapters, more complex in order to develop
the moral problems that Bilbo faces in those chapters with the several apparently conflicting fidelities he discovers he has assumed in his journey. But no
matter how complex or simple that style may be, it is an eminently verbal
style, more dependent in its effects upon its texture of rhetoric and sonics than
upon its images. Furthermore, its images do not clash with one another, as
Lewis's do; dwarves, trolls, eagles, and dragons come from the same storehouse
of the kind of story Tolkien is telling, the European fairy-tale. He is in this regard much more conservative in his materials than is Lewis. Only two figures
jar with this assessment. One is Bilbo himself, but hobbits, of which he is the
representative figure, are assimilated so thoroughly into the style in the first
pages that we may not notice that hobbits were never a part of the kind of
story from which dwarves proceed, though the reference to golf almost gives
the game away (26). The other figure that jars is Gollum; and there is no help
for it, except insofar as his function here is to give Bilbo a magic ring, which
does belong to this sort of story. Gollum, then, remains as a figure who is the
occasion of the next great quest that awaits Tolkien, the search in *The Lord of
the Rings,* the major quest one could argue, for what it means to be a Gollum;
the shattering answer to that quest is the discovery that a Gollum is a hobbit,
and thus Tolkien's narrative comes full circle—we suspect that the Gollum
came from the same place as the hobbit in his comfortable hole. A correlative
answer, however, to what it means to be a Gollum was already constructed in
The Hobbit when Tolkien discovered or overheard the style of Gollum's

speech. His appearance is sketched in; but it is his style of speech, regressive and horribly childish, a parody of the childlike style of the first chapters of that book, by which a reader is most likely to identify him. Once more, style precedes image in Tolkien's creation.

Having said so much, we need to qualify our description of Tolkien's procedure by admitting that he does mention an umbrella. In *The Lord of the Rings* Lobelia hits Sharkey's ruffians with her umbrella before they carry her off to the Lockholes (3.293). No such instrument is mentioned in *The Hobbit*, but it might very well exist in a work that mentions tea-time. In any case, both Lobelia and Bilbo do need an umbrella, for they wear clothes; and given Bilbo's pride in his clothes, we can assume with some confidence that Lobelia is careful in her clothes also. One of the odd things about Mr. Tumnus's umbrella is that he has very little need of it since he is, as any self-respecting faun should be, naked. Tolkien's umbrella may be anachronistic, as so much in the Shire is, but Lewis's umbrella is absurd.

I read Tolkien for the complexity of his moral vision, what he is pleased to call his applicability (*LotR* 1.5), but man shall not live by morality alone. Lewis, who believed in the lucidity of his moral universe, wrote of something more than that universe because through his images he created a range of meanings, often surreal, of which his conscious mind would probably not approve. Some of them we have cautiously touched upon. In this light let us return to the lamp-post shining in the darkness of the wood by virtue of its gas and by virtue of having been produced in a lamp-post factory in order to overcome the infamous fogs of late-nineteenth century London. In 1878 Robert Louis Stevenson wrote a nostalgic essay on gas lamps, praising the "warm domestic radiance they cast," in contrast to the new electric light that should shine "only on murderers and public crime, or along the corridors of lunatic asylums" (13.169). But like electricity the lamp-post depended on an intricate technology, centering on the gas works, which foiled the attempt of revolutionaries to extinguish the lights of a modern city (Schivelbusch 110–12). Through the lamp-post in the wood Lewis juxtaposed modernity and the fairy-tale in a baffling fashion; the witch, not quite as primitive as the one whom Hansel and Gretel meet, knows what shall appeal to an English child when she offers Edmund a piece of Turkish Delight.[5] These various meanings, however, shall be done away with when the wood shall later be renamed the Lantern Waste: the waste in which the lantern,

---

5. In 1870 Dickens mentions the confection in *Edwin Drood* (vd. "Turkish" OED).

something other than a lamp-post, for a lantern does not usually throw as much light as a lamp-post and a lantern is made for perambulation, is to be found; or it is the place where a lantern is a waste or where a lantern shows that a waste is to be found. Something has happened, something inexplicable, to that cozy wood in which Lucy met Mr. Tumnus; now it is a waste. The end of the world is near when a lamp-post devolves into a lantern.

II

Au fond du miroir le double se confond
qu'on ne consulte davantage,
tandis que, dans son lit, le sombre moribond
aux souvenirs qui vaguement s'en vont,
en défaillant arrache son image.

Celui du miroir et lui qui meurt,
sont-ils tous deux d'accord à disparaître?
Ou, dans la glace, restera, peut-être,
un être à son tour provocateur?

[The double in the mirror is confused
because we don't consult him anymore,
while in his bed the sombre moribund
with memories that vaguely vanish
tears off his image as he wastes away.

The mirrored and the dying one,
have they both agreed to disappear?
Or, perhaps, will there remain in the mirror
one who, in turn, provokes?]
                (Rilke, *The Complete French Poems* 244–45)

In the light of these various skirmishes, what are we to say of Lovecraft's imagination? At first blush we might be tempted to associate him with Breton's surrealism. His imaginative life often begins in the images of a dream, often enough that he institutionalized that part of his life in a commonplace book, though nothing mentioned in that book takes place in a common place; but he is so careful to render that dream in precise rhetorical terms (cf. "The Statement of Randolph Carter," "Nyarlathotep," and "The Outsider," early stories based to a greater or lesser extent on actual dreams) that his work is not a synthesis of the two modes. Rather, given the material of the dream, he feels a strict compunction to convert that material into linguistic forms. He is thus closer to Tolkien than Lewis, whose style is always unashamedly utilitarian; a man proud of the precision displayed in his arguments he wishes to say what he wishes to say, no less and no more. Tolkien and Lovecraft always wish to say more.

Not that Lovecraft would have approved of either of these two gentlemen. Given his disapproval of Chesterton we can imagine only too well what he would have thought of a work like *The Lion, the Witch and the Wardrobe*; and he would probably have seen through to the basic Christianity of Tolkien's work as well. On the other hand, he might have acknowledged the level of terror that Tolkien works with in the patterned imagery connected with the Black Riders and the Eye of Sauron. He was not, however, interested in eucatastrophes of any sort. No, as far as material is concerned he would not have felt any kinship with these two representatives of the Inklings.6

Be all that as it may, this matter is not as simple as it seems. Lovecraft did very much admire E. R. Eddison on the strength of the man's style (*SL* 2.171), and that fantasist had been very cordially received by the Inklings. But it is not simply a question of Eddison's style. A few days later Lovecraft praises the book because it combines "some gloriously imaginative phantasy with an exquisitely lyrical prose style" (*SL* 2.174). Let us not press this point too greatly, but it is as though he praised Eddison for the two qualities we have noted in Lewis and Tolkien. Still, in 1933 Lovecraft picked up a remaindered copy of "that magnificent phantasy" *The Worm Ouroboros* (*SL* 4.144). Two months later he writes, "There is nothing else quite like it— even by the same author. It weaves its own atmosphere, and lays down its own laws of reality" (*SL* 4.156), words that we can suppose might as well describe the work of Tolkien. Eddison forms something of a bridge between the aesthetics of Lewis and Tolkien and the aesthetics of Lovecraft.

This question of aesthetics is not unimportant for Lovecraft, for he often asserts that the only justification of any particular story is not its subject but the way that subject has been handled, usually considered under two categories, the shape of the story and its style. The subject, however, is not unimportant to Lovecraft; he knows what he likes, and what he likes is the weird tale. Let us consider again his introduction to "Supernatural Horror in Literature": "The oldest and strongest emotion of mankind is fear, and the oldest and

---

6. In the question of a relation between Lovecraft and Tolkien we should note that both were excoriated by the same literary caretaker of the canon, Edmund Wilson.

strongest kind of fear is fear of the unknown. These facts few psychologists would dispute, and their admitted truth must establish for all time the genuineness and dignity of the weirdly horrible tale as a literary form" (*D* 365). There is much that might be objected to in these claims. First, though Lovecraft doubtless feared many things, he was not as an adult a fearful man; his letters attest too much to his charm and humor for us to believe that his fears overwhelmed him in his day by day life, except perhaps in his dreams, but those fears he was able to overcome with his ready pen transcribing them in his notebooks, letters, and stories. I think that in fact several psychologists in his day would have disputed the priority of fear; for instance, though Lovecraft disagreed with Freud upon points of detail, he did accept Freud's case as a point of argument that sexuality was extremely important. The true point of this introduction is to assert the pertinence and worth of the weird tale. Despite his belief that we lived in a universe where the significance of humanity was as nothing, he also believed firmly in the seriousness of his intentions in writing this kind of story and in the importance of this kind of story for the human condition. More broadly, he agreed with Lewis and Tolkien that the work of fantasy possessed its own justification.

Having said all this, what we may ask is his central image? Some might argue, feeling that I have too quickly dismissed the surreal quality of Lovecraft's fiction, that the monster is his central image, whether that be Cthulhu or perhaps even more strikingly Wilbur Whateley. Ingenious as Lovecraft is in his descriptions of his monsters, however, I do not sense anything oneiric in their construction; for they are constructed as Lovecraft conscientiously adds here a tentacle, there a claw, and there a scale and a bit of slime. If it were not for the atmosphere of the work, we would laugh like a reader of the first lines of Horace's *Ars Poetica*, in which he ran through a short catalogue of monsters composed of different animal and human parts and concluded, "Spectatum admissi risum teneatis, amici?" [if you saw such a picture could you hold back your laughter, my friends?] (l. 5). Lovecraft's creatures are meaningful, but in themselves they are depthless. The exception is the ticklish night-gaunt, but it does not function powerfully in the fiction except perhaps in *The Dream-Quest of Unknown Kadath*. They are more frightening in Lovecraft's dreams than in his writing.

No, what truly reveals the nature of his imagination? The answer to this question is not difficult, given how often I have earlier dealt with one scene obsessively. We must return to the conclusion of "The Outsider" in which the narrator discovers himself in a mirror. Just as Lewis discovered in a dream much of the material that became *The Lion, the Witch and the Wardrobe,* Lovecraft discovered the climactic moment of "The Outsider" in a dream: "Fear of *mirrors*—memory of a dream in which scene is altered and climax is hideous surprise at seeing oneself in the water or a mirror. (Identity?)" (MW 89). What is it then about mirrors, water, and pictures, this problem of identity, that makes them so fearful?

A mirror is a human artifact that mimics the effect of looking into the surface of calm water. An act of hybris is connected with an artifact that smoothly and perfectly appears to reflect the scenery in which we find ourselves; the water shaken by the air, always shaken by the air, reflects only a broken image, but the mirror reflects no broken image. There we cohere. We learn early as children that this apparent scene does not in fact exist behind the mirror as our various experiences with stereoscopic vision would persuade us, perfect though the image is. Thus the scene in the mirror is at once radically solid—it does not merely exist, it exists with depth—and it does not exist at all. Yet all our experience insists that things possess depth, though not a depth that we can exhaust. In a very immediate and naive fashion the mirror raises the question of existence and reality.[7]

Another problem arises with the space within the mirror. At one point in his study of space Bachelard considers the imagery of weightless houses, those houses that however well-rooted like "to have a branch that is sensitive to the wind" (52) and aspire out of the earth into the air and find a new space everywhere, in a peony or a chalice (55) or even, he concludes, in a mirror. But the lines that he cites by Jean Bourdeillette to illustrate this space are dark:

> Le chambre meurt miel et tilleul
> Où les tiroirs s'ouvrirent en deuil
> La maison se mêle à la mort
> Dans un miroir qui se ternit
> [The room is dying honey and linden
> Where drawers opened in mourning
> The house blends with death
> In a mirror whose lustre is dimming] (56)

---

7. The stereopticon was an important domestic entertainment at the turn of the twentieth century; and this imagery of stereoscopic vision is thematically important to Joyce (cf. *Ulysses* 3.418–20) and to Proust, as Roger Shattuck has shown (40–83), and provides another contact between Lovecraft and the Modernists.

The felicitous space to which Bachelard had addressed himself in this study (xxxi) is changed in the mirror into something discomforting. When I look into a mirror I am the same self as I always was, because the only exterior self I have ever known is in the mirror; but the space behind me, the space in the room I inhabit, is not the same. Its reversal multiplies the space in the room, but at a severe psychic price.

Perhaps as important as these ontological questions are the aesthetic questions that the mirror raises. In the Ars Poetica Horace had summarized Greek thought in his insistence that poetry should be "ut pictura" [like a picture] (l. 361), a famous tag that controls the aesthetic arguments for the next nineteen hundred years, through the Age of the Enlightenment; and during that time the image of the mirror was often used as well as the picture until the work of the Romantics, when the lamp and the Aeolian harp became the favored models of art (Abrams 58–69). Lovecraft is picking up, therefore, a rather archaic image when we find the mirror and the painting coming to the center of his fiction. But there is a radical difference between Lovecraft's mirror and the two-dimensional surface of the painting. Since his mirror is stereoscopic, three-dimensional, its realism is an act of trickery as the painting never is, trompe l'oeils notwithstanding. Given its stereoscopic nature, something remarkable happens in the event that Lovecraft portrays; if we can here leave aside the time-reversal implied in the terminal climax, the narrator of "The Outsider" sees something that we the readers do not expect. In the original dream the surprise seems to belong to the narrator; in the story the narrator has no expectation, for he has no idea what he looks like, but even so he does not like what he sees. Who would? The point is that we expect that the image in the mirror will show a person who is reasonably human rather than this rotting mockery of the human. The shock of the story lies between what is human, according to the realism that we expect in the mirror, and what is actually human, the corpse. But as far as the story is concerned the mirror does show precisely what stands upon its weakened legs before it. This aesthetic obeys the ut pictura, but it shows something that Horace would never have expected and that as far as the first lines of the Ars Poetica are concerned, to which I earlier alluded, he did not believe it should show. Lovecraft, however, is not playing for laughs nor for weirdness per se, so his art is in fact radically different from that of the classical world and of the Enlightenment.

One further implication lies in the mirror that we have tacitly admitted. It exists to show the self. That is to say, no mirror is only a mirror; it comes complete with a self because it has a human function and depends upon a person who shall look into it, rather like the forest that Bishop Berkeley imagines; and so Lovecraft's imagination always turns on a confrontation with the bald, naked, unadorned, though not quite unmediated, self. He is in that regard very different from Lewis and Tolkien. Lewis's lamp-post has nothing to say about the self, though it does return Lucy, Edmund, Peter, and Susan to what they actually are in the world of the Blitz—children, but their group identity as children barely touches what it is to be a self. Tolkien has some concern with the self, but that identity is tangential to the literary task of reconciling the hobbit and the Gollum, those complex entities through whom the self is at last realized.

"The Outsider," however, takes one further step that brings its effect beyond either the classical world or the world of fear that he had affirmed in that misleading introduction to "Supernatural Horror in Literature," for the protagonist accepts himself as the mirror has revealed him. More than acceptance, it is an image to which he continues to return, as though he were in some fashion in love with the image. This possibility leads us to compare the story to two famous classical myths, one ascribed to Aristophanes in the *Symposium* and the other occurring in Ovid's *Metamorphoses*; we have referred to them before, but they will not release us. The myth that Aristophanes tells comprises one of the several praises of love that we find in Plato's masterpiece, but we are at some loss to say how we should judge it; true, Aristophanes is a great comic playwright, but this does not quite seem like comedy, not to the sensibility of the later Western world, and the Neoplatonic figures of the Renaissance took its imagery very seriously. He recounts how once upon a time each human was composed of three sexualities, male-male, female-female, and male-female; but upon their rising up in revolt against the gods, Zeus struck each of them through the center so that these eggs now found themselves mutilated and in an agony to find the lost self. This is love, whether gay, lesbian, or hetero, the search for the self, not to overcome difference but to find fulfillment in that part of the self that seems to have become autonomous. This is the point of Rilke's rhetorical question about the self in the mirror: "Ou, dans la glace, restera, peut-être, / un être à son tour provocateur?" Notice, incidentally, the doubling of the "être" across the pause between the two lines, as though being were never being unless by chance it doubled and reflected upon its self.

In Ovid's account of Narcissus this reflection befalls the protagonist, the young man who dies because he has fallen in love with himself and punningly complains that "inopem me copia fecit" [abundance made me poor] (3.466). The only difference is the ontological difference of the self and the image, which the self cannot overcome. Aristophanes promises that some shall find the lost self, but Ovid, also a comedian, discovers here a tragedy, for Narcissus has found himself and dies for it. But as he dies he becomes the occasion of the Middle Ages' taking him for the exemplum of self-love and a warning against self-obsession. Perhaps, however, in Lovecraft there is no escape from self-obsession and the death that at last we die of, we die for.

What is it we die for when we look in the mirror? The Outsider looked at himself in the mirror to discover that he was already dead, in a manner of speaking. What he looked like before his death we have no idea. Was he once young and handsome? Consider this quatrain, "Suleika spricht," from Goethe's *Westöstlicher Divan*:

> Der Spiegel sagt mir, ich bin schön!
> Ihr sagt: zu altern sei auch mein Geschick.
> Vor Gott muß alles ewig stehn,
> In mir liebt Ihn, für diesen Augenblick.
> [The mirror tells me I am beautiful!
> You tell me that it is my fate to age.
> Before God everything stands eternal,
> So in me love Him, for this blink of an eye] (2.41)

The tragedy of the mirror is only overcome in this significant moment, this blink of an eye, that combines eternity, that is to say every individual death, and this moment of imaginative, complacent fulfillment. We must not forget that the Outsider does move beyond the moment of the mirror, now that he has a self at last, to join the company of "the mocking and friendly ghouls" (DH 52).

Something else happens in the mirror. Hawthorne left a note for a story he never wrote that points towards this moment: "An old looking-glass. Somebody finds out the secret of making all the images that have been reflected in it pass back again across its surface" (169). Nothing is lost in the mirror. When we step aside from it our reflection steps aside also, to disappear behind the frame, but not to vanish, just as an actor steps aside behind the proscenium only to reappear later. Lovecraft left notes in his *Commonplace Book* about a story in which a reflection in a pond would live for the sake of revenge (MW 90) and another story in which a face would be present in a mirror in the cellar (91). The mirror preserves our self-love and self-obsession, but it also preserves our immortality, just as in another mode the portrait does. Perhaps that unwritten story contains one of the truths in "The Thing on the Doorstep": the rotting corpse of Asenath in the cellar reveals the actual, inner face of Derby, the ineffectual aesthete, just as the mirror reveals the truth about the Outsider and the portrait the truth about Dorian Gray.

One further moment in the mirror occurs that extends beyond the subject, the fact that the mirror accepts and doubles any and every object. It resembles the scholastic understanding of the soul that is capable of accepting all forms and thereby infinite in its reception of the images that it can contain (Aquinas 1.80; 1.84). We shall never know, then, what images shall appear to us out of the mirror, behind us or at our left or our right side. The mirror contains every surprise.

Thus, we think, Lovecraft's imagination was liable to operate, always playing upon the confrontation of the self within the mirror and probing its reality. But what did he think of the work of art, the form that it would take and the effect that it would have? Did it look like a lamp-post or a tree? And if it looked like a mirror, did his mirror depend upon Horace as a late Romantic? Did it illuminate or burgeon or multiply? Did it threaten or immortalize? For an answer to those questions we need to turn to those stories in which he describes art works, and that is in fact one of the major themes of his stories.

"The Picture in the House" seems to be quite direct about the purpose of art, or at least the art in this story. It is pornographic. The old man confesses that the picture does "tickle" him; the word does not go so far as to say that he has an erection or an orgasm when he contemplates the murder, butchery, and devouring of long pig, but it certainly suggests that he experiences some sort of arousal, an awakening of the ancient blood and flesh that he urges the narrator to share and that the narrator does indeed share, for he admits, "I experienced some shame at my susceptibility to so slight a thing" (*DH* 119). This narrator has certain pointed comments in the opening of the story about the Puritans who suffered from their desires and hid them away until the desires became something even more shameful (117). The old man is very old, but he is caught at an early stage of development, the stage at which the story explicitly appeals to the reader, drawing the reader back into that primitive life. We should not miss the Freudian cast of this analysis, at a time when Lovecraft admitted in a letter that he has begun to study Freud. Here we find art driven by the oral stage of development. The psychological basis of the art, however, does not matter to the validity of the art. The question of "so slight a thing," if properly managed, for instance so slight a thing as a short pulp fiction, can work upon various levels of desire and form.

So much for the picture of the shambles, no matter whether it is, as we argued earlier, a sham, a shame, or a *semblable*. But then there is the other picture, the one "drawn wholly from imagination and careless descriptions" that "represented negroes with white skins and Caucasian features" (*DH* 119). That is no doubt a sham, a shame, and a *semblable* also. I do not wish to deal with the psychological implications of the picture but with the fact that it is neither careless nor a mere production of the imagination. The engraver is a realist, but realists can only see as they are trained to see; so this engraver can only create a picture of the African world based upon the European world that he knows. This picture deals in what we can only call homely details; and let us keep in mind that Lovecraft is writing only upon what he sees in the copy of Huxley's *Man's Place in Nature* that lies before him.

This picture forces me to digress and admit that if there is a surrealistic quality to Lovecraft's work it lies in his ability to describe out-of-the-ordinary moments in terms of quite homely imagery. The door out of which Cthulhu erupts looks like a barn-door, a trap-door, or a cellar-door (*DH* 151), depending we must assume on the angle from which a person sees it or the attention a person gives to it, rather like the vase or silhouettes conundrum of Gestalt psychology. The path the Dunwich Horror takes to its refuge in the Cold Spring Glen is "as though a house, launched by an avalanche, had slid down through the tangled growths of an almost vertical slope" (179), suggesting both the creature's size and its erratic movements in a world it does not understand. The most splendid examples of Lovecraft's ability to seize upon a homely image in an extreme situation, however, lie in "The Shunned House" in his comparison of the vampire's elbow to "a mammoth soft bluewhite stovepipe doubled in two" (*MM* 261) or in *At the Mountains of Madness* his comparison of a shoggoth to a line of subway cars on the Cambridge line, its stations lovingly called out, in Boston (100) or to a piston in a cylinder (101). In all these cases it is the tension implicit in the comparison that makes it work: a cellar-door fits oddly next to the orientalia of so much connected with R'lyeh; a house is so solidly there, unlike the invisible Horror; the stovepipe is so radically different from the human form; Antarctica is so far from our familiar Boston; and the enormous, pseudo-organic, "protoplasmic" (101) shoggoth is so different in nature from a steel piston. Within the list of art works that I am analyzing, these comparisons are miniature art works, and what we learn from them applies to the more conscious presentations of art in the stories.

I have already discussed at length the problems of the paintings that Pickman creates from his experience, mediated by the photograph. One of the points of the story seems to be that art of this nature, a brilliant realism, can only be created through a mediation; despite the arrogance of the claim that the artist creates directly from nature, whether that be the exterior or the interior world, the artist needs the experience of other art before submitting to inspiration, which we have already discussed as one of the divine manias. The other point of several of Pickman's paintings is that humor, albeit of a rather sardonic and satiric nature, is not only permissible in this sort of thing, the weird art or the weird fiction; humor may be a necessary component. Humor, however, is not a simple matter. It is often aggressive, as Pickman's certainly is; and it may be, *pace* Freud, a sublimation and release of a particular pain. What is Pickman's pain? It is, I believe, his heritage, betrayed slowly to the reader, that he is not himself human but a changeling; more specifically, he is as his name reveals a ghoul. As a changeling he was handed over by his actual ghoulish parents when he was only a child to occupy the bed of a human baby. Was that good for him or not? What does the child now think of those parents, be they ghouls, who have deserted him? Once more we stand at the beginning of the story of Oedipus, exposed by his parents. If the primal scene in which most of us meet our origin is unbearable, what shall we say of the primal scene enacted by ghouls? Which is worse, the primal scene or exposure? Pickman turns the anger that consumes him, evident in almost every sentence of his monologue, against the human race; but if we wonder at the origin of that anger, its most apparent source lies in the ghouls that deserted him to the mercies of the obtuse humans.

One aspect of "The Music of Erich Zann" is its repeated allusion to the difficulty of this music. To live near it and enjoy it the narrator must climb a "steep" street, a word repeated several times; and then there is the difficulty of language, for not only is Erich Zann German in a French city, presumptively Paris, but he is dumb—his only language is his music and the feverishly composed notes that he scrawls for the narrator only for them to be lost in the wind from the window. This problem of language extends to the street name, Rue d'Auseil, which makes little sense in French; and the narrator confesses that he has never been able to find the street on maps of the city. "Rue d'Auseil" first of all signifies street, though in English "rue" suggests a particular herb as well as remorse. "Auseil" is more difficult. Robert M. Price suggests that "seil" can be heard as sill, referring thus to both the doorsill over which the narrator must step to enter the tenement and the windowsill through which the music pours ("Erich Zann" 13–14); similarly, Donald R. Burleson suggests that word sounds very like "au seuil," "at the the threshold," inviting entry and denying it also (*Lovecraft* 75). It is possible, however, that the narrator has misheard the name, which actually is Rue d'Asile, the street of the refuge or sanctuary; to hear the sort of music that Zann hears and to make the sort of music that Zann makes it is necessary to retire from the world. In addition, let us note the resemblance of the word to the French "seul," alone, a loneliness that haunts both Zann and the narrator. Each man needs to be singled out in order to experience the music that sounds on the other side of the windowsill. In German, however, Seil means rope. This is the street of the rope, the place where you can hang yourself, as Gérard de Nerval did, in the loneliness and remorse of an irrational despair that engulfs you from the outside where your terrible muse dwells.

It is the central image, however, the image of the mirror, that remains important in this story. As Zann plays, the narrator hears as it were in counterpoint to his music the music that plays outside the glass window that, in the climax of the story, shatters at the impact of the storm outside, the music that carries away the confession Zann attempted to write, the explanation of his secret and of his art. Before it shatters that window functions as a mirror, albeit a mirror hidden behind a sash. Though the narrator does not emphasize the point, we are aware how clearly a window functions as a mirror at night when all is dark outside and the room in which we stand is lit. This art, then, both presents the self and shatters the self; it possesses that erotic component that, following Leo Bersani, we have previously identified as *ébranlement*, the shattering of the self in an erotic encounter (Waugh, *Monster* 153–570). To say that we desire art is to say too little; we are attracted to it because it offers both a reflection of the self and an erotic shattering of the self. To use our earlier language, there is a moment at which the two ecstasies, that of art and that of eros, merge.

It is impossible not to consider the relation of Lovecraft's story with the classic sketches that Hoffmann made of the eccentric musical genius Johannes Kreisler. Lovecraft was probably not familiar with the details of this work, for in 1923 he wrote that "all of Hoffmann [was] still ahead" of him (*SL* 1.214), so he may not have known that it was something of an open secret that Hoffmann was treating Kreisler as an alter ego, the double as a projection of the self. Several details in the story of Erich Zann are very like those in Hoffmann's *Kreisleriana*, in which an eccentric musician is described. I think we can attribute these details to a common architype of the musical genius, but the details are nonetheless striking. In the first chapter the narrator says he has no idea where Kreisler was born or who his parents were (3.363) and confesses that the man has now vanished; there is no closure to his life (3.364–65). There is something directly demonic about his playing, for twice the narrator compares him to Faust carried off in the mantle of Mephistopheles (3.365, 432). The words that Kreisler uses to describe Beethoven's music, "Unge-heuer," "Furcht," and "Entsetzen" [monsters, fear, and horror], introduce the realm of "Riesenschatten [. . .], die auf und ab wogen, enger und enger uns einschließen und uns vernichten" [giant shadows that surge upward and downward, that lock us into narrower and narrower spaces, and annihilate us] (3.386). This is the art of terror and sublimity that is to reign through the nineteenth century. The great master of this art was Liszt, so it is perhaps not odd that the last air Zann plays is "a wild Hungarian dance" (DH 89).

In considering Lovecraft's story we must first notice that the narrator is himself a double of Zann, for the narrator is a "broken" figure (DH 83), living an "impoverished life as a student of metaphysics" (83). At that time he was "not himself" (84). When, owing to the good will of Zann and of the land-lord, a paralytic gentleman by the name of Blandot, he receives a cheap room on a lower floor, it lies ambigouously between "an aged money-lender and [. . .] a respectable unholsterer" (87). Zann, who is dumb, unable to speak or communicate in any immediate way, writes in a bad French that is "laboured" or "execrable" (87), words that suggest that the narrator is himself French; so if we need to accept Zann's words with some caution we need to accept the speaker's words with as much caution. The most important detail, however, in this doubling is the Rue d'Auseil that lies across a river "bordered by pre-cipitous brick, blear-windowed warehouses" (84). This steep hill, "consisting in several places of flights of steps" (84), strongly resembles the steep hill that led eastward to the area where Lovecraft had been born and lived most of his life. The city in this story—call the city Paris, which never had such a Left Bank such as this—is a mirror image, a double, of Lovecraft's Providence, as we realize when the narrator hears "a calm, deliberate, purposeful, mocking note from far away in the West" (89). But rather than the city that the narra-tor expects in this story, he finds only a cosmic void; the source of the art and the source of life is revealed as a great nothingness.

The oddest detail in this pervasive doubling lies in Zann's face, which the narrator says twice is like that of a satyr (DH 85, 86). Immediately after he al-ludes to this resemblence he says of himself that with "a certain capricious-ness" he wished to look out the covered window. Dr. Johnson only notes that the word "capricious" comes from the French word "capricieux," but the OED derives it from the Latin "capro," goat ("Capriccio"). In attempting to look through the window, driven by an "odd fascination" and a "curious desire" to see into the source of Zann's art, the narrator behaves like a double of Zann. If we are to consider this imagery in a mythological fashion we should note that here the figure of Pan, who is half goat, reasserts itself into our work; this desire, then, reaffirms the erotic nature of the art. The narrator of this story is behaving exactly like the narrator of "The Picture in the House." We understand the anxiety that the musician feels as the narrator approaches the window; it is the same anxiety that Pickman had felt toward the room that contained a well through which the sources of his art ventured.8

The music that Zann plays has one further odd aspect. His viol in the climax of the story is "night-baying" (DH 90), though we cannot say whether it is baying for the night or the music incarnates the night baying. In any case, the narrator flees that "ghoulish howling" (91). Lovecraft wrote the story in 1921, and in 1922 he wrote "The Hound"; it is as though in the earlier story he used the language metaphorically that in the next year he was to use literally, both the language of the hound and the language of the ghoul. This music is related in an obscure fashion to the devouring impulses of the two aesthetes in the later story. More generally put, Lovecraft insists here and in other stories on the aggressive nature of art.

The most remarkable work of art in Lovecraft is the portrait that Joseph Curwen engaged Cosmo Alexander to paint of himself on a wall-panel of his home in Olney Court. It was one of the gestures he made to present himself as an aristocrat among the other aristocrats of Providence mercantile society; he had, after so many years had passed since his arrival from Salem, truly arrived. The portrait affirms that he has arrived, but that purpose is quite short term. The portrait also grants him a quasi-immortality, that life after death that so many patrons have hoped for when they applied to Rembrandt or Stuart for the performance of their portraits. Curwen, however, hopes for an immortality that transcends that of mere art. Cosmo Alexander would have probably been shocked that his painting had to be reduced to "fine bluish-grey dust" (MM 234) for Curwen to manifest himself in the flesh, such a coarse, loose flesh that was all that could be reconstructed from his essential salts. Either the portrait achieves immortality, or the subject; never both. But the painting of Joseph

---

8. *Webster's Dictionary* derives *caprice* from "*capo* head + *riccio* hedgehog," as though the fancies of a capricious person sprouted like the needles of a hedgehog ("Caprice").

Curwen exists upon two levels, in the painting itself and in Lovecraft's own oblique rendering of the man, in which he works like Balzac in Arthur Symons's symbolic description of that energetic art through which, "stepping out of the canvas, as the sombre people of Velazques step out of their canvases at the Prado, is the living figure, looking into your eyes with eyes that respond to you like a mirror" (113). As we said, here with complete appropriateness, Lovecraft's imagination centers upon the self that so yearns to step out of the mirror and cannot. But Joseph Curwen does.

The painting itself seems quite satisfactory. The narrator assures the reader that Cosmo Alexander must have had some competence, since he was a teacher of Gilbert Stuart. It shows Curwen seated before a window in which his ships, the foundation of his wealth, appear. He wears a wig and possesses "a thin, calm, undistinguished face, [. . .] a lean, pallid visage" (MM 155) that has nothing to recommend it as far as this description is concerned but that electrifies his descendent through the "precise duplication" of his own features (155). The portrait becomes a mirror. But would this portrait have assured Curwen immortality if no magic were involved? Though the narration insists upon Alexander's competence, that "undistinguished face" that is later called "colourless" (163), this of a man who in person boils over with a blinding energy, suggests that Alexander may not have truly seen the remarkable man he was painting.

In "Medusa's Coil" the theme of the art-work finds a fitting climax as the young artist Marsh paints a fateful work depicting Marceline as the whore of Babylon (Rev. 17), nude and holding "a monstrously shaped goblet in one hand, from which was spilling fluid whose colour" the father finds impossible to identify (HM 192). It is a purely generic work, though we note that the erotic element is very obvious here. Marceline, however, though she is "the key" to the work just as she was "the key" to Marsh's genius, is only one part of "a vast composition" (192). The father, who is not sympathetic to this kind of art, finds it difficult to interpret this scene, whether she imagines the scene or whether the scene conjures her into being, whether it is an interior or an exterior, whether the buildings are of stone or of "a morbid fungous arborescence" (193). It seems to share the ambiguity of the ground/figure constructions of Gestalt psychology in which two appearances advance and retreat. The only certainty the father has is that the Witches' Sabbat it portrays "wasn't Egypt— it was behind Egypt; behind even Atlantis; behind fabled Mu, and myth-whispered Lemuria. It was the ultimate fountain-head of all horror" (193). The painting has the quality of a mirror, creating a profound illusion of infinite space behind its surface, reaching back or behind itself to an active source of aggression; and the longer he looks at the work, the more "those monstrous, dilated eyes," the synecdoche of this new space, seemed to watch the father and her hair seemed to lift off the surface to attack him.

Both the father and the narrator attest to one other quality of the painting. It turns the observer to stone, as though the myth of the Medusa had come true; but this quality we recognize as the effect of all great art, absorbing the attention of the observer so completely that it strikes into oblivion every object that surrounds it (Adorno, *Minima Moralia* 75–76). One other quality the painting exhibits arises from the father's assurance that it guards against the resurrection of Marceline (*HM* 197). The painting takes the place of reality. It has not slain Marceline, but in some fashion it is intimately involved in her being supplanted by its heightened truth.

One further point about the title of this story. Once we become aware that a painting is an intimate component of the narrative we realize that a further context of the story is Géricault's famous painting *The Wreck of the Medusa*, so prophetic of the new sensibility in Europe and of the convulsion that was shortly to shake the continent at the fall of the Bastille. Death, despair, and a meticulous technique even to the details of the water-drops on the livid flesh combine to turn the observer to stone; in this sort of art, history, a fortuitous history, and myth work toward one end that is not, as a Hegelian would have it, the revelation of *Geist*. Though Géricault could not have painted the work without *Geist*, in this work *Geist* is overturned by terror.

I have been upon the verge of saying that Tolkien has his mirror just as Lovecraft has; or to say this in another way, each man sees something in the mirror that he cannot surrender or betray. Tolkien sees an elf, and Lovecraft sees a dream. They insist in the same way upon the existence of what they see there. In all his various comments upon his elves Tolkien only twice lets slip the fact that he does not truly believe in elves[9]; and I am not sure that Lovecraft ever admits that dreams are only dreams, certainly not the Freudian dream that arises from the desires and fears of the dreamer, rather than narratives that exist within a world that grants them a substantial, autonomous existence. This is something about the two of them that I believe we

---

9. In the essay "On Fairy-Stories" he argues that it is true we seldom meet elves "even if they are only creations of Man's mind" (*Monsters* 113); and in a 1954 letter he concedes that, "if I were pressed to rationalize, I should say that [elves] represent really Men with greatly enhanced aesthetic and creative faculties" (*Letters* 176).

must find utterly admirable, the way that the creative force within them will not betray the image. Elves exist; and dreams exist; and nothing more is to be said. Or rather, everything remains to be said, because these fictions in Vaihinger's and Adler's sense exist in order to discover other concepts and values. Elves exist in order to discuss mortality and immortality and the fall; dreams exist in order to investigate the autonomy of the horror that the imagination insists upon revealing. In this sense Tolkien and Lovecraft are speculative authors. Because in contrast Lewis is dogmatic, he never spoke in this fashion about Narnia.

Lewis, Tolkien, and Lovecraft have very different attitudes toward the stuff of the story. Lewis is writing a history of a world, but his history is very carefully controlled by the attention he pays to his typological models in the Bible. Tolkien is also writing a history with biblical overtones, but he much more pays attention to the developing details of his own world, controlled by the philological invention that presents itself to him; speculation and the hard facts of philology intertwine. Both Lewis and Tolkien conclude in apocalyptic fictions, but Tolkien continues the history into a post-apocalyptic world. In part they are thus responding to the challenge of Bishop Berkeley that in various ways resonates through much of fantasy. If the fictional world is so radically different from the world in which we live, how are we to ascertain its existence, reality, or authenticity? Lewis provides a lamp-post to which smidges of reality cling and, more interestingly, the death of the children. The hard-headed Tolkien provides an intricate system of manuscripts, calendars, and linguistic analyses. Lovecraft provides those details that we discussed when we considered his work as historical fiction, the manners and tongue and architecture of New England, that specific place in its three-hundred-year existence. It is the history of Providence and New England that arrests his attention, and in that arrest his art blooms. And at the conclusion of his stories we are still on the edge of apocalypse.

"An Exquisitely Low and Infinitely Distant Musical Note": German Romantic Opera and Lovecraft's Aesthetic and Practice

> Painted emblems of a race,
> All accurst in days of yore,
> Each from his accustomed place
> Steps into the world once more.
> (Gilbert and Sullivan 440)

H. P. Lovecraft had little interest in music, as he freely admitted; despite his two years' practice on the violin his interest rose no higher than comic ditties (*SL* 1.75–76), though in 1931 he allowed that Wagner's "Ride of the Valkyries" had its merits (*SL* 3.342). Having admitted that Lovecraft was not greatly interested in classical music, I must admit something more complex, that his stories do bear interesting resemblances to a series of three German Romantic operas that may enlighten us about certain points in his stories. There is no question here of influence. Lovecraft may have heard of Weber's *Der Freischütz* and Wagner's *Der Fliegende Holländer*, but he never heard them or saw them; and it is very doubtful that he ever heard of Marschner's *Der Vampyr*. These three operas, however, are tightly connected among themselves, and thus a close examination of their librettos and music present us a complex collection of texts that provide a remarkable context for a number of Lovecraft's stories. I propose to examine these three operas first as examples of the weird in German Romantic opera and then to treat some of Lovecraft's stories, especially *The Case of Charles Dexter Ward*, within their context.

I

Hier, unter diesen Trümmern, ist die Zisterne [Here, under these ruins, is the cistern]. (Beethoven and Popelka 2.1)

When Carl Maria von Weber's career began, he had already adumbrated ideas for the opera *Der Freischütz,* ideas based upon a group of superstitions that he had heard as a child. These include the notion that the devil will help a man make six bullets that shall always hit their mark but that the last bullet, the seventh, belongs to the devil, who aims it wherever he wishes. Two other superstitions are important for the opera, one the belief in the Black Hunter and closely associated with it the belief in the Black Horde, superstitions fused in Weber's music.

Before any opera comes the overture, often a light-hearted concoction based upon melodies in the work. Mozart in *Die Zauberflöte* and Beethoven in *Fidelio* changed all that; and Weber follows their lead in an overture that begins in a mysterious melody in the horns, perhaps suggestive of the German woods, emblematic of supernatural threat in the collection of *Märchen* that the Grimms had recently assembled. Consider the beginning of "Hansel and Gretel": "Vor einem grossen Walde wohnte ein armer Holzhacker" [In front of a great wood dwelt a poor woodcutter] (67); this woodcutter has little hope against the immensity of the forest that confronts him. Having established that forest world the overture passes into a music that is much darker, threatening, and tumultuous, using materials based upon the appearances of Samiel and upon the conclusion of Act II, which is the central scene of supernatural terror. Only at the end of the overture is the material connected with Agatha, alluded to very lightly before, now heard in full, a joyous music that promises the protagonist salvation.

The curtain rises upon a chorus that announces the conclusion of a shooting contest, the triumph of the peasants over the hunters, the triumph of the agricultural world over the aristocratic past; the audience that does not know the opera is disconcerted to learn that the winner of the contest is not the protagonist, Max, who has just failed miserably and must bear the friendly teasing of the crowd, shamefully wondering, "Sind denn die Sehnen dieser Faust erschlafft?" [Are the nerves of my hand asleep?] (1.1).[1] The reason for his failure is obscure, both to himself and to his comrades, but in the third act the

---

1. In this chapter the quotations from the operas are cited by act and scene.

reason is clearer when Kuno, the father of Agathe, Max's fiancée, suggests that he shoot before she arrives because her presence might distract him. In this act Kuno innocently sings, "Leid oder Wonne, / Beides ruht in deinem Rohr" [Pain or joy, / Both rest in your barrel] (1.2). He cannot hit the mark because of sexual anxiety. Since these various details make the phallic significance of the gun in this work obvious, we must keep this thematic strand in mind. At this point also the opera reveals its hierarchical structure. The characters who count in this society are the prince and Kuno, the *Erbeförster*, the hereditary head forester. The old people maintain a social, moral, and metaphysical authority, while the young, Max in this case, are too liable to err.

The next moment of significance is Kuno's account of how the contest, the *Probeschuß*, began in the time of his ancestor Kuno, who at the instigation of the prince shot a deer that bore on its back a poacher—a common punishment at the time—but both prince and Kuno took pity on the man, and in the last act, balancing this moment at which society created itself, pity shall once more play a significant part. This account also reveals that people jealous of the ancestor's shot suggested he had recourse to a "Freikugel" [free bullet], giving the librettist an opportunity to explain the superstition of the seven bullets upon which the opera is based; a person who applies to the devil is allowed six shots that shall strike any target he desires, but the last shot belongs to the devil. But who can say whether this shot belongs to the devil, to God, or to chance? This is a version of the Faustian bargain. Faust in the various versions trades or wagers his soul for knowledge and experience. The huntsman trades his soul for the perfect shot; Max trades his for Agathe.

So far the opera has been light in tone, taking place on a quotidian, social level; but the overture promised tragic possibilities that now take form in the figure of Kaspar, in Kuno's forthright words an unsavory "Tagedieb, ein Schlemmer, ein falscher Würfler" [an idler, a glutton, a cheat with dice] (1.2), who likes to defend his language and opinions as a former soldier who fought for Tilly "und war beim Magdeburger Tanze" [and was at the dance at Magdeburg] (1.5). This careless phrase reveals the depravity of the man, for the sack of Magdeburg became infamous as an example of the violence of the Thirty Years War.

Kaspar is a sorry character. His song of temptation, rollicking as it is, promises only wine, dice, and a barmaid. The line that insists on"dies Trifolium" [this three-leaf clover] is a casual blasphemy, no more. Nevertheless the music, a disturbing melody sung to an insistent, obsessive beat, is such as had not been heard in previous operas, and so we should pay closer attention to the words. In the first stanza Kaspar sings that in this vale of tears nothing would be right

> Trüg' der Stock nicht Trauben;
> Darum bis zum letzten Hauch
> Setz ich auf Gott Bacchus' Bauch
> Meinen festen Glauben.
> [If the stock did not bear grapes;
> So until my final breath
> I will set on God Bacchus' belly
> My fast belief.] (1.5)

Marschner in *Der Vampyr* also makes a theme of the grape. For now, the accent upon the stomach of Bacchus must strike us as questionable. It is much more forthrightly blasphemous than most of the language in praise of Bacchus.

The second stanza begins in an imitation of the lines in Goethe's *Faust* (ll. 2540–52) that parody the doctrine of the trinity, but here the attack also centers upon the Eucharist to insist once more upon the virtue of the grape: "Eins ist eins und drei sind drei, / Drum addiert noch zweierlei / Zu dem Saft der Reben" [One is one and three are three, / So add just two more sorts with them / To the sap of the vine] (1.5). However one adds up the trinity or, in addition, the doctrine of the two persons of Christ, the grape remains the grape, an intoxication that redeems us from these problems. Kaspar then praises cards and dice, the worship of chance in human life, and the further chance of "ein Kind mit runder Brust" [a girl with a rounded breast], for all these bring us "zum ew'gen Leben!" [to eternal life] (1.5). The third stanza has nothing to add but a summation. Kaspar's trinity, that saves us "Seit dem ersten Übel" [since the first trouble] (1.5), is the grape—stupefaction—chance, and a casual sexuality.

This chance, however, that Kaspar praises is threatening to Max. Earlier, after he failed in the shooting contest, it had seemed to him that "Unsichtbare Mächte grollen" [invisible powers rumble] (1.2) that somehow "umgarnen" (1.4) him in a web. He asks, like Mr. Gardner in "The Colour out of Space," "Für welche Schuld muß ich bezahlen?" [For what guilt must I pay?] (1.4) and more bluntly, "Verfiel ich in des Zufalls Hand?" [Have I fallen into the hand of Chance?] (1.4). Questions like these lead to the great question, "Herscht blind das Schicksal? Lebt kein Gott?" [Does blind fate rule? Is there no God?] (1.4). The possibility of a meaningless chance is a persistent theme in this opera.

The material threat in the opera is the mysterious figure of Samiel, appearing and disappearing to a simple yet threatening motif, "three soft strokes of a drum below an unchanging dismal chord" (*NNDB*, "Carl Maria von Weber"), and never singing; he speaks, but uses few words. Thus he is utterly abnormal in an opera in which all of the characters except him sing. He stands "von beinahe übermenschlicher Größe, dunkelgrün und feuerfarb mit Gold gekleidet. Der große, mit einer Hahnfeder verzierte Hut bedeckt fast das ganze schwarzgelbe Gesicht" [of almost more than human size, clothed dark green and gold the color of fire. His large hat decorated with a rooster feather covers almost his whole dark-yellow face] (1.4). The dramatis personae identifies him as "der schwarze Jäger" [the Black Hunter], but the characters in the action only warn against that figure. Thus he remains simply Samiel, a demonic figure.

But if he is *der schwarze Jäger, der wilde Jäger,* or *der grosse Jäger* [the Black Hunter, the Wild Hunter, or the Large Hunter], what does that signify? Jacob Grimm argues persuasively that this figure in folklore who guides "der wütende Heer" [the raging horde] descends from the god Wotan (2.765–93). In the libretto that great hat, but not its flamboyant feather, concealing the face of Samiel is certainly a detail we often see in Wotan, hiding his maimed eye, a theme that Wagner uses in *Der Ring.* That color dark-yellow, however, is anomalous. The libretto may be suggesting a relation between the figure of the *wilde Jäger* and the *wilde Mann* who stands in the square of so many German towns, hefting an uptorn pine tree, and also upon the shields of many families in southern Germany, clearly a fertility figure (Grimm 1.402). These details perhaps assure that despite the threat of damnation that Samiel casts across the action the marriage still takes place. Max needs to have his naive confidence shattered and plowed under in order to re-establish his life within a new mode.[2]

To convince Max that it is possible to make a miraculous shot through the use of the natural powers, Kaspar persuades him to shoot an eagle out of the sky, despite its height and despite the gathering shadows of evening. It is a shot that in his most confident days Max would consider impossible, but he brings the eagle down, a woodsman Prometheus, and agrees to join Kaspar at midnight in the Wolfsschlund to forge the magic bullets; but despite his success, the uncanny shot dampens his spirits and his confidence.

---

2. The name Samiel belongs to one of the ambiguous devils in the system of the Kabbalah; in some traditions he is Satan, the accuser, in others the angel of death (Scholem 385–88).

The second act opens with Agathe and her friend Ännchen, who is nailing onto the wall a portrait of the original Kuno that has fallen and injured Agathe. Understandably the young woman regards the accident as an ill omen; Ännchen, however, an incorrigible, jolly character, will not accept that. For her the world is simply the world; though she is conventionally religious, she does not believe in a supernatural world that is operative here and now. But despite her laughter this motif of the portrait is important here and in Wagner's *Der Fliegende Holländer*. In both operas the portrait is not fully alive, yet its life is clearly an extension of the life of the person it represents. The ancient Kuno is attempting to warn Agathe, but the only way that he can do this is by wounding her. After some conversation between the two women, Max arrives to tell Agathe with considerable hesitation that he is going to the Wolfsschlund to retrieve a deer he has killed. Though the action does not make much of this moment, we should note that he does lie to his fiancée and is thus already in the snares of Samiel.

The Wolfsschlund scene makes this opera famous as one of the first that plays with the Gothic materials that had for years enthralled the Romantic generation. It opens with stormy music upon a scene filled with stricken trees, ravens, and owls "mit feurig rädernden Augen" [with fiery wheeling eyes] (2.4). Kaspar is revealed drawing a magic circle while a chorus of invisible spirits sing words that shall be significant in the last act: "Eh' noch wieder Abend graut [. . .] / Ist sie tot, die zarte Braut" [Before the evening grows gray again [. . .] / She will be dead, the tender bride] (2.4). Hell is so confident. In one of the longest appearances of Samiel, he answers the invocation of Kaspar, who refers to the "Frist" of their bargain, the time that Samiel has allotted him in return for his service (2.5); with some equivocation Samiel agrees to the bargain that Kaspar would now like to strike so that he can exchange Max's life for his. This interchange clarifies Kaspar's motive in the first act. He is a drunkard, just as Kuno had said, an addict, dependent upon Samiel for his life, and a dealer; in order to live he has to addict others, and Max in his present state, so anxious to make the perfect shot and feeling pressured by a society and a bride that expect so much of him, is an easy victim. His entrance is greeted by a figure that he identifies as the ghost of his mother, warning him to flee, a parallel to the portrait of Kuno that tries to warn Agatha. Max advances, however, and in a powerful music that Kaspar counts off the two men forge the magic bullets.

The last act opens on an entre-act of strings and horns establishing the lovely day that follows the storm. This lyric piece, however, is followed by a short scene in which two hunters merrily discuss Max's success as the *Probeschuß* begins. Max, however, is not encouraged and desperately tries to obtain more bullets from Kaspar. The second scene returns to Agathe as she prepares to receive her bridal wreath. Ännchen, unfortunately, enters to say that the portrait has fallen down once more; and the box of the bridal wreath reveals only a funeral wreath. Once more Ännchen explains the incident as mere accident, but hardly has she calmed the chorus when the portrait falls again with a great thud.

The third scene begins as the first act had upon a sharpshooting contest, in which Max using the magic bullets has already proven himself. Now comes the decisive moment. Kuno points out to him a pigeon to aim at, but as he fires Agathe appears, crying out that she is the pigeon and falls, struck by his bullet—for she is a pigeon like the other leading ladies of these operas, symbols of divine power. When Max confesses his sin and receives the harsh judgment of the prince, the hermit steps in to insist upon mercy. Samiel reappears, seen only by Kaspar, who dies cursing heaven. They bear his body away to cast like offal into the Wolfsschlund, and the opera ends on a hymn to mercy and heaven's grace. Nothing could be more satisfactory.

But we do have second thoughts. The prince shows mercy so that in a year's time, another span of time, Max and Agathe can marry and he can become the new Chief Forester. No one casts a glance on the death of Kaspar, for everyone knows that something is wrong with him, though they have endured his company for some years. The most successful character, then, is Samiel, for he gains the soul of Kaspar. Though everyone believes in the existence of the Black Hunter no one sees him, and thus no one except the audience acknowledges his victory; but he would have been victorious whether he captured Kaspar's soul or Max's. All that he has lost is the destruction of the society that he had threatened through their despair at the death of Agathe; but the devil does live to work another day. The conclusion of the opera, despite its happy music, does not achieve a conclusion.

We must mention one technical aspect of the opera. Besides being a Gothic tale in which the fantastic and the numinous are at play, the opera is a *Singspiel*. It is not through-composed, as Wagner does in the *Holländer* with its recitatives; the arias, duets, and choruses of *Der Freischütz* and *Der Vampyr* are connected by spoken dialogue, as we find in *Die Zauberflöte* and *Fidelio*; and this dialogue, often profane in nature, operates against the sacred nature of the music as such. But we see a clear development among these operas. *Die Zauberflöte* is lightened by the comic role of Papageno; and earnest as it is in the dungeon of the second act, the first act of *Fidelio* is lightened by the roles of Jaquino and Rocco and by the bitter-sweet comedy (see the quartet "Mir ist so wunderbar"), as Marcellina falls in love with the transvestite Leonore. The world is more somber yet in *Der Freischütz*, but the various hunters' choruses establish a solid world of normality. Weber's opera and Marschner's share public moments of celebration, based on the popular treatments of hunting songs and drinking songs.

Der Freischütz is based upon a superstition restricted to a relatively small area in Germany. The next opera, Heinrich Marschner's 1828 work *Der Vampyr*, composed to a libretto by his brother-in-law Wilhelm August Wohlbrück and based upon John Polidori's "The Vampyre," takes up the famous and widespread superstition of the vampire. As Weber's work had demonstrated, the operatic stage was now very open to librettos that can only be understood from the viewpoint of the fantastic. Rooted in the myth of Orpheus (e.g., Monteverdi and Glück) and elaborated in such works as *Die Zauberflöte* and *Fidelio*, the opera as an art-form often generates works in which a descent to the underworld for the sake of a beloved underpins the narrative. So it is in Marschner's work, though the descent is ironic insofar as it is played out as the threefold descent of the vampire in search of his conquests.

Given these points, one framework for our study is the position the opera holds to other works of horror, for it is very self-conscious. First, there is the immense importance that Goethe's *Faust I*, published in 1808, had assumed in German culture. Then there is the significance in Europe of John Polidori's 1819 novella, which had been frequently adapted for the stage, especially in France where Nodier, Carmouche, and Jouffroy adapted the novella in 1820, and it was that adaptation, perhaps modulated by Heinrich Zxchokke's story "Die Tote Braut" and the translation "Der Vampyr oder die Totenbraut" by Heinrich Ludwig Ritter (Peter), that Wolhbrück took as the basis for his libretto (Mucci, "Heinrich Marschner and His Vampyre"). So popular does the figure of the vampire become that Goethe has the Night Poets and Graveyard Poets excuse themselves from the masque in *Faust II* "weil sie soeben im interessantesten Gespräch mit einem frisch entstandenen Vampyren begriffen seien, woraus eine neue Dichtart sich vielleicht entwickeln könnte" [because at that moment they had become engaged in a most interesting conversation with a recently resurrected vampyre, out of which a new genre could possibly develop] (l. 5298).

From a musical point of view four works are significant to Marschner's work: Spohr's *Faust*, a very loose adaptation of Goethe's drama; *Der Frei-schütz* of course; Mendelssohn's *Die Erste Walpurgisnacht*, a setting of Goethe's 1799 semi-ironic poem; and in 1830 Berlioz's *Symphonie fantastique*. Each of these works at crucial moments becomes a celebration of the demonic (Mucci, "Heinrich Marschner and His Vampyre"). Goethe's poem, which explores the origin of the Walpurgis in pagan celebrations, shows how often "ein Altes, Gegründetes, Beruhigendes durch auftauchende Neuerungen gedrängt, geschoben, verrückt und, wo nicht vertilgt, so doch in den engsten Raum eingesprengt werde" [an old, established, comforting tradition may through emerging novelties be repressed, marginalized, crazed and, where not destroyed, yet confined within the narrowest space], though it may "lodert noch einmal in Glanz und Wahrheit hinauf" [flame into splendor and truth] (Letter to Mendelssohn, 9 September 1831, ctd. in Alt, *Anmerkungen* 16). From within the Walpurgis, demonized by Christianity, pagan truth may shine forth, as it does without distortion in the *Klassische Walpurgisnacht* of *Faust II*. Finally, it is useful to realize that Wagner rewrote an aria in Marschner's opera for his brother-in-law and that the aria that opens Act III influenced the ballad Senta sings (Bauer 22, 576), crucial for the musical voice of that opera. *Der Vampyr* exists within an extended family with a great variety of attitudes towards the demonic.

Given the wealth of literary and musical pressures on Marschner's opera, it is not surprising that it differs greatly from Polidori's novella. The action of the novella moves from contemporary London, where extended scenes establish Lord Ruthven's resemblance to the popular notion of Byron; thus he is a Byronic hero despite Byron's own attempt to distance himself from the novella. The action then moves to Greece and back to England, where Aubry attempts to confront his friend. In Greece Ianthe, Aubry's butterfly soul, tells him "all the supernatural tales of her nurse" (34); thus he learns of vampires and realizes that her words provide "a pretty accurate description of Lord Ruthven" (34). When Ianthe dies, however, Ruthven cares for Aubry and extracts from the young man an oath to say nothing of him in England, dies, and apparently rises again under the light of the moon. Upon Aubry's return to England he finds his sister, whose "step was not that light footing, which strays where'er a butterfly or colour might attract" (39); the narrative insists that she is not his butterfly soul. Nevertheless, as her brother sinks into apparent madness she is attracted by the charms of the reborn Lord Ruthven; and when Aubry dies she yields to the lord and, in the last sentence of the work, "glut[s] the thirst of a VAMPYRE!" (43). Polidori's story has no happy ending.[3]

Nodier's melodrama applies to this loose narrative the Aristotelian unities of space and time. The scene is seventeenth-century Scotland, perhaps because of Byron's Scotch connections, and opens with a prologue in which Ituriel, the spirit of the moon, and Oscar, a prophetic bard and hermit, discuss the nature of vampires, especially that of Lord Rutwen who shall be reduced to nothingness unless within thirty-six hours he can add one more crime to his others by seducing another victim (*Oeuvres Dramatiques* 37–39). The first act introduces first the comic characters Brigitte and Scop (for in this genre of the melodrama comedy finds itself at home), who discuss vampires at length. Then Aubry and his sister Malvina enter; she recounts a dream that touches on the singular nature of the vampire much more eerily than the previous scenes. At the conclusion of the act Lord Rutwen appears to the joy of both brother and sister and is swiftly engaged to her, insisting that they be married before the end of the next day. But hearing that Edgar and his beloved are to be married, he goes with Aubry to that marriage. The second act introduces Oscar once more, who sings a marriage song that praises married love rather than, as the refrain says, "l'amour qui donne la mort" [the love that gives death] (90–92). When Rutwen seduces Edgar's bride Lovette, Edgar shoots him, but in the climax, Rutwen swears Aubry to an oath not to tell Malvina what has happened and faces a rising moon that floods him in light. The last act focuses on the marriage of Malvina and Rutwen, to Aubry's confusion and chagrin, for he now suspects the real nature of Rutwen but feels himself constrained by his oath. Only in the last moment does the striking hour release everyone from the compunction of the monster, Malvina faints, and the vampire is consigned to "le néant! Le néant!" [nothingness! nothingness!] (125).

Wohlbrück's libretto differs from both these works though it depends on them. Like Nodier's melodrama, it profits from the dramatic necessity of compression and acts itself out within twenty-four hours; it may be extravagant, but it obeys the unities. The first act, analogous to Nodier's prologue, provides

---

3. Polidori had taken the name Ruthven from Caroline Lamb's novel *Glenarvon*, a *roman à clef* about her relationship with Byron. She was apparently aware that Lord Grey de Ruthyn had initiated Byron into homosexual relations when the young man was fifteen (Davenport-Hines 244–45). Though neither Polidori nor Marschner were aware of this background, the gay subtext of the vampire figure has reverberated thereafter.

important background, but its owls, witches, and frogs lack the poetic imagination of Nodier's dialogue between the spirit of the moon and the figure of Oscar. The opera opens with Ruthwen's bargain with the Vampire Master for one more year of life if he succeeds in gaining three victims before midnight of the next day (1.2); he hurries to the seduction of Janthe, who returns from Polidori's work with no explanation of her Greek name; when Ruthwen is wounded by Janthe's father, he swears Aubry to silence and regains his strength under the full moon. After a dramatic pause in the second act that presents the main plot of the threat to Malwina, Aubry's beloved (into whom Wolhbrück has transformed Aubry's sister with the ease that the Romantic period exercised with the theme of incest), the action moves in the third act to the seduction of Emmy, Wohlbrück's name for Lovette, an act in which much is invented for the opera. The last act almost concludes with the forced marriage of Malvina to Ruthwen—her parallel to Aubry's serious sister is even clearer in this act—but Aubry at last breaks his oath, the vampyre is struck by lightning, and all ends happily. In purely literary terms the opera would seem to be a prostitution of Polidori's work and an elaboration of Nodier's; but as we shall see it *is* an opera and moves with its own logic.

Let us begin with a structural point. Ever since Goethe had invented his Walpurgis Night for *Faust I*, an attempt to make a spectacle of Faust's experience of evil, the scene had become a model for many works to follow, an integral part of the tradition. Satire and phantasmagoria, Goethe had placed his Walpurgis Night essentially at the penultimate point of *Faust I*, immediately before the heart-rending scene of Gretchen's madness in prison and her redemption. Weber places his demonic scene at the center of the work in the conclusion of Act II, as the protagonist bargains with the devil for a means to win his beloved; but Marschner places his Walpurgis Night at the direct opening of the work. Since Wagner's Dutchman has already sworn himself to the devil, intimations of the Walpurgis Night are scattered throughout that opera. All these works conduct a celebration of evil, "les inexplicables solennités de leurs fêtes nocturnes" [the inexplicable solemnities of their nocturnal revels], as Nodier writes in his psychological fantasia *Smarra* (33). This is the moment in which the irrational and destructive powers are highlighted as the highest good. Beyond that generic purpose, Marschner's scene has a variety of purposes. Besides being a celebration of evil, it introduces us to information crucial to the plot: Wohlbrück's Lord Ruthwen makes a Faustian bargain with the Vampire Master that in return for a year of life he will bring three sacrifices to his master within twenty-four hours. This is the "Frist" so important to Kaspar; the opera plays out within a shorter time than Nodier's melodrama.

This bargain provides the spine of the work, as Ruthwen proceeds to the seductions of Janthe, Emmy, and Malwina. After the seduction of Janthe, the scene introduces Aubry and the bargain he has made in the past with Ruthwen and concludes with the eerie scene in which the wounded Ruthven is held up to the light of the moon, a potent motif recalled from Polidori. Most of the supernatural action of the opera occurs in the opening and conclusion of the first act.

Yet we must not be too certain of this reading. In the complex finale of the second act, accomplished through a quartet and a chorus, the characters differ on how they interpret the metaphorical thunderstorm that arises in their language. Aubry and Malwina regard it as a storm sent from heaven, an expression of anger against the imposition of Ruthwen; but he regards it as a storm sent from hell to support his plans. How is the audience to interpret the storm? At the end of the fourth act a second storm arises that strikes Ruthwen dead with a thunderbolt. According to the stage directions the Vampire Master rises, Ruthwen falls destroyed at his feet to be carried off to the "Hochgelächter der Hölle" [mocking laughter of of hell]; as flames leap up the spectators stand "wie versteinert" [as though turned to stone] and well they might since the scene reminds us strikingly of the conclusion of *Don Giovanni* (4.6). Ruthwen sings, "Gottes Donner wirft mich nieder" [God's thunder casts me down] (4.6), and we certainly feel inclined to accept this moment as a response to our question; but we must not be too confident in believing that the scene confirms our belief in a beneficent supernatural world. Given the presence of the Vampire Master, the action more likely ascribes the thunderbolt to hell than heaven. Thus the opera destabilizes our confidence in the beneficence of the supernatural world. A contemporary critic of Nodier's play objected that "toute la pièce représente indirectement Dieu comme un être faible ou odieux qui abandonne le monde aux génies de l'enfer" [the entire piece indirectly presents God as a weak or hateful being who abandons the world to the spirits of hell] (ctd. in Summers 294). In the prologue Oscar had confessed that a power, "dont il ne nous est pas permis de scruter les arrêts irrévocables" [whose irrevocable judgments we are not allowed to scrutinize] (37), permits monsters to exist. Nodier's father, we recall, had been one of the judges during the Reign of Terror with the guillotine at his disposal.

A number of times Ruthwen refers to the inaudible and invisible presence
of spectres that abet his actions. In the extended climax to the second act he
addresses the "Stimmen der Hölle, die mich umklingen" [voices of hell that
ring around me] (2.6), and as he approaches his seduction of Emmy he invokes "Die ihr mir unsichtbar schwebet, / Jubelt, bald wird sie euer sein"
[you that invisibly surround me, / Rejoice, soon she shall be yours] (3.5). In
the aria that Wagner was to recompose, Aubry sings:

> Doch jetzt umgibt mich dunkle Nacht,
> Ich verzweifl' an Gottes Macht;
> Unheilbringende Dämonen
> Scheinen die Schöpfung nur zu bewohnen.
> [But now dark night surrounds me,
> I despair of God's power;
> Ill-health bearing demons
> Appear to inhabit creation.] (3.10) .

The witches and spirits that vanish after their Walpurgis Night are still palpable presences.

The status of the thunderbolt matters to our understanding of the opera's
genre. Doubtless it is marvelous, as Terry Heller following Todorov understands the category, in that supernatural events are "accepted as normal" by
the characters and by the audience for the sake of the aesthetic effect (11),
though the characters do need to be reminded in Emmy's ballad what a
vampire is. As Carolyn Abbate puts it, this opera like several others of the
period plays out the myth of intrusion, in which something monstrous from
outside our normal life inserts itself shockingly among us (130). But within
the framework of the marvelous and the intrusion, there is at the least a fantastic moment as the audience hesitates between deciding whether heaven
or hell or chance lies behind the thunderbolt (12). This dilemma, moreover,
leads to another dilemma. To believe that the thunderbolt is mere chance
denies that the moral world is supported by the supernatural world and perhaps to deny that the supernatural world exists; but to affirm the supernatural world is also to affirm the possible existence of so threatening a creature
as a vampire. In short, God allows the damned to walk among the living.
Something of this dilemma is acted out in the manuscripts of Nodier's work,
in one of which an "ange des amours" appears in the final tableau, in another of which this figure is the "Ange exterminateur" (126).

The fascination and fear that the vampire excites indicate the basic ambivalence a reader finds in this kind of story. After discussing the congruities
among Todorov's marvelous, Otto's *mysterium tremendum et fascinans* in his
treatment of the numinous, and Freud's *Unheimlich* (14–31), Beth McDonald concludes, "The vampire represents a character caught on the margins of
existence, one who has passed beyond being human but has not crossed the
threshold into death. To be a vampire is to be in a state of suspended transcendence, caught at the edge of both the physical and the spiritual worlds,
an insider and an outsider at once" (36). Just as in *Don Giovanni* we are un-
certain where the moral and artistic center of the work lies because the Don
is so much more imaginatively written than Ottavio, so in Marschner's work
we find that Ruthwen is more powerfully imagined than Aubry.

The numinous character of Lord Ruthwen is established at the end of the
first act when he is lifted up to the "grellheller Mondschein" [dazzling
brightness of the moon] through theatrical machinery. This moment is in
striking contrast to the Walpurgis Night that opens the act. The "Molche,
Kröten, schwarze Katzen, / Kobold, Hexen, Teufelsfratzen" [Salamanders,
frogs, black cats, / Cobolds, witches, devils' pranks] (1.1) that the chorus invokes are all very well, but they are not equal to this quiet moment of Ruthwen's elevation to the moon. We recognize witches and demons, but the
vampire is anomalous, a fashionable parvenu in the realms of the *ungeheim-
lich* and the *heimlich*. Elevated *ex machina*, this vampire finds himself be-
stowed with a mysterious light that seals his numinous power.

One reason for the apparent segregation of the supernatural material to
the beginning of the first act—and we must now agree that this segregation
is only apparent—arises because the structure of the three seductions forces
us once more to consider Mozart and Da Ponte's *Don Giovanni*, which was
often treated as a *Singspiel* in Germany where the recitatives were performed
as spoken dialogue (Meyer 33), a treatment that emphasizes the comic
scences of Leporello and Mazetto. The resemblance is all the closer when we
consider the details of the three seductions. Janthe has been seduced before
she appears on stage; she has yielded to the fascination Ruthwen exerts and
is ready to fall. Emmy meets Ruthwen on stage and only yields to his charm
with great hesitation and fear, despite the fact that she is engaged. She is a
court attendant, not a peasant like Marcellina, who is about to be married to
another peasant; but Emmy is not of Janthe's or Malvina's class, as her familiar name indicates, and she falls easily to Ruthwen's charms in a duet whose
words are reminiscent of "La ci darem la mano." The outcome of this seduc-

tion, however, is very different from the comedy that Da Ponti and Mozart concoct, for like Janthe before her Emmy dies. If it were not for the fortuitous thunderbolt at the end of *Der Vampyr* we would have to consider it a tragedy. How long, we wonder, can Malwina hold out against her father and the chorus as they insist that she marry Ruthwen? She stubbornly refuses, but the conclusion could have been quite different. The conclusion of *Don Giovanni*, on the other hand, assures us that the Don has received a just punishment, since he refuses the opportunity the stone statue offers of repentance. He does have the possibility of repentance if he transgresses his nature; the debate about that opera in part hangs on the question whether the audience is being invited to affirm his Promethean decision or to condemn him. In *Der Vampyr*, however, Ruthwen can simply not repent; free will is no longer available to him.

This comparison of the two operas leads us to another consideration when we realize that the Walpurgis Night and the rape of Donna Anna occur in the same place in the action. Marschner's Walpurgis Night contains no overt sexual materials, but the Walpurgis Night in Goethe does. Marschner's music invites us to this understanding, however; and the action immediately glides into the seduction of Janthe.

The seductions of Janthe and Emmy are a part of the theme that John Mucci considers the major theme of the opera, the arrogance of the aristocracy. "The sacred honor of the upper class," as Mucci describes it with some irony, is subverted by the plot as Ruthwen rather like Don Giovanni or like the Duke in *Le nozze di Figaro* proceeds upon actions that are clearly demonic. And Ruthwen is not simply an idle aristocrat; he is an ambassador to Madrid, with special prerogatives and responsibilities (2.6), to which he appeals for the necessity of his swift marriage, and thereby he assures the unity of the action; the aristocracy is utterly on the side of a monolithic unity. This theme of the power of the aristocracy is, however, by 1827 rather old-hat, whatever the aristocracy may think; various revolutions lie in the offing. Their power had already been laid out in extreme light in the Gothic novels of the Marquis de Sade, and the *droit du seigneur* is simply a melodramatic plot device in *Le nozze di Figaro*.

The theme of the aristocracy is dejeune today, but we cannot ignore how often the democratic American public is seduced by the pageantry of the British monarchy. Perhaps Lovecraft in his gestures to King George touches upon a deep paradox in our being; we hanker after that hieratic order and style, above all style, at the same time that we draw away from it as an evil in our past, but an evil at the moment at which we became what we are. Nothing is as dead as aristocracy; but anything that is not as dead as dead should be is a vampyre—and what is more vampiric in our political arrangements than colonialism?

This theme of the arrogant aristocracy is subsumed into the theme of the Byronic hero. Polidori, of course, was drawing from the model. But so many Byronic heroes are to follow, several of them vampiric in nature like the Count of Monte Cristo with his unnatural pallor that causes a lady to remark that he greatly resembles a vampire—he could indeed be Ruthwen himself "en chair et os" [in flesh and bone] (1.412; ch. 34). Professor Aronnax never needs to interpret the pallor of Captain Nemo, since the Captain obviously spends so much time removed from the sun. Like the vampire he avoids the sun through most of the novel. Like a vampire he seems compelled to commit his phallic acts of violence; and like a vampire he sighs at the end of the work, "Dieu tout-puissant! assez! assez!" [omnipotent God! enough! enough!], yearning for a death or a release from his compulsive acts (610; 2.22). The Byronic hero as vampire has little free will. All these figures represent an erotic, implacable force that masquerades as human but in truth is very little human at all.

This theme of the arrogant aristocracy is reinforced and generalized in the theme of the double, introduced when Lord Ruthwen claims that he is his brother, not the wicked duke that Aubry believes him to be. At first Aubry accepts the double at face-value, then realizes that Ruthwen must be lying. The audience is assured of Ruthwen's identity by a sequence in which everyone including the chorus comments upon the nature of his glance, "Schneidend, wie ein gift'ger Pfeil" [cutting like a poisoned arrow]; for Aubry it is "beeinflussend" [influential] and "zurückhaltend" [restraining], and at the conclusion of this act "Ruthwen bannt Aubry durch seinen Blick" [Ruthwen binds Aubry with his glance] (2.6). A number of times he exercises a mesmeric power that operates upon various levels. As McDonald says, it indicates the numinous power of the vampire, a doorway into a power that cannot be explained in natural terms (4–5). It is also the sign of the vampire's power over the ego of Aubry, who only regains his self-possession when he rejects Lord Ruthwen's command, "Gedenk an deiner Schwur" [think of your oath] (2.6). That imperative, then, is not so much an admonition to adhere to an aristocratic ethos but a ritual command that asserts the vampire's numinous and uncommon power.

The chorus, however, that plays the part of an infatuated herd determined not to understand what is really going on, continues to believe in the double: the man who stands before them must be the brother of Ruthwen, not Ruthwen himself. And thus the fatal significance of the double, an accusation of the selfhood of a character and thereby an accusation of each individual in the audience, continues to bear its meaning upon this stage. The double is abroad and walks among us because we want it.

Now we need to look more closely at the different women in the series of seductions. When Janthe falls into Ruthwen's arms, announcing remorsefully, "Ach, und heimlich konnte ich [meinen Vater] verlaßen, mit Tränen wird er am Morgen sein Kind suchen und nicht finden" [alas, and secretly I could desert {my father}, with tears in the morning he will search for his child and not find her] (1.5), she prepares another major theme of the work, the authority of the patriarchal power and the opposition its children offer. The theme stands out all the more in Janthe who has a mother whom she mentions, but the woman never appears. Every bride in this opera suffers from a tyrannical father. This theme shall remain potent throughout the operas of the nineteenth century, as we can see in such representative works as *Rigoletto* or *Die Walküre*. Janthe's father and Malwina's are tyrants, insistent upon the fulfillment of their dynastic aspirations. Malwina's father, however, shows a few signs of remorse for his tyranny in the last act as Ruthwen presses insistently for the consummation of the marriage before midnight. The further aspect of this theme is that much of the dialogue in *Der Vampyr* works in terms of apprehension and anxiety; its chief topics are the tyranny of the father and the possible existence of the vampyre. So strong is this parallelism that we cannot ignore the possibility that the vampyre is the father or, perhaps more meaningfully, the father is the vampyre.

Despite the parallel that I have outlined between Emmy and Marcellina, they differ in one remarkable way, the ballad of the vampyre that Emmy sings at the beginning of Act III, which she learned from her grandmother. Though it is merely "ein altes Märchen" [an old fairy-tale], the atmosphere of the music with its dragging rhythm returns to the supernatural mode at the beginning of Act I (3.2). Moreover, there is a special illusion when a character in an opera, surrounded by a music that the audience assumes the character cannot hear, asks an on-stage audience to listen to a song (Abbate 166). The song takes the place of the dream that Malvina recounts in the first act of Nodier's play, but it operates upon an *unheimlich* level. With no foreknowledge but perhaps with an unconscious premonition, Emmy sings what shall happen to her by the end of the act: the "bleiche Mann" [pale man] with remarkable eyes shall lead the girl away, both the girl in the ballad whose mother warns her so carefully and Emmy who sings the song but who has no mother to warn her. And as she concludes, the chorus repeats her refrain: "Nun geht sie selber, glaubt es mir, / Umher als grausiger Vampyr!" [Now she herself, believe me, goes / Around as a gruesome vampire!] (3.2). As the music trails away, Ruthwen enters and surprises them. Their terror, however, they attribute to their surprise, and very soon Emmy asks, with a touch of coquetterie that shall destroy her, "Also meinetwegen seid Ihr gekommen, gnädiger Herr?" [so you have come on my account, Lord?] (3.2). With ease he assumes his role as his suppositious brother, the lord of the castle, with all the graces attendant thereon. The ballad, then, maintains an ironic distance upon the action that the action itself belies. The vampire is not "ein altes Märchen." He is a real and present danger in the contemporary world.

Lord Ruthwen is so confident of his power that in a startling aria in this same act he brazenly reveals himself to Aubry:

> Nun gehst du, ein grausiger Leichnam, einher,
> 　　　Bestimmt, dich vom Blute Derer zu nähren,
> 　　　Die dich am meisten lieben und ehren.
> [Now you walk about, a gruesome corpse,
> 　　　Fated, to nourish yourself on the blood of those
> 　　　Who love and honor you most.] (3.9)

This is a family affair. He drinks the blood of his wife, sons, and daughters. No hope exists for him, for he is compelled to perform these acts that are a remarkable complex of violent incest: "Du mußt es saugen, das teure Blut" [you must imbibe it, the precious blood] (3.9). After this confession, however, he still possesses the power that the music bestows to defy Aubry to make any use of the confession. He is abject and defiant.

Ruthwen's compulsions are connected to a theme already suggested, the way in which the supernatural threat of hell pervades the *mise en scène*. Not only through the asides of Lord Ruthwen, this spiritual presence manifests itself in an apparently innocuous drinking song, Marschner's version of a folksong that is one of the innovations of the opera, reminiscent of Kaspar's song in *Der Freischütz* that he admits is a "Schelmenliedlein" [a little song of a rascal] (1.5). The only reprimand the singers in *Der Vampyr* receive is from a wife who complains they are drinking too much. Their song begins:

Im Herbst, da muß man trinken!
Da ist die rechte Zeit;
Da reift uns ja der Traube Blut
Und dabei schmacht der Wein so gut;
In Herbst, da muß man trinken!
[In Fall you have to drink!
That is the right time;
The blood of the grape ripens then for us;
That's when the wine tastes really good!
In Fall you have to drink!] (2.1)

Thereafter the stanzas proceed, taking the audience through the four sea-
sons with the refrain, "Im Sommer [Summer, Winter, and Spring] muß man
trinken." There is no escape: "The blood warms us. [. . .] The blood cools us.
[. . .] The blood refreshes us." In this rollicking ballad, sung by three happy
drunkards, there is no escape from the cycle of blood. Since the blood of the
wine is emphasized in these four stanzas, we cannot help but compare this
jolly but obsessive drinking to the drinking of the vampyre, who must drink.
Muß implies not only a *have to* but a *compulsion*, a drive that permeates the
opera from the Walpurgis Night upon which the curtain rises to the thunderbolt at which it falls. But whether that thunderbolt is a *deus ex machina* or
a *diabolus ex machina*, who shall say?

But though this song is one of the strengths of the opera, it also indicates
one of the opera's weaknesses. Together with Emmy's "altes Märchen," her
ballad of the vampire, and Ruthwen's furious confession that also occurs in
the third act, it forms a literary climax with which the ensembles of the last
act, energetic as they are, cannot compete. The third act is the peak of the
work. Thus the structure of *Der Vampyr* is flawed in a way that Nodier's
melodrama is not, but despite that flaw it represents a remarkable moment
in the history of the vampire. Its ironies and uncertainties make it a work
that must be considered beside such later classics as "Carmilla" and *Dracula*.

By his own admission Wagner had the examples of Weber and Marschner
already in mind when he wrote and composed *Die Feen*, his first opera (1.80).
Der Freischütz was based upon a superstition that Weber was probably familiar
with from an early age, *Der Vampyr* upon Nodier's reworking of Polidori's novella. The material of *Der Fliegende Holländer* is more complex. Wagner knew
of the story from Heinrich Heine, but its landscape, the inescapable, tumultuous ocean, was first brought home to him in a storm crossing from Riga to

England at a time when his relationship with his art and with his wife was in jeopardy. The ship was the *Thetis*, with a figurehead of the goddess raising her arms to heaven in supplication for the lives of sailors (Hansen 87). "Hier," Wagner wrote, "tauchte mir der 'Fliegende Holländer' wieder auf: an meiner eigenen Lage gewann er Seelenkraft; an den Stürmen, den Wasserwogen, dem nordischen Felsenstrande und dem Schiffgetreibe, Physiognomie und Farbe" [Here the "Flying Dutchman" once more emerged for me: from my own situation it won psychic power; from the storms, the waves, the northern coasts and tossing of the ship physiognomy and color] (1.88). We seldom think of Wagner as a local colorist, but he needed the storm to realize the thematic possibilities that Heine had elaborated in his satiric recasting of the story; it was Heine who added the seventh year encounter with a woman dedicated to the Dutchman's salvation, a theme Wagner found congenial for his purposes in many of the operas he was to write thereafter. At this point in his memoir Heine drops away, though once Wagner had arrived in Paris he met Heine and they became friends, for Heine was one of those people you had to meet (Hansen 94–96); but now for Wagner the story of the Dutchman became an archetypal folk legend, very similar to both the story of Odysseus and the story of the Wandering Jew (1.93–95). Musically and thematically, this was the opera in which Wagner became Wagner.

Nevertheless, he could not become Wagner without this spiritual father Heine, a Jew who had submitted to baptism for advancement; but Wagner was very good at dropping friends once their usefulness was at an end. We recall the old baseless rumor that Wagner's father was Jewish and Adorno's more nuanced comment that Wagner may have portrayed his own fears of the significance of his appearance, his large head and slight stature, in his description of Mime in *Siegfried* (*In Search* 16–17)[4]; these fears seem all the more justified when we consider that he was born in the Jewish Quarter of Leipzig (May 12). In his essay *Das Judentum in der Musik* he concludes in the penultimate paragraph by excoriating Heine, announcing that "er war das Gewissen des Judentums, wie das Judentum das üble Gewissen unsrer modernen Zivilisation ist" [he was the conscience of Jewry, just as Jewry was the bad conscience of our modern civilization] (13.29); but then, in an odd anticlimax, he writes:

---

4. Some commentators find the notion that Mime is an anti-Semitic caricature inexplicable; but though Mime, his brother Alberich, and Alberich's son Hagen are dramatically compelling characters, I think that the details of the anti-Semitic code are too apparent to be denied (Žižek xiii–xv).

Noch einen Juden haben wir zu nennen, der unter uns als Schriftsteller auftrat. Aus seiner Sonderstellung als Jude trat er Erlösung suchend unter uns: er fand sie nicht and mußte sich bewußt werden, daß er sie nur mit auch unsrer Erlösung zu wahrhaften Menschen finden können würde. Gemeinschaftlich mit uns Mensch werden, heißt für den Juden aber zu allernächst soviel als: aufhören, Jude zu sein. Börne hatte dies efüllt. Aber gerade Börne lehrt auch, wie diese Erlösung nicht in Behagen und gleichgültig kalter Bequemlichkeit erreicht werden kann, sondern daß sie, wie uns, Schweiß, Not, Ängste und Fülle des Leidens und Schmerzes kostet. Nehmt rücksichtslos an diesem, durch Selbstvernichtung wiedergebärenden Erlösungswerke teil, so sind wir einig und ununterschieden! Aber bedenkt, daß nur eines eure Erlösung von dem auf euch lastenden Fluche sein kann: die Erlösung Ahasvers,—der Untergang! [We have one more Jew to mention who appears among us as an author. Out of his perculiar position as a Jew he comes among us seeking redemption {Erlösung}: he doesn't find it and becomes aware that he will only be able to find it with our redemption to true men. Becoming a man in society with us however means to the Jew just as much as to cease being a Jew. Börne has fulfilled this. But immediately Börne also learned that this redemption cannot be achieved in contentment and an indifferent cold complacence but that it costs, as it does us, sweat, need, anxiety, and an abundance of sorrow and pain. Take part recklessly in this work of redemption that gives rebirth through self-destruction, then we are agreed with no difference between us. But remember that your redemption from the heavy curse upon you can only be the redemption of Ahasuerus, shipwreck and ruin!] (13.29)

Though this breathtaking passage is ostensibly about Ludwig Börne, a friend with whom Heine had quarreled, Wagner's outline of his career closely approximates Heine's, and the reference to Ahasuerus returns us not only to the medieval legend of the Wandering Jew but to Heine's version of the Flying Dutchman and Wagner's version in which the protagonist, yearning so desperately for the mercy of that repeated word "Erlösung," literally "goes under" in a shipwreck. The Dutchman, however, unlike Heine and Börne after his "Untergang" rises with Senta into a supernatural light.

The opera opens with a storm in the overture whose nature is not specified until we learn in the ballad that Senta sings in the second act how connected its motif is with the agony of the Dutchman. This overture has something of the shape of the overture to *Der Freischütz;* the archetypal storm, which is associated with the sea that the Dutchman combats and with himself, occupies most of the overture, alternating with the music of some of the songs, until the music of redemption, that soars in a very different color, concludes it. The first act begins with a purely natural heaving storm as the ship of a merchantman, Daland, comes ashore not far from his home in Norway. Telling the Helmsman to keep a good watch he goes below. Left by himself the Helmsman sings the first song that Wagner employs as local color, a simple song such as a sailor might sing of longing for the beloved and the promise of a gift he shall bring her, a scene in small of the Dutchman's own condition. Falling asleep the Helmsman makes way for the storm motif of the overture and the appearance of the spectral ship and its captain. A pale man in black clothes, he steps on land and begins his first aria, a meditation upon his condition that concludes in this nihilistic appeal:

> Wann alle Toten auferstehn,
> dann werde ich in Nichts vergehn.
> Ihr Welten, endet euren Lauf!
> Ew'ge Vernichtung, nimm mich auf!
> [When all the dead rise up
> I will perish in nothingness.
> You worlds, cease in your tracks!
> Eternal destruction, receive me!] (1.2)

Let us here confess to a problem that we have. The phrase "der fliegende Holländer" refers both to the ship and to the man who possesses no name in the opera. Having a name is a rather touchy affair in Wagner's works. Lohengrin only announces his name under pressure in the last act, Siegmund has good reason to call himself Wehwalt until his sister sings out his name in the highest register at the end of the act; Parsifal does not know his name until Kundry reveals it in the second act of Wagner's last opera; and her actual name is something of a problem also—Klingsor addresses her as with various names, but the first is "Namelose" [nameless] (2.1). Wagner is aware of the magical nature of a name, its close association to the person who bears it for good or ill and the mistake that person might make if the name is pronounced and thus its power depart. In this opera Wagner has made a conscious choice to suppress the protagonist's name that in the tradition is Vanderdecken, but clearly the statement "Vanderdecken heiß' ich!" will simply not fly. The only name he has, "der fliegende Holländer," is something of an oxymoron, for it confesses that he belongs to Holland, the hollow land or low land, referring physically to the fact that the Netherlands lie beneath sea level, at the same time that it asserts that he flies. He is very swift, uncatchable, and not to be outraced, someone who literally flies and belongs to the sky, but also someone who is of the earth and the hollow earth at that. Full of energy he is also empty. It is no wonder that this walking contradiction is nameless. The other point to this name, the identification of the protagonist with Holland, shall be made more interesting later. For now let us note that the Jews of Europe found their securest home in the tolerance of the Netherlands. The synagogue was safe in Amsterdam and The Hague and provided rich subjects to Rembrandt's portraits. The Dutchman is a distant cousin to Spinoza.

This nameless man, then, deracinated but Dutch, who is as much his ship as himself and who reserves the power of his name throughout the opera, steps upon land, potent as Lovecraft writes in his Dutchman's breeches and his insolent bloodroot (*DH* 63), announcing "Die Frist ist um" [the span of time is up] (1.2). Once more, as in *Der Freischütz* and *Der Vampyr*, a certain span of time, so many years no more no less, so many bullets, so many hours, is connected with a bargain. This bargain, however, as we learn from Senta's account in the second act, is utterly reckless and perhaps involuntary, spoken by a man not aware that the devil will take him at his word. Despite these difficulties, the audience of the first performances of the opera recognized him as the Byronic hero, pale in black clothes, with something of an air of the vampire about him, an aspect of his character that the plot develops, for he is searching for the one woman, out of so many that he has encountered, who will die for him, as at the end of the opera Senta does; she is redeemed, yes, but the other women who could not be true are damned (May 32).

Carl Dahlhaus analyzes the initial monologue into three parts, an account of past history, a prayer for release, and an outburst of despair, but claims that it has no immediate cause (29). This is true and not true; when the nameless man steps out of his ship he steps out of a state of eternity in which the ship runs back and forth across the oceans with no goal except endurance until the time has come once more, that moment when "die Frist is um," to encounter the chance on land that someone may love him; he has not, however, truly entered time until he meets Daland and learns that the man has a daughter; it is the social life of the land that implies time as we know it. The monologue arises in a place between eternity and time. He inhabits the space of the daemons that exist between immortality and mortality.

Time is the place of satire. The conversation between the Dutchman and Daland satirizes the greed of Senta's father, who is only too ready to offer his daughter to this unknown man for the sake of the treasures that the man orders his crew to produce from the bowels of their ship. The lyricism of the Helmsman is here debased. The music is jaunty, but the fact of the transaction is transparent; and so with a good wind behind them they depart for

Daland's home and the completion of the bargain.

We have of course realized in this first act that the Dutchman is a version of Ahasuerus, the man who goes under many names but who has committed the same blasphemous act of urging Jesus, the cross on his back, to go a bit faster and not rest, to receive the answer, "I am going, and you will wait until I return" (Anderson 19). So the man is condemned to live throughout human history and observe its eternal futility. We should add, however, that there are two perspectives upon his meaning, preserved in the German name of the legend, *der ewige Jude*, and the French name, *le juif errant*. The one name asserts his eternity, his inability to escape his fate and society's inability to escape him; this version, then, is open to a variety of anti-Semitic fantasies. The other name asserts his wandering fate, passing through all human cultures and observing their various despairs (Anderson 54). One minor version of the legend is appropriate to the moment in which the Dutchman offers Daland great treasure, for Ahasuerus, under whatever name, often has the intuitive gift of pointing out where hidden treasure lies, whether for good or ill (Anderson 27–28). As far as a specific model of the Dutchman's first aria is concerned, we should probably go to Christian Schubart's rhapsody, "Der ewige Jude," in which Ahasuerus rages about his inability to find death until, at the end of the poem, an angel says to him, "Gott zürnt nicht ewig" [God is not angry forever], and promises him forgiveness; this very striking reversal to the legend undoubtedly influenced both Heine's playful version of the Dutchman and Wagner's treatment.

The second act opens in Daland's home where the women are spinning, an archetypal scene in German drama, and one that establishes like the choruses in *Der Freischütz* and *Der Vampyr* the local color. One the other hand, the repeated address in this chorus to the "gutes Rädchen" [good wheel] (2.1) may point at the same theme as the drinking song in *Der Vampyr*, the circular nature of time, which is a very different matter from the Dutchman's experience of time as a "Frist." Senta, however, takes no part in their song. She is already abstracted from this social life, looking at a painting on the wall in which the Dutchman is delineated exactly as the audience has seen him in the first act, pale in black clothes. The center of this act, indeed the center of the opera, is Senta's ballad of the Flying Dutchman, which according to Wagner was the first music that he wrote for the work. It contains that motive that we have already wondered at, whether ocean or Dutchman, and the other motive associated with the *Erlösung* music at the end of the opera. It also establishes Senta as already dedicated to the story of the Dutchman; she is for him, on his side, before she ever learns that the legend is true. Her feeling of its truth is confirmed by her suitor Erik who tells her of his dream in which her father brings home a man, pale in black clothes, at whose feet she falls and then rises to kiss him passionately. At this moment in Erik's account that she elaborates as he tells it the man himself, pale and in black clothes, walks through the door, accompanied by her father who rather heartily introduces them and then bows out; Erik has hopelessly rushed out earlier. The act concludes in a long and complex duet in which we cannot say that the Dutchman or Senta speak to each other; rather, they conduct a common meditation upon their experience of meeting, he with the certainty that this is not so much love as redemption, she with the certainty that a great magic has brought her to this act of mercy that means redemption for him.

Let us pause to consider certain words that the Dutchman and Senta use to describe this redemption. In his first aria he calls it his *Heil*, his health or wholeness or salvation; he is wounded. Senta calls it *Erlösung*, that has a cognate in the English word "release"; he needs to be untied from his unhappy state, he needs deliverance. Wagner came to regard this word from the standpoint of Buddhism, in which the release from the illusions of the world is the great goal. As Bryan Magee describes the situation of the Dutchman in this light, he "is motivated chiefly by the desire to escape from his prolonged and chain-like existence" (178).

The third act opens on a *gemütlich* scene in which the sailors of Daland's ship are making merry with the women of the town passing the bottles around while next to their ship looms the Dutchman's ship, maintaining a stubborn silence despite the invitations of the joint chorus to join in the festivities and despite the sympathy the women express for their condition. When the women leave, however, the darkness spreads from the ship and a threatening chorus warns their captain that he must either be lucky with this girl or suffer his fate once more; and they seem quite confident that he shall fail. This scene, another supernatural moment in the play in which evil is celebrated, opens a difficult question. It is all very well to accept the fate of the Dutchman, given his arrogant gesture and defiance of the devil—but why do the members of the crew suffer this fate of eternal wandering if they have in no way taken part in his gesture? We have no immediate answer to this question as far as Wagner's libretto is concerned.

Keeping in mind the theme of the Wandering Jew, let us turn to Coleridge's *The Rime of the Ancient Mariner* because it directly addresses this problem. At first the crew believe that the Mariner's attack on the albatross has saved them from the threat of the ice, so they say that what he has done is quite right; later, when they find themselves becalmed beneath the punishing sun, they say that what he has done is quite wrong. They are moral opportunists; and something of the same can be said of the Dutchman's crew. Secure in their own power as we can see when they drive away Daland's people, they mock their captain's chances of ever finding a woman who will be true to him. They would never have had the temerity to challenge the devil as he had done, but they have sufficient temerity to challenge women's fidelity. So they were damned before the captain ever committed the trespass for which he suffers.

After this scene the opera rushes to its conclusion in another confrontation between Senta and Erik that convinces the Dutchman she does not love him. He steps aboard his ship once more, announces that he is indeed the flying Dutchman, that he is indeed the cursed man she thought him, and gives the order to set out once more. But she will not accept his departure, leaping into the sea with the words that she is true to death. A cataclysm sinks his ship, and she and he are seen in the distance, in a bright light, ascending into the sky. The music that concluded the overture and concluded Senta's ballad now concludes the last act.

A number of comments need to be made about particular themes in the opera. First, the opera picks up the conviction important to the Romantics and to Lovecraft that dreams are important to a global notion of reality. When the Helmsman falls asleep the Dutchman arrives on the winds of the storm. In the second act, when Erik tells Senta of his dream in which he sees her collapse in the arms of the Dutchman, the Dutchman walks through the door with Daland. In the third act the crew of the Dutchman's ship remain stubbornly asleep, but when they awake the storm awakes also. Put in another way, the opening monologue "Der Frist ist um," Senta's ballad, and the sailors' chorus are the supernatural centers of the three acts. The Dutchman's aria, however, is introduced by the Helmsman's simple song "Mit Gewitter und Sturm," which implicitly introduces the erotic element of the Dutchman's fate and which thus forms an integral part of it. From another aspect we can consider the appearance of the Dutchman's ship and his aria the oneiric dark side of the Helmsman's imagination as he falls asleep. In the chorus of the third act the crew of the Dutchman's ship cannot appear until after the women depart; and a dread of women on behalf of the supernatural is a theme in the three operas.

II

"Ne deeth, allas! ne wol nat han my lyf;
Thus walke I, lyk a restelees caityf,
And on the ground, which is my modres gate,
I knokke with my staf, bothe erly and late,
And seye, 'leve moder, leet me in!
Lo, how I vanish, flesh, and blood, and skin!
Allas! whan shul my bones been at reste?'"
(Chaucer, *The Pardoner's Tale* 727–33)

One of the technical similarities between Lovecraft's works and Wagner's is the leitmotif, which we meet also in Weber's musical treatment of Samiel's appearances.. This term has come to indicate several ways by which a musical phrase may function in an opera, and there is no doubt that Wagner's practice in *Der Fliegende Holländer* is relatively primitive when compared to his later practice, but he was already using a form of it in *Das Liebesverbot*. Despite, however, the extent to which Lovecraft employs the leitmotif, we should also note that several modernists are also influenced by Wagner in their various ways; such authors as Eliot, Joyce, Lawrence, and Mann all employed the leitmotif, which thus became a part of the cultural atmosphere after Wagner's work. Lovecraft is one of many in this regard.

The leitmotif can function in a variety of ways. It may be a mere mnemonic, reminding the audience of a previous occurrence of an audial or verbal gesture; as such it may function as an intensive or atmospheric device, probably the real effect of the motif that accompanies Samiel. More interestingly, when it is varied it calls attention to the difference between itself and earlier occurrences, sometimes asking the audience to pay attention to the moral change; this use shades into its establishment of major themes. In addition, it may function as a structural device that overarches the chronological time of the work and binds it into one complex significance. We should also note that in a verbal text it may be difficult to distinguish between the leitmotif and the rhetorical figure of anaphora; the main difference would seem to be that anaphora works within a relatively short passage, whereas the leitmotif may well occur throughout the work, in Wagner's *Ring* through some fifteen hours of the performance.

Lovecraft's leitmotif serves a variety of purposes. Often it is simply the anaphora that Lovecraft had learned from his eighteenth-century masters. Most of the time when it is used extensively throughout the work it is a question of atmosphere, but his atmospherics may serve other purposes as well. The leitmotifs in "The Hound" are structural and thematic, as well as nods to *The Hound of the Baskervilles*. In *The Case of Charles Dexter Ward* the delicate placing of the phrase "fine bluish-grey dust" early in the first part, at the end of the third part, and at the end of the story (MM 109, 174, 234) nicely shapes the narrative. In "The Call of Cthulhu" the various descriptions of the creature serve both moral and thematic ends, and the repetition of various words connected with "piece" is a careful indication of the theme of the piecemeal. In "The Music of Erich Zann" the description of him as a satyr serves as we have seen various purposes, descriptive but also thematic, mirroring him in the narrator. In "The Colour out of Space" the phrase "the blasted heath" establishes a great range of thematic concerns as we have seen. The usefulness of the leitmotif lies in its variety of purposes that refuse to lull the reader into any complacence.

Before we turn to the conflicts in Lovecraft's stories let us examine the group experiences that they record. In the operas the chorus represents a communal normality, the normal appetites of nourishment, sexuality, and advancement; they are often not aware of what is happening before them, but as best they can they comment and encourage the protagonists. The composers are fond of them but treat them with some irony. That is certainly the attitude that Lovecraft adopts toward the community in "The Lurking Fear," composed of squatters who are "simple animals, [. . .] gently descending the evolutionary scale because of their unfortunate ancestry and stultifying isolation" (DH 186). They are an early study in a communal backwoods decadence that Lovecraft studies in greater detail in "The Dunwich Horror," as we have already seen in the dramatic soliloquies he invents for them; but in that story this community proves to some extent capable of handling the danger that threatens them once they are given a capable leader. Despite these clear limitations, however, in "The Outsider" the community that the protagonist finds in the castle represents everything desirable, though after it runs from him he finds a more congenial community in the company of the ghouls. In "The Rats in the Walls" the English community that the protagonist did approach rejects him also, not because of his appearance but because of the house he represents; and they do not turn out to be wrong in their judgment.

The Case of Charles Dexter Ward delineates two Providence communities, one in 1770 and one in 1926, and the contrast is strong, for the normative community of pre-Revolutionary days proves very capable of defeating, at

least for a time, the danger that threatens them; but in the days of a confident democracy only one man stands against the danger and defeats it. The
normative community, of course, is subject to complaisance, as we can see in
"Pickman's Model" in which the members of the Art Club, the people of
Newbury Street, Back Bay, and Beacon Hill, cut Pickman; but cutting a man
like that who can simply retire to the slums of the North End and restore
himself is not an effective strategy. The various communities in "The Call of
Cthulhu" are effective within a certain sphere, especially the Louisiana police led by Inspector Legrasse. The backwoods squatters, however, are utterly
ineffective; but the community of Cthulhu, mongrel and decadent as it are,
clearly represents an energy that may well achieve its goals someday in an
apocalypse that threatens the end of time. This is not a normative community at all, whether in values or in discourse. In "The Shadow over
Innsmouth" we find Lovecraft's most detailed treatment of this anormative
community, which at first is described as though it were simply another version of the decadent, ineffectual community but is revealed as something
much more threatening and exciting, so much so that at the conclusion of
the story the narrator elects to join it.

One of the striking touches in "The Colour out of Space" is the isolation of
the Gardners that is rendered all the more extreme by the presence of the
community in Arkham to the east, just far enough away to have no comprehension of the sufferings of the Gardners until it is too late. At the beginning of
the story the three wise scientists come from Arkham to investigate the thing
that has befallen the Gardners, but despite their technologies and theories they
have nothing to say; theory can go only so far. At the end of the story six men
come to the farm, led by a seventh, Ammi; they are three police officers, "the
coroner, the medical examiner, and the veterinary" (DH 72), once more the
professionals who represent the best in the community; and they fail even more
spectacularly to comprehend what has happened. In Lovecraft the normative
community is well-meaning and deserving of salvation, but hopeless.

We need to observe one other aspect of all these communities. Eric in
Der Fliegende Holländer, Aubry in Der Vampyr, and Ännchen in Der Freischütz argue that a love aimed at the other world should not and does not
exist. The normative community supports the Sosein of the world and refuses
to admit the possibility that any other world might exist. In Lovecraft, then,
the shock is considerable when another world and another geometry invades
the flat surface upon which we Euclidian creatures are accustomed to live.

Thereafter the *Sosein* is highly suspect; but whether a love capable of salvation exists is a totally different problem.

The Dutchman has sworn an oath that commits him to an eternal conflict with the storming waters. There are a few storms in Lovecraft's work, for instance before the revelation of Cthulhu, but most of the time his ocean landscapes are treacherously placid. Often in the tradition the ocean is the emblem of chaos. W. H. Auden draws a close comparison between the ocean and the desert and argues that in most Romantic literature "the sea is the real situation and the voyage is the true condition of man" (12). Only love, a love that totally believes in the existence of the beloved and rescues him from nonexistence can equal and overcome the existence that the audience's perception—a touch of Berkeley—grants him. Is there anything in Lovecraft comparable to that love and perception? Yes, a reader perceiving his characters; we are the audience of this desolation, maintaining these characters and participating in their horror. But does love exist as a redemptive agent? We have investigated the presence of erotic mania in the stories, but that is a very different thing from *Erlösung*, whether we understand it in the sense of *Der Freischütz* or in the sense of *Der Fliegende Holländer*; *Erlösung* is not demonic. No, love as a redemptive agent does not exist in Lovecraft's stories, but neither does its opposite, hatred—worse than that, we are faced by the universe's indifference. If Senta did not exist, nor the audience, only the storming waters would exist, the symbol of non-existence, and no land, a state that the audience can only imagine at some remove. Lovecraft, however, takes this imagery one step further when he imagines an ocean whose bed has lifted above the waves to the light of day. If the storming waters are a symbol of non-existence, then this landscape deepens its meaning into a state beyond non-existence, that upon which non-existence depends, the undifferentiated muck of the ocean abyss. We shall have more to say about this in our last chapter, in which this non-existence invades our individual humanity.

To these comments we should add that in the operas and in Lovecraft there is one further emblem of chaos, the forest. This is most evident in *Der Freischütz* because it is so faithful to its *Märchen* background in which the forest often appears as the site of the great threat, though it also appears as the place of great allure. In Lovecraft we see the forest functioning in this way first in "The Picture in the House," which associates its analysis of Puritans with the backwoods in which they live isolated (*DH* 117). This imagery is announced clearly in the opening paragraph of "The Dunwich Horror":

"The trees of the frequent forest belts seem too large, and the wild weeds, brambles, and grasses attain a luxuriance not often found in settled regions. At the same time the planted fields appear singularly few and barren" (*DH* 156). This language recurs in "The Colour out of Space," though in that story the luxuriance of the forest becomes the false luxuriance of the fields that turn into barren dust. The forest also exerts an active presence in "The Whisperer in Darkness" and "The Thing on the Doorstep." The world that the Puritans attempted to tame is always on the verge, like Birnam Wood, to march back upon the tidy fields.

Each of the operas is concerned with a *Frist*, a firmly appointed time in which something will happen and at the end of which something else shall happen. The word is closely related to the English word "first," and both lie within the lexical range of the words connected with travel, such as "fare" (Pokorny 813). It may imply a set space of time, it may also imply a delay, or even more it may imply a grace. Karl Barth uses the word as an indication of each individual's given and appointed time that moves from a specific birth to a specific death; the *Frist* is the shape and span of an individual's life, to be used an individual decides (3/2.672). In the economy of heaven each person has only so much time, no more, no less, a span of time available only to the God who created it out of his eternity. Kaspar's anxiety for his *Frist* (2.5), yea so many days and no more, is echoed in *Der Vampyr* and in *Der Fliegende Holländer*, in which the first aria of the protagonist begins portentously "Der Frist ist um" (1.1). The time is up, the seven years are past, and the Dutchman once more receives the grace to set his foot on land. Is there an anxiety of time in Lovecraft? Given our anxieties, it is difficult to agree with Barth when he insists, "Es gibt keinen Gott Kronos" [there is no god Kronos] (3/2.547), a false, idolatrous god who usurps the place of the God who dwells in eternity; for many people the passage of chronological time is inexorable.

The time given the Dutchman is the same as that given Ahasuerus and Kundry. Like every other person he is born and grows up, and until the moment of his dire mistake he leads a presumptively normal life; but at that moment his life breaks off from normality. We only know the story of his act from Senta's ballad: trying to round a cape in a storm he swears, "In Ewigkeit laß ich nicht ab!" [For all of eternity I will not stop trying!] (2.1). He has attempted to break the boundaries of the time given him. We each of us, in Barth's analysis, attempt to do this, naturally desirous of a life that is "unergründlich und unerschöpflich" [bottomless and inexhaustible], but we can only achieve it through our relationship with God and our neighbor (3/2.673).

We shake at the bars of our prison in time, boundaries that we conceive of as bars that are the conditions through which we exist as subjects and individuals (3/2.683–87). When the Dutchman attempts to achieve such a life without conditions he projects a god that is a devil; and thereby the given time is disarticulated into a mere chronological time with none of the density it might otherwise have achieved; once more Kronos is the god of our linear, thin time. Unlike every other person, the Dutchman finds his past increasing daily and out of all bounds to contain. Though he is still human—he eats and drinks and sleeps and desires—the past that he remembers and forgets makes the life he leads inhuman: little wonder that a person who leads that life may become as unbalanced as Kundry in *Parsifal* does. With that in mind we can ask whether Joseph Curwen is actually sane and whether the officials in Providence, though they cannot recognize who or what he is, may have done well to incarcerate him in the asylum. Certain other people have also questioned the sanity of the old man in "The Picture in the House," who does age but who like Curwen has this great amount of time behind him; on the other hand, Curwen goes out among people, a well-respected man if only as a merchant, whereas the old man apparently stays in his ramshackle house and lets his food come to him, so all his memories are in the story effectively of the far past. Curwen has no interest in the past, except for his connections with those old friends with whom he exchanges formulae and essential salts.

The future that the Dutchman expects is very different from that of human experience, for every mortal expects that he or she will die, perhaps rather soon by accident, perhaps in a few more years indicated by the biblical three-score years and ten. Though according to Barth that time is allotted, appointed, and determinate, we do not know the when or how of our death, only that we are approaching it day by day. We may not be truly convinced of that death in our gut, but we politely acquiesce in its probability. But for Ahasuerus and the Dutchman, as the incomprehensible years stretch behind them the horror of eternity stretches before them, an eternity that the Dutchman had arrogated for himself in his oath. This is not the state that Kaspar or Lord Ruthwen suffers, whose lives are ladled out in dribs and drabs as they bargain year after year for the *Frist* that they had been offered and that still stands appointed.

The real anxiety about time for Lovecraft is to be found in "The Shadow out of Time," for if the situation of its narrator Nathaniel Peaslee is indeed out of time, too late, with no more time available, it is also a mere shadow. "Life's but a walking shadow," Macbeth complains tendentiously as he approaches the conclusion of his allotted *Frist* (5.5.23). Much more pressingly history becomes not simply a shadow to Peaslee; it becomes transparent to his prophetic mania. Whatever has happened to Peaslee—and there is some question about that—it is striking that several people question his sanity; and doubtless he takes up psychology and anthropology because of his own anxiety on that point. He loses time; through no fault of his own he finds himself literally abstracted from his time, the time that he thought he possessed, which is of course our time too, but given nothing but an ambiguous insight to repay him for that loss, though of course on some level of personality unavailable to him he takes part in a time much more spacious than we can imagine or grasp. It is as though, without our being able to be conscious of it, the human condition had indeed tapped into a space and time "unergründlich und unerschöpflich." That space and time, however, if it is indeed a space and time that possesses its own authenticity and authority, becomes in his own circumscribed time a language that is clumsy, certainly not persuasive; he is babbling out of his time in the same way that Joseph Curwen does in the 1920s. Both of them speak the same alien tongue that was to alienate some of Lovecraft's readers after his death. Peaslee, however, much more cast out of his own time than Lovecraft ever was, must insist upon his experience on faith until he meets his own hand on the manuscript.

We cannot lose sight of that moment in *Der Freischütz* and *Der Fliegende Holländer* in which a portrait takes part in the action. In the case of Weber's opera the portrait insists upon falling, demanding that Agathe and Ännchen pay attention to the moral world around them that is about to step out of the *Sosein* world. In the case of Wagner's opera the portrait stands stiff and obdurate in its own right, but beneath it the Dutchman steps out, the image of himself in the portrait. No one steps out of a portrait, but as the epigraph from *Ruddigore* suggests, this is no peculiar tropos. On the contrary, the operas rationalize a moment inherent in the imagery of the portrait and mirror, in which it is not simply the portrait that is remarkable but the space that the painter has created and the space in which the figure lives, that illusion of a three-dimensional space. Let us now think of that space as something peculiar to the person, a space that the person brings with him as he steps out of the frame, or at the least, in the case of *Der Freischütz*, as a space that is already a potent possession of the person in the frame. Though Kuno hangs upon the wall with the heads of the deer that he and his descendents have killed, with no detail specified, he himself still possesses a life that is represented by the spatiality of the portrait. The portrait of the Dutchman in the second act has a bit more detail. It is "das Bildnis eines bleichen Mannes mit dunklem Barte und in schwarzer spanischer Tracht" [the picture of a pale man with a dark beard and in black Spanish garb] (2.2). The Spanish garb gives the painting that historical depth that it might otherwise lose. In both cases this is the terrible attraction of paintings that they share with mirrors, the illusion of a space that does not exist and that lends the figures within them the energy and reality that otherwise they might lack. Sometimes, however, if the figure is to step from the portrait the background must be hidden. In *The Hound of the Baskervilles* Holmes must hide the hat and ringlets in the portrait of Hugo Bakerville to allow the likeness of Stapleton to spring from the canvas and reveal him as "a throwback, which appears to be physical and spiritual" (879), rather like Joseph Curwen.

The two pictures in "The Picture in the House" possess this reality, perhaps all the more so since they confess that they cannot achieve the reality that a later experience with Africa demands. Instead, they present only that reality that the people of the time can imagine, Caucasian faces fixed upon black bodies; but within that rude space and empowered by it the axe in the shambles goes chop, chop, chop. After the narrator has discovered that he is oddly susceptible to these pictures that as it were place him, as a white man, in the center of the action, his reaction to the other pictures in the room, the eighteenth-century engravings in an edition of *Pilgrim's Progress*, is simply to find them "grotesque" and dismiss them (DH 119).

The portrait of Joseph Curwen has none of the clumsiness of the artist in the Pigafetta volume. A sedate, rather cool Joseph Curwen is presented, "thin, calm, undistinguished," within the background, a background well-established in this work, "a window with wharves and ships beyond" (MM 155). The spatiality here encompasses the ships that have assured Curwen's power in the eyes of his contemporaries; it presents his public, horizontal space, not that vertical space in which his laboratories and dungeons and his hold on the essential salts of history lie. In that sense the spatiality of the ships is misleading, like the ringlets of Hugo Baskerville. But the painting of the portrait announces to his contemporaries, as Curwen had intended, that he was a force to be reckoned with in the social world; but as none of them understood, he secretly meant the portrait to assure his immortality. For many sitters the portrait means no more than this, their victory over time, though each in his heart of hearts knows he shall die; but Curwen means this victory quite literally: through the magical space of his portrait he shall live. The portrait of the Dutchman, which he has had apparently no part in creating, exerts the same effect upon Senta, compelling her to give life and salvation to the man it represents.

In "Medusa's Coil" another portrait is achieved, and here the background, that three-dimensional, perspectival triumph over the flat world that we might otherwise imagine we live in, reveals even more depth. This depth is not only spatial but temporal, for it reveals the past of Marceline in the Great Zimbabwe and what lies behind it and her future in the apocalyptic world of the last judgment. And here something occurs that was implied in *The Case of Charles Dexter Ward* but never made a part of the narrative. The energy of that three-dimensional world receives an active manifestation; Joseph Curwen steps out of the frame, and Marceline's hair reaches out to the watcher. That three-dimensional world, whether achieved by tricks of perspective or the fact of the mirror, illusion as it is, yet receives through our stereoscopic eyes the immediate, physical assurance of its existence; and that existence surrounds and enables the person in the mirror. He looks like the self but is not as a careful study reveals; but at the same moment that he is not the self he achieves his own autonomous existence and is only too liable, much too liable, to reach out and destroy us. One glance at a mirror was enough to traumatize the Outsider. This depth of the mirror that usurps the everyday space that we are so certain lies behind it is one more reason why mirrors are so dangerous.

Last in this sequence of paintings let us consider the glancing reference Wilmarth makes in "The Whisperer in Darkness" to the landscapes Leonardo da Vinci creates as the mysterious Noyes drives him through the New England landscape. Da Vinci's mountains, toppling in a mad defiance of gravity, are mere backgrounds, seen "through the vaultings of Renaissance arcades" (*DH* 248); that is to say, they are doubly framed and distanced by the frame of the painting and by the arcades. But "we were burrowing bodily through the midst of the picture, and I seemed to find in its necromancy a thing I had innately known or inherited, and for which I had always been vainly searching" (248). Once more what might have been a mere two-dimensional surface gains depth, in part through the driver's determination to burrow "bodily" into the landscape, in part through Wilmarth's confession that he wishes to find that death in the painting for which he had been "vainly searching." In addition, this peculiar space within this landscape functions as a preparation for the immense spaces that the whisperer will sketch within his darkness.

Very well. Having noticed the significance of the painting, a near cousin to the mirror, in *Der Freischütz* and *Der Fliegende Holländer*, what shall we say of *Der Vampyr?* Lord Ruthwen introduces the theme of doubling when he invents the fiction of a brother who looks exactly like him, a brother so different that he several times insists upon that fictional existence. But after *Dracula* we expect a moment in the opera when the treacherous mirror will appear in which the vampire is revealed as nothing; he shall not appear at all, and thus his non-existence and lack of soul shall be revealed. It is as though in referring to his brother Lord Ruthwen had invented the mirror that shall betray him. For he has to confess to Aubry the fact that he has no soul; it was lost in that alternate world of the mirror long ago. When we stare into the pictures in that ramshackle house in the wilds of western Massachusetts and find ourselves tickled and aroused we admit that in some odd fashion we take part in the actions of the picture, hacking away at the human parts in the shambles and dreaming of new recipes that shall whet our appetites; no matter how crude the picture may be, the picture as mirror invites us into its eerie three-dimensional world—and we should not ignore the possibility that its very crudity is an invitation to correct and expand it just as we struggle with the image of a landscape in a lake shaken by the wind. As for the portrait of Joseph Curwen, a nice example of the correct portrait, whatever the bargain for his soul may have been, he had in fact bartered his soul away long ago, and so the portrait that should have rendered him in a three-dimensional reality instead renders him flat and "undistinguished" (MM 155). He has no spacious room for a soul to play and expand in, but that is probably not the fault of the artist who could only play with what he found. He found nothing, so the picture is simply *comme il faut*; and though he does cut quite a figure in twentieth-century Providence, his language makes him something of a sideshow, a flat example of what happens to an eighteenth-century man in the contemporary world to which he cannot belong. The effect is rather different in "Medusa's Coil." Here the portrait is too spacious; the exuberance of the details, the arabesques of the various black masses and witches' sabbaths, the references to Zimbabwe, the worlds behind it, and the world outside, and the overwhelming presence of Marceline and her hair in the foreground, as though she were a radical and opulent version of an odalisque by Ingres—all this demands too much room and apparently finds it, so that the soul itself has no room in which to play. If there is a soul here, it is overwhelmed.

The portraits in *Der Fliegende Holländer, The Case of Charles Dexter Ward*, and "Medusa's Coil" have one thing in common: the subject steps out of the frame and gains reality. But in each case the subject has already wandered a good deal. The theme of the Wandering Jew, so evident in Wagner's opera, influences Lovecraft's two stories, for Joseph Curwen certainly needs to be a wanderer, though a strange fatality seems to bind him to the sacred city of Providence, and Marceline, in a way that she herself does not seem to be aware of, certainly not after she becomes besotted with Marsh and unworthy of her heritage, has been a wanderer also. They are each wanderers *manqués*; though each steps out of the frame neither can go far beyond it.

We must consider these portraits and mirrors from a different perspective in order to suggest something else about the lives that these characters live. First, let us recall that the portrait in *Der Freischütz* is of Kuno, the ancestor of the Kuno in the opera, except that the Kuno in the portrait knows more than his descendent, who is as much of this daily world as Daland is in Wagner's opera. There is neither mirror nor portrait in *Der Vampyr*, but as I said we are aware of the folk belief that a vampire cannot be reflected in a mirror. Yet there is something suggestive in Lord Ruthwen's being lifted up to the moon, as though it were a mirror with its own glowing light within, through which he gains a new life more potent as far as the stage is concerned than the putative day that the Vampyr Master has granted. The portrait in Wagner's opera doubles the Dutchman, who as it were steps out of the portrait; and yet he does not, so his image broods above his courtship of Senta. More to the point, he stepped out of the portrait as soon as he stepped on land, where no one except Senta can recognize him as the figure of legend, though everyone that he encounters on the sea knows him for what he is; but she recognizes him not through fear but through faith.

These three figures, Kuno, Lord Ruthwen, and the Dutchman, enjoy serial existences. They live, and do not, and live again. It is rather like the life we each regain when we look in a mirror. For that is a stunning moment! Every time I look in a mirror I see myself again, as though in this moment I and the mirror not only fulfill our function; as it gives me back to myself I recognize myself in my image and rejoice in it. Of course we all experience in various degrees of awareness a serial existence in the various circadian rhythms of organic life. The major rhythm that is inescapable between wake and sleep is signaled by a day that is as we have come to expect and a night that is not as we ever expect, whether in fear or expectation—and Lovecraft seems to have looked forward to his dreams and feared them in equal measure—or simply a blank; but whatever our individual experiences may be, we are liable to concur in the classical tag that sleep is the brother of death. Night by night we are inured to our death, and this is either a serial existence or not. These are the details of our lives upon which the operas and Lovecraft's fictions are based.

A detail in some of the legends about the Wandering Jew elucidates the kind of serial existence that we actually have in mind, the radical experience of dying and coming to life again. One of the earliest stories, in which the man is called Cartaphilus, faces the question of how the man lives out the eternity to which he is condemned and asserts that once he arrives at the age of 100 he suffers a transformation and returns to the age of 30 when he encountered Jesus and spoke those crucial words, "Go quicker" (Anderson 19). In this story he ages, becomes young again, and knows that he will once more suffer the ills of slowly aging; and as an old man he knows that he will once more suffer the exuberant foolishness of youth. Most of the other stories prefer to think of the Wandering Jew as eternally old, but for our purposes this legend presents a classic version of serial life. Another existence of the serial existence of the supernatural, quite aside from the legend of the Wandering Jew, is the description that Spenser gives of Duessa's witchlike life when at the prime, perhaps every spring, "When Witches wont do penance for their crime" (1.11.40.5), she is revealed to be in truth an ugly hag. It is an existence that shifts between age and youth, because the protagonist believes that he or she has exacted some bargain from the evil powers, whereas in fact those powers have laid a subtle trap for the sinner.

The old man in "The Picture in the House" may be the first of Lovecraft's characters that experiences a serial existence, though we have no idea what kind of life he leads between his various butcheries. It may well be a vicarious existence; that is to say, he is sustained most certainly, if he is not mad, by the butcheries and by the pictures themselves that tickle his imagination and his body also. From this point of view he does not need the blood; the pictures are enough.

Joseph Curwen gives the clearest example of this kind of character. Though he doubtless would have preferred living year after year, he does not seem to care that he will have to skip a few years, from 1773 to 1926, in order to take up his life as he had left it. What a shame he did not have an opportunity as Charles Dexter Ward to sit for his portrait. But would a cubist treatment have served his purpose? The difficulty for him, which he does not seem to have anticipated, is that given the motion of history, its various cultural and linguistic transformations, he is certain to seem a fish out of water in his new life; but perhaps in the eighteenth century he had little awareness of how swiftly history can move once it is powered by such technologies as the cotton-gin, the textile factories, and the automobile. This is not a problem that arises for the characters of Romantic opera, but it is a very serious problem for Curwen. Given Lovecraft's realistic premises, an eighteenth-century man, despite the fact that he has lived in Lovecraft's favorite epoch and culture, will seem quite mad in the twentieth century. These are ironies that cut in two directions, whether the satire operates upon our century or whether it operates upon the simplicities of that earlier age. Curwen has no moral problem, however, in causing the death of his young descendent, just as Kaspar had no problem in offering Samiel Max's life, Lord Ruthwen no problem in taking the lives of the women, and the Dutchman apparently little problem in the deaths of the women who can not be faithful.

In *Der Freischütz* the Faustian bargain with evil is made for the perfect shot, and the demonstration of that shot is its ability to strike down an angel from heaven, the eagle that Max hits; the other side of that bargain is that in truth it is for the sake of the beloved, to win her—the other aspect of this victory, that Max can become the new *Erbsförster*, is not as important as the new relationship of love and trust after the death of his mother. In *Der Vampyr* the bargain is made for more time, for just a little more of life; and on the other side, where the man is unconscious of the bargain, we yet sense that it does have something to do with the beloved. In *Der Fliegender Holländer* the bargain is made to overcome the chaotic element and at last to come to rest, but even more it is to find the beloved who will sacrifice herself for the sake of a demented soul. This is a wide range of motives, but the main goal of these bargains at the least has to do with love and relationship, not with knowledge or experience as we find in the classic bargains. In a new form the Faustian bargain is basic to these operas.

There are of course many sorts of bargains, as we can see from the difference between Marlowe's and Goethe's. The one is quite objective, though that very objectivity makes an audience wonder why Faustus, with an objective devil before him with an account of the hell he lives in, should decide recklessly to sign the parchment in his blood. Goethe's Faust has no problem because he does not believe in hell or heaven and because, more significantly, he recognizes that the voice of Mephistopheles is the human voice, that niggling skeptical voice that will not allow any sentiment of love or transcendence to remain unexamined. We may in this regard consider Karl Barth's analysis of the human compulsion to break the boundaries of space and time appointed to our condition in order to realize fully our relationship

to God and our neighbor (3/2.681); the Faustian bargain may have two outcomes, a denial of this relationship as in Marlow's *Doctor Faustus* or a surprising fulfillment of it in Goethe's *Faust II*. This perception allows us to
understand the peculiar nature of that insistent motif in the overture to *Der
Fliegende Holländer* that we could not specify. The Dutchman is not combating the waves or the devil; he is combating the waves of passion and non-
existence within his own heart. He is himself and the waves, so in the overture, without the audience being aware yet of these various meanings it suffers the indiscriminate agony of the protagonist who has not yet stepped
ashore. This is the reason the Dutchman needs *Erlösung;* he needs to be untied and released from himself.

In "The Dunwich Horror" Wizard Whateley has made a bargain off-stage
with Yog Sothoth in which he handed over his daughter to be the conduit of
Yog Sothoth's child. We can wonder whether either was aware that she
would give birth to twins; certainly Wilbur is very helpful, perhaps necessary,
in the care of his twin. But being human, more human than the Horror, he
becomes impatient and dies in the library. More mysterious are the goals of
Wizard Whateley, who breaks the boundaries of space and time not for his
own sake but in order it seems to allow Yog-Sothoth an entry into this world,
more perhaps in order to show that it can be done than for any other reason.
He is a techie of the first order. In *The Case of Charles Dexter Ward* the young
man makes a bargain with his ancestor by the very act of exorcising him from
the portrait. This ancestor, incidentally, has some relation to Goethe's stylish
Mephisto, but he shares that self-blinded devil's limitations. What does Ward
gain from the bargain? Some knowledge, but it is a knowledge that proves fatal because the devil with whom he makes the bargain is his ancestor and his
double. A parley with one's self in this story is fatal. In "The Shadow over
Innsmouth" Captain Obed has made the bargain through his marriage for the
sake of the gold, but the bargain seems to be one that once enacted is carried
through by his descendants—once your ancestor has made this bargain there
is no way "to the third and fourth generation" (Ex. 20:5) to gainsay your
blood inheritance—something of the problem that Charles Dexter Ward
faces. For the narrator in "The Shadow over Innsmouth," however, it is no
longer a matter of gold but of transfiguration and eternity, and that hell to
which you have been sold is rather a place of glory—or so at least it seems.
Karl Barth argues that our means of transcending the restlessness and Angst
we suffer within the boundaries of the *Frist* is through our living our life in our
realization that our connection to God is "unergründlich und unerschöp-

flich"; this is certainly the narrator's expectation as he looks into that abyss where his ancient ur-grandmother lives. Like the Dutchman, the narrator has been released from that which was human in him.

In a more speculative mode, the Faustian bargain may also stand behind "The Outsider"—why is he as he is? Has someone sold him as the price of a fuller life, the person who is now his contrary and perhaps his father? We ask this remembering that in *Der Vampyr* and *Der Freischütz* the bargain is demanded by another for his own selfish sake, to substitute another for the self. This is essentially what Joseph Curwen has done in *The Case of Charles Dexter Ward*, offering up his descendent for his own fuller life. A striking moment in *Der Freischütz* is Max's shot at the eagle in the dusk, a miraculous achievement that seals his fate and makes him a dark Prometheus; blood usually seals the bargain, but here it is sealed by blood from heaven.

In this regard to the bargain, it is interesting to see that among the many tales told of the *wilde Jäger* and the *wütende Heer* one tale seems absolutely factual of a man addicted to hunting who upon his death-bed defies Heaven if only he can continue his life of the hunt—the priest at his bed-side then says, "So jage bis an den jüngsten tag [sic]!" [So hunt until the day of judgment!] (Grimm, *Deutsche Mythologie* 769). This is not the most significant of stories from the viewpoint of mythography, but it does indicate that a parallel can be drawn between the story of the *wilde Jäger* and the story of the Dutchman. Both involve a bargain that defies Heaven and the chaotic world, whether in the woods or on the sea. As an indication of this mythic closeness George Anderson spends a good deal of space describing the richness of the stories that concern the *wilde Jäger* and the *wütende Heer*, stories that indicate the ambivalence of the myth, whether it indicates a punishment wrought upon the spectral figures or upon the mortals that suffer beneath the horror of the hunt. It is at once a hunt, a pursuit, and a flight (5–8). A further story, recounted by Karl Blind in his interesting comparison of Wodan, the Wild Huntsman, and the Wandering Jew, tells of a huntsman who, because he would not allow Jesus to drink from a river, is condemned to roam a line of seven mountain towns through seven years. Whoever sees him and calls out will be condemned to eat horse-flesh; that is to say, he must repeat the ancient pagan rites (181–82). So the hunt is also a temptation to join the Walpurgis Night.

Not far removed from the fate of the condemned hunter is the fate of the vampire and of the ghoul, who are one and the same, except for the vampire's extraordinary strength that he loses during the day; and Ruthwen needs the moon in order to regain his strength. Though Lovecraft scorned the traditional tropes of the weird tale such as ghosts, he does employ a variation of the vampire in two stories. The immediately striking detail in "The Shunned House" is that the vampire is not an aristocrat, for the upper class was surely such a vampire in Polidori's work and in Bram Stoker's. But this conception is new in its day, for before those stylish and upper-class manifestations of the blood-sucker the peasant, ragged and needy, appeared as the vampire. So Lovecraft returns the theme to its original when in the records we read of Jacques Roulet utterly squalid, "covered with blood and shreds of flesh in a wood, shortly after the killing and rending of a boy by a pair of wolves. One wolf was seen to lope away unhurt" (MM 249). As the story unfolds, however, the vampire is much greater than the peasant horded in lice; he is a pageant and a legion, something much greater than the individual suffering self. So the later story "The Colour out of Space" seems to imply that the universe outside our universe is a vampire, as the old trope escalates beyond human comprehension; the thing in the well needs the lives of the Gardners to gain the strength to ascend and regain that state of the outside from which it has come. The price it pays, however, for there is always a price, is to leave a part of itself behind, something that Ammi had seen "feebly rise" (DH 79), only to sink back into the well where it now lurks, perhaps full of malice because of its failure. It shall not possess new strength in the light of the full moon as Lord Ruthwen had.

Curt von Westernhagen contrasts *Der Fliegende Holländer* to Weber's and Marschner's works by noting that in it "the supernatural, the miraculous or demonic elements, were not external forces but proceeded directly out of the characters of the protagonists" (66). What are we to say of Lovecraft's work in this regard? It is something of a mixed bag, but a development is fairly clear. Certainly the early work leans heavily upon the miraculous; yet often the miraculous is simply a sign of an internal process that depends upon heredity, and that process is often more intimate than the protagonist who is destroyed by it can perceive. This would seem to be the case in "The Tomb," "The Rats in the Walls," and *The Case of Charles Dexter Ward*. In each of these stories the protagonist is overtaken by a hereditary propensity that he does not fully understand; but if he did fully understand it his knowledge would still do him no good. He understands just enough to realize that he has no hope. In Lovecraft's later works because of the science-fictional identification of the monsters and spirits as ultra-dimensional entities the only element that strikes us as supernatural, the use of dreams, was not so to either Wagner or Lovecraft.

In *Der Freischütz* we have seen how the Black Hunter shades into the Wild Man as a fertility figure and that Lord Ruthwen plays out the part of Don Giovanni. What are we to say of Wilbur in "The Dunwich Horror"? He is no erotic Lord, but he possesses a magical vitality that is indicated by his swift growth; and when he dies we are told that below his waist there lies a "sheer phantasy" that is "teratologically fabulous" (*DH* 174). Fortunately the narrator proceeds then to a detailed description of what lies below Wilbur's waist: "The skin was thickly covered with coarse black fur, and from the ab-domen a score of long, greenish-grey tentacles with red sucking mouths pro-truded limply" (174). Many readers have often laughed at these phrases, which seem an expression of the stylistic extremities that Lovecraft is fond of; but we should take them seriously as an indication of Wilbur's peculiar virility. From a distance he might look like a satyr, creatures noted for their sexual power because below the waist they are goatlike. The tentacles are phalluses, limp now in death, combined with the vagina dentata of male nightmares. He is a Pan figure, bisexual and potent like Aleister Crowley's vision of Pan that we noticed earlier, but he also embodies the imagery of his own fear. Thereby he is a failed fertility figure, for he dies too early for any sign of his potency to take effect, unless the true effect of his fertility is the release of his brother, who reveals Wilbur's failure in his own hollow invisi-bility. Nevertheless, this brother possesses a power that cannot be denied.

Having considered Wilbur as a fertility figure, we must see the Outsider in that light too. He has risen out of his sepulchre in search of revelry and light, and when he finds that revelry he causes a panic that is surely the equal of Pan's. His sexuality has been a cause of some dispute that I do not believe we have settled yet (Waugh, *Monster* 115); and it is possible, if we cannot settle this question, that we must confess that his sexuality trespasses the usual categories. At the end of the story, despite his horror at what he is, whatever that might be, he nevertheless joins in the revelries that are avail-able to him "with the mocking and friendly ghouls" (*DH* 52). He is certainly "a stranger in this century" (52), but he does have his own community, out-cast and abnormal itself, that accepts him; after all, though he is dead he is not dead enough to be food.

We have earlier observed that in these operas the plot often suggests something not quite right in the community it represents. In *Der Freischütz* the bullying nature of the chorus at the beginning of the first act is one of the causes that drive Max to supernatural aid. In *Der Vampyr* the drinking song enacts the cycle of blood. In *Der Fliegende Holländer* the chorus of the spinners is either incredulous or sentimentally taken by Senta's ballad; or in the battle of the choruses in the third act we witness the antagonism between the mortal life of the land and weird life of the sea. Most important however, these operas emphasize that despite the attempt of the protagonist to live and suffer alone, the community is always a significant milieu that the protagonist cannot escape.

There is a dark side to this theme of community, for an apparently minor theme of the three operas is the communal joy of inebriation; but that joy is highly qualified. Kaspar's song praising wine, dice, and barmaids is unearthly in the setting Weber gives it; Marschner's song implicitly praises the blood that the vampyre drinks; and the song the sailors sing is rebuffed by the mocking chastity of the Dutchman's crew. Though the songs seem to testify to community, the effect they have seems to move towards isolation. In Lovecraft's stories a few drinking songs occur, such as in "The Tomb" in which an aristocrat from the eighteenth century warbles a few notes of revelry; but these songs are reprehensible, written by an author who distrusted alcohol profoundly. We shall later examine this problem in his work at length, but now we can see that his attitude parallels that of the operas.

More generally, Lovecraft is often concerned with the community within which his characters live. This is of course a function of his depiction of New England life, which from the time of the Puritans unrolled within a communal context. Though so often his protagonists are isolated and solitary, the importance of community is very evident in *The Case of Charles Dexter Ward*, "The Dunwich Horror," and "The Shadow over Innsmouth." These communities, however, differ among themselves greatly. The community of Providence is well-knit. They understand each other, their strengths and their weaknesses; they have a rational understanding of their various self-interests; and they have a self-understanding that finds itself easily turned against a man who they perceive is utterly inimical to the *Sosein* life they lead, though he has not yet attacked them. We might wonder in fact whether he would ever attack them. The community of Dunwich we have earlier seen is characterized by its communal monologue; they are always speaking to each other and maintaining themselves in that communal discourse. In the language we have already used, they have no other speech than normal discourse, though clearly they need someone like Dr. Armitage who can bridge the gap between normal and abnormal discourse if the Horror is to be dissolved from the dimensions of this world. As for the community of Innsmouth, unlike the two other communities, it has no interest in communicating with the outside world. At the stage of historical presence when the story occurs it is truly losing everything it had once gained through the Deep Ones so that any advantage it can gain from its former bargain is now purely individual; though the narrator is ready to plunge into the depths of the ocean and gain the glories that his ancestors promise him, his achievement, if it is indeed an achievement, means nothing for the city of Innsmouth that he leaves "croaking, baying and barking" behind him (DH 359). But before he leaves, the community of Innsmouth on land is no more, for the community that exists outside it has decided that Innsmouth must be destroyed because of the danger it represents. From the point of view of that outside community, despite its rationalisms, the community of Innsmouth is composed of the Walpurgis Night and nothing else.

One of the constants in these operas, harking back to Goethe, is the Walpurgis Night, but they are as different from each other as they are different from the poet who inspired the episode. In Goethe we have two of these moments, one in the first part of *Faust* and the other in the second. The first Walpurgis Night celebrates a barren sexuality and abortion, looking forward to Gretchen's murder of her baby[5]; a real evil is celebrated here, but it is diluted by satiric elements and by Mephistopheles' refusal to bring Faust to the summit of the mountain. The second Walpurgis Night celebrates the search for perfect human beauty and the four elements within the context of evolutionary change. As Goethe makes explicit in the satiric poem "Die Erste Walpurgisnacht," the Christian world sees the celebration of the natural world as a pagan expression that is a vision of evil. The Wolfsschlund scene in *Der Freischütz* opens significantly with the apparition of Max's mother, warning her son away from the magic that shall make his aim Promethean; Kaspar of course denies that it is evil but only an employment of the occult natural world. This Walpurgis Night then celebrates the death of the mother and her impotence against the count of the bullets that asserts the power of demonic precision; there is a touch here of that quintessential Romantic anxiety about a Newtonian clockwork corpuscular universe. The opening scene of *Der Vampyr* celebrates the bargain that the vampyr makes with the devil. Most complicated of these scenes is that which opens the third act of

---

5. Lovecraft could have found these traditional themes enunciated in the witches' sabbath celebrated in the "grotesque witch-dances" of Robert Burns's "Tam o' Shanter" (D 373). As a late letter (SL 4.344–46) demonstrates he is quite acquainted with the traditional Walpurgis Night, referring to materials from Margaret Murray (109) and the "Walpurgis" entry in the *Encyclopaedia Britannica*.

Wagner's opera, when silence of the crew of the Dutchman's ship rebuffs the sexual challenge made by the women's chorus and they summon a storm that silences the good cheer of Daland's men. They despise *Erlösung*.

Lovecraft has his version of the Walpurgis Night, but it is quite different from those of the operatic world, for he is not really interested in the categories of magic and nature or of sexuality and nature. In fact, he does not believe in the innocent nature that is celebrated by the Transcendentalists nor, quite, in the fallen nature cursed by the Puritans. His nature is fallen, surely, but only because it is the world of Darwin, sharpened by Spencer, in which Nature is always at war, always bloody, always in danger of devolution and incoherence; the odds in fact are much more in favor of decadence than of improvement. As for Christianity, its problematic seldom appears explicitly in his works. The celebration of the Walpurgis Night, then, is allowed to proceed as it will; and something seems to have happened to the celebration when it came to New England, because his versions of this moment are certainly celebrations of the utterly alien that human safety must perceive as evil. We have earlier noted that the feast on the circumference of the universe also takes place at the center; but the Walpurgis Night is eccentric.

"The Festival," "The Nameless City," "Under the Pyramids," "The Horror at Red Hook," "The Call of Cthulhu," "The Shadow over Innsmouth," and "The Thing on the Doorstep" play out this moment in very similar ways. Usually it is staged as a pageant of hybridism, but often this pageant becomes as in "Tam o' Shanter" a pursuit. The protagonist of the work has looked upon that which he should never have seen and must assume an immense guilt. In "The Nameless City" the protagonist affirms that the mummified creatures that he finds "were of the reptile kind," only to insist then that they cannot be compared to "the cat, the bulldog, the mythic Satyr, and the human being" (D 104), though those comparisons do spring to mind. Later, after he descends further, these creatures pursue him, now restored to a semblance of life that is "hate-distorted, grotesquely panoplied, half-transparent" (110). In "The Festival" the celebrants mount "a horde of tame, trained, hybrid winged things that no sound eye could ever wholly grasp, or sound brain ever wholly remember. [. . .] not altogether crows, nor moles, nor buzzards, no ants, nor vampire bats, nor decomposed human beings" (215). Indeed, it is not possible in this language of negation to grasp at all the size, much less the shape of these beings, which seem at least to veer between the human and the ant. The protagonist flees, "before the madness of my screams could bring down upon me all the charnel legions these pest-gulfs might conceal" (216), because the wax mask of the central celebrant has slipped and revealed his true nature, which is not given the reader to know. This pursuit, then, and this climax are foiled before they can begin.

"Under the Pyramids" is complex in the various stages of its pageant. First comes Houdini's dream that has faded in its details but that finds its justification in his awareness of "certain perverse products of decadent priestcraft—*composite mummies* made by the artificial union of human trunks and limbs with the heads of animals" (D 234). In the climax he does see these creatures, in which Lovecraft seems to have let himself go—this was, after all, merely a ghostwritten story—in such details as the hippopotami with human heads; at the sight of the five-headed creature that turns out to be the paw of a sphinx he turns and runs, but no pursuit follows for this was, Houdini assures the reader, only a dream. Though this pageant is composed of "hybrid blasphemies" (D 241), it remains oddly unsatisfyingly. "The Horror at Red Hook" has a different problem. Here, when the pageant is identified as "the foetor of hybrid pestilence" that destroys nations (D 260), we realize the racist and anti-Semitic direction of the story that narrows its possibilities; and the object of worship, whether identified as Hecate, the Magna Mater, Gorgo, Mormo, or Lilith, no longer possesses the cosmic implications of Lovecraft's other work. Also, one does wonder how this classical worship has arrived in New York, a question that is no problem in "The Rats in the Walls." In "The Shadow over Innsmouth" the pursuit becomes inadvertently a pageant as the narrator watches what he attempts not to watch, creatures whose "forms vaguely suggested the anthropoid, while their heads were the heads of fish. [. . .] They were the blasphemous fish-frogs of the nameless design" (DH 361). Though the word hybrid is not used here, the intent of this imagery is clear—an intent that the history of the town also points at in the interspecies' matings, first the Kanakas and the fish people and then the Innsmoutheans and the fish people.

A more peculiar Walpurgis Night, quite different from the pageant and pursuit, occurs at the center of "The Call of Cthulhu" when the police disperse the rites being celebrated in the bayous by a "hybrid spawn" of "mongrel celebrants," a crowd of "mix-blooded" people, many of them "mulattoes" (DH 138–39). Just as we would expect. The dance however is a ring-dance, circling widdershins in opposition to the sun around "a great granite monolith" surmounted by a figurine of Cthulhu "incongruous in its diminutiveness" (138). The hybrids that we have come to expect are choreographed according to the material that Lovecraft found in Margaret Murray's work, such details as the widdershins direction (135) circling around a phallic stone (131). Her theory rationalizes the hybridism through the fertility dances of the witches that they often performed in the costumes of the animals that the cult needed to increase (130). This dance, then, in contrast to the other Walpurgis Nights we had observed, is a fairly mild sort, despite the scaffolds on which bodies hang head-downward, desacralized emblems of the hanged man in the Tarot deck. It is a hodgepodge in which fertility symbols and anti-fertility symbols clash. We are forced to wonder whether here Lovecraft's source, Murray's suggestive work, had overpowered his own powerful, controlling image of the pageant, even though so much else in the novella, especially its verbal texture, works so well.

In "The Dreams in the Witch House" we have allusions to perhaps the most normal Walpurgis Night in Lovecraft's work; it is even given its proper name and assigned the proper date of May 1st. It is attended by a proper witch, her familiar, and the Black Man. Children have gone missing in the past, and it is clearly feared that they are being sacrificed to the devil. Though so much else in the story is remarkable, especially the extended journeys through non-Euclidean space, this Walpurgis Night is quite conservative. It is this contrast between a rather humdrum Walpurgis Night and an extravagant intergalactic journey that makes this story something of a puzzler, a work that is not quite achieved, despite the fascinating outlines of an erotic mania that we studied earlier.

The Walpurgis Night as we have seen is frequently held on the top of a mountain; Faust and Mephistopheles climb the Harzberg where the celebration was traditionally held. But in Lovecraft's work, as Lévy demonstrated, the way down is often identical to the way up, and this principal holds in fantasy work in general. Thus we turn once more to the Wolfsschlucht, which Wagner, summarizing the opera, describes in these terms as Max approaches it:

> [D]umpfes Ächzen und Stöhnen durchwehte, bei voller Windstille, das breite Geäst der alten Tannen, welche von selbst ihre schwarze Häupter hin und her bewegten. Am Saume angelangt, blickte er dann in einen Abgrund, auf dessen Tiefe sein Auge nicht dringen konnte: Felsenrisse ragten da empor in der Gestalt menschlicher Glieder und scheußlich verzerrter Gesichter. [Dull moans and groans blew through, the wind completely still, the broad branches of the high pines, which of themselves moved their black heads back and forth. Arrived at the edge, he looked into the abyss that his eye could not plunge to its depths: the outlines of cliffs towered up in the form of human limbs and horribly contorted faces.] (8.8)

Now we have read of such places in Lovecraft, whether in the trees that sur-

round the Gardners' doomed house and the well next to it that has no bottom in "The Colour out of Space" or in the Glen into which Wilbur's invisible brother goes for refuge in "The Dunwich Horror." It is, as Edward Derby
says, "The unholy pit where the black realm begins" (*DH* 287). This is a *locus nefandus*, a place of horror that must not be spoken of and that nevertheless a narrator or protagonist cannot cease from attempting to describe. This
abyss is the same as Dante views early in the *Inferno*:

> For certain, on the brink
> I found me of the lamentable vale,
> The dread abyss, that joins a thunderous sound
> Of plaints innumerable. Dark and deep,
> And thick with clouds o'erspread, mine eye in vain
> Explored its bottom, nor could aught discern. (1.4.6–11)

Thus whether one has ascended to the top of the *locus nefandus* or whether
one has descended, there is no end to this place and nowhere to find a place
to stand with any assurance. When the legion climbs into the hills to put
down the celebration of that primitive cult in the Roman dream, the ascent
becomes increasingly vertical until in the climactic moment the sky is
snuffed out (*SL* 2.195–96). Just as there is no bottom below us, there is no
end to the universe above us either; and that is the very quality that renders
this a *locus nefandus*. With no end to it, we cannot rationalize it according to
any measure, much less in words.

Dante's universe does have an end, in the genitalia of Satan that Dante
must take hold of, following the example of Virgil, in order to turn upside
down and begin his ascent. But this center, rough and ready-made as it were,
not really a locus accommodated to words, recalls Augustine's problem with
the question of evil. It is finally not a rational question and not to be answered by rational means. The *locus nefandus* is unspeakable.

Nevertheless, it is to be celebrated in great numbers, with great fre-
quency, and with great energy. Here, as Lovecraft's works accumulate, we
find the several names of the the myth that he is sharing with his friends in
Weird Tales. The problem with these names is that they do not share a narrative despite Derleth's insistence—and in this regard he is undoubtedly
wrong. In the various stories, every time the *locus nefandus* is approached,
the protagonist ejaculates the names without suggesting any coherent structure among them. Rather than an orderly procession of the gods, it is a rout.
In this regard Lovecraft's practice was quite different from that of his co-

participants, who were intent upon creating some sort of shared, structured myth, and their practice makes it relatively easy for the later authors to create the mythos. In Lovecraft's practice all structure and coherence breaks down in the *locus nefandus*. Nevertheless, what should not be spoken in the *locus nefandus* and what these several points we have made insist cannot be spoken is in fact perfectly well spoken, the horror that Lovecraft feels in the face of a hybrid society; this is not the past, neither Goethe's past, an idealized classical world devoted to the celebration of nature, nor Margaret Murray's past, an anthropological cult of the pre-classical world that is still alive in the present—it is the world of urban immigration that Lovecraft, the last outpost of the eighteenth century, found such an affront.

I want to conclude on a more speculative theme, one suggested by Wagner's anti-Semitism and his relation to the man I earlier called his spiritual father, Heinrich Heine. In *The Case of Charles Dexter Ward* there is no doubt that Joseph Curwen, though of good birth and having the tongue "of a learned and cultivated Englishman" (MM 124), is in fact something of a vampire. He bears the telling pallor and the "black satin small clothes" (155) and feeds on the knowledge of the men he has captured in their essential salts. To that image of the vampire, however, I would like to add the stereotype of the Jew; he is partially assimilated into the society of Providence, but it will not accept him because it realizes that he observes it with a "cryptic, sardonic arrogance, as if he had come to find all human beings dull" (120). He has the same aggressive laughter that Kundry, the female Ahasuerus, is shaken by in the second act of *Parsifal*; this is the same laughter that Wagner resented in Heine (cf. Ross 71). In the most charged language that this nameless narrator employs, a voice that seems to speak for the society of Providence in the 1700s and the 1920s, Joseph Curwen was "a pathetic, a dramatic, and a contemptible thing" (MM 124), The reasons for this judgment remain vague, and thus the language functions as a code for another judgment that he cares not to voice. Despite this social judgment, however, the clever Curwen is able to contract a marriage to a woman of an "unquestioned position" (125) through the power of his wealth. This coded language opens the novel. Curwen seems much older than his twenty-year-old descendent whose place he has usurped, his intense intelligence has "been twisted into strange and grotesque forms," and his chill, dry skin is "exaggeratedly coarse and loosely knit" (108). He has the skin of a Jew (cf. Julius 46–47). Consider now the position of Charles Dexter Ward, discovering that his ancestor is—what? What is worse within Lovecraft's imaginative universe, to discover that one's ancestor is an erudite, necromantic vampire or to discover that he is a Jew?

All these speculations bring me back to the problem of Lovecraft's father, whom his son often characterized as an English gentleman, a man who despite being born in Rochester, New York was "something of an Englishman himself" (*SL* 1.31), whose "extremely precise and cultivated British voice" Lovecraft believed he could still remember (*SL* 3.362). I have previously noted the similarity of names in Lovecraft and his friend Samuel Loveman, but I did not ask what now seems to me the next question that Lovecraft surely asked: What kind of a name is Lovecraft? He insists that his line goes directly back to Tudor times, perhaps to the name Lovecroft (*SL* 2.182; 3.360), but there is no evidence to support his account (Joshi, *HPL: A Life* 2). Although Kenneth W. Faig Jr. in great detail traces the name of Lovecraft's line back to a great-great-great-great-grandparent, Will Lovecraft, a weaver living in Broadhempston in Devon in 1699 (32), neither the name Lovecraft nor Lovecroft appear in Reaney's dictionary of English names; Loveman, however, is an ancient English name (221–22). On the other hand, although the Guggenheimers report neither Lovecraft nor, surprisingly, Loveman as Jewish names, they do list a large group of names based on compounds of "love" and "Löwe" (474–75). Despite such evidence as he has, Lovecraft has no doubt of his origin; he insists to Richard F. Searight, "Of its Saxon source there is no doubt" (38). We have come, however, to view all such insistences with our own skepticism. He says a number of times that his people were traditionally weavers, which Faig's material does attest to. Now the trade of the weaver, a very traditional trade, was not open to the Jews that Oliver Cromwell in 1655 invited to migrate to England. First came the wealthy Sephardic Jews who settled in London; only later did the poorer Ashkenazis arrive, who often took up the work of itinerant pedlars and who by 1750 were three-quarters of the Jewish population in England (Felsenstein 51). Into neither of these cultures can we imagine the Lovecrafts fitting. So I do not mean to suggest that Lovecraft may have had Jewish ancestors—he very likely did not—but I do wonder whether he feared the possibility, in part given the similarity of his name and Loveman's, and whether his insistence stemmed from that fear. This is the problem of origins. No matter how intensive our genealogical studies may be, there comes either that point at which we discover we know nothing or we discover that one of our ancestors is a horse-thief, an ichthyic-batrachian monster, or Joseph Curwen.

Filiations and Affinities

Lovecraft, a Citizen of Rome

Then the chief captain came, and said unto him, Tell me, art thou a Roman? He said, Yea. And the chief captain answered, With great sums obtained I this freedom. And Paul answered, But I was free born. (Acts 22:27–28)

It has become a commonplace to say that Roman literature and culture was extremely important for Lovecraft. Rome was, as it were, bred into him, for Providence is the city of seven hills, the representative of Rome in the New World. In 1895 the city touted itself in this fashion:

"Providence, built like Rome upon its seven hills, fanned by gentle breezes from the ocean, with its freedom from serious epidemics, its great wealth, large banking facilities, large and varied industries, its nearness to other great commercial centers, [. . .] is not excelled by any other city in the United States for residence and business purposes." (Society of Architectural Historians)

Lovecraft referred to that civic conceit of the seven hills of Providence at the conclusion of *The Dream-Quest of Unknown Kadath* (MM 401). At a very early age in his grandfather's library he delighted in the work of the Augustan Age, material difficult to comprehend without a knowledge of the classics. Though at first he was indiscriminate in his love for both Greek and Roman literature, writing a version of the *Odyssey* when he was six years old (AT 3–5), he soon began to favor the Roman world. As a young man he translated the opening lines of the *Metamorphoses,* and near the end of his life he translated Horace. He was familiar with several Latin poets, even Antias and Lucan (AT 398, 403), but it is his intimacy with a small number of Latin authors that we wish to investigate, observing how he sought to build an image of himself as a Roman, just as at other points in his life and in other moods he attempted to see himself as a Teutonic brute or as an English gentleman.

But various problems exist in his attempt to see himself in these ways. The Pax Romana, whether in 20 BCE or in 1700 CE never really existed. Defining the period from 1680 to 1776 as Augustan begs a number of assumptions, whether in the government of Octavius Caesar or in the governments

267

of Charles II, William and Mary, Anne, or the three Georges. The Pax Romana was quite relative, for Octavius and his generals waged various wars
from Persia to Germania; and in the experience of Britain 1700 years later
we need not mention the Dutch wars, the wars of Marlborough, or the
Seven Years War. Undoubtedly Lovecraft identified himself with the cultural achievements of the great Tory authors, but we need to keep those
achievements within the context of the colonial, expansionist efforts of the
Whigs that were to lead to the American Revolution.

The Teutonic brute is a very different sort of beast. Did it ever exist? The
various Viking tribes conducted a series of depredations upon Western and
Eastern Europe, but they were at last cast back, beginning at the battle of
Clontarf. In England the Vikings were assimilated into the kingdom of Yorkshire; beyond that the Teutonic brute is as much a construct of political
propaganda, such as we can see in the Third Book of the *Dunciad*, as the
gentleman of the Augustan period. During the late 1910s and early 1920s
Lovecraft is constructing a self-image that is based upon two remarkable,
contradictory fictions. In this chapter I am only concerned with his Roman
projections, but it is well to keep in mind that the Teutonic brute was not far
from his mind and inflected his Roman imagination.

I

Et iam summa procul uillarum culmina fumant
maioresque cadunt altis de montibus umbrae.
[And now in the distance the high roofs of the houses smoke
and large shadows fall from the high mountains]
(Virgil, *Ecl.* 1.82–83)

Before we discuss the various Roman writers that interested him, we must
acknowledge the context of the five authors who introduced him to things
Roman at different points in his life. Very early he read Thomas Babington
Macaulay's *Lays of Ancient Rome*, which he was still enthusiastic about later
in his life (*SL* 1.314–15), quoting from memory such potent lines as "The
priest who slew the slayer / And shall himself be slain" (*SL* 2.331). Macaulay's work is peculiar. We cannot imagine that the monarchist Lovecraft approved of the great Whig history of England; but the *Lays of Ancient Rome*
offers a history of Rome that can easily be regarded as a justification of the
Empire to come, toward which Lovecraft had ambivalent feelings. He preferred the Republic, but the image of strength that the Empire projects was

highly attractive. More specifically, Macaulay's work has a peculiar structure; each ballad, vivid and energetic in the style of *Boys' Own Paper*, is introduced by an essay on the possible origins of such a ballad. Lovecraft may have been impressed by the dichotomy between the rationalist essays that reason away all miracles and the simple, headlong belief of the poems.

Two short passages in De Quincey, as he prepares to discuss his opium dreams, provide Lovecraft with imagery that he often repeats in his letters. First is De Quincey's comment that he "had often felt as solemn and appalling sounds, emphatically representative of Roman majesty, the two words so often occurring in Livy, *Consul Romanus*; especially when the consul is introduced in his military character" (848). In his dreams pageants connected with the court of Charles I would dissolve into "the heart-shaking sound of *Consul Romanus*; and immediately came 'sweeping by,' in gorgeous paludaments, Paullus or Marius, girt around by a company of centurions, with the crimson tunic hoisted on a spear, and followed by the *alalagmos* of the Roman legions" (849). Lovecraft is very sensitive to these images drawn from the Republic and the triumphant shouts of military authority.

Two authors even more important for Lovecraft's imaginative treatment of Rome are Arthur Machen and Arthur Weigall, one in the novel *The Hill of Dreams* and the other in an archeological work titled *Wanderings in Roman Britain*. From both authors Lovecraft believed that he gained a sense of everyday Roman life in the frontier of England after the Roman conquest (e.g., *SL* 4.373–74), but that is not quite so as far as Weigall is concerned, who intends to demonstrate the heterogeneous character of Roman blood (20), at one point describing the "little *half-caste* children from whom we are descended" (102). Lovecraft accepts this point, since by the time extensive Roman colonization took place the Roman stock itself had become as vitiated and as mongrelized as he felt the American people threatened to become (*SL* 2.282). If, then, he is to imagine a Roman genealogy for himself, he prefers to choose or invent someone from 60 or 70 CE and give him "a good ancient name derived from the equestrian order of the original Roman people," tracing the line "through half-Celtic Roman provincials & early Cambrian bards and scholars—until I arrive at a full-fledged Welshman" such as Machen describes (*SL* 2.283). The project is a solace that evades the late mongrel Roman and the modern mongrel American. Lovecraft dreams of his Roman identity through Weigall in the loosest possible manner, perhaps as much through the architectural features of the legionary camps that Weigall expends most of his space describing.

On the other hand, much in Weigall may have spoken to Lovecraft directly, such as Weigall's description of a contemporary English farmer who aids the archeologists because "he sees [. . .] that since the genius of England is rooted in her British and Roman past, the dead who lie beneath his fields have a claim upon him both as a man of understanding and as a patriot" (97). In addition, Lovecraft may well have been moved by Weigall's account of the Ninth Legion, which "marched into the Lowlands and so passed utterly out of existence. It was never heard of again, nor did a single man come back to tell how or where it was annihilated" (101). This is the kind of story that Lovecraft was indeed to experience in a dream shortly after he read Weigall's book.

The impressions that Lovecraft believed that he gained from *The Hill of Dreams* are even more problematic. He was well-disposed toward Machen, but *The Hill of Dreams* concerns daily Roman life in the most tangential ways. At first the book seems an impressionistic *Bildungsroman*, an uneasy mixture of satire and ecstasy: a young man called Lucian comes of age in Wales, suffers the insults of other young men, the shame of the pubescent body, and inchoate sexual longings, as he retreats into ancient, useless knowledge, haunted by a recurrent, visionary experience of a Roman fort overlooking his valley. The book ends in his isolation in a nightmare London where he dies, attempting to achieve a career as an author. Much of this might have appealed to Lovecraft as a mirror of his own experience. The protagonist is like Randolph Carter, an expert dreamer who sits "secure on the throne of ivory and gold" (150). These visionary dreams form the main body of the novel. The sound of a boy in the school band practicing his bugle becomes "the note of the Roman trumpet, *tuba mirum spargens sonum*, filling all the hollow valley with its command. [. . .] In his imagination he saw the earthen gates of the tombs broken open, and the serried legions swarming to the eagles" (59–60). Perhaps more telling for Lovecraft's Roman dream is Lucian's vision in which "The Celt assailed him, beckoning from the weird wood he called the world, and his far-off ancestors, the 'little people' crept out of their caves, muttering charms and incantations in hissing inhuman speech: he was beleaguered by desires that had slept in his race for ages" (65). One could claim that the book is more about the desire for faerie than the desire for the legions. Lucian's dreams of Roman life are likely to debouch into fantasies of Sappho (123), synaesthetic orgies that recall the more lurid expressions of British decadence (127), or meditations upon Mithras, Isis, and the more occult religions of the East (133–34). No, the novel does not concern everyday Roman life in Britain.

Finally we should consider the impact of Gibbon's monumental history and its potent title, *The History of the Decline and Fall of the Roman Empire*. It is possible that Lovecraft was familiar with the work by the time he was twelve years old, for in 1902 he had written a poem, "On the Ruin of Rome," that in clumsy hexameters strikes Gibbon's pose on the tragic fall of the city (AT 12). Lovecraft thoroughly agreed with Gibbon's thesis that the reason for the Empire's decline and fall was the slow rot of Christianity, expressed most powerfully in Gibbon's fifteenth and sixteenth chapters; Gibbon and Nietzsche are agreed in their critique of the baleful influence that the irrational beliefs inherent in Judaism and Christianity had upon the classical world. Perhaps more impressive to Lovecraft is the immense depth of Gibbon's historical view, sweeping through 1,500 years, though we have little evidence that Lovecraft was ever interested in the intricacies of Byzantine culture; once Rome fell in 493, a thousand years before the fall of Byzantium, his interest moved to the energy of the Nordic tribes. If he could not be a Roman he would rather have been an ignorant Teuton, dreaming of weird creatures in the Northern woods, than a hyper-sophisticated Greek. We see, then, in his interest in Gibbon another indication that a study of history is often for Lovecraft an essay in self-identity.

As we turn to the Roman authors that Lovecraft discusses, we discover that he has a wide variety of reasons to read them and that, needless to say, some writers are much more significant to him than others.

Take, for example, the three poets who deal with the cosmos, Ovid, Lucretius, and Manilius. Surprisingly, Ovid resonated strongly for Lovecraft. Though the proem of the *Metamorphoses* is something of a patchwork of various influences—hardly philosophic at all—Lovecraft frequently quotes a particular phrase from this passage: the early universe is "rudis indigestaque moles" (1.7), which in his early translation he renders as "raw unfinish'd mass" (AT 5). In playful moods he uses the phrase to describe cottage cheese (SL 3.190) and to describe the noise of his rooms invaded by steam heat (3.410). And he uses the phrase as the title of his essay on Eliot's *Waste Land* (CE 2.63). The phrase seems to function for Lovecraft as the expression of the chaos of the universe that invades our world in its most intimate experiences; it does not express a cosmic vision but a satire of our everyday failures. In two other poems he employs an epigraph from the *Metamorphoses* (AT 215, 308) and writes a satire, "Gryphus in Asinum Mutatus," explicitly "after the manner of Ovid's *Metamorphoses*" (202).

Lovecraft is also twice concerned with one other work by Ovid, the *Ars Amatoria*, as an example of a work that the modern world in its concern with

censorship is too stupid to touch—along with such other pornographic classics as the *Decameron* and the Old Testament (*SL* 3.266). In another mood
he baits Whitman, who "copies Ovid's filth without his grace" (*AT* 193). Art
is all. Lovecraft asserts that the contemporary mind "gets on finely with [the]
Ars Amatoria, but doesn't understand what the tale of Baucis and Philemon
in the same author's *Metamorphosis* [sic] is about" (*SL* 4.285). Lovecraft uses
Ovid's erotic masterpiece to bait the philistine, but he prefers the later work,
for reasons that we shall soon explore. Besides these references to the creation story and the old couple, other sections of Ovid's masterpiece may have
occupied Lovecraft, though the work is seldom horrific or weird. Take for
instance the lengthy section devoted to the cave of Somnus, which was to
call forth from Spenser an ornate stanza of emulation in the first book of *The
Faerie Queene*. It is possible that a few sections of *The Dream-Quest of Unknown Kadath* find their ultimate genesis in Ovid's passage. More horrific is
the descent to the house of Invidia, a filthy and disgusting scene that Ovid
works up with great gusto. Most interesting to Lovecraft, I think, was the
climax of the work, the long passage, some four-hundred lines, in which Py-
thagoras announces that all is in flux:

> Neque enim consistere flumen
> nec levis hora potest, sed ut unda inpellitur unda
> urgeturque eadem veniens urgetque priorem,
> tempora sic fugiunt pariter pariterque sequuntur
> et nova sunt semper; nam quod fuit ante, relictum est,
> fitque, quod haud fuerat, momentaque cuncta novantur.
> [Neither can the river stand still
> nor the light hour, but as a wave is driven and moved by a wave
> at the same time arriving and moves the one before it,
> thus equally our times fly and equally follow,
> eternally made new, for what was before is abandoned,
> what hardly existed is made, and all moments are renewed].
> (15.181–85)

Originating in the Lucretian emphasis on flux, this passage insists upon
change as an inescapable aspect of human experience, whether in the
macro- or the micro-universe, and thus functions as the capstone for Ovid's
wonderful, shifting narrative.

Lovecraft's discoveries in the *Metamorphoses* are patent and hidden. It is
patent that any work that deals with bodily transformations should be of in-

terest to an author influenced by the recent claims made by Darwin. Evolution finds its imaginative correlative in a work that traces the continuous transformations that the earth has endured from the creation of the world to our own day, *pax Augustana*. And without pressing the point too greatly, we recognize that we are dealing with an author who in the Augustan peace suffered a radical transformation in his own life when Caesar exiled him to the shores of the Black Sea. Ovid is an exemplary author, in his grandiose theme and in his own life.

In contrast to Lovecraft's involvement with Ovid stands his involvement with Lucretius, whom he does not mention often in his letters. Keeping in mind that philosophy and poetry should not be distinguished in an imaginative writer, we might argue that Lucretius more works upon Lovecraft as far as his philosophy is concerned than his art. His references to Lucretius are almost overwhelmingly philosophic and perfunctory; he is one in a line of atomistic thinkers, Leucippus, Democritus and little else (cf. *inter alia* SL 2.160, 227, 270, and 336; and 3.146 and 300). In an early letter Lovecraft writes that certain authors, especially Plato, Lucretius, and Emerson, happen to be literary figures through their culture and brilliance, though it was the philosophic content that mattered most to them (*SL* 2.142). The power of such phrases as the "flammantia moenia mundi" (1.73) finds no resonance in the letters—though the phrase may, as I have argued elsewhere, find a resonance in the fiction, as has his vocabulary of the wall and the vortex (Waugh, *Monster* 54–55). But though this imagery proves fruitful for Lovecraft's language, it is difficult to separate Lucretius from the other atomists. Lucretius tells few stories, and therefore he almost seems a dead letter for Lovecraft the artist; he simply illustrates what the Providence author wishes him to illustrate. He does not excite the man, though paradoxically he does excite the thinker, especially the religious thinker. Lucretius is the Roman poet *par excellence* who determinedly disbelieves in the effectual power of gods and who denies thoroughly any belief in immortality. "Nil igitur mors est ad nos" [therefore death is nothing to us] (3.830), he announces, and he argues this proposition with every argument available at the time. The young Lovecraft, determined to find an escape from the First Baptist Church of Providence, must have found an agreeable soul in the works of Lucretius. In 1920 he wrote a poem, "On Religion," clearly influenced by Lucretius's work, as this couplet demonstrates: "Hope, effort, fame, to empty chaos tend— / Atoms on atoms, reeling without end!" (AT 240).

The last cosmic poet we wish to consider is Manilius. This is perhaps the most surprising poet to find Lovecraft interested in, for Manilius's poem, the

Astronomica, is not at all a work on astronomy as we understand it but a work on astrology; but as S. T. Joshi has pointed out, Lovecraft adverts to Manilius a number of times in his column on astronomy in the *Providence Evening News* ("Notes" 380), six times in fact (CE 3.129–307). Most of the time he is quoting from the translation of Thomas Creech, sometimes with a slight error as though he were quoting from memory. The final reference to Manilius, however, is through his own prose translation. Here is the original: "An maior densa stellarum turba corona / contexit flammas et crasso lumine candet, / et fulgore nitet collato clarior orbis?" [Or does a greater crowd of stars weave / its flames to a crown and shine with the dense light / and this circle gleam brighter in gathered splendor?] (1.755–57). This passage, like the others, shows that the *Astronomica* is more than a technical discussion of astrological intricacies, though it is certainly that. Through lovely descriptions of the constellations and the Milky Way it is a paean of praise to the coherence and order of the universe, insisting through the myth of the gigantomachia that divine understanding is capable of defeating the monstrous energy of chaos. This is a myth that in Manilius's hands plays in two different ways; on the one hand it celebrates reason and coherence, but politically it praises the coherence of the Augustan rule. But Manilius is not a simple optimist. He is quite aware of discord and transience, and though truth does exist it is hidden deeply away from our ability to discern it:

> Sic altis natura manet consaepta tenebris
> et verum in caeco est multaque ambagine rerum;
> nec brevis est usus nec amat compendia caelum,
> verum aliis alia opposita est et fallit imago
> mentiturque suas vires et munera celat.
> Quae tibi non oculis, alta sed mente fuganda est
> caligo, penitusque deus, non fronte, notandus.
> [Thus nature remains hidden in deep darkness
> and truth in the blind labyrinth of things;
> neither is the exercise short, nor does heaven like shortcuts,
> one thing is opposed to another, and the image fools us,
> counterfeits its strengths and conceals its gifts.
> Not with your eyes but with deep understanding must darkness
> be put to flight, and god found within, not outside. (4.303)

In this worldview no knowledge is won without great effort; we can imagine that Lovecraft would have appreciated this noble expression.

At least as interesting as these three authors for Lovecraft is Horace, upon two counts. First, the entire attitude that Horace represents in his odes is congenial to Lovecraft, a measured and ironic attitude that refuses to take himself or life too seriously; only art and local traditions are important to this cosmopolitan. Twice in the *Odes* he skeptically pokes fun at astrological pretensions (1.11 and 2.17). Lucretius is a much fiercer poet than Horace, and Lovecraft never assumed that ferocity within his letters. Horace is not a tragic poet, as is Lucretius; and his Epicurean attitude is very congenial to Lovecraft in most of his poetry, though he does employ lines in praise of wine as an introduction to his poem "The Power of Wine: A Satire" (AT 200). Twice he uses lines from the *Ars Poetica* as epigraphs to poems (AT 234, 383) and once three lines from the *Epodes* (AT 97). It is not out of character that in 1936, near the end of his life, he translated one of the lighter of Horace's erotic odes, with the distancing subtitle, "Translated by a Gentleman of New-England" (AT 180). There is that problem with the bibulous Horace; though he believed in moderation he was hardly an English gentleman.

More interesting for us in Horace's work, when we consider Lovecraft as a weird writer, are the epodes, satires, and letters that concern Canidia, in some poems simply an old hag who sells simples and charms, in others a witch who on the model of Medea is capable of sacrificing children to the dark goddess. Leaving aside the critical argument that labors to elucidate the purpose of these poems, we find here material that would have interested the man who was going to write "The Dreams in the Witch House." In the most harrowing of these poems, Horace allows the victim, a young boy, to speak before the witches sacrifice him for the sake of his organs. Canidia, like Medea, can bring down the stars and moon, and Keziah can fly through four-dimensional space; these witches have powers that can disrupt the cosmic order. It is remarkable, I believe, that in his compendious essay "Supernatural Horror in Literature" Lovecraft's list of the Latin authors that seem to him most representative of the genre does not mention Horace; yet he is often free to quote Horace in other contexts. Either he regarded these pieces as thoroughly satiric and thus beneath his concern, or he repressed them from his own concern because they were too close to him. On the whole the first possibility seems more probable, given the enormous, conscious generosity that he showed in other questions of debt. These pieces are simply too anomalous for a reader who treasures the Epicurean Horace. If the witches represent mere superstition, it is yet a superstition that seems to have some power in Horace's world. On the other hand, in his letters Horace does di-

rectly deny any validity to the supernatural world: "Somnia, terrores magi-
cos, miracula, sagas, / nocturnos lemures, portentaque Thessala rides?"
[Dreams, magic terrors, miracles, tales, / nocturnal lemurs, Thessalian por-
tents you laugh at?] (*Epist.* 2.2.208–09). Nevertheless, this particular scorn
for superstitious phenomena does not include the name of Canidia. The attraction Horace holds for Lovecraft is quite complex.

Perhaps the most famous witch in Roman literature, however, is Erictho,
whom Pompeius Sextus consults in Lucan's epic *The Bellum Civile*, also
known as *Pharsalia*. Most of the sixth book deals with this encounter, an occasion for Lucan to expatiate at length on the details of witchcraft as the
popular Roman mind envisioned it. This passage includes an ornate invocation of the gods of the underworld, especially Chaos "innumeros avidum
confundere mundos" [eager to destroy innumerable worlds] (6.696), a passage very like Lovecraft's treatment of such entities as Azathoth or Yog-
Sothoth. At the climax she resurrects a dead man and charges him, "Vel
numina torque / vel tu parce deis et manibus exprime verum" [Either torture
the deities / or spare the gods and wring the truth from the ghosts of the un-
derworld] (6.598-99). This is a blasphemous attempt to rip knowledge out of
the hands of the gods, an attempt that Joseph Curwen would have admired
and a cosmic magic that lies closer to Lovecraft's imagination than that of
Horace's poor hag. In addition, later in the ninth book in the description of
Cato's heroic leading of his army across the viper-infested desert of Libya,
Lucan develops an extensive account of how those serpents sprang from the
blood of the Medusa, whose look not only turns people into stone but im-
prisons their souls in those stone bodies. As we observed in an epigraph to
one of his poems (*AT* 403), Lovecraft was not unaware of Lucan, the
nephew of Seneca.

The Roman poet with whom Lovecraft is most concerned throughout his
life is Virgil, although it seems that he has two Virgils in mind, by both of
whom he is saturated. One is through his mother, since through her his ancestry is "immediately rural" (*SL* 3.316), a flavor that he attempts to recapture through reading such things as *The Farmer's Almanacks*, James
Thomson, and Robert Bloomfield, a poet-ploughman like Burns and Clare
who was in his heyday even more successful than they, Hesiod, and the
Virgil of the *Eclogues* and *Georgics* (*SL* 3.317), to which Lovecraft makes
several casual allusions. The poem "Quinsnicket Park" is introduced with an
epigraph from the *Georgics* (*AT* 267), as is the poem "Ver Rusticum" (*AT*
293). The other Virgil is the author of the *Aeneid*, which his uncle had trans-

lated (*SL* 5.329). "The Prophecy of Capys Secundus," a parody of Macaulay's manner in *The Lays*, is introduced by lines from the *Aeneid* which are rather too solemn, as Lovecraft knew, for the occasion (*AT* 364), a ploy he uses to introduce "The Feast" (371). Twice he parodies the famous opening of the *Aeneid* (*AT* 371, 397), and once he tells a joke on himself by referring to the famous phrase "lacrymae rerum" (*SL* 5.226), a phrase that he inserts more seriously into a lengthy passage in which his pastoral note is fused to his sense of loss and the passage of time (3.317–18). But what really moves him is not the Virgil who laments; it is the dream of power that seems sanctioned when Anchises prophesies the future of Rome:

> Excudunt alii spirantia mollius aera
> (Credo equidem), vivos ducent de marmore vultus,
> orabunt causas melius, caelique meatus
> describent radio et surgentia sidera dicent:
> tu regere imperio populos, Romane, memento
> (hae tibi erunt artes), pacisque imponere morem,
> parcere subiectis et debellare superbos.
> [Others will hammer the breathing bronze more softly
> (I think so indeed), and bring living faces out of marble,
> they will orate causes better, describe the motion
> of heaven with a rod and talk of the rising stars:
> you, Roman, remember to rule the peoples with authority
> (these will be your arts), to impose the manners of peace,
> to spare the downcast and beat down the proud.] (*Aeneid* 6.847–53)

It is a matter of some debate what Virgil intended by these lines. Certainly they express that distrust of the clever Greeks that we find elsewhere in the epic; Lovecraft forthrightly says, "I think of Greeks as cultivated but somewhat sycophantic aliens—good tutors of rhetoric and philosophy, but a little servile, unctuous, ratlike, sharp, and effeminate" (*SL* 4.333). A cynic might well argue that Anchises urges Aeneas/Augustus to spare those whom he has already subjected and to beat down those who oppose him; but we must not ignore the phrase, so firmly expressed in the Latin, "to establish the manners of peace, / to spare the downcast." Jupiter speaks with the voice of authority that the Trojan race, as Romans, should "totum sub leges mitteret orbem" [submit the world to laws] (4.231), not simply Roman law but a law that is transcendent. The purpose of empire, of sparing and of beating down, is ostensibly peace, though it is more likely that a poet will desire peace than that a ruler will; on the other hand, as though he were speaking for the nation Virgil often expresses the hope that the civil wars that had plagued Rome for so long should now cease with the accession of Augustus. This is the historical framework of the passage.

Twice, however, Lovecraft develops an ecstatic reading of this passage, compelled by his own prophetic stance that moves in a different direction. In 1923 he writes at length to Frank Belknap Long about the *"asthetick of strength"* to be found in Roman architecture, explicitly embodied in the three lines of Anchises' exhortation that Lovecraft claims the Romans fulfilled. As "conquering despots" they represented an "ebullient domination"; the city of Rome is "earth's supreme apotheosis of dominion" (*SL* 1.276). In 1931 he writes to James F. Morton in something of the same tenor, alluding to the "haughty dominance" of Anchises' lines; and he repeats the theme again in 1931, once more writing to Long, speaking of the Roman *"aesthetic of power"* and citing the Anchises passage in full (*SL* 3.313). And in other passages it is again the power of the Roman army that excites him (*SL* 1.315). His poem "1914," an exhortation to England that opens with an epigraph from these lines, concludes in the hope that "the mighty Empire shall become / A world itself—the deathless heir of Rome!" (*TA* 398). It is as though he were reading the Nietzschean will to power as well as the modern colonial imperative into Virgil; he never mentions such defeats as the battle of Cannae. He cannot take to heart such a Virgilian line as that which expresses the labor of establishing Rome, "tantae molis erat Romanam condere gentem" [such an effort was expended to found the Roman people] (1.33), and so he ignores that a better description of Virgil's work might be that it represents the aesthetics of piety—a responsible attitude toward the gods above and the gods below, to our ancestors and to our descendants, and to the society within which we live. We cannot escape the impression that a wilful misinterpretation of Anchises' lines occupied Lovecraft most of his life. There is a certain pathos in his reminiscence of having "sported" when seven years old the name L. Valerius Messala and torturing Christians in the amphitheatre (*SL* 3.313).

One other aspect of the *Aeneid* may have a different kind of impact upon Lovecraft's fictions—the way by which Virgil three times represents a history through the pictures on the walls of temples. In the first book Aeneas finds the history of Troy represented on the walls of Juno's temple in Carthage and realizes that he will find sympathy here; this is the scene that climaxes in the phrase, "sunt lacrimae rerum," leading to the supposition that piety is a more important response to tragedy than Stoic ataraxia. In the sixth book the pictures on the walls of the Sibyl's temple represent the inability of Daedalus to deal with the tragedy of his son's death. Given these models, it is possible that when Lovecraft gives the history of an alien race through the pictures graven on the tunnels that lead to their civilizations, as he does in "The Nameless City" and At the Mountains of Madness, he does so to lend an epic flavor to the narration. In addition, these depictions often encourage the lacrymae rerum, a piety toward a monstrous fate that finds its epitome in the statement that bears witness, "Whatever they had been, they were men!" (MM 96). In this case Virgil has provided Lovecraft with a noble model. In the seventh book Aeneas' embassy to Latinus meets him in a temple that displays the ancient kings, a list that moves into the religious myth and the folktale; throughout the Aeneid Virgil is fond of an antiquity that presents the history of a people in an atmospheric blue tint.

This aspect of Virgil surely appealed to Lovecraft in the story of Cacus that Evander recounts in the eighth book. Aeneas and his cohorts have arrived at the upper Tiber, the future site of Rome, looking for allies. The king invites them to a religious service that he assures them, in an anti-Lucretian passage, has not been established by superstition but by an immediate experience of savage perils (8.185–88). Lovecraft, we imagine, read this passage with a double engagement, on the one hand scorning Virgil's dismissal of Lucretius and on the other hand admiring Virgil's respect for tradition. Evander then describes, in highly impressionistic terms, the appearance of the semihuman Cacus who terrorized the people, hanging the faces of the men he has slain at the entrance to his cave (8.194–96), before the appearance of Hercules. When the monster, the son of Vulcan and thus himself semidivine, stole Hercules' cattle, employing the trick that Mercury had used when stealing the cattle of Apollo (cf. Horace's ode 1.10), Hercules with little finesse tore apart the mountain that shielded the cave in which the monster took refuge. Several phrases up to this point have emphasized the weird darkness of this cave that lies beneath a "saxis suspensam [. . .] rupem" [cliff suspended upon rocks] (8.190), under a pile of "disiectae [. . .] moles desertaque montis" [scattered heap and deserts of the mountain] where the "scopuli ingentem traxere ruinam" [stones dragged down a great ruin] (8.191–92). I think it not forfetched to believe that Lovecraft, who often argued the power of atmosphere in the weird tale, found some support in Virgil's practice. Hercules of course does not adopt the intellectual stance of so many of Lovecraft's protagonists; more like Robert E. Howard's Conan he attacks, using a tree to uproot the cave of Cacus and leave it bare to the sun, which reveals it as a complex underworld:

> At specus et Caci detecta apparuit ingens
> regia, et umbrosae penitus patuere cavernae,
> non secus ac si qua penitus vi terra dehiscens
> infernas reseret sedes et regna recludat
> pallida, dis invisa, superque immane barathrum
> cernatur, trepident immiso lumine Manes.
> [The cavern and great kingdom of Cacus lies discovered,
> and the shadowy cavern lies open to its depths,
> not otherwise than if the earth should gape violently
> and unlock the infernal seats and pallid kingdom
> hateful to the gods, the immense pit be seen
> and the ghosts shudder at the light let in.] (8.241–46)

The rhythm of this passage, its repetitions and half-rhymes, is very suggestive of the style that Lovecraft employs at his climaxes that are a blend of the weird and the sublime. To these details we should add the allusion to Homer that Virgil contains in the alliterative phrase "trepident immiso lumine Manes." Consider this passage, then, from "The Rats in the Walls":

> It was a twilit grotto of enormous height, stretching away farther than any eye could see; a subterranean world of limitless mystery and horrible suggestion. There were buildings and other architectural remains [. . .], but all these were dwarfed by the ghoulish spectacle presented by the general surface of the ground. For yards about the steps extended an insane tangle of human bones at least as human as those on the steps. Like a foamy sea they stretched, some fallen apart, but others wholly or partly articulated as skeletons; these latter invariably in postures of daemoniac frenzy, either fighting off some menace or clutching other forms with cannibal intent. (DH 41–42)

The depth and height of the scene, the "ghoulish spectacle" of the bodies, the suggestion of cannibalism, and the immense energy of this internal world—all these details have affinity with the cave of Cacus.

Last let us consider the moment when his penates appear to Aeneas to give him one of the several prophecies of the third book. In a book that is often weak the scene has a remarkable power, in part because it is one in a series of nocturnal scenes in the Aeneid that emphasize rest:

> Nox erat et terris animalia somnus habebat:
> effigies sacrae divum Phrygiique penates,
> quos mecum ab Troia mediisque ex ignibus urbis
> extuleram, visi ante oculos astare iacentis

in somnis multo manifesti lumine, qua se
plena per insertas fundebat luna fenestras.
[It was night, and sleep lay upon all the creatures of earth:
the sacred effigies of the gods and the Phrygian household gods
which I had borne with me from Troy
out of the fires of the city, I saw stand before my eyes
in a dream, manifest in much light, which the full moon
poured through the open windows] (3.147–52)

"Multo manifesti lumine" is the phrase that indicates the difference between
Virgil and Lovecraft, for though Aeneas feels fear, "talibus attonitus visis" [as-
tonished at such a sight] (3.172), he also receives important information that
sustains his journey. Such passages in the Roman poet are the fantasizing of an
enlightened mind that still feels the sway of the numinous. In this regard we
can argue that fantasy as we understand it first arises among the Roman authors; both Ovid and Horace in very different ways tell this kind of story,
though the numinous is losing its power in the context of their irony. Employing a very sophisticated meter Catullus tells this kind of story when he describes the self-castration a young Roman inflicts on himself when he takes
part in the rituals of Cybele, a poem to which the protagonist of "The Rats in
the Walls" refers with trembling (DH 37). It is telling, I believe, that the Romans tell ghost stories; consider once more the third, fifth, and fifteenth Epodes of Horace, with their gruesome and nasty allusions to witches who
sacrifice young children, and Apuleius' Metamorphoses, which opens with an
extended story of witches and ghosts and which features a protagonist who
like so many Lovecraft protagonists is determined to learn of occult matters
and who does so at his peril. We might, indeed, take this protagonist, eager to
travel to Thessaly, "originis maternae nostrae fundamenta" [the base of our
maternal origin] (1.2), because of his fascination with the theme of witchcraft,
"nimis cupidus cognoscendi quae rara miraque sunt" [too desirous of knowing
things that are rare and miraculous] (2.1), as symptomatic of Lovecraft's protagonists and of Lovecraft's own condition as he deals with weird fiction. The
theme of the witch as ghoul, so important to Lovecraft (Waugh, Monster 20–
22), is central to both Horace and Apuleius. Even the sober Stoic Seneca invents such moments in his tragedies, for instance the extended presence of the
ghost of Laius in Oedipus.[1] The Greeks did not tell this kind of story because

---

1. In 1931 Lovecraft cites a famous epigram from Seneca's Hercules Furens (ll. 251–52) in
conjunction with a reference to Seneca's Medea (SL 3.251).

they still more than half believed in the integrity of their myths. And for this reason the fantasy story disappears during the Middle Ages, the ages of belief, only to return during the Renaissance in the hands of Pulci, Boiardo, and Ariosto. This is, I believe, the more profound reason for the affinity Lovecraft feels for the Roman authors. I am not convinced of any direct influence that Catullus, Apuleius, or Horace exert upon Lovecraft, despite his familiarity with them, but I suspect that these materials may have offered an additional sanction to such stories as "The Dreams in the Witch House."

Lovecraft has another reason for appreciating the Romans, one not so immediately apparent in his letters. Several Roman authors—but not Virgil—express a profound anti-Semitism that must have been agreeable to him. And how wrong was he in finding authority for his anti-Semitism in the Romans? The historical roots of anti-Semitism are murky, but there is some evidence that the Romans did feel differently about the Jews than they did about their other conquered peoples, feelings intensified by the growth of Christianity. As Gager and Schäfer make clear, for some years scholars have surveyed signs of anti-Semitism in Latin culture, attitudes that the Romans inherited from the Greeks and Egyptians. In the case of the Romans, however, these attitudes are powered by the fear that Judaism might be accepted in Rome because it is indeed attractive, especially in its forthright monotheism. In the oration *Pro Flacco* Cicero describes Judaism as a "barbara superstitio," opposed to the values of Roman *religio* and *mos* of the *res publica* (67). According to St. Augustine, Seneca describes the Jews as a "sceleratissima gens" who have been received in every part of the earth; so ubiquitous are they, and by inplication so persuasive, that "victi victoribus leges dederunt" [the conquered give laws to their conquerors] (6.11). They are the most dangerous example of the *superstitio* demonstrated by other Eastern peoples (6.10). As late as the fourth century we can see these attitudes at work in an otherwise pleasant poem by Rutilius Namatianus. Though he claims that Rome made a city of what had once been a world (1.66), this hegemonic vision is threatened by the Jew, whom he attacks for not eating the food that others eat, for his sabbaths, and for his circumcision. The climax of this long passage is a couplet that imitates Seneca, "latius excisae pestis contagia serpunt, / victoresque suos natio victa premit" [the contagion of this plague, though excised, creeps widely, / and the conquered nation oppresses its conquerors] (ll. 397–98). The most thorough and well-known outline of Roman attitudes can be found in the beginning of the fifth book of Tacitus's *Histories*, in which he sketches the history and beliefs of the Jews. Here we find the charges that the Jews in their exclusivity hate the rest of humanity with a "hostile odium" (5.5). Moses had established "novos ritus contrariosque ceteris mortalibus" [new rites contrary to other mortals] (5.4); moreover, their rites and feasts are based upon a *mos* that is "absurdus sordidusque" (5.5). So widespread is this antipathy that in his old age Seneca confesses that he gave up vegetarianism at the urging of his father because it was associated, however unjustly, with "alienigena sacra" [foreign rites] accused of superstition (*Ep.* 108.22).

This is the background to Gibbon's attitude toward the Jews:

> From the reign of Nero to that of Antoninus Pius, the Jews discovered a fierce impatience to the dominion of Rome, which repeatedly broke out in the most furious massacres and insurrections. Humanity is shocked at the recital of the horrid cruelties which they committed in the cities of Egypt, of Cyprus, and of Cyrene, where they dwelt in treacherous friendship with the unsuspecting natives; and we are tempted to applaud the severe retaliation which was exercised by the arms of the legions against a race of fanatics, whose dire and credulous superstition seemed to render them the implacable enemies not only of the Roman government, but of human kind. (2.78)

The Jews he claims, not the Romans, were moved by malice and prejudice against the Christians (2.88–89), and in a footnote he holds "the malice of the Jews" responsible for the pagan riots against the Christians (2.101).

These various passages, most of which Lovecraft was doubtless familiar with, provide the background to his reading of Juvenal. It is not surprising that Lovecraft, given his satiric turn of mind, should be attracted to Juvenal. A number of perfunctory references attest to that author's authority in the picture he draws of Roman decadence. More interesting is a letter in 1927 when Lovecraft cites the famous line "Syrus in Tiberim defluxit Orontes" (*SL* 3.62), which he misquotes slightly from memory, and uses to draw a parallel between Juvenal's Rome and his own recent experience of New York City: "It is not America—it is not even Europe—it is Asia & chaos & hell— the sort of stinking, amorphous, hybridism which Juvenal noted in Rome" (*SL* 2.101). He makes the same point in 1929 at greater length when he discusses his desire to be descended from "Roman stock," but not from the time of the Empire when that stock "had become as vitiated & mongrelised as the American people now threaten to be" (*SL* 3.282). His evidence for that mongrelised state is again Juvenal's lines:

> *Jampridem Syrus in Tiberium defluxit Orontes, et linguam et mores et cum latrinae chordas obliquas nec non gentilia tympana secum vexit* . . . . Or as Gifford trans-

lates it—or rather paraphrases it—

> "Long since the stream that wanton Syria loves
> Has disembogued its filth in Tiber's waves;
> Its language, arts; o'erwhelm'd us with the scum
> Of Antioch's streets, its minstrel, harp, & drum." (SL 3.283)

These two passages suggest another reason for Lovecraft's preference for
Roman culture, because it seems to represent to him the same kind of animus against the cultures of the Near East as he felt, an animus recently exacerbated by his experience in New York. Thus Juvenal becomes an
authority for Lovecraft's anti-Semitism. And thus Gifford's paraphrase, with
its obnoxious word "disembogued," not really suggested in Juvenal's lines
where the word "latrinae" does not appear, becomes justified by imputing a
sewer life to the Semitic world. Note how often in Lovecraft's stories the underworld is characterized in part as a sewer, especially in his most overtly
anti-Semitic story, "The Horror at Red Hook." In any case, the suggestion of
Juvenal's lines is reinforced by a passage in which Tacitus charges the Christians and the Jews of infecting Rome: "per urbem etiam quo cuncta undique
atrocia aut pudenda confluunt celebranturque" [for through the city all that
is atrocious and shameful flows and is celebrated] (*Annales* 15.44). All sewers lead to Rome—or to Providence. There is one exception to these attitudes in the skeptical Ovid when in the *Ars Amatoria* he lists the various
temples where a young man might pick up a young lady and includes "culta-
que Iudaeo septima sacra Syro" [the sabbath celebrated by Syrian Jews]
(1.76). Ovid, unlike these several other Roman authors, comic skeptic that
he is, has no problem with the religions or the peoples from the east.

There is one other aspect to the language the Latin authors use in regard
to the Eastern rites, especially the Phrygian celebrations of the Great Mother
Cybele, which Lucretius describes in these alliterative lines: "Tympana tenta
tonant palmis et cymbala circum / concava, raucisonoque minantur cornua
cantu, / et Phrygio stimulant numero cava tibia mentis." [The taut timbrel
thunders from palms, and the concave / cymbals, horns threaten with raucous song, / and the hollow flute excites minds with Phrygian numbers]
(2.618–20). According to Catullus, Attis celebrates the Goddess thus,
"niueis citata cepit manibus leue tympanum" [excited she takes in her white
hands the light timbrel] (63.9), and later in the poem "leue tympanum re-
mugit, caua cymbala recrepant" [the light timbrel bellows again and the hol-

low cymbals crackle] (63.29). Catullus uses a similar language when he announces the arrival of Bacchus to the deserted Ariadne:

> Plangebant aliae proceris tympana palmis,
> aut tereti tenuis tinnitus aere ciebant;
> multis raucisonos efflabant cornua bombos
> barbaraque horribili stridebant tibia cantu.
> [The timbrel lamented to the palms of the leader,
> or brought forth a thin whine from rounded bronze;
> the horns blew raucous booms
> and the barbaric flutes whistled a horrible song.] (64.261–64)

Note how Catullus employs the Lucretian "palmis" and "raucisonos" in a
new phrase. When the women tear Orpheus apart in the *Metamorphoses*,
they do so to the music of "infracto Berecynthia tibia cornu / tympanaque et
plausus et Bacchei ululatus" [of the Berecynthian flutes and the weak horns,
/ of the timbrel and clapping and the Bacchic lament] (11.16–17). Not surprisingly, Ovid uses the same language when describing the approach of
Bacchus: "Tympana cum subito non apparentia raucis / obstrepuere sonis et
adunco tibia cornu / tinnulaque aere sonant [when suddenly the invisible
timbrel / made a raucous noise and the flute / rang out bronze to the crooked
horn] (4.391–93). The timbrels, drums, and flutes, discordant and deep, belong to all the ecstatic cults. Associated with wine and the East, with all that
is not rational from the perspective of sober, philosophic Rome, the provoca-
tive blood-lust of the music announces radical change. And in Lovecraft the
drum, the cymbals, and the flute obsessively characterize the clumsy music
played in the court of Azathoth. At the conclusion of "Nyarlathotep" we
hear "the muffled, maddening beating of drums, and thin, monotonous
whine of blasphemous flutes [. . .]; the detestable pounding and piping"
(MW 34). In *The Dream-Quest of Unknown Kadath* Azathoth sits "amidst the
muffled, maddening beat of vile drums and the thin, monotonous whine of
accursed flutes" (MM 404). In the sonnet "Azathoth," monsters in the court
of chaos dance "insanely to the high, thin whining / Of a cracked flute" (AT
73). The excitement of the classical music has been transposed to a different
key, the joy castrated to a music purely instinctual. The irrational temptations and terror of the Great Goddess accompany the worship of the chaos at
the center of the universe; but that chaos fundamentally qualifies her music.
Or, to put this another way, the only divinity that Lovecraft implicitly acknowledges is the irrational numen that the classical world worshipped un-

der the names of Cybele and Dionysus, the one transformed into a force
even more threatening and the other watered down into a sinister intellect
that eschews the grape. The pagan world, despite Lovecraft's praise, cannot
live in the modern world.

We need to ask to what extent Latin authors are present in the stories
themselves. A simple survey gives us a swift answer—not as much as we might
expect, given what we have already said. In the early story "The Tree" the epigraph, "Fata viam invenient" (D 50), derives probably from the *Aeneid*, in the
optimistic lines Jupiter speaks on the reconciled future of the Trojans and the
Latins (10.113). "The Tomb" has an epigraph also from Virgil, the ambiguous
line that Palinurus speaks in his afterlife, hoping that "Sedibus ut saltem
placidis in morte quiescam" [at least I might rest in a quiet seat] (D 3). In the
same story Jervas mentions his reading of Plutarch upon Theseus as the young
hero finds the signs of his paternity under a rock (D 6). This reading, however,
is rather ironic, as is the Virgilian epigraph, since there is no rest in this tomb
and since Jervas's paternity does not initiate a heroic life. "The Festival" is introduced by an epigraph from Lactantius, "Efficiunt Daemones, ut quae non
sunt, sic tamen quasi sint, conspiceanda hominibus exhibeant" (D 208), a
phrase that is related to a similar sentiment in the Latin epigraph with which
Coleridge introduces *The Rime of the Ancient Mariner*. Both suggest a pneu-
monology in which the universe is filled with spirit.

Finally in this survey we must note the various references in "The Rats in
the Walls" to Catullus' poem on the voyage of Attis to the Magna Mater and
his self-castration (DH 29, 37, and 45). This may be the story in which Lovecraft most consciously makes use of Latin materials, this cautionary tale
against Eastern cults and irrational dispossession; but this learned and perverse poem is central to this story. In his letters Lovecraft does not seem interested in the Catullus so desperately in love with the unfaithful Lesbia,
though he does in 1927 write the poem "Hedone," in which Catullus attempted to revive in his heart the dreams of conquest "But found his
deaden'd soul bound fast / To foetid flesh and charnel fire" (AT 173). Catullus is also at work in "Medusa's Coil," in which the reference to the hair of
Berenice probably depends upon Catullus' learned translation of a poem by
Callimachus. The only references to Catullus lie in these two remarkable poems that represent the Roman poet's desire to fulfill the Alexandrian aesthetic of Callimachus—no doubt a fascinating aesthetic but not the language
of naked revelation for which we read Catullus today. Catullus, then, does
seem to have an influence upon Lovecraft's imagination, orbiting within

Lovecraft's imagination of the decadent world of his beloved, stalwart Rome in the late Republic, and thus it is a minor influence that admits the power of the erotic world. As Lovecraft grows older and begins to elaborate his own mythic world he depends less upon the classical world for his inspiration.

II

[. . .] et iam nox umida caelo
praecipitat suadentque cadentia sidera somnos.
[and now the moist night comes down
from heaven and setting stars urge us to sleep] (Virgil, *Aen.* 2.8–9)

Finally, let us examine the stories that Lovecraft produced to give body to his Roman obsession. But we do not possess them as stories. Two or more that he wrote as a boy, some of them based on dreams, were lost by the time he described them in his letters. Some of the first dreams may have been excited by "a handbook of Roman Antiquities" he wrote during 1905 (Joshi, *HPL: A Life* 72); it was during this period, he later wrote, that most of such dreams occurred, though they never wholly ceased through the rest of his life (*SL* 2.189). Half the stories that he wrote during this period concerned "strange survivals of Roman civilization in Africa, Asia, the Antarctic, the Amazon Valley, and even pre-Columbian North America" (*SL* 4.336). One that he did save for years, clearly close to his heart, based on a dream in 1904, dealt with a Roman legion where Providence was later to stand at war with the Native Americans and "a gradual blood-mixture" that led to the aquiline features of an otherwise Mongoloid race (*SL* 4.336). Their ruins are discovered "during the digging of a sewer-main"—once more that motif!—"and the dreams it inspired in one lone student" (*SL* 4.336), who shall clearly return as Wilcox in "The Call of Cthulhu" or as Gilman in "The Dreams in the Witch House." The idea of writing such a story was still with him in 1929 when Elizabeth Toldridge sent him a clipping about a Roman coin found in an Indian grave. In the story he would have had the forgotten colony at war with a Mayan or Aztec culture "and perhaps suffer extirpation in a desperate battle, or sink amidst an earthquake" (*SL* 3.27). Perhaps the story seemed too much an imitation of H. Rider Haggard or perhaps too much an imitation of the fate of the Lost Colony in North Carolina, for Lovecraft never wrote it.

More fascinating is a dream that he described in great detail in a letter to Bernard Austin Dwyer, but never came to elaborate and shape as a story. We cannot be certain why he never carried through. One difficulty he felt was how to handle the chronological terms, reconciling the Roman Republican calendar with that of the black sabbath (SL 2.215–16). Since he never wrote the story, we can only speculate upon its main parts through his indications of how he might have written the story, recognizing that a dream no matter how detailed is not the story for which it would have provided the material—yet he had in the past used some of his dreams, most notably in "Nyarlathotep," "The Statement of Randolph Carter," "The Outsider," and "Celephaïs" (SL 2.202). Lovecraft was accustomed to living off the gifts of his dreams.

But this dream, he felt, needed a frame. A month after the dream he planned to write a frame, in which contemporary archaeologists discover fragments of an ancient disaster; one of them then dreams of the disaster, Lovecraft's dream proper (thus perhaps obviating problems of historicity), only to wake and discover that his friends have died in mysterious circumstances. It is quite possible that Lovecraft might have wished to elaborate this frame a good deal; but if he had he would have faced the problem that he had never lived in Spain and thus one of the great virtues of his work, its local specificity, would have been difficult to create. He had not felt such problems in earlier works like "The Hound" or "The Rats in the Walls," but his later meticulous aesthetics would not have permitted such a cavalier treatment.

A further difficulty we may speculate was that certain phrases have an interesting resonance. At its opening the people of Pompelo are afraid "of the doom which they felt about to fall upon their town" as an act of revenge (SL 2.191); and when the soldiers arrive they discover "there was indeed an air of monstrous doom upon that town" (SL 2.194). Lovecraft seems to be using the language he had already used in "The Doom That Came to Sarnath." That story is in many ways quite different from the dream, above all in that fact that it does not use a historical location as the Roman dream does—but it is a story of a nameless revenge upon a town. Doubtless Lovecraft would have revised the dream heavily had he written the story; and we recognize how often he returned to early themes and narratives and elaborated them into new shapes. Nevertheless, this verbal echo does suggest that the stories might have been too akin.

As for the dream, a very striking aspect is the fact that the protagonist of its first-person narration falls asleep at least four times in its course, once to another nightmare. In few stories of his mature period are dreams so foregrounded, both in the original dream in which the protagonist sleeps to wake three days before the action proper begins and in the frame Lovecraft might have written. This may be one reason that he could not continue the story;

it expresses a growing doubt in what Burleson called oneiric objectivity: "The theme that there is at best an ambiguous distinction between dreaming and reality—that the world of deep dream may be as real as, or more real than, the waking world" ("On Lovecraft's Themes" 136). In the story as Lovecraft imagined it, a strong tension would have existed between the dream and the realism the place demanded. It is as though the dream acknowledged its own status, were attempting to say four times, "This is a dream," and felt a great compunction not to get to the point; the protagonist is eager to climb the mountains in order to confront the mystery, but his unconscious is not. In a clear example of Freudian ambivalence, the unconscious goes kicking, albeit not screaming, toward the confrontation it desires where the celebration of chaos is underway. Perhaps to that extent Burleson is quite right, because the dreams that the protagonist suffers know better than he what lies ahead in the dream of the primary dreamer.

This problem raises a further problem Lovecraft faces in writing his Roman dream as a story. He does, in the story, wish to maintain that it is a dream, and thus (*pace* Burleson's argument) he no longer seems to believe in his dreams as he once had. Consider how few stories from 1928 on, in contrast to his earlier period, are cast as dreams; "The Dreams in the Witch House" is not an exception to this remark, since its dreams are cast within the framework of science fiction. The frame will not work imaginatively. But if it will not work, he finds himself cast back upon the plot's facticity, which in his first, meticulous account is immense. But once he had renounced the power and authority of dreams, Lovecraft became a local writer. Dreams after all, as Joyce realized and hence the difficulty of *Finnegans Wake,* do not obey the categories of space and time. Now, in dealing with his Roman dream, Lovecraft felt that he needed to become a local writer of Roman Spain, as far as his imagination is concerned—but not as far as his reason is concerned, which demanded that he swat up more realistic details, as though he had been there. He cannot, however, be there in the sense that he had been in New England from his earliest years and needed to return there to save himself from his New York catastrophe. It is an insoluble problem, so his dream, looking forward to the problem, demands that he fall asleep in the dream.

How are we to interpret the story if we do not have the privilege of these biographical details? If we simply read a story in which the protagonist is always falling asleep and suffering, as he tells us without providing any detail, nightmares? This protagonist, Lucius Caelius Rufus, bears a fine equestrian name, just the sort that Lovecraft was later to imagine as one of his ancestors

(*SL* 2.283). Perhaps he had in mind Marcus Caelius Rufus, a young friend of Cicero with a dramatic career that moved from party to party as Caesar rose to power. Fortuitously, the second and third elements of his name mean "heavenly" and "red." This is a name that Manilius could have set among the constellations. The man has a reason to sleep, attempting to recover his divine connection.

The other main character of the story is Cnaeus Balbutius, the legatus of the XII Legion. The name Balbutius, as Lovecraft knows as he plays with the name, is rather similar to Balbus, the Iberian Roman who became rich constructing public works in Rome, of such an ill-repute that Cicero had to defend him, just as upon occasion he had had to defend Marcus Caelius Rufus also. Though there is no indication that Balbutius suffers from this affliction, the root of the name means "to stutter"; and a number of failures in communication do occur in the story. Balbus is of sufficient interest that Joyce was to make him a central figure in *Finnegans Wake*.

A further aspect of the narration is that it follows an arc of moving from a civilized world, one in which the protagonist often goes through the motions of civilization, to a primitive world in which the Vascones are terrified of the *Miri nigri*, which spoke "amongst themselves a language that neither Roman, Celtiberian, nor Gaul [nor any other people in the Roman *orbis*] could understand" (*SL* 2.190). In the civilized world Lucius reads Lucretius, speaking with his family and writing in the garden; in the primitive world only gestures are used to communicate. Balbutius, in contrast, reads "a shabby copy of Cato's *De Re Rustica*" (*SL* 2.193). The legatus is a conservative man, interested in the solid Roman virtues of the farmland two centuries before.

This mention of Lucretius is remarkable, for as we have seen Lucretius is otherwise not of great imaginative interest to Lovecraft. But Lucretius is a part of the characterization of this protagonist, who is thus revealed as a Roman rationalist, open to the foreign ideas of certain "advanced" Greeks who oppose the tradional piety of the Roman *religio*. Early in the dream the protagonist reads this line from the *De Rerum Natura*: "lunaque sive notho fertur loca lumine lustrans" (5.575). Lucretius here is arguing the nature of the moon's light, which either proceeds of itself or, as the line says, illuminates the land with a bastard light. This is the light that ill illuminates the main action of the story, when the cohort led by its uncomfortable guide advances up the mountain to confront the cultists, climbing through a valley so steep that it is at last precipitous. If we remember that in a dream the way up is the way down, we realize that this is an underworld that the cohort is moving through. From this

point of view the Lucretian line may be a substitute for the Virgilian passage
that describes Aeneas' descent into the underworld:

> Ibant obscuri sola sub nocte per umbram
> perque domos Ditis vacuas et inania regna:
> quale per incertam lunam sub luce maligna
> est iter in silva, ubi caelum condidit umbra
> Iuppiter, et rebus nox abstulit atra colorem.
> [They were going darkly through the shadows of night
> and through the empty homes of Dis and his void kingdom:
> as through an uncertain moon beneath malign light
> one journeys in a wood, when Jupiter buries
> the sky in shadow, and black night removes all color.] (6.268–72)

Here again we find the heightened phasing—"sub luce maligna" and "rebus
nox abstulit atra colore"—and the artful varied repetitions (*umbram-umbra,
regna-maligna,* and *est iter-Iuppiter*) that are so much a part of Lovecraft's mature style. But even that malign light of the moon, that bastard light as Lucretius puts it, is absent in Lovecraft's dream, for the soldiers begin their
ascent in the dark of the moon.

The great question the dream presents is whether the cohort should be
sent to suppress the *Miri nigri*. Balbutius and Lucius are agreed upon this
point, the latter feeling that good governance and the trust of the populace
are threatened by these alien ecstatics in the mountains. Lucius' mother
Helvia does not approve of his participation in the military work—he is, after all, a civil servant—but when the operation is approved "my joy was extreme" (*SL* 2.193). Since Lucius' father is never mentioned in the dream, it
is hard not to compare the situation to that which Lovecraft and his mother
faced when he attempted, against her successful opposition, to sign up for
America's entrance into the Great War. To this extent the dream patently
manifests Freud's notion of the wish-fulfillment; but at the catastrophic end
Lucius pays severely for this fulfillment and for ignoring the wish of his
mother. Even more striking is the interest that the rationalist Lucius shows
in "terrible and forbidden" matters, possessing a large library in which the
Hieron Aegypton takes the part of the *Necronomicon* as that preeminent work
in horror (*SL* 2.192). Once again we see that he desires the horror that he
means to exterminate, just as his ancestors had "broken up the widespread
orgies of Bacchus in Italy" (*SL* 2.198).

In the climax the soldiers do not actually see what destroys them—but what is there to see in the kingdom of Hades? Instead, they are swept by a panic that strips them of all Roman reason and power, the qualities that Lovecraft most admired in his ideal Roman culture. Only one ancient soldier retains his Stoic calm in the face of the faceless terror. His words conclude Lovecraft's account of the dream: "*Malitia vetus—malitia vetus est—venit—tandem venit*" [the old evil—the evil is old—it comes—at last it comes] (*SL* 197). It is clear that no one shall return from this expedition, one reason perhaps why Lovecraft felt that he needed the frame in which the dreamer wakes to find that something horrible has happened to the Spanish archaeologists. When we think of Spain in this period, however, it is not horrors that happen to archaeologists that spring to our attention but the horrors of the Civil War. Lovecraft's dream occurs before the Civil War began, and I do not wish to suggest that the dream is prophetic. Still, Lovecraft read widely in political affairs, so it is not far-fetched to invoke Plato's suggestion that poets know more of the world's events that they are individually aware of and to opine that Lovecraft's story, the story he never wrote, can be applied to the Spanish cataclysm. Think of Lucius as a serious and selfless falangist and of the *Miri nigri* as the Republican forces, keeping in mind that Lovecraft did not care for the communist Republicans but he also felt some ambivalence concerning the Catholic fascists (*SL* 5.392).

Let us probe further the identity of this *malitia vetus* that has come upon the expedition, that has not only come upon it but has "at last" come upon it, as though that *tandem* implied a thing expected despite anything that might be done. Earlier Lovecraft informs Dwyer that it is known in the area as the *Magnum innominandum*, "a neuter gerundive form of sound Latin etymology, though not found in the classics" (*SL* 2.190). Most properly we would translate this phrase "the great thing that must not be named," but it is unclear whether it must not be named because of a prohibition or because it in fact has no name: must it not be named, or can it not be named? Lovecraft had of course explicitly dealt with this theme earlier in the story "The Unnamable," and now his dream returns him to the theme as though it had not been fully explored. In that story, when the entity arises from a tomb for a brief moment of destructive power, Randolph Carter and his friend Joel Manton experience it in different ways. For Carter, his "fancy peopled the rayless gloom with Miltonic legions of the misshapen damned," but Manton has a fuller experience of "a gelatin—a slime—yet it had shapes, a thousand shapes of horror beyond all memory. There were eyes—and a blemish" (*D* 207). The congruity between their experiences is undercut by this last detail.

The blemished eye recalls that eye described earlier in the story by Cotton Mather, set in the face of "the beast that had brought forth what was more than beast but less than man" (*D* 203). That which cannot and must not be named, because it belongs to two categories of being, also cannot and must not be named because it looks upon the world in a distorted fashion. The blemish belongs to the language of mockery that is so important to Lovecraft's vision of humanity. But whatever the entity is now, whether beast or "a thousand forms of horror," is "beyond all memory," exciting an infinity of visionary experiences that Carter's word, "fancy," is too weak to express.

We find, then, that this blemish, a mote in the eye, belongs also to the two men: Manton, the believer in the supernatural, who cannot bring himself to believe in the unnamable; and Carter, the skeptic, who finds that he does believe in that which he cannot name, if only through the fact that the word he bandies about so rhetorically does point at it. And this relationship between the skeptic and the believer is repeated in Lovecraft's dream, but with a reversal of roles. The protagonist of the dream now takes the role of the believer rather than of the skeptic; and the other, the rough and ready Balbutius, takes the role of the skeptic. Nevertheless, no matter how these roles are transformed, the blemish in the eye remains, so that they do not see the *malitia vetus* that descends upon them, though it does descend upon them "at last," obliterating their words.

Lovecraft's dream creates a powerful narrative rhetoric for expressing the *Magnum innominandum*. The Romans have colonized a Celtiberian people that speak their own language. To the north of them live the "restless Vacones, only a part of whom were thoroughly Romanised" (*SL* 2.190); but to the north of them, in the mountains, live the *Miri nigri* with a language utterly alien to any of the others. The landscape presents three grades of inexpressibility. The third grade, the truly inexpressible, is represented through the steepness of those mountains, ascending at the conclusion of the dream into the cold sky that says nothing. In an analogous fashion, the dreams of the protagonist had warned him that he was approaching a dream landscape in which his secret dreads would take shape to destroy him.

Such was Lovecraft's Roman dream, in which he discovered a protagonist such as he had written of before; but transposed to a Roman scene, which Lovecraft so much more admired than the twentieth century America in which he lived, his concerns seem to take on a new point and clarity. It is a shame that he never shaped this dream into a story in which he would have made it so much more his own.

Lovecraft Speaks French, in a Manner of Speaking

> Here, then, in this revolt against exteriority, against rhetoric, against a materialist tradition; in this endeavor to disengage the ultimate essence, the soul, of whatever exists and can be realised by the consciousness; in this dutiful waiting upon every symbol by which the soul of things can be made visible; literature, bowed down by so many burdens, may at last attain liberty, and its authentic speech. (Symons 5)

Here is the program of Symbolism as Arthur Symons understood it. Lovecraft freed himself at last from rhetoric, but he was always a materialist. On the other hand, he did work at freeing from the narrative through his interest in rendering the atmosphere of the story, its interiority and soul. He was never sure that he had attained "the soul of things" or an authentic speech, since he feared that he had been too influenced by the conventions of pulp fiction, but there is no doubt that he was as powerfully influenced by the Symbolist movement as Clark Ashton Smith had been. France permeates his fiction.

Consider some of his characters: Charles le Sorcière, Jacques and Etienne Roulet, Marceline Bedard, and Joseph Curwen's "incredibly aged French housekeeper" (MM 119). It is a dramatis personae of horror in Lovecraft's stories. A small but striking number of his villains are French, and it is a small window into the workings of his imagination to ask why. His different feelings toward French culture and French literature were of course qualified by his Anglophilia. On the one hand, his attitude toward the French authors of the Renaissance and the Enlightenment never varies from one of affirmation, as we can see in even so small a detail as the presence of Pierre-Louis Montagny from the time of Louis XIII among the elite selected by the Great Race in "The Shadow out of Time" (DH 396); yet his knowledge of the literature of that time seems quite minimal. His attitudes toward later French literature are more complex.

French architecture, however, was in his own backyard across the street from the First Baptist Church, the Fleur-de-Lys Building that was modeled on the seventeenth-century Norman and Breton style and built in 1885 (Gaer 265). Fortunately he had no problem with the Normans, given their conquest of England. In January 1926 he had written his aunt Lillian that he had no problem with the assimilation of "such French-Canadians as are of Norman extraction" (ms., JHL). His attitude changed remarkably in 1932 when he visited New Orleans and Quebec and experienced an architectural and cultural conversion. Upon his visit to New Orleans he wrote, "I stayed there over two weeks & came to like it immensely" (SL 4.86). This is the New Orleans in which he sets "Through the Gates of the Silver Key" and introduces the amiable mystic Etienne-Laurent de Marigny.

In the seventeenth and eighteenth centuries, he wrote, we fought the French culture as it crept from Quebec and the Mississippi Valley (SL 3.59)—a culture that he respected, but alien to his culture, which in 1929 he identified as *ours* in his frequent royal *we*. Nevertheless, in the same letter he wrote,

> I hate a jabbering Frenchman with his little affectations & unctuous ways, & would defend the English culture & tradition with my last drop of blood. But all the same I can see clearly that the French have a profounder culture than we have—that their intellectual perspective is infinitely clearer than ours, & that their tastes are infinitely farther removed from animal simplicity. What Anglo-Saxon could have written Balzac's *Comédie Humaine* or Baudelaire's *Fleurs du Mal*? It is only in *poetic* feeling of the main stream that we excel the French. (SL 4.78)

So far he apes the attitude that Anchises expresses against the Greeks. After invoking the great names of English poetry and the battles of the Hundred Years War he concludes, "The Frenchman is our superior, god damn him, but he'll never set foot on an inch of English soil"—as though in this latter age any French government had such an idea (SL 3.78–79). In 1933 he repeats these sentiments, contrasting the respect that the English always held for French culture to the scorn that the Americans have for things German, both in the Great War and now—1933—at the inception of the Third Reich. In a less rhetorical mode he wrote in 1936, "My only real favorites [in continental literature] are Balzac, Gautier, Flaubert, de Maupassant, Baudelaire, Leconte de l'Isle, and a few other Frenchmen. . . . This may or may not be because my basic tastes are Graeco-Roman—hence oriented toward that culture from which French culture is derived." On the other hand, he feels more interested in weird fiction that is Gothic rather than Celtic. "I not only lack but dislike the Celt's whimsical angle toward the unreal world" (*SL* 5.265). Nevertheless, the themes to which he feels attracted are those that appear in the cultural traditions of Greece and Rome, traditions that France of all nations seems to have most fully developed, rather than the themes of the northern nations. As far as French culture, then, is concerned, Lovecraft seems to have lived in a powerfully ambivalent situation, seeing it as alien to Germanic and Anglo-Saxon feelings but superior in terms of intellect; perception and culture remain attractive to a heart that has become aware of its deficiencies. On the other hand, once he truly experienced the French cultures of the New World he felt rather different.

Let us pause for a moment and survey the French authors that appear in his letters. He mentions Rabelais once, but never Villon, Ronsard, Montaigne, Pascal, Molière, Corneille, or Racine; the French Renaissance and Neo-Classicism are truly closed books to him. He is aware of Diderot, Voltaire, and La Mettrie, but he never speaks of Rousseau; and that is probably just as well. He despises the Romantics, but he approves of Gautier and Baudelaire, of Balzac, Flaubert, Maupassant, Zola, and Huysmans. He mentions curtly Mallarmé and Verlaine prefers Lautréamont to Rimbaud ("Letters to Lee McBride White" 34) though he mentions both along with Baudelaire in "Medusa's Coil" (*HM* 175). The truth is that a determined decadent, who has every *raison* for his condition, is much more appealing to the rational side of Lovecraft than an author who seems to be the incarnation of chaos.

Broadly speaking his feelings for French literature are rather like his judgments of English literature. He despised French Romanticism in precisely the same way that he despised English Romanticism, at least that form of it which as fiction appears as Romance. Thus he despises Hugo and Dumas, whom he links with Scott, Dickens, and Stevenson, because in their sentimentality, bombast, or mawkishness (*sic*) there is "something 'non-vital' about the overcoloured representation of *what purports to be real life*" (*SL* 2.90). He contrasts these "*contradictions of known truth,*" which are "always ridiculous" to his own attempt at "*excursions beyond truth or excrescences upon truth*" (*SL* 3.147). We need to gloss this remark, however, by saying that to Lovecraft's mind the truths that Romance contradicts are psychological truths, whereas the truths that Lovecraft attempts to extend are the contemporary laws of nature. As he later put the matter, "The *one* form of literary appeal which I consider *absolutely unsound, charlatanic, & valueless*—frivolous, insincere, irrelevant, & meaningless—is that handling of human events & values & motivations known as *romanticism*. Dumas, Scott, Stevenson—my gawd!" (*SL* 3.193). He has nothing good to say about Dumas, and I find no evidence of any influence; neither the Count of Monte Cristo nor Jean Valjean stride through Lovecraft's fiction, though I suspect that he might have approved of the upright Javert.

As far as Hugo is concerned, however, although Lovecraft mentions him very little, whether in the letters or in the fiction, more needs to be said. The only work mentioned in "Supernatural Horror in Literature," rather grudgingly, is *Hans the Icelander*. Conspicuous in its absence is *The Hunchback of Notre Dame*, which nevertheless gave Lovecraft one of his chief images for describing Hell's Kitchen and which thereby functions in a section of *Fungi from Yuggoth* (Waugh, "Structural and Thematic Unity" 163). But Lovecraft has transformed the significance of the imagery. In Hugo the people who inhabit the Court possess a positive revolutionary force, if only they are able to be informed by knowledge; in Lovecraft, Hell's Kitchen represents all that is evil in contemporary society, a revolutionary force that he fears. This difference in political outlook in the two men may be the reason why *Les Misérables*, Hugo's novel that is the most direct expression of his socialist faith, is not mentioned at all by Lovecraft, even though its most famous scene, the descent into the Paris sewers, would seem to be an attractive model for those several descents that occur in Lovecraft's works. But there is a difference. In Hugo that descent is regenerative; in Lovecraft it is revelatory but shattering.

Yet to return for a moment to *The Hunchback of Notre Dame*, I cannot help but think that certain aspects of that work have another impact on Lovecraft, specifically on "The Outsider." The disfigured protagonist who tries to leave his sepulchral home for the sake of beauty and light but who thereby realizes all the more shatteringly what he is, this travesty of the human figure, meets his *semblable* in Quasimodo. The fact that Quasimodo is drawn out by the figure of Esmeralda, another person living upon the margin of society, and that in the epilogue of the novel their bones crumble into one another indistinguishably also indicates a congruence to Lovecraft's narrator, who is drawn out of the self through an anima aspect of the self. Frere Frollo reappears in the punishing conscience of the Outsider. The aspects of the novel that Lovecraft cannot use are on the one hand the light-hearted poet who so quickly sublimates his desire because his desire is so slight and on the other hand the frank sensuality revealed both in the lieutenant and in Esmeralda herself; even more Lovecraft may not have approved of Hugo's coy allusion to Homer in order to mitigate that sensuality.

The French poet who most concerns Lovecraft is Baudelaire. In the early 1920s he is clearly praising Clark Ashton Smith when he calls the Californian "an American Baudelaire—master of ghoulish worlds no other foot ever trod" (SL 1.163), just as when he compares Samuel Loveman to Baudelaire (SL 1.166). At the same time, however, he is placing some distance between himself and the French poet when he writes, "The Freudianism of such decadents as Baudelaire mildly amuses me. [. . .] I have yet to find in Baudelaire, great as he was in the domain of the hideously imaginative, any trace of this terrible realisation of the mysteries beyond the stars" (SL 1.172–73). Unlike him, the decadents he felt argued for a metaphysical importance of the human being in the cosmos, so he was not as moved as other English and American decadents were by Baudelaire's "Les Litanies de Satan." Nevertheless, he realized that Baudelaire was in command of his own decadence. To his friend Dwyer, who had apparently suggested an "unholy feast," Lovecraft told the story of how "a trifle exasperated by the ostentatious 'shockingness' of [a] young man, Baudelaire 'went him one better' by asking gravely—'Have you ever / tasted young children's brains? They're quite delightful, and taste exactly like walnuts'" (SL 2.105–6). Lovecraft had come to appreciate the irony that is so much a part of the Baudelairean style and subject, an irony that qualifies and elevates his decadence.

Obviously Baudelaire is not unimportant to Lovecraft. There are more references to him in the Selected Letters than to almost any other figure. He appears as an authority of the weird in "Supernatural Horror in Literature." And his name appears as an indication of a character's tastes in "The Crawling Chaos," "Herbert West—Reanimator," "Hypnos," "He," "Medusa's Coil," and "The Thing on the Doorstep." In the fifth installment of "Herbert West," that which takes place in the fields of Flanders, the protagonist whose scientific interest has by now degenerated into "a mere morbid and ghoulish curiosity and secret sense of charnel picturesqueness" has become, "behind his pallid intellectuality, a fastidious Baudelaire of physical experiment" (D 155).

Among other reasons for Lovecraft's admiration of Baudelaire would be his attitude toward cats, revealed in a number of poems to which we can compare Lovecraft's story "The Cats of Ulthar." I will say nothing of those several letters in which Lovecraft describes how he charms and tames wild cats to lie in his lap and nothing of his essay on cats (and dogs). It is a persistent theme, as though no one but he could truly communicate with these beings that are in touch with "cryptical realms" (MM 314). Baudelaire's cats are quite complex. For one thing, they are sexualized hermaphrodites, whose loins are full of stars; one of them like his mistress has eyes "profond et froid" (110). The monologuist in "Autumn Lament" by Mallarmé says fondly "my cat is a mystical companion, a spirit" but then sensuously plunges his hand into the cat's fur in a sublimation of a lost mistress (ctd. in Symons 68). Lovecraft's cats are resolutely male, but unsexual.

So let us examine those stories in which Lovecraft treated cats more extensively. One is "The Cats of Ulthar," with a suggestive title that recalls the Latin *ultor*, which means avenger, and the Latin *ultra*, which means beyond. And in this story and the novel that extends it, *The Dream-Quest of Unknown Kadath*, cats are revengers from beyond our *Sosein* world.

"The Cats of Ulthar" is a short and simple story written in 1920, some four pages long, which achieves precisely what it intends, no more and no less, a cautionary tale that warns against the mistreatment of cats. The first paragraph, however, is a short prose poem celebrating the cat, distilling and extending material from Baudelaire's poems:

> The cat is cryptic, and close to strange things which man cannot see. He is the soul of antique Aegyptus, and bearer of tales from forgotten cities in Meroë and Ophir. He is the kin of the jungle's lords, and heir to secrets of hoary and sinister Africa. The Sphinx is his cousin, and he speaks her language; but he is more ancient than the Sphinx, and remembers that which she hath forgotten. (D 55)

The repetition of the word "forgotten" emphasizes that the cat is the emblem of the enigmatic bedrock of truth that lies beyond human consciousness. In this mythology the cat is best recognized through its association with Egypt, but its origins are lost in the heart of "hoary and sinister" Africa. The cat must be both honored and feared. The dark side of the cat appears in Marceline in "Medusa's Coil," for she is characterized as one of the great cats, a tiger or a leopard (HM 172, 188), and this description of the cat's antecedents is very like the description of the painting in that story. The age of the cat, so deep in time that its origin is no longer known, is emphasized in the earlier story when the "dark wanderers" appear in Ulthar (D 56), the patent equivalent in this fantasy to gypsies, who receive their name in our world from the belief that they come from Egypt.

The significance of the story that follows, however, as Lovecraft writes of the orphan who has lost his cat and who pronounces a revenge upon the couple who torture cats, is its recasting of Lovecraft's childhood biography. For he, the young boy who lost his grandfather, his father, and his childhood

home, also lost his pet black cat called Nigger-Man (Joshi 59)—that is to
say, it was a cat that according to its name was connected to Africa. As Joshi
has well said, "Nigger-Man's loss perhaps symbolized the loss of his birth-
place as no other event could" (59). He never learned what became of the
cat, and this existential ignorance is symbolized in the story by the couple
that steals cats who live in a small hovel "darkly hidden under spreading
oaks at the back of a neglected yard" (D 56). In the story the young boy
takes the extraordinary revenge that any child might dream of, enchanting
the cats of Ulthar to devour the couple. And having invoked this revenge,
the boy leaves the city with his dark tribe before the revenge takes place.
The adults of Ulthar are quite at a loss, not knowing what they should think
of these events; so they pass a law, as humans are accustomed to do when
they are at a loss, that no one shall kill a cat in Ulthar. The cats become
wards of the state.

This fantasy is expanded early in The *Dream-Quest of Unknown Kadath*, a
passage probably written in 1926, when Randolph Carter, Lovecraft's frequent alter ego in the early stories, is aided in his quest by an army of cats
that rescue him from the loathsome toad creatures that live on the other
side of the moon, because cats are aware of "cryptical realms," and "it is to
the moon's dark side that they go to leap and gambol on the hills and con-
verse with anciet shadows" (MM 314). Often Lovecraft suggests that cats
are sensitive to the unknown; in "The Colour out of Space" the five cats
that Mrs. Gardner treats as pets have the good sense to leave the doomed
farm early. The cats in The *Dream-Quest*, in Lovecraft's paean of praise, are
"black, grey, and white; yellow, tiger, and mixed; common, Persian, and
Manx; Thibetan, Angora, and Egyptian," as he grants them every multicul-
tural glory that he detested in his beloved New England, for over them hovered "some trace of that profound and inviolate sanctity which made their
goddess great in the temples of Bubastis" (MM 323). They aid Carter because he knew their language from of old and because, when he passed
through Uthar on his dream-quest, he had paused to help a small black kit-
ten and fed it a "saucer of rich cream" (MM 324) before he left. The loss of
his Nigger-Man is still at work in these passages.

Earlier, in 1923, this treatment of Nigger-Man had taken a more serious
turn in "The Rats in the Walls," in which the main character has nine cats,
presumptively rich in their 81 lives, but the most important of them, in fact
the only one named, is Nigger-Man. This is the first cat to sense that something is dreadfully wrong in the abbey that the main character has rebuilt to

be the perfect simulacrum of its past grandeur, albeit with the modern additions of electric lights, in order to compensate him for the loss of the Southern plantation of Carfax when he was a child. That is to say, the several losses that Lovecraft had suffered as a child, projected as the defeat of the South thirty years before he was born, is played out in the background of this story and associated with a cat.

The first point we should note in all these stories is the affection they express for cats. So often we are too liable to think of Lovecraft as rather chilly unless with friends of a like mind, but there is good evidence that he was capable of immense affection. After Nigger-Man he never owned a cat, but he became the confidant of every cat in the neighborhood willing to play his game of confidence, as I dare say most were.

In contrast to French Romanticism, French realism is for Lovecraft the great triumph of French literature, represented by such figures as Balzac, Flaubert, de Maupassant, Zola, and Proust. French poetry is not so overwhelming, certainly not the national achievement that he sees in English poetry (SL 4.383). Balzac, of course, is writing at the same time as the Romantics, but as Lukacs realized Balzac likes Scott precisely because Scott is not a Romantic. Balzac has some of the attitudes of the Romantics, but he treats them within a solidly realized world. In 1932, giving literary advice to E. Hoffmann Price, he wrote, "Dreiser is the boy to study when it comes to dealing with life—he or Balzac or Zola or de Maupassant" (SL 4.114). Later that year, again to Price, he says that Balzac is a universal artist like Shakespeare (SL 4.119). A year later, emphasizing that he can only write weird tales, that that is his only talent, he exclaims, "I'd certainly be glad enough to be a Shakespeare or Balzac or Turgeniev *if I could!*" (SL 4.267). Taken together these passages testify to admiration but to no great love or knowledge. We should note that there is no indication of a work by Balzac in Lovecraft's library, though in "Supernatural Horror in Literature" he pays tribute, in no great detail, to *The Wild Ass's Skin*, *Seraphita*, and *Louis Lambert* (D 391). To this extent he is ahead of many American critics, who for many years, because their notion of realism was rather constrained, did not appreciate Balzac's extension of it into a supernatural realm; several years later they began to see the significance of these works in Balzac's worldview. Nevertheless, in this regard Lovecraft much preferred Gautier, who captured "the inmost soul of aeon-weighted Egypt," and de Maupassant, whose "Horla" had a strong influence on his own thought and work (D 392)

One of the surprises in Lovecraft's letters is his slighting of Huysmans, though he writes of him at length. He seems to indicate in the early twenties some scorn of the author, or at least of the decadent imitations of the famous novels *A Rebours* and *Là-Bas*. His references to Huysmans in "The Hound" and "The Rats in the Walls" are vague. More interesting by 1930 is his reference to des Esseintes and Durtal, the protagonists of Huysmans's two novels, in "Medusa's Coil" (*HM* 175). Though he mentions Huysmans, "a true child of the eighteen-nineties, [. . .] at once the summation and finale" (*D* 392) in conjunction with Baudelaire in "Supernatural Horror in Literature," the reference is quite curt in comparison to his treatment of other authors. Though by 1930 he does refer to the novels in a more detailed fashion in the letters, albeit without any specific details (*SL* 3.155), it is only in late 1932 that he mentions buying a copy of *A Rebours* (4.91). It is quite possible that he read Huysmans in the twenties, but there is no doubt that he took pains to distance himself from that decadent.

The French novelist with whom he seems most involved is Proust, whose every volume he recommends to his friends. At first he perfunctorily groups him with other modernists of whom he disapproves (*SL* 2.249), but shortly thereafter he sends a copy of *Swann's Way* to Frank Belknap Long, accompanied by a lengthy poem (2.255–57). Writing to Derleth in 1930, an obscure comment seems to distinguish between Proust and Joyce (3.142). A year later, in 1931, he is much more detailed in his praise of Proust, "a sensitive perceiver, [. . .] the one real novelist of the last decade or two," who has needed to create a language that bypasses the stereotyped phrases of the great tradition (3.343), though he certainly "inherits many qualities from the main tradition of the French novel" (3.383). A year later he characterizes Proust as "one of the evokers of wistful reminiscence who symbolise universal things in particular memories" (4.90–91). In 1933 he confesses that he has not read any more than *Within a Budding Grove*, though he feels that he must proceed on "at least through *The Guermantes Way*," feeling that "he captures significant avenues & details of life that everyone else has overlooked or understressed" (4.259). More specifically, he feels that "no writer has more magnificently captured the sense of time than Proust. [. . .] I can comprehend Proust's sensation finding his friends aged after a long absence from them" (4.353), a passage followed by a lengthy rumination on his own perceptions of how much has been transformed in friends and locales since his own childhood. Though he never read it, Lovecraft seems here to have leapt ahead to the climax of Proust's work in *Le Temps retrouvé*. I suspect that this is one of the centers of Lovecraft's interest in Proust, the sense that here was a man who had truly confronted the ache of loss that memory reveals to us, sustained in the life that we live in time. But he confesses that he has still not read *Cities of the Plain;* we can imagine the difficulties he might have faced in Proust's exploration of the Gay experience, though of course he had read the passage relatively early in *Swann's Way* in which Mademoiselle Vinteuil desecrates the home of her dead father with her lover (123–25). By 1935, however, he seems to have cooled in his enthusiasm, for he says this in comparing Proust to Balzac: "Many try to put Proust ahead of [Balzac] today, but I believe Proust is too narrow in his field & and too specialised—even abnormal—in his psychology to take first rank" ("Letters to Lee McBride White" 37). That seems to have been the extent of his Proustian experience, but despite the fact that he did not read the complete work he seems to have intuited rather sharply its direction and its fundamental concerns.

So many scenes in the first three volumes must have been striking to him: the description in the early pages of the experience of falling asleep, followed by the meditation upon the woes of childhood; the meticulous treatment of class; the retrieval of memory through the aroma of the madeleine dipped in the cup of tea[1]; the meditations upon the different effects of art in the works of Vinteuil, Elstir, and Rachel; Marcel's reaction to the death of his grandmother, which surely recalled to Lovecraft his feelings at the death of his grandfather; the fragility of the self revealed in the way that people seem utterly different as time passes. We have questions to which probably no answer is possible. Did the magic lantern screen of the early pages strike him, and did that scene appear comparable to the screen of "Nyarlathotep" or the one mentioned in "The Horror at Red Hook"? Did the account of the Dreyfus affair cause him in any way to reconsider his anti-Semitism? What did he make of Marcel's growing obsession with Albertine, and how did he react to the inescapable realization that the entire work besides being a meditation upon time was also a meditation upon sexual and erotic obsession—or did he merely exclaim, "How French!" and shrug his shoulders? And in a more specific, literary aspect, does the Proustian experience of childhood and time color "Through the Gates of the Silver Key"?

Lovecraft's encounters with French culture and French literature affected

---

1. In 1919 Lovecraft wrote a fragment in his "Commonplace Book" that is analogous to Proust's scene and indicates his sensitivity to this kind of moment: "Peculiar odour of a book of childhood induces repetition of childhood fancy" (*MW* 89).

other stories besides those I have already mentioned, "The Alchemist" for instance, that Lovecraft wrote in 1908 when he was eighteen years old, presumptively not long before the breakdown that assured his failure to gain his high school degree. As we read it today we are acutely aware of how many stories written years later this story seems to prefigure, most obviously "The Outsider," "The Rats in the Walls," "The Dunwich Horror," and "The Thing on the Doorstep." We are only interested now in the fact that it takes place in France in the thirteenth and nineteenth centuries, and that its characters are French.

This France, however, is a generalized landscape. Except for the names, Antoine the narrator, Michel Mauvais and his son Charles le Sorcière, and the Count Henri and his son Godfrey, this might as well be anywhere in Europe as described by Edgar Allan Poe—there is a smidge of "The Fall of the House of Usher" about the story. Though the action proper takes place in the nineteenth century there is no reference to the swift and violent changes in public life from the French Revolution to the Franco-Prussian War. Everything is focused inward on the fate of the family.

Two aspects stand out in the narrative. This is a story about the father and son relationship. The narrator Antoine lost his father before he was born, and since his mother died in childbirth he was raised by an old servant called Pierre who dies immediately before the main action begins. "Thus," Antoine writes, "was I left to ponder on myself as the only human creature within the great fortress" (D 332). The Count Henri attacks Michel Mauvais and kills him because he suspects the alchemist has killed his son Godfrey; and this murder leads Michel's son Charles, who "had for his parent a more than filial affection" (331) despite the probability that Michel had burned his wife alive, to kill the count. The violent paternal and filial love that attempts to overcome death drives the story. This theme of the father and son relationship is supported by the possibility that the narrator, Antoine de C——
——, receives his name from Lovecraft's having noticed in the *Encyclopaedia Britannica* the names of a French Calvinist theologian Antoine Court, a man credited with restoring Protestantism in France, and his son the scholar and mythographer Antoine Court de Gebelin.

But who is the alchemist of the title? Yes, Charles le Sorcière has discovered the elixir of life and perhaps the means of transmuting base metals to gold, but the narrator Antoine is "as wrapt as had been old Michel and young Charles themselves in the acquisition of daemonological and alchemical learning" (D 332). Since he is now ninety years old, as he tells the reader in the third paragraph of the story, his encounter with Charles "in the ancient Gothic doorway" (334), a lengthy and impassioned description of a Struldbrug that looks backward at Roderick Usher and forward to the Outsider, shows him, the young man, the horror that he shall be in sixty years.

According to this story the French, whether of the protagonist or antagonist, are addicted to secret knowledge probably after the example of Nostradamus; and in this story the search for secret knowledge is intimately connected with the father and son relationship that is so intimate that it excludes the mother.

Dr. Elihu Whipple and his nephew, the heroic protagonists of "The Shunned House," trace the evil of that story back to a remarkable family of French Huguenots who had been driven to Providence from Frenchtown because of "their ardent Protestantism—too ardent, some whispered" (MM 248). We may pause at this passage to wonder why Lovecraft decided that these characters should be Huguenots; in fact the only large body of French in Rhode Island at that time were Huguenots, a Calvinist sect that came to various parts of America in the period of the late seventeenth century. Some had gone at first to Holland but found that country too tolerant for their taste. The phrase "too ardent" may suggest a Calvinism that resembled that of the Puritans in the Bay Colony, in the 1600s rivals of Rhode Island for the heart of New England. The Roulets, then, are suspicious because they are French and because they appear to be rigid Calvinists, the very sort of religious thinking that Roger Williams had fled.[2]

There is another possible reason for the presence of the Huguenots in the story. If the inspiration of the story began for Lovecraft in the shunned house, not far from it stood St. John's Episcopal Church, which had once been King's Church, founded in part by Gabriel Bernon, a Huguenot refugee who donated a part of his land for its establishment (Gaer 268). The church later became St. John's Church, with a cemetery that Lovecraft was fond of visiting. I think it quite possible that the propinquity of the four sites, the shunned house, St John's Church, its cemetery, and Mrs. Whitman's house that Edgar Allan Poe visited, formed the inspiration of Lovecraft's story.

Of course there is the vampirism. The superstitious Ann White from Exeter is convinced that "there must lie buried beneath the house one of those vampires—the dead who retain their bodily form and live on the blood

---

2. According to S. T. Joshi, Lovecraft found the name Jacques Roulet in John Fiske's *Myths and Myth-Makers* ("The Shunned House" 293).

or breath of the living—whose hideous legions send their preying shapes or spirits abroad by night" (MM 245).[3] That word "legion" reappears when the creature under the house takes hold of Dr. Whipple and transforms him into "a charnel-house and a pageant" (258); as significantly the word "hideous" had earlier appeared in the casual reference to the "sumptuous but hideous French-roofed mansion" that Archer Harris built in 1876 (243). This famous house is quite striking, as much a part of the eccentric styles to be found in Providence as the Fleur de Lys Building; but there seems no reason in this story to call it hideous except for that word "French." The word "hideous," incidentally derives from the Old French words "hisdos" and "hisde," meaning repulsive or very ugly; an additional meaning, significant for this story, is "terrific on account of size; tremendously or monstrously huge" ("Hideous" OED). Two years after the writing of "The Shunned House" the narrator of *The Case of Charles Dexter Ward* mentions "the hideous indistinct mumbling of the incredibly aged French housekeeper that served Joseph Curwen" (119). We should not make too much of this pattern, for "hideous" is one of those words in his vocabulary of the weird that Lovecraft is liable to use quite broadly; still, it does seem to have an apt application here.

Nevertheless, despite these various reasons for condemning the vampire, the narrator has another view of the "ill-favoured" family (MM 252). It is the experience of the family's ancestor Jacques Roulet, rescued from the stake to be confined in a madhouse by the mercy of a proto-Enlightenment justice, that both Dr. Whipple and his nephew suffer in their dreams, the one "with a crowd of angry faces framed by straggling locks and three-cornered hats frowning down on him" and the other "with hostility surging from all sides upon some prison where [he] lay confined" (256). Whatever lies beneath the house, monstrous, vampiric, French, it is nevertheless human and suffers as humans do. It is not simply justice that destroys it through the anonymous nephew's hands; it is mercy.

The location of "The Music of Erich Zann" is no more specified than as the city, but the street, the Rue d'Auseil, identifies it as a city in France. But France in this story provides the scene as the country of exiles, for though the narrator seems to be French as I have previously argued he is leading an "impoverished life" (DH 83), and the protagonist, Zann, is German; it might be a truer description of the story to say not that it is Lovecraft's French story,

---

3. Faye Ringel Hazel places this case in the context of a public anxiety in Exeter about tuberculosis, but her psychic vampires were not French (14–17).

then, as to say that it is his European story. He has precedence for such a treatment in Hoffmann's stories about Kreisler and Poe's about Dupin.

It is useful to keep this international flavor of the story in mind when we find ourselves forced to confront the possible meanings of the proper names Erich Zann and Rue d'Auseil. Zann, which appears to be German (a notion we accept provisionally because he seems more comfortable in writing in German than in French), could suggest "Zahn," tooth, a slight support for Robert M. Price's suggestion that Zann has parallels to the ghoul Pickman (13–14). If that resemblance seems far-fetched, however, all the more far-fetched since Lovecraft had very little German, the notion which I have elsewhere advanced, that *Zann* recalls the Italian word "zanni" though missing the final, phallic "i," becomes more attractive (*Monster* 46); Zann is a person missing something, most obviously his voice, some means of verbal communication, and so he is reduced to his music and to notes in very bad French.

French culture is tangential to "The Call of Cthulhu," but one of its subplots takes place in the bayous of Louisiana. The three representatives of that culture are strikingly different from each other. Inspector Legrasse is a thoroughly professional gentleman, but his full name, John Raymond Legrasse, indicates that he is not deeply immersed in the French life. Then there are the squatters who look to the police to protect them from the cultists; these squatters are "mostly primitive but good-natured descendants of Lafitte's men" (*DH* 136). At a crucial moment they refuse to approach the place where the cultists are dancing. These people are a "hybrid spawn," to whom the word "mongrel" is often applied (*DH* 138). More particularly, they are "men of a very low, mixed-blooded, and mentally aberrant type. Most were seamen, and a sprinkling of negroes and mulattoes" (*DH* 139). The most one can say of this description of the bayous of New Orleans is that it is at once innocent, possessed of the innocence of children, and ignorant.

In "A Shadow over Innsmouth," one of Lovecraft's most intensely imagined New England landscapes, a minor figure is the French governess and guardian of the protagonist's mysterious great-grandmother who had been educated in France. This governess, a "very taciturn" lady who could perhaps "have told more than she did" (*DH* 363), had had the tact to warn her charge against wearing the Innsmouth gold pieces in New England, though she apparently added that "it would be quite safe to wear them in Europe" (365). For a quick moment in the story New England decadence and French exoticism reinforce one another.

The family of the de Russys in "Medusa's Coil" had moved from Louisiana to southern Missouri but still maintained, as the grandfather says, "the old French tradition of the family" (*HM* 170), hence their reason for sending young Denis to the Sorbonne where he stayed in the Rue St. Jacques as Charles Dexter Ward was to stay some twenty years later when he pursued dangerous research in the Bibliothèque Nationale. Unfortunately, Denis there fell in with "the aesthetes—the decadents, you know. Experiments in life and sensation—the Baudelaire kind of chap. [. . .] They had all sorts of crazy circles and cults—imitation devil-worship, fake Black Masses, and the like" (170). The old man has no sympathy with such doings, but he deprecates the danger; these are the sorts of things that young people do. Unfortunately, this penchant of the French for the latest intellectual fad—not at all like the stolid English—does lay Denis and his friend Marsh open to the temptation that Marceline represents. Furthermore, it is a culture that has no concern as the Americans do about the possibilities of miscegenation. Fortunately this is a possibility that the grandfather, who speaks like an English gentleman in the passage we just examined—"chap" indeed!—cannot imagine. But the story intimates that this is one other danger inherent in French culture. Years earlier in 1915 Lovecraft had written à propos of European culture in general, "I believe that certain stocks have greater assimilative powers than others. The Gallo-Basque stock with Latin infusion, which constitutes the bulk of the French population, is much more receptive to alien blood than is our colder and more Northern Teutonic stock" (*SL* 1.17–18). The conclusion of "Medusa's Coil" reads like a demonstration of this assertion.

As in "Medusa's Coil," French culture, more specifically French decadence, is the background to "The Thing on the Doorstep," for this is precisely the literature that the young Derby is reading—Baudelaire is mentioned obliquely—and that sets him upon his path as a weird poet. A warning in fact is embedded in the narrative, for the narrator Upton mentions that a "notorious Baudelairean poet," a correspondent of the protagonist, "died screaming in a madhouse" (*DH* 277). By the time that he wrote this story Lovecraft had taken a more cosmopolitan attitude toward Baudelaire, but the story still suggests that one can not be too careful about what one reads.

Written after Lovecraft's visit to New Orleans, "Through the Gates of the Silver Key" takes place in that lovely French city. Despite his distaste for writing the story at Price's urging, it may also render something of his experience in reading Proust, for here is Lovecraft's own attempt, through the mysteries of geometry, to recapture the solidity of time as an experience. This is not the manner or style of Proust, but the aim is the same. It is, however, the manner of Descartes, who transformed arithmetic into geometry.

As we consider these two influences upon Lovecraft's work, the French deposit and the Latin, we need to acknowledge that it is not simply a question of influence but of love, a love surpassing that of a man for woman, a love so great that Lovecraft needed to set some of his stories within the beloved milieus; and in this attempt, as far as the French stories were concerned he succeeded, but he did not succeed in the life of Rome, though he did sketch a story that took place in Roman Spain, on the margin of Rome, a story that gave him the opportunity to draw an ideal image of himself as Lucius Caelius Rufus. All these stories, those within the French world and that within the Roman, attest to his vision of a world outside the Puritan New England with which he conducted such ambivalent exchanges, a world that threatened to break through into the world of New England or the world of the blessed South. It meant to break into our world. Our world, however, is bracketed in these stories, for it means nothing more distinct than a Western tradition that has reached its apotheosis in that very particular Rhode Island mode of New England life. For I do believe that, however gropingly, Lovecraft knew how parochial he was.

Epilogue

In contrast to the impact that French literature and culture exerted upon Lovecraft, the presence of German literature in his work is rather minor, as a glance through "Supernatural Horror in Literature" demonstrates. This is perhaps surprising for a person who was so insistent early in his career upon his identity as a Teutonic barbarian; but the war to end all wars put paid to those aspirations when he found that he had to side with England and thereby with France. In any case the flower of German literature does not have any barbarian tinge about it. Lovecraft did give a nod toward Goethe, especially "The Bride of Corinth" and *Faust* (D 371, 373), but the one he barely mentions and his extravagant praise of the latter is belied by the fact that in his library he owned only *Part I* and a volume of the poetry, a volume that would hardly have excited his interest since the Victorian translations and the exclusions (little of the *Roman Elegies* or of the *Venetian Epigrams*) give a decidedly poor impression of Goethe's range or intelligence. Lovecraft never mentions such poems as "Erlkönig," "Der Zauberlehrling," "Der

Getreue Eckart," or "Der Totentanz." If he misses such works by Goethe, is it any wonder that he misses so much else in German literature?

It is no surprise then that he sketches a dismissive picture of Hoffmann and turns to a long account of Fouqué's *Undine;* he mentions Bürger, but only in the context of Scott's translations from German balladry. As for the Gothic novel, after a long account of *The Castle of Otranto* he writes that "German romance at once responded to the Walpole influence, and soon became a byword for the weird and ghastly" (DM 375), but then turns his attention to English imitations. He does not mention Tieck, Novalis, Chamisso, or the Grimms, significant figures in the history of the new treatment of supernatural materials that began with German romanticism.

The presence of later German literature in Lovecraft's account is also meager. He treats at some length Wilhelm Meinhold's *The Amber Witch* and Gustav Meyrink's *The Golem* (DM 391, 394), but he only mentions Hanns Heinz Ewers (DM 391). Voilà, c'est tout! Madame de Staël might as well have never written.

Why does Lovecraft have so little to say of German literature, a literature that he implies was the fountainhead of the weird in the transition from the eighteenth to the nineteenth century? First, obviously, he is dependent on translations since he had only half-year of the language in school and found it "absolutely repulsive to [his] Latin-based taste" (*Letters to Richard F. Searight* 40); and at the time he was writing the translations of German literature still presented a culture very much filtered through a Victorian sensibility. I think the real truth of the matter is, however, that when Lovecraft was beginning to educate himself French literature represented the cutting edge of Western culture; it seemed both the most critical and the most contemporary. For someone like Lovecraft, eager to associate himself with what was most advanced in intellectual achievement, the French occluded the Germans. The only exception to the picture we have drawn is his response to German philosophy and science, especially his reading of Schopenhauer, Nietzsche, Haeckel, and Freud; but these are the figures who might have seemed least German to a writer in the 1920s, least German because they are so resolutely critical of traditions that appear obscurantist. Reading "Supernatural Horror in Literature," I receive the impression that the German writers of the weird were important historically but hopelessly old-fashioned. In concentrating upon the French Lovecraft perpetuates the prejudice that German culture is dull.

Lovecraft and O'Neill: The New England Haunts

It is a more natural impulse than it may seem to study the relationships between H. P. Lovecraft, the father of modern weird literature, and Eugene
O'Neill, the first great exponent of experimentation on the American stage
in the twentieth century. It is not simply that Lovecraft appreciated O'Neill's
work, speaking very approvingly of *The Emperor Jones*. There are several
striking correspondences between their lives, their opinions, and their works.
They were, for better or worse, our first American expressionists, who then
became something else because of their families and their homes. In claiming
this I am saying no more than Norman Gayford has already said about Lovecraft's relation to the Modernists. We never escape the age in which we are
born, try as we will; and few authors tried as desperately or as futilely as
Lovecraft to escape his age. It did not help him to write "Long live King
George" at the conclusion of his letters.

I

I once was as meek as a new-born lamb;
I'm now Sir Murgatroyd, ha ha! (Gilbert and Sullivan 436)

O'Neill was born in 1888 in a hotel in Manhattan when his father, an actor famous for his Shakespearean roles, was on tour. This was two years before Lovecraft was born on Angell Street in Providence, Rhode Island; and
we might think that a great contrast lies already in these two places, and we
would be right except that O'Neill's father was to buy a house in New London, Connecticut, where the family was to spend its summers when the tour-
ing season had abated, no more than sixty miles from Providence. O'Neill
thus became as much a New Englander as Lovecraft; and though in later
years he was to flee the area it becomes the scene of many of his works. And
in so far as both states abut upon the Atlantic, it is natural that Lovecraft

and O'Neill have a deep engagement in their works with the ocean. Both authors express a deep fidelity toward their common place. There is one profound difference, however, in their attitudes toward New England. Lovecraft through his mother had a deep relationship toward the Yankee, Puritan tradition; but O'Neill, the son of an Irish immigrant, always felt like an outsider in that tradition and repaid the scorn of the Yankee with his own scorn. For Lovecraft, the son of Yankee failures, it was pressingly important to be a gentleman, an attitude that would have disgusted the bohemian O'Neill. Thus there is a great difference between the two men in the tone of their lives. Until O'Neill needed to restrain himself or die he lived as a man driven, thrown into rage, whereas from his early years Lovecraft lived as a man restrained and constrained. Only very slowly, very slowly indeed, did he loosen the reins on himself.

O'Neill was athletic and proud of his body as several photographs of him as a young man demonstrate, though he had to suffer a bout of tuberculosis to shock him out of his early dissipation and though at the end of his life he suffered severe debilitation; laid waste by various mysterious ailments as a young man Lovecraft was not athletic at all, though as an adult he hiked miles through cities to enjoy the architectures peculiar to them. Both men were anti-Semites, though O'Neill expresses only the genteel, unexamined animus of the society of his day (Gelb 145, 608) whereas Lovecraft is virulent in his language; but O'Neill did make anti-Semitism one of the themes of the play *Lazarus Laughed*. Each man has an argument with the received religion of his family, O'Neill against Roman Catholicism and Lovecraft with the Puritanism of the Baptist church; O'Neill, however, did not go as far as Lovecraft in espousing the position of an atheist. Both men at an early age felt the impact of Nietzsche, though O'Neill remained an agnostic with several indications of vitalist thought. And O'Neill like Lovecraft preferred American popular music, especially that of the player-piano, to the European classical tradition (Gelb 198).

They were both autodidacts. I have already had a good deal to say about Lovecraft in this matter (*Monster* 162–78), which I will only summarize here. First, it is quite possible that an autodidact has attended school, but he or she depends much more upon private sources of knowledge (e.g., family libraries). Thus the autodidact approaches institutional, normal discourse with a skeptical eye. O'Neill's early career marks him as an autodidact. His early education was interrupted by his father's theatrical wanderings as the Count of Monte Cristo. In his first seven years he learned backstage life, and "saw more of the country [. . .] than most people see in a lifetime" (Black 60). We cannot ignore the fact that he received a first-class education in the theater as the son of his father, though he rebelled against the theater that his father represented as well as against his father; and despite the dramatic separation of the father's library and the son's library in A Long Day's Journey into Night, his father's library provided the basis of his education (Gelb 142). Like Lovecraft, some of that rebellion can be seen in his literary tastes, picking up decadents such as Wilde, Fitzgerald, and above all Swinburne; we can hear the echoes of that rebellion in taste in Ah, Wilderness! and in A Long Day's Journey into Night, authors that Lovecraft also appreciated, though for a time he went beyond them to the French Symbolists and Decadents. When Lovecraft saw the film Ah, Wilderness in 1936 he wrote that it "made [him] homesick for the vanish'd world of 1906!" (Letters to Alfred Galpin 221), a comment that attests to the closeness he felt to O'Neill's world. A friend introduced O'Neill to "The Hound of Heaven," which in time he learned by heart; it did not return him to Catholicism as the friend had hoped (Gelb 387–88), but clearly the argument with God that lies at the poem's heart concerned him as greatly as it did Lovecraft. As should be no surprise O'Neill also read widely in the dramatists who preceded him, Shaw, Ibsen, Hauptmann, and Strindberg; and like Lovecraft he found Nietzsche very much to his taste, though he added to the perceptions of Das Geburt der Tragödie, Jenseits von Gut und Böse, and Also Sprach Zarathustra the work of Freud, especially Beyond the Pleasure Principle. He received a good education in a variety of private schools—Black insists that he received a good formal education, and that is doubtless true (83)—but though he attended Professor Baker's class in drama at Harvard he never earned a college degree, having been dismissed from Princeton at the end of his freshman year (Gelb 229); his education lay in his own hands. Later his attitude softened when the famous playwright bowed his head to an honorary degree at Yale, where in later years he was happy to accept a seat in the box of President Angell (Black 341); New England is a small world.

Despite these congruencies in the works they read and in their early personal tastes, we can see an interesting difference that comes clear in their fictional self-images. The two young men in Ah, Wilderness! and Long Day's Journey face two different responses to their decadent reading; in the one case, the problem is moral, in the second case it seems to be moral also but turns out to be aesthetic. When Edmund convinces his father that there is some fine writing in the decadents' work, something that a performer could roll around on his tongue, Mr Tyrone's objections are calmed. Lovecraft's

young men, Randolph Carter, Charles Dexter Ward, and Edward Derby display an early taste for the decadents, but their parents have no objection;
and given this lack of friction we may doubt whether Lovecraft's mother
ever uttered an objection either. She may of course have had no interest in
his reading; it was up to him by a slow personal process of trial and error to
realize that the decadent world of the previous generation did not really represent his world. None of the parents in O'Neill's plays, serious and solemn
as those parents are, objects through ridicule. Lovecraft had to craft his own
ridicule through the means of parody before he could free himself of the ha-
bitual gestures of the decadent world.

A writer has to go further than a mere rebellion in taste. Once it was
clear that his reading would not do the trick, O'Neill's rebellion took several
forms, an early inclination to alcohol that expressed itself in several episodes
of binge drinking and rage and an early promiscuity to which his older
brother introduced him. The most creative rebellion, however, was his decision to go to sea as a common seaman, a life that in time lead to his tuberculosis. We shall examine shortly the wealth that O'Neill discovered in that
experience at sea that led to his first confrontation with his yearning for
death and his recoil from it. Yet despite these self-destructive actions and
despite his shyness, many people said that O'Neill had a gift for friendship
and human community, although most of these friendships were epistolary as
were the friendships that Lovecraft constructed (Black 63).

Lovecraft's rebellion never expressed itself in alcohol or promiscuity; in
this respect the two men are drastically different, for Lovecraft early became
a vocal advocate of abstinence—the difference is so great that we must later
examine its expression in their works. As far as sexuality was concerned, it is
clear that though Lovecraft had no great moral problems in that regard his
taste in such matters was low; it is possible, I believe, that he would have expressed a distaste. And he hated the sea. His rebellion was first expressed in
his various breakdowns and withdrawals, until the death of his mother allowed him the major rebellion of marriage with Sonia Greene and a move to
New York City, where he was to see O'Neill's work.

More interesting, O'Neill like Lovecraft had an argument with America,
which we can trace in *Ah, Wilderness!* when O'Neill's alter ego Richard exclaims, "Darn the Fourth of July, anyway! I wish we still belonged to England" (2.209). Had Lovecraft ever seen this play, though late in life he saw
the movie, he would have leaped on the stage to embrace the young man. I
think we can assume that it is unlikely that anyone in America outside of

New England would understand this sentiment because only in New England is the connection to old England still alive. New England informs their works. The place, history, dialect, and characters of New England we meet at every turn. We need not list the stories Lovecraft wrote that take place in New England—the list would be too long—but we can point out that besides Rhode Island the stories also take place in Massachusetts, Vermont, and Maine. But O'Neill's plays that take place in New England are remarkable: "Rope," *Desire Under the Elms, Mourning Becomes Electra, Strange Interlude, Ah, Wilderness!, Long Day's Journey into Night, A Moon for the Misbegotten,* these plays are filled with the people and tongue and types of New England life. Something of this New England attitude can be seen in the cutting analysis of American business in *The Great God Brown* and in Marsden's thought about "this adolescent country" (1.120). As a gentleman Lovecraft did his best to avoid being soiled by commercial considerations and starved; O'Neill of course was very successful.

Technically the two men have in common their use of the dramatic monologue. I have earlier in this book considered the case of Lovecraft in this matter, so let us now consider O'Neill. In "Before Breakfast" in 1916, early in his career, he constructed a one-act play upon a woman's monologue to her off-stage husband, an experiment that he was to expand upon in several of his plays thereafter, most notably "The Emperor Jones," *Strange Interlude, The Iceman Cometh,* and *A Long Day's Journey into Night,* so much so that it becomes a mark of his style (Gelb 589). This is striking at a time when his models for the modern play, Ibsen, Strindberg, and Wedekind, are avoiding lengthy monologues and expanding the place of dialogue in their works. O'Neill is returning to the examples of Aeschylus, Shakespeare, and—dare we say it?—the theater of his father. Normand Berlin cites above all the example of Shakespeare (14), and rightly so, but we must not minimize the examples of the Greeks and of his father's work, though he himself would have surely minimized the latter.

Last in this cursory comparison of the two men's lives it is important that both men contemplated suicide. Years after the event Lovecraft reported that when he was fourteen years old he contemplated suicide at the death of his grandfather and the dissolution of the family home. O'Neill, when he twenty-four and at one of the lows in his alcoholic degradation, downed a bottle of veronal in Jimmy the Priest's dive, the bar and hotel that later served as a model for *The Iceman Cometh.* With some experience both men go on in the works they survive to write to depict suicides, the final choice for those who have no hope; and hope is very long to come by in either of the two men's worlds.

Given all these biographical details it is perhaps not strange that Lovecraft appreciated O'Neill's work that he was able to see when he lived in New York; his residence there was not utterly the hell that he liked to portray later. Among other good experiences it enabled him to see O'Neill's work on the stage during the playwright's first Broadway successes. In May, 1922 he saw the famous production of *The Emperor Jones* to which he responded very favorably, writing to Frank Belknap Long, "It is a thing of terror, ably presented. O'Neill strikes me as the one real dramatist of America today—starkly tragic, and with a touch of the Poe-esque" (*SL* 1.173). A month later he repeats his judgment, adding that he had some familiarity with O'Neill's famous father (1.187–88). I believe that several elements of the play appealed to Lovecraft, above all the theme of regression. But the moment that spoke most directly to him is the appearance of the Little Formless Fears: "They are black, shapeless, only their glittering eyes can be seen. If they have any describable form at all it is that of a grubworm about the size of a creeping child. They move noiselessly, but with deliberate, painful effort, striving to raise themselves on end, failing and sinking prone again" (O'Neill 3.189). Their mockery is "like a rustling of leaves. They squirm upward toward him in twisted attitudes" (3.190). After Jones fires his gun they run into the jungle again, but his attempt to claim that they are wild pigs falls flat. "What you think dey is—ha'nts?" he asks himself (3.190). Lovecraft would have thought no; they were night-gaunts. He saw his own intimate fears being played out on O'Neill's stage.

Two years later he saw the larger work *All God's Chillun Got Wings*, the first act of which the mayor had banned and which the director read on the stage; again Lovecraft felt it was a very powerful work and affirmed that O'Neill was "perhaps the only American dramatist of note now living" (*SL* 1.348–49). Further, he commented on the symbolic use of the mask in the final acts. It is interesting that the two plays that Lovecraft did see and responded to with such pleasure, given his casual racism, concern themselves directly and sympathetically with black protagonists. O'Neill seems to have sympathized deeply with Harris, the protagonist of *All God's Chillun*, seeing in his relation with Emma something of the fate of his own parents; and he was Black Irish.

After a few more years of passing references, with little chance to see more plays since he had repaired to Providence, Lovecraft railed against the ban of *Strange Interlude*, though he had not seen it and did not plan to since he was certain that it would be a bore (SL 3.266). It is a shame he did not attend. In the first few minutes he would have seen one version of himself as the reclusive Professor Leeds, hidden in the classical world of his library, "a cozy, cultured retreat, sedulously built as a sanctuary where, secure with the culture of the past at his back, a fugitive from reality can view the present safely from a distance" (1.3); and another version of himself as Charles Marsden, "an Anglicized New England gentleman" who "speaks with a careful ease as one who listens to his own conversation" with the stoop to his shoulders of a man muscularly weak, "who [. . .] has always been regarded as of delicate constitution" (1.4), carefully and precariously distanced from his sexuality. In the second act Lovecraft would have seen a third version of himself, the scientist Edmund Darrell, who "has come to consider himself as immune to love through his scientific understanding of its real sexual nature" (1.33). A major theme of the play is how these three New England types with the best will in the world destroy a passionate woman who is their daughter and friend and lover. Perhaps Lovecraft might have been bored, but he might also have seen himself as in a glass darkly.

In 1932 Lovecraft confessed that he did not really do drama, perhaps because of his disinterest in human individuals, despite his great admiration for Dunsany and O'Neill; and given his great admiration for Dunsany this is great praise indeed (SL 4.72). In 1934, in a long letter to J. Vernon Shea, he recalled with pleasure the performance that Charles Gilpin gave in *The Emperor Jones* and concurred a few pages later with Shea's opinion of O'Neill's use of the song "Bedelia" in a play, an instance he remarked of O'Neill's "reminiscent accuracy" (SL 4.363 and 4.365). Having seen the film of *Ah, Wilderness!* in 1936, not many months before his death in 1937 he adds O'Neill approvingly to his list of political radicals in the cultural life of America (5.405). The impression we receive is that though he was excited by *The Emperor Jones, All God's Chillun Got Wings*, and the film version of *Ah, Wilderness!* and retained a respect for O'Neill throughout his career, he did not follow the details of the career closely. That would have been difficult to do, of course, once he had returned to Providence.

Given the closeness of these details of their lives I want to examine a number of themes in their works as a series of dialogues between the two authors. We shall begin with the apparently most intimate details, their attitudes toward drink and sexuality. Then we shall investigate the works that play out attacks against the mother and attempt to mount responses to the

father, the terrible old man. Finally we will consider their treatments of the
quest, their attitude towards the sea, and their attitude towards the haunted
life. We are thus moving from the personal toward the universal.

II

> Oh, Whiskey drove my old man mad!
>   Whiskey! O Johnny!
> Oh, Whiskey drove my old man mad!
>   Whiskey for my Johnny! (O'Neill 3.210)

Lovecraft and O'Neill are both obsessive personalities; one shall drink, or
not, and the other shall not. Each floats upon a private pain that cannot be
put aside and that must be dealt with rigidly. We can guess at that private
pain with no great assurance, though each man worked at his own trauma,
so we shall not guess at it here.

The question of alcohol is fraught because it serves so many purposes. As
wine or beer it may be the only thing to drink when the water is bad. In the
religions of the world it serves a variety of cultic, liturgical, or social purposes. A society may employ it as a source of elation or merriment, a loosen-
ing of its various inhibitions; this elation may edge into a defiance of society,
a comic or obsessive rebellion, as we see in much that is brilliant in the poetry of Robert Burns. Alcohol may be a means of deadening pain as an an-
aesthesia when none is available—witness amputations before World War
I—or it may be a means of deadening psychic pain. It may be the water of
life; it may be the water of death. The great dividing line in these possibilities
occurred when humanity discovered the process of distilling, thus rendering
the drink much more potent and much more potentially addictive, the effects of which began to be evident in England and America during the eighteenth century.

In order to understand O'Neill's and Lovecraft's responses to alcohol we
need to consider the background of the temperance movement. When Norman H. Clark analyzes the background of compulsive drinking in America he
argues that the most influential cause is social instability: "by the fall of the established church, by the rush for cheap land, by the complex impact of the
cotton gin and the textile factories, [. . .] by the windfalls of economic and
geographic mobility and of unlimited moral freedom. The migrations of thousands of people westward after 1814—and the continual surges of migration
and immigration, of settlement and dispersion" (29). To this list of social dis-

ruption let us add the cataclysm of the Civil War, the defeated economy in the South, and the inflations, panics, and depressions of the Gilded Age. A further social problem arose in a society that demanded that men be strong, courageous, and self-reliant (Clark 34). Inhabited by strong, silent men who would never complain but who might imbibe too much rum, whiskey, or gin, it was a spasmodic century that O'Neill and Lovecraft entered at its conclusion, and their families suffered from much in this catalogue of instability.

Granted this challenge, the temperance movement had three kinds of arguments that it employed throughout the century. Perhaps the most important was the moral argument that alcohol threatened the cohesion of the nuclear family; the most graphic example of this argument was to be found in Timothy Shay Arthur's novel *Ten Nights in a Barroom*, soon converted into a lurid melodrama that concluded in an act of drunken patricide (Clark 40–43). Next in importance and in the long run perhaps the most persuasive was the hygienic argument, first represented in one of the earliest temperance tracts, *An Inquiry into the Effects of Spirituous Liquors upon the Human Body*, written by Dr. Benjamin Rush, one of the signers of the Declaration of Independence, who discriminated between distilled and fermented beverages and demanded the control of the former (Blocker 7; Pegram 13–15); it soon, however, became difficult to distinguish between the effects of distilled liquors and fermented liquors. The third argument was the religious argument, mounted steadily by the evangelist churches, the Methodists, Baptists, Congretionalists, Presbyterians, and Quakers, which believed in the enthusiastic inspiration of the Holy Ghost but also in the rationality of the Word that should not be disrupted or corrupted by material means; throughout the nineteenth century the temperance movement could count on these churches for energetic support. The Roman Catholics, the Episcopalians, and the Lutherans were much more cautious in their support and often antagonistic. Let us note immediately that though Lovecraft most often availed himself of the hygienic argument, he did grow up within a Baptist church.

The temperance movement was not monolithic in its history. Though several groups were evangelical in their roots and propelled by the enthusiasm of the Second Great Awakening, important groups like the Washington Temperance Society were indifferent to religion (Clark 32–33). In 1836 the American Temperance Society adopted teetotalism as its goal, moving beyond the condemnation of distilled liquors. An important force in the movement was Neal Dow, who in 1851 worked to promoted the first prohibition law in the nation in the state of Maine; but as a corollary to his perception of the weakening of the social fiber that he remembered as a child, he also joined those opposed to the immigration of the Irish Roman Catholics (Clark 39). Between 1845 and 1855 most of the immigrants were Irish and German, both of which exacerbated the temperance anxieties of the evangelicals (Pegram 32–33). In the 1850s "some prohibitionists welcomed the promise [made by the Know-Nothings] of excluding the immigrant vote and thereby removing an obstacle to prohibition's triumph, and some Know-Nothings seized upon prohibition as a tool to discipline the immigrant hordes" (Blocker 57). During the 1880s and early 1890s a popular temperance speaker, Edward B. Sutton, argued that the pope had instigated the Catholic immigration that Sutton feared would shortly take control of the governance and education of the Western states. Often in its history the temperance movement became connected to a bigotry that objected to the new immigrants (Clark 79–80, 88–89); during the triumph of Prohibition in the 1920s, the Ku Klux Klan associated its own program of a pure white America with the perceived purity of Prohibition (Pegram 172–73). In the 1870s a rather different direction, though not that different given the Klan's demand for purity, was taken by temperance leaders who "came to believe that heredity caused some drinkers to drink to excess" (Blocker 57). Shades of Zola in *L'Assommoir!*

A very different direction in the movement was represented by the founding in 1874 of the Woman's Christian Temperance Union, the most powerful of the societies led by women, which in the 1880s and 1890s, though never formally adopting a socialist platform, became broadly and deeply interested in radical change. Here we see the most nuanced expression of the moral argument. A group with which the WCTU was associated, the National Prohibition Party, in 1872 called for a prohibition amendment to the constitution as well as amendments for a federal income tax, direct elections of senators, and women's suffrage. In 1876 they added platforms against polygamy and prostitution (Clark 70) and in 1892 platforms to support an end to lynching, a progressive income tax, and equal pay for equal work by men and women (Blocker 101).

For a time it seemed as though the prohibition movement was firmly wedded to a broad reform program, despite its threads of populism and bigotry, but the WCTU and the Prohibition Party failed because these broad aims at the turn of the century seemed too radical. It was the Anti-Saloon League that succeeded in advancing the 18th Amendment because it had only one aim, that of Prohibition, which it advanced by a total neutrality between the Democrats and the Republicans, though most of its members were

Republicans, and a vocal appeal to evangelical support (Blocker 102–6). More quietly it exploited the differences between rural values and urban (ethnic) values (112). Its program found support in a plethora of studies that advanced the hygienic argument and in increasing anxieties about the recent immigration of Jews and Italians and in the growing consumption of beer based in the German-Americans (Pegram 89–96). In 1913 the ASL decided to force the issue of the amendment by 1920 because it feared that the census of that year, given the immigration patterns, might well have prevented its passage (138–39). America's support of the Allies in World War I turned American sentiment against the German-American breweries and furthered the acceptance of the amendment (144–45).

Against this background, as far as Lovecraft and O'Neill are concerned, it is good to point out that in the 1880s Rhode Island passed Prohibition but soon repealed it (Pegram 79); and only it and Connecticut did not ratify the 18th Amendment (Clark 129). For them it was important that the conscience should remain free of Federal coercion.

O'Neill's alcoholic addiction, as an Irish-American of Irish immigrant descent, is threefold: first, there is the response of the Irish to English repression and its impoverishment of Irish society, a repression and impoverishment that for centuries seemed endless; second, the response of the Irish to WASP repression in America; and third, O'Neill's response to his father's behavior, according to most accounts careful in his professional life but both inviting and repressive as far as his son's behavior was concerned. "It's a good man's failing," as Mr. Tyrone tritely remarks (Long Day's Journey 135) It is as though a triple fatality were laid upon O'Neill's life.

It is a subject to which the plays often return. One of the early one-acts, *The Long Voyage Home*, takes place in a bar. Drinking is important in *The Moon of the Caribbees, Ah, Wilderness!*, and the two late plays *The Iceman Cometh* and *Long Day's Journey into Night. The Iceman Cometh* takes place relentlessly in the bar, which different characters call a morgue (3.580), the last harbor, and a graveyard (3.587); it is the place that is just this side of death, and we shall have more to say of that death later. It was a scene that O'Neill had known intimately and that he made good use of.

In vino veritas. Lovecraft is too good a student of Latinity not to be aware of this classical tag. This is the overt function of liquor in his stories, as a release of truth. In *The Dream-Quest of Unknown Kadath* Randolph Carter drinks "ceremoniously" from a potation of fermented sap that the zoogs offer, well-aware of social niceties to no apparent detriment to his soul—but of course he is a Boston gentleman (MM 309)—and takes "another gourd of moon-tree wine" when he leaves (310). He does commit, however, "a wicked thing" with the wine, inebriating the priest Atal so that "robbed of his reserve, poor Atal babbled freely of forbidden things" (312). When Carter tries this ploy on a merchant from the black gallies the man drinks to no effect, but Carter passes out from a sip of the wine that the man proffers in return (317). We see this motif preeminently at work in "Pickman's Model," where the narrator needs several shots before he turns to coffee at the end of his account, and in "The Shadow over Innsmouth," where that narrator needs almost a quart of whiskey to open the thirsty lips of Zadok Allen. The stories would not have been possible without liquor. In "The Thing on the Doorstep" Derby also needs a bit of whiskey in order to speak with his friend Daniel Upton who, as Derby knew, would have a bottle handy. The narration does not dwell on the point, but Upton is a social drinker. The narrator of "Pickman's Model," Zadok Allen, and Edward Derby all need a drop or two, perhaps three or a gallon, to speak; and they speak rather well with it under their belts. Of course the narration often implies that they say things that for the safety of the human race should not be said. The truth for Lovecraft is terrifying. It needs to be told, but it also needs for the sake of humanity's psychic well-being to be repressed; but truth always trumps fear in these stories, even at the risk of liquid courage, and *mirabile dictu* we come away from the experience unscathed. Do we not have the impression that Lovecraft's narrations are perhaps too sober, especially the late narrations upon which he exercised such care, and that this is a failing that some of his disciples, Fritz Leiber for example, corrected, though the correction almost destroyed Leiber? In asking such a question we are of course brought round to O'Neill.

For O'Neill alcohol was also associated with a truth that needs to be told, but that was not at all the whole story. He knew that his own relation to alcohol was complex. His binges were often violent, wrecking the rooms in which he lived (Black 92, 105). In the plays alcohol often functions as a means to tell the truth, but that truth is also aggressive; the speaker means to wound, then repents and claims that that truth is one-sided—an equivocation. This wound and repentance controls the rhythm of Tyrone's and Jamie's language in *A Long Day's Journey into Night*. Lovecraft does not seem to be aware of this violence in his stories, but that is perhaps just as well.

In the plays of O'Neill, however, the same characters also drink to dull the truth and to forget it, to achieve oblivion for one more day. This is the main function of liquor in the somber *The Iceman Cometh,* and it is at work in *Long Day's Journey into Night.* At this stage alcohol has of course another purpose, an attempt at suicide. Not without reason a doctor who presided at Dylan Thomas's death established that he died of "a severe insult to the brain" (Brinnin 277). This was a part of the pattern that developed in O'Neill's life from 1909 to 1912 when he attempted to hurry the process by ingesting a number of veronal tablets (Gelb 329–30). The aggressive behavior, the destruction of rooms and the attacks on friends turned inward towards what was truly hated, the self and whatever lay within the self.

The theme of alcohol runs through Lovecraft's letters, though he seems to be less intense upon the subject when he is older. One of his first statements on the subject in 1916, "It is the deadliest enemy with which humanity is faced" (*SL* 1.26), leaves no room for discussion. More interesting is this explanation: "It was in the sombre period of 1896 that I first became a temperance enthusiast. Somewhere I discovered an old copy of John B Gough's *Sunshine & Shadow* & read & re-read it, backward & forward. From that time to this, I have never been at a loss for something to say against liquor!" (*SL* 1.35). Both the book and the author, as Lovecraft testifies, are arresting. Born in England, Gough came to America in 1829 when he was twelve to make his fortune, but in his late teens he became an alcoholic and suffered from his addiction for some seven years until he "took the pledge" and became an enthusiastic and successful lecturer on the subject. Having written several books, among them an autobiography ("Gough, John Bartholomew" *Encyclopaedia Britannica*), he returned to England in 1878, the return that he recounts in *Sunlight and Shadow or, Gleanings from My Life Work.*

The book begins with a good deal of Gough's Anglophile complacency in his reception, acknowledgments of the prelates and aristocrats that have received him, and details of their wealth. Lovecraft probably read these chapters in the context of his own Anglophilia, in which they reinforced his belief that an English gentleman must not be drunk. But just when a contemporary reader might be tempted to turn from the work in disgust Gough begins to recount with great relish his meetings with Cockney gamins, cabmen, and pickpockets; here we realize, as the proto-narrator in Lovecraft must have realized at the bare age of six, that Gough was a great humorist and raconteur, surely a part of his success as a lecturer and an indication of his broad mind. The book does have several chapters devoted to his belief that only total abstinence will save an individual from the destruction wrought by alcohol. It destroys the body (207), but it also destroys the mind; a long pero-

ration details the lunacy that alcohol leads to (447–48), a passage that resonated in several of Lovecraft's later comments. Much of the rhetoric of these
chapters, like much of the rhetoric throughout the temperance movement,
centered upon the drunken fathers that abuse families, and I think it quite
possible that this rhetoric increased Lovecraft's anxieties about his father
and made alcohol doubly reprehensible and taboo. But lest we think that
such passages are merely signs of middle-class culture, let us recall the conclusions of Joyce's "Counterparts" and "The Little Cloud" in which a drunk
father abuses his children. In 1923 Lovecraft advised Frank Belknap Long to
avoid tobacco and rum, which "merely aggravate nervous susceptibility and
disturbance, coarsen the mind and physique, harden and debase the appearance and every facial expression, and in short ruin every vestige of that virtuous delicacy and fine honour which alone give aesthetick value to the
emptiness called life" (SL 1.273). He has extended Gough's arguments to
outline the danger of alcoholism to the decadent life and turned away from
Baudelaire's words in Le Spleen de Paris: "Il faut d'être toujours ivre" (338).

One other aspect of Gough's attack on alcoholism is striking. He insists
that drunkenness is the major cause of poverty. After citing the opinions of
several British and American aristocrats and editors he concludes, "The
people know that drunkenness and consequent improvidence is the cause of
seven eighths of the poverty here and in Great Britain" (151). He then applies this opinion to the Irish situation, where, as Lord Longford argues, "If
all classes or individuals [. . .] would spend on relieving the wants of their
poorer neighbors, to their own credit, what they now spend on whiskey, to
their own destruction, it would be less necessary to make frantic appeals to
the government, to the landlords, or to private charity" (153). The "Irish
Ecclesiastical Gazette" is of the same opinion: "Those who discourage emi-
gration, temperance, and honest industry, and foster in the Irish people the
insane earth-hunger, the waste, the improvidence, the love of political excitement, rather than patient, plodding industry,—the sin, the misery, the
nation's degradation, lie at their doors" (153). This aspect of Gough's thinking would have appealed to Lovecraft who had little patience with "the slip-
pery sons of Saint Patrick" (SL 1.23)

Several of Lovecraft's friends did drink, but only one man had a serious
problem with alcohol, Hart Crane. Still, when Lovecraft comments in 1924
that Crane "has an unfortunate predilection for the wine when it is red" (SL
1.349), the comment is slightly comic; the touch is light, as though he were
willing to concede Crane's foible. In 1930, however, he writes an extended

lament for Crane, whose poem *The Bridge* he genuinely admires (*SL* 3.151–52): The remarkable aspect of this passage is its profound sympathy; he no longer condemns the man as weak of will but seems to understand the pressures that could have brought Crane to this difficult pass from which he could not escape.

In 1928 upon the matter of policy he speculated whether Prohibition was quite worth all the money and time spent in its enforcement, since, after all, drunkenness was not as antisocial as such crimes as murder or robbery. Though he still found alcohol personally repugnant—he never changed in this regard—and though he still found alcohol dangerous in "an orderly and delicately cultivated civilisation," he clearly moderated his views to maintain the argument at this level (*SL* 2.229–30). He maintained something of the same tone in 1932 as he wrote an extended discussion of the advantages to be gained by granting the lower classes alcohol to assuage their misery; yet he added, "I have a physical loathing for the smell of alcoholic beverages of all kinds, from beer to claret, and port to whiskey, a whiff of any one of them is almost an emetic to me" (*SL* 4.59).[1] In the same year in a letter to Howard he alluded to the "artificial paradise" of alcohol and asserted that he would approve of Prohibition if there were any means by which the law could work, though it had become clear that it cannot (*SL* 4.50–51). But in 1935 he returned to his chief anxiety and his chief misunderstanding: "I've never been able to understand the psychology of drink—just why people consider it desirable to spend most of their time in the clutch of a poison which sends them back several million years along the evolutionary scale!" (*SL* 5.93). That is the great danger; alcohol is simply an opportunity, a much too tempting opportunity, of falling back into what the race was thousands, no, millions of years ago. He had not read Freud on *Civilization and Its Discontents* on the burdens of maintaining our modern society and would probably have found its arguments unpersuasive.

In *The Case of Charles Dexter Ward* the newspaper reports a case of graverobbers and Sergt. Riley opines that the empty grave was the repository of bootleggers (*MM* 169), an ingenious suggestion when Prohibition was still in force; doubtless Lovecraft in his propagandistic mood must have found the detail only too apt, the connection between alcohol and the grave; but the

---

1. S. T. Joshi in a lengthy analysis of Lovecraft and the temperance movement emphasizes the point that Lovecraft's repugnance to alcohol may well have been based on constitutional grounds (*HPL: A Life* 144).

truth of the story affirms something more interesting when it connects alcohol and the tomb of the immortal Joseph Curwen. This connection is also to be found in the early story when Jervas sings a drinking song much more appropriate to the eighteenth century rake he resembles. Both stories imply something magical about drink. It has secret powers to overwhelm the human race; it is the first weapon of the Old Ones; and it is very attractive.

Lovecraft's fear of alcohol is at least as great as the fear that his characters suffer in the face of various genealogical disasters and in the face of his monsters. We have before suggested that this fear has an anti-Semitic component (Waugh, *Monster* 89–92), but now we might suspect that it has also a component of the fear of alcohol that we have outlined. In this light the various stories in which a character needs various alcoholic infusions to speak of the horrors take on a new significance; the drink invokes and adds body to creatures, which are delirium tremens incarnate, the delirium tremens that is an inescapable madness.

III

> And if the Babe is born a Boy
> He's given to a Woman Old,
> Who nails him down upon a rock,
> Catches his shrieks in cups of gold.
> (Blake, "The Mental Traveller" 9–12)

Parallel to Lovecraft's and O'Neill's attitudes toward alcohol are their attitudes toward sexuality. O'Neill had considerably more sexual experience than Lovecraft, but his experiences and their expressions are strongly colored by a sentimentality we do not find in Lovecraft. On the one hand, in O'Neill we find a rich display of earth-mothers in the brothel, and on the other hand the cold-hearted, sober, withholding women—who secretly take morphine. In Lovecraft, as we have seen, the women represent either a highly threatening and ecstatic sexuality or a pallid asexuality. In either case the authors have a deep suspicion about the mother, and both need to dispose of her.

O'Neill often perceives her as smothering (Gelb 514). The great example of this is in *Desire Under the Elms*, which begins with this remarkable description of the elms that lean over the house:

> Two enormous elms are on each side of the house. They bend their trailing branches down over the roof. They appear to protect and at the same

time subdue. There is a sinister maternity in their aspect, a crushing, jealous absorption. They have developed from their intimate contact with the life of man in the house an appalling humanness. They brood oppressively over the house. They are like exhausted women resting their sagging breasts and hands and hair on its roof, and when it rains their tears trickle down monotonously and rot on the shingles. (1.202)

The passage immediately calls up problems of language. How is this description, the "sinister maternity," the "crushing, jealous absorption" or the "appalling humanness," to be realized upon any stage? This language exceeds naturalism in the same way that Lovecraft's language of the blasphemous and the eldritch exceeds rationalism.

Nevertheless, the language returns us to the jungle into which Jones flees. Smithers warns him, "Ternight when it's pitch black in the forest, they'll 'ave their pet devils and ghosts 'oundin' after you. You'll find yer bloody 'air'll be standin' on end before termorrow mornin'. [. . .] It's a bleedin' queer place, that stinkin' forest, even in daylight. Yer don't know what might 'appen in there, it's that rotten still" (3.185). Though Jones deprecates these fears, they do destroy him, and in the light of the passage in *Desire Under the Elms* we must suspect that this strong phallic man is in fact still subject to the maternal principle.

As in O'Neill, Lovecraft's women are mothers that must be overcome. In looking at this theme we must obviously be careful of reading these stories back into Lovecraft's own life. Lavinia, Asenath, and the Witch Keziah are not Sarah Phillips Lovecraft nor, for that matter, Sonia Greene, though both women provided models for these characters. Lavinia loves her son extravagantly, perhaps because he is the only person in the family with whom she can have any relationship; her father is more than her intellectual equal, and he has pandered her to a monster. How much, then, does she love Wilbur? We recall that semi-incestuous moment when she and he are seen atop Sentinel Hill, not long after his birth, celebrating the rites of Halloween unclothed, where "they darted almost noiselessly through the underbrush" (*DH* 161). The adult Wilbur treats her "with a growing contempt" (168), obviously to her distress, until she dies in mysterious circumstances at Halloween, the victim of a "probable matricide" (170) and her soul is captured by the whippoorwills. Only later does the narrator agree that Wilbur has killed his mother. We have no idea why he has done that unless to his mind it was the only way to break his dependence on her extravagant allures. We must imagine that for a Yankee, even a Yankee who is an alien half-breed, there is something ecstatically attractive in an albino mother.

Something of the same story seems to occur in "The Thing on the Door-step" if we decide to read that narrative in a purely naturalistic fashion, paying no attention to its insistence that thought and consciousness can be transferred. Edward Derby has been brought up much too closely by his parents, so that there is little escape possible from his home. Only after his mother's death, when he is thirty-four, does he experience "a sort of grotesque exhilaration, as if of partial escape from some unseen bondage" (DH 279) and goes forth into the world where he meets Asenath when he is thirty-eight. Daniel Upton explains in the Freudian language of the day: "The perennial child had transferred his dependence from the parental image to a new and stronger image" (DH 282). This is a very slow maturation, but it is not difficult to read it and the language that glosses it as Lovecraft's commentary upon his own life with his mother until she died when he was thirty-one, to marry Sonia Greene shortly thereafter. His marriage in effect ended in 1925 with Sonia going to Cincinnati, and Derby explains the end of his marriage as due to Asenath going west. Sonia of course really did go west, and their marriage then died a natural death without their ever resorting to a divorce; and Asenath really did go west, since the phrase can mean that she died. Derby is in a much more dire relationship than his author; Asenath is a terribly domineering personality, so the only way out that he can imagine, the only effectual divorce, is to shoot her and bury the body in the cellar. He cannot, however, bear the guilt and so he cracks up, shouting as the physicians hustle him off to the asylum, "It'll get me . . . it'll get me . . . down there . . . down in the dark . . . Mother, mother! Dan! Save me" (DH 297). These shrieks are ambiguous. I imagine that most of us would suppose that he wants either his mother or his friend Daniel Upton to save him from his mental breakdown, but we might also think that it is his dead mother down in the dark with the dead body, because he transferred his dependence upon his mother to Asenath. More profoundly, he shot his mother when he shot his wife. And then there is the case of Walter Gilman, who if he did not in fact kill Keziah twists the chain of a crucifix around her neck "enough to cut off her breath" (MM 292); as we have earlier argued, she functions as his mother in that story.

These three matricides, the one actual, the other unconscious, and the third symbolic, invite us to consider other matricides. Nero has his mother killed, with whom he had earlier conducted an incestuous relation, as gossip, a persistent gossip, informs us, and Orestes kills Clytemnestra for the sake of his father. Nero justifies his murder in order to escape his dependence upon a mother who insists upon her own political power. This is a superstitious, literal-minded murder, from which the narrators draw back in horror; but in order to justify the murder and to admit his guilt Nero stages and acts in *Agamemnon,* the *Choephoroi,* and *Oedipus Rex* (Champlin 96). But his mother indicates the horrendous nature of the murder when she holds out her belly to her executioners and says, "Ventrem feri" [Strike my womb] (Tacitus, *Annales* 14.8), a moment that Seneca seems to allude to in the death of his Iocasta as she apostrophizes the sword with which she kills herself in the climax of the tragedy: "Hunc, dextra, hunc pete / uterum capacem, qui uirum et gnatos tulit" [This, right hand, strike this / capacious womb that bore both husband and sons] (ll. 1038–39).

So it is logical for us to call to mind the situation of Oedipus, for though Jocasta kills herself in both Sophocles' play and Seneca's, we may view her death as a wish-fulfillment on the part of her son. Seneca, indeed, blackens his Iocasta's guilt by the words of the ghost Laius, who says, "maximum Thebis scelus / maternus amor est" [the greatest desecration of Thebes / is maternal love" (ll. 629–30), and later refers to his son in these words, "implicitum malum / magisque monstrum Sphinge perplexum sua" [an intricate evil, / a monster more convoluted than his Sphinx] (ll. 640–41). This passage allows us to consider the death of the Sphinx at the hands of Oedipus before he enters Thebes and the death of his mother before he leaves as somehow connected, perhaps the same moment; and this is the theory Robert Graves suggests in his belief that "the Sphinx, overcome by Oedipus, killed herself and so did her priestess Iocaste" (2.13). Orestes can only justify his murder by appealing to Apollo, the god of male rationality that O'Neill, reading Nietzsche's *Der Geburt der Tragödie,* might well distrust. The murder that Aeschylus finds at best ambiguous, at most justifiable, O'Neill finds impossible; he cannot bring himself to write it, though it lies at the heart of *Mourning Becomes Electra,* his attempt to rewrite Greek tragedy in a modern mode. Orin cannot kill his mother, but he and his sister drive their mother to kill herself, an act that Orin cannot escape the guilt of and so he kills himself also. However, by an ingenious slight of hand it is the daughter Lavinia who bears the true guilt of the death of their mother.

If Orin is weak, he is nevertheless heroic, just as Orestes, Oedipus, and Wilbur Whately are heroic, for in the *Choephoroi* we are told of Clytemnestra's dream in which she gives birth to a snake, with which Orestes immedi-

ately identifies himself (ll. 526–34). This imagery says more than he understands, though it is possible that Nero understood this language, for it places
Orestes in the same relation to his mother that the hero bears to the Great
Mother (Harrison, *Prolegomena* 325–31). In Lovecraft's work we return at
once to Wilbur Whateley, holding in reserve the phallic power of himself in
his pants, but necessarily killing his albino mother, the Great Mother, the
White Goddess. When he is barely a year old there is "something almost
goatish or animalistic about his thick lips" (*DH* 162). When he is four and a
half "his lips and cheeks were fuzzy with a coarse dark down, and his voice
had begun to break" (165); sexual discrimination has appeared early. When
he is fourteen years old he is more than seven feet tall, a walking phallus,
"and shewed no signs of ceasing its development" (169). Still, there is no
sign in the years until his death that Wilbur has become a sexual totem in
the community. Two events, I think, account for that repression: first, he
has killed his mother, an attack on the Great Mother that must inflict a
wound on the phallic power of the son; second, perhaps more important but
less evident, influenced by his grandfather Wilbur has embarked upon a
highly intellectual education under the sign of Apollo that prevents any development of the Dionysian aspect of his being. He suffers thereby a double
wound that suppresses any development of the natural, sexual side of himself. He needs to keep himself inside his pants, he is determined to keep himself inside his pants, and he has no alternative but to keep himself inside his
pants. He has internalized his own castration.

In *The Iceman Cometh* the relation between Parritt and his mother takes
place in the past off-stage. After Hickey says that his wife is dead but before
he confesses that he killed her, Parritt comments upon Hickey and his own
mother: "It's that queer feeling he gives me that I'm mixed up with him some
way. I don't know why, but it started me thinking about Mother—as if she
was dead. [. . .] I suppose she might as well be. Inside herself, I mean. It must
kill her when she thinks of me" (3.666–67). The fact is that she very probably guesses that her son betrayed her to the police; and his later insistence
that the betrayal "had nothing to do with her! It was just to get a few lousy
dollars!" convinces Larry and the audience that the betrayal had everything
to do with her and certainly has a matricidal component. Parritt's suicide occurs on the same level as Orin's does.

The aggression toward the mother becomes in both authors an aggression
toward women in general, so often the representatives of morality. For
O'Neill women are sometimes too sexy, like Mrs. Mannon in *Mourning Be-*

comes *Electra*, or too repressed like the white bitch in *The Hairy Ape;* but at either extreme the woman threatens the man, either to address the sexual challenge or to retreat from it. Every extreme repulses him or collapses into his ambivalence. These feelings in *The Iceman Cometh* are concentrated when at the moment that he murders her Hickey blurts out to the wife who has condoned his violent drunkenness, "Well, you know what you can do with your pipe dream now, you damned bitch!" (3.716). This moment reverberates through the play. One aspect of it is Parritt's decision to kill himself, out of the guilt that he feels for betraying his mother; and thus she has her revenge upon him, just as Christine Mannon has her revenge upon her son. That curse, "You damned bitch!" the moment of murder and the moment at which the protagonist says No to the repressive, pervasive society that surrounds him, needs to be applied to "The Thing on the Doorstep," in which Derby murders his wife because he fears her growing influence over him. If we choose to read that story as a realistic account of a marriage gone very wrong, Asenath is no worse than the pious Evelyn.

One of the first characteristics of New England life upon which O'Neill and Lovecraft are agreed is the landscape that is filled with terrible old men who are obsessed by their identification with a hard God. In using this phrase "terrible old men" I of course have in mind Lovecraft's early story; but I also have in mind the Italian word *terribilità*, a phrase often applied to the work of Michelangelo, for there is something demiurgic about the aspirations of these men The first terrible old man in O'Neill's work appears in the one-act *Recklessness* in which Mr. Baldwin arranges the death of his young wife's lover, which leads to her suicide. The outstanding example of the terrible old man is Ephraim in *Desire Under the Elms.* At the end of the play he says: "I kin hear His voice warnin' me agen t' be hard an' stay on my farm. [. . .] I kin feel I be in the palm of His hand, His fingers guidin' me. [. . .] It's a-goin' t' be lonesomer noew than ever it war afore—an' I'm gittin' old, Lord—ripe on the bough. [. . .] Waal—what d'ye want? God's lonesome, hain't He? God's hard an' lonesome!" (1.268). He insists that he is only as hard and as strong as that God, albeit with a strength that can conquer any man, especially his sons. Yet at the conclusion of that play, despite his attempt to display his virility with the blessing of his hard God, he has been undone by the Oedipal desire of his son Eben. Abraham Bentley in the one-act play *The Rope* is the same sort of man, old and sick but full of a titanic rage that expresses itself in quotations from the prophetic rage of the Bible and determined to prove his virility by his marriage to the young town harlot almost immediately after the death of his wife. Both men are produced by the demanding Puritan tradition of New England. Both Cabot and Bentley, however, are weak-sighted and cannot really see, neither others nor themselves (Gelb 632).

One of the surprises in O'Neill's treatment of this theme is Professor Leeds in *Strange Interlude*, a very mild-mannered gentleman. Before the play has begun, however, he has persuaded his daughter's fiancé not to marry her before he goes to war and so at his death she is left desolate. He admits that he did wrong to interfere in their love, but it is too late. Though he dies after the first act his presence lingers and is one of the reasons that she so desperately tries to believe in a God who is a woman; but this theology doesn't work when in the ninth act she is an old woman and surrenders to the patriarchal power of her dead father.

Another surprise in O'Neill's treatment of this theme is Brigadier-General Ezra Mannon in the first play of the trilogy *Mourning Becomes Electra*. We expect a terrible old man; every utterance of the other characters prepares the audience for his imminent, powerful arrival. His wife says, "I couldn't fool him long. He's a strange, hidden man. His silence always creeps into my thoughts. Even if he never spoke, I would feel what was in his mind and some night, lying beside him, it would drive me mad and I'd have to kill his silence by screaming out the truth" (2.40). But the war has changed him; he wants to be soft, to be loved. He is not the Agamemnon we expect and his family expects.

One of the most impressive of these terrible old men in O'Neill's work is James Tyrone in *Long Day's Journey into Night*. Though he insists upon his Irish Roman Catholicism, that is not the important magic in his life. No, it is his connection to the stage, which still possesses enough power that it impresses his son in the last act, when Tyrone can still overcome his besotted state to give a star turn as he unscrews the bulbs in the chandelier. No performance of this play has it right unless it presents this terrible old man, despite the chorus of his sons deriding his authority, as a man still powerful and potent though in ruin. Above all, of course, he is Irish, in touch with the self-defensive blarney of the island, from which his sons have chosen to distance themselves; this Irishness is consciously removed from the world of the "Yanks" that his mother served and that still rankles after those many years.

Lovecraft's terrible old men are not Puritans, they are not Yanks; they are the contraries of Puritans, which is to say that they are in rebellion against the dogma but are nevertheless the bearers of its tone, its confidence, its authority, and its anger. Besides that, they are more sexual than they would ever confess, but that sexuality is a mark of their desire; the repression of the Puritan is beginning to crack in them. Both Wizard Whateley and Ephraim Waite, for instance, are engaged in breeding programs that have various goals, one of which is certainly to perpetuate their own patriarchal image and voice; and in order to accomplish this each man has engaged in an attack upon his daughter, Waite through psychological rape and Whateley through the act of the pander. At the climax of "The Dunwich Horror," when we least expect it, the face of Wizard Whateley appears atop the alien horror, albino in the guise of his daughter but nevertheless himself. Ephraim lives on in his daughter, though we grant that in Ephraim something utterly alien also lives on, an entity that cannot be disentangled from Ephraim's mundane existence, as though here the complexities of the Oedipal and Electral complexes had taken upon themselves a purely impersonal, abstract quality. Though half-mad, these two men possess the weight of authority that allows them to wait out the ages. It is difficult to say whether the terrible old men possess a power or are possessed by it; it is easy to say that the id disguised as the superego has utterly usurped whatever ego may have once existed, but that interpretation ignores the confusion of identity that seems to rage in these stories.

Lovecraft's first study of the terrible old man is in the short story that bears that title, though his name is never given; few in Kingsport know his name, and no one knows how old he is. He is simply terrible, old, and solitary. The story says nothing of a wife or mother or daughter. But he has given birth to something, if we notice that the later terrible old men we shall look at often have sons. This old Yankee has immigrant sons, though he will not accept them nor they him. Three criminals "of that new and heterogeneous alien stock which lies outside the charmed circle of New England life and traditions" (DH 273) decide to attack him because he "is reputed to be both exceedingly rich and exceedingly feeble" (272). He demands and deserves their attack, and their Oedipal essence rises to the challenge. The attack will be easy, they believe, not only because he is feeble; he is also quixotic, his house surrounded by "large stones, oddly grouped and painted so that they resemble the idols in some obscure Eastern temple" (272), a religion to which he presumably succumbed when he was, as some believe, the captain of a clipper ship in the East Indian trade, and in that house he holds conversations with bottles that bear the names of men who were once his crew—perhaps; the narrator assures the reader that anyone who observes these conversations "do not watch him again" (273). This happens to the three men, whose bodies are found the next morning "horribly slashed as with many cutlasses, and horribly mangled as by the tread of many cruel boot-heels" (274). Who has done this? The old man, so terrible and unhuman in his yellow eyes, yellow perhaps like cat's eyes, or the crew that he has summoned in his need? We can only resolve the question by saying that the Terrible Old Man—the phrase is always capitalized to emphasize his power—"leaning quietly on his knotted cane and smiling hideously" (274), has the power to summon that crew to wreak his bidding or he has the power to do whatever he wishes. Circled by the power of the stones that he has pried out of the unforgiving New England soil, he is "stubborn and perverse" (274), maintaining a reserve that is impenetrable and invulnerable, both by nature and, ironically, by the very fact of his feeble old age (275).[2]

In "The Picture in the House" the old man of the establishment was a Puritan once, as the prologue of the story argues, but he is not a Puritan any longer; he is simply an old, hungry man. He no doubt has hopes of eating the young narrator, but first he has to justify his actions. It is as though his monologue served the purpose of an appetizer; and the most interesting part of this need, besides his historical references, is his use of the Bible, his insistence that the violence of the holy word justifies the sadistic violence he is about to employ. The Bible tickles him and speaks through him.

Joseph Curwen never looks old, but he is very old indeed as his skin indicates. He pretends to be a member of one of the established churches, but he rather easily changes denominations when it suits his social ambition, which is itself a guise for his secret activities that grant him his true authority. He begets a child only in order to have a descendent in the future whose existence he can usurp. For the truly terrible old men the child does not exist for itself but to engrandize their fathers; make no mistake, the mild Delapore is a terrible old man.

The relationship with his descendent Charles Dexter Ward has already preoccupied us and now preoccupies us again. Curwen steps down from the frame of his portrait and usurps his great-great-great-grandson's life, in the same way that Laios usurps the life of Oedipus. For we can think of that event between the father and the child in the same way; the biological imperative lies with the child and all its potentials, not with the father whose life is well-nigh over but who insists that no threat, imaginary as it certainly is pace the oracle, shall loose him from his life and power. From this angle we

---

2. Carl Buchanan makes a strong argument for the Oedipal nature of the three immigrants' attack, comparing the story to the Oedipal situation in O'Neill's *Desire Under the Elms* (22–40).

need to consider Ward's relationship with his actual parents, that Dr. Willett, the ancient friend of the entire family, is so eager to protect. They are introduced relatively late in the novella, long after the remarks about the care that Ward's nurse lavished upon him (MM 113). Only fifty pages into the work do we learn the colorless information that his father is a cotton-manufacturer "with extensive mills at Riverpoint" (155). It is as though his father and mother performed the relaxed care that Oedipus met in the parents who adopted him, Polybus and Merope; but the family is not as carefree as it seems. The researches that Ward undertakes lead his mother to a near breakdown, removing her from the main plot of the novel; and his father seems oddly ineffectual, not able to accomplish the descent that Willett undertakes.

But when the portrait is discovered the relations between his father and his mother change. "She did not relish the discovery," the narrator writes, for there is "something unwholesome about it" (MM 155). It is as though Merope had been transformed into Jocaste, who is so passionate in attempting to persuade Oedipus not to pursue any further the secret of his birth. Nor is this so surprising since the presence of Joseph Curwen lies within her family tree; it is through her that his baleful influence reaches, and it is her that his existence accuses.

One of Lovecraft's most remarkable terrible old men is Wizard Whateley, but before dealing with him we need to deal with his grandson Wilbur, for every father has a son or daughter just as every son and daughter has a father. The last sentence of "The Dunwich Horror" is a minor masterstroke, bearing something of the weight and pathos of the last sentence of "The Outsider." I have considered them both in the light of the terminal climax (Waugh, *Monster* 111f.), but I have not analyzed its effect until recently when I saw that the two sentences are actually related in several ways. In the one sentence the protagonist discovers a mirror that reveals him for the first time. In the other sentence a speaker reveals a mirror relationship between the protagonist Wilbur Whateley and his twin brother, the invisible Horror of the title. At the end of "The Outsider" the protagonist says that he has put forth his hand, without wishing to, "and touched *a cold and unyielding surface of polished glass*" (DH 52). The mirror has no pity for the pitiable rotting corpse it reveals. At the end of "The Dunwich Horror" Dr. Armitage, who "chose his words very carefully" (197), says of Wilbur Whateley and the creature that he and his friends have just destroyed, "*It was his twin brother, but it looked more like the father than he did*" (198). In both cases the italics announce the importance and oddity of the sentences—these are terminal climaxes, inviting the reader to readjust any judgment the reader has made; but they are also something more.

For instance, if we take note that the two sentences can be taken to announce a similar situation, we see that the Horror and the "cold and unyielding surface" are similar to each other and function in the same way. The Horror, invisible and apparently a great emptiness, is like the surface of the mirror, cold and unyielding—so unyielding that it can knock down houses with great ease. And also, more significantly, the Horror mirrors Wilbur and his great lack, like the mirror as it reflects the Outsider: "deathwards progressing / To no death was that visage" (Keats, *The Fall of Hyperion* 1.260–61). Given these congruencies, one may speculate whether the banishment of the Horror is as conclusive as it appears.

Wilbur not only lacks something, the sentence announces; he is a failure. We had already understood him as a failure in the previous narration, but in various superficial ways: he cannot lay his hands on a decent copy of the *Necronomicon*, which no decent librarian will provide him, whether in Arkham or in Cambridge; he is ripped to shreds by a dog; and thus he cannot complete the revelation of his brother. But the failure to which this sentence refers is much more profound. His brother looked more like his father than he did. He is not as much a part of his family, that is to say the family of the mysterious entity Yog-Sothoth, as he seems to have wished. This is not his fault; it results from the accident of his birth. This is, nevertheless, an existential guilt that no amount of learning can relieve him of, earnestly though he tries to achieve that learning. The Outsider is a failure also, in that he fails to join the bright revelry as he had so much desired; on the other hand, he does join the dark revelry of the ghouls, and perhaps that undesired success is better for him as he is. He is most a failure in what he least expected, that he shall not live; and though he has ineffable memories of his previous life, he has no way to possess those memories—he shall always be as he is, stripped of much of his mind and body, but not wholly.

We do wonder which of the Whateley brothers was the eldest. There is no answer to this question, but the story of Jacob and Esau comes to mind, one of them the eldest but the other clever enough to take the heel of his brother in birth and thus to have a hand over his brother in so many of their encounters thenceforth. They are twins, but a great difference lies between them, not simply the difference of their appearances. Esau is a hunter, whereas Jacob is a man of the tents. More importantly, their father Isaac loves Esau, something of his opposite, more than the clever Jacob (Gen. 25:24–34). The lesson of the story is that even the least esteemed can become the most esteemed; the obverse of the story is that the most esteemed may become the least. Since we have no idea what kind of regard or attention Yog-Sothoth has toward his sons—such words as "regard" or "attention" may not apply at all to that entity—we have no indication how to read Lovecraft's story within this model.

And then, more pressingly, there is the problem that Wilbur's twin brother looks more like his father than he did—which is to say that Wilbur does not look like his brother, who is so much more powerful than he is. Like and unlike the Outsider, who looks into a mirror and sees himself for the first time such as he had never expected to see himself, Wilbur looks into the mirror but does not see himself at all. Of course in looking into his brother it is understandable that he does not see himself, for his brother is invisible. But that is his twin brother. So in looking into his brother he sees himself in fact more profoundly, for he discovers himself as a vast emptiness. If we understand him as such an emptiness, his desperation to accomplish the task his grandfather bequeathed him and the pathos of his situation are further increased.

If he had seen himself as he is in the flesh, unclothed, though Wilbur is very careful throughout his adult life to clothe himself very tightly from the neck down as though he were ashamed of himself, he would have seen his divided body, human above the waist and "sheer phantasy" below. With some irony we might recall these lines in the mad mouth of Lear:

> But to the girdle do the gods inherit.
> Beneath is all the fiends'; there's hell, there's darkness,
> There's the sulphurous pit, burning, scalding
> Stench, consumption! Fie, fie, fie! pah! pah! pah! (4.6.123–26)

Lear is of course referring to his wicked daughters, though his language attempts to describe the sexuality of all women. Wilbur is a man, thoroughly phallic in some of the language that describes him but hysteric in other parts of the language. Consider this description: "from the abdomen a score of long greenish-grey tentacles with red sucking mouths protruded limply" (DH 174). It seems remarkable that Wilbur was able to contain all this in his pants. The first division in the psyche is between being human and being monstrous. But other divisions follow, here as we see between the genders, a division from which Wilbur cannot save himself given his probable murder of his mother.

All this discussion has something dreadfully wrong about it, the way that it ignores the presence and necessity of Lavinia; but as the sibyls and witches in David Jones's In Parenthesis say, "The Lord God may well do all without the aid of man, but even in the things of god a woman is medial—it stands to reason. Even the gigantic dynion gynt and mighty tyrannoi of old time must needs have had mortal woman for mothers, if demi-gods or whatever father'd them—it stands to reason" (214). Whatever indeed! We need, then, to pay attention to Lavinia. She is, the narrator informs us, "one of the decadent Whateleys, a somewhat deformed, unattractive albino woman of thirty-five," who gives birth to a boy perhaps more deformed than she that she "was heard to mutter many curious prophecies about" (DH 159). She has given birth "In the midway of this our mortal life" (Dante, Inf. 1.1), a significant time—a proud mother, just the sort of mother a deformed child would desire. The narrator, however, says rather condescendingly that she was "apt to mutter such things, for she was a lone creature given to wandering amidst thunderstorms in the hills and trying to read the great odorous books which her father had inherited through two centuries of Whateleys" (DH 159). They are closed books to her, so she probably has no idea what her father has in mind for her. Until that moment she "was fond of wild and grandiose day-dreams and singular occupations." Though we suspect she is defective, her father does show "some trace of pride" in her and claims, "Lavinny's read some, an' has seed some things the most o' ye only tell abaout" (160). In truth, however, he has pimped her to Yog-Sothoth so that she can give birth to the twins. He respects her more than Ephraim Waite respects Asenath, for to him the very fact that she is a woman makes her unworthy of his intellect and goals.

We must not ignore the implications of the rest of this family tragedy, though we often do. When Lavinia is of no further use to Wilbur he apparently kills her, probably for various reasons. She has no reason to stop the naked liturgies that she and her son have celebrated on the top of the hill, liturgies that may provide the only pleasure she has in life and that affirm her connection to the Horror, whereas he, now come of age, has every reason to stop them. But what young man of a certain age wants to dance naked with his mother? And how shall he convince her? What with her "wild and grandiose day-dreams" she is not a convincible person, so from his point of view, in this most practical sense, she has to die, for he cannot any longer reveal himself as he actually is. As a human being, however, she is simply what she is, which of course Wilbur can no longer admit to the world nor probably to himself. So the old Eve has to die, and we are complicitous in that death insofar as we are eager for the story to proceed.

Just as there are two sons, there are also two fathers, Yog-Sothoth and Wizard Whateley. Let us call them the spiritual father and the intellectual father. The language of the *Necronomicon*, naming Yog-Sothoth the gate, the key, and the guardian of the gate (*DH* 170), imitating the language of the gospel of John, clearly aspires to a religious statement; though we must apply a physical interpretation to the nature of Yog-Sothoth it is impossible not to use such a language for an entity that transcends space and time as we know it. Wizard Whateley, thoroughly human, is at first the educator of Wilbur, initiating him into his identity, but like his son-in-law Yog-Sothoth he also transcends space and time in his death, for the whippoorwills do not catch him and he seems to return in the first climax of the story in Curtis Whateley's description of the face on the top of the Horror, "*a haff-shaped man's face [. . .], an' it looked like Wizard Whateley's, only it was yards an' yards acrost . . .*" (197). The effect of this passage is peculiar, both diminishing the old man and magnifying him.

"The Shadow over Innsmouth" has two terrible old men. One is Captain Obed Marsh, who for the sake of the gold that the Deep Ones can provide establishes a new religion in his home town, the Esoteric Order of Dagon, and who pimps his daughters just as Wizard Whateley had done to perpetuate the new religious order. The other, oddly enough, is Zadok Allen, the last of Lovecraft's terrible old men because he speaks with such authority. It is difficult to make him speak; even with the liquor in him he has a strong compulsion to speak in riddles since he fears the retribution of the community. But he must speak because he was there. He has a history to deliver and a prophecy. A part of what he has to say is simple enough: "Mene, mene, tekel upharsin" (*DH* 334), the message on the wall that Daniel interprets, "Mene; God hath numbered thy kingdom, and finished it. Tekel; Thou art weighed in the balances, and found wanting. Peres; Thy kingdom is divided, and given to the Medes and Persians" (Daniel 5.26–28). And Zadok Allen is right; not long after the events of the story the Federal agents arrive to arrest the Innsmouthers, take them to concentration camps, and dynamite the town (*DH* 303). Like every other terrible, old man Zadok Allen possesses and is possessed by his private connection to God.

In contrast to these terrible old men let us consider for a moment Nahum Gardner in "The Colour out of Space," who has nothing of their *terribilità* and whose relations with God are at best tentative; he is not confidential with the Old Testament God of New England and cannot summon him to his defense, much less to any attack, and so he and his family slowly fall apart. Most of Lovecraft's terrible old men survive, and if they do not their ends are memorable. The Gardners die not with a bang but a whimper. In this decline and decease—no tragedy certainly—Lovecraft is writing more closely to T. S. Eliot than he might have wished.

With Mr. Gardner in mind we admit that there are other fathers and father-figures in these stories who are quite different from the terrible old men. Besides the rather helpless fathers of Charles Dexter Ward and Edward Derby, certain elderly men behave heroically. Francis Thurston's grand-uncle Professor Angell would not have wished his own death on his grand-nephew. After Dr. Whipple dies valiantly his nephew avenges him. Dr. Willett, who brought Charles Dexter Ward into the world (MM 109), avenges the death of that hapless young man. Although his wife divorces him, his son Wingate defends Nathaniel Peaslee and accompanies him on his trip to the Great Down Under where he learns the truth of his condition. These several tender relations suggest that the terrible old man is not at all Lovecraft's final word on the father; instead, they reveal how important to Lovecraft those relations were in which he played the role of a grandfather to several young men.

IV

The holy blisful martir for to seke,
That hem hath holpen, whan that they were seke. (Chaucer 419)

So they left that goodly and pleasant city which had been their resting place near twelve years; but they knew they were pilgrims, and looked not much on those things, but lift up their eyes to the heavens, their dearest country, and quieted their spirits. (Bradford 50)

The image of the pilgrim is embedded in the first lines of Chaucer's *Canterbury Tales*, where the rime riche assures us that sickness and searching are the same thing, and in Bradford's history of the Plymouth Plantation that tells the reader before the Puritans have ever crossed over from Holland to England once more to embark for New England, only recently given that comfortable name, that they have resolved to take no place for their final resting unless it is that place outside this physical world. So we need to change our perspective. We have already treated the young men in these plays and stories as readers. Let us now think of them as questers, as pilgrims. In O'Neill's work the great questers are the Emperor Jones and Hank the hairy ape. They do not wish to be questers—Jones thinks that he is running away from a disastrous situation without realizing that he is plunging into his racial history, something that though he must die for it he must uncover and discover, and Hank does not realize that his apparent quest, to confront the white bitch, is actually aimed at the discovery of his own identity. Viewed from this perspective, it is not so clear that the death they suffer is a tragedy, unless that identity lies beyond them. To their group in Lovecraft's work we should add Wilbur Whateley, who is searching for the final text that shall validate his murder of his mother, an albino that we might consider a parody of the white, deadly white, woman in Hank's quest. We leave aside the white whale for which Ahab quests because those white whales are liable to mean too much

Before we consider those early works, however, the two most evident quests in O'Neill's later work, *Marco Millions* and *The Fountain*, are the most disappointing. Written at the same time, they are the sort of historical spectacles that his father performed in; they tempted O'Neill away from his great strength in the details of the contemporary world. A third play at the same time, *Lazarus Laughed*, has the same problems, but it is not as evidently a quest. Lazarus has his vision of overwhelming life at the beginning of the play, and so he is upon no quest; it is rather everyone who meets him, hidden in their hundreds of masks, that are forced to begin a quest out of the life each of them lives.[3]

But though the three plays resemble externally his father's spectacles, *The Passion* and *Joseph and His Brethren*, they work strenuously against those conventional pieties. The theme to which they all return is the ferocity of life that transcends all middle-class values. So the tone of the plays often wobbles uneasily upon the satiric, most notably in *Marco Millions* whose chief quester is too complacent to realize that he is on a quest, though he journeys from Venice to Cathay and back again, never affected by cultural differences or by the possibility of love. He insists that he has a soul though he has no idea what that might mean, and in any case the great Kaan doubts very much that he has any such thing. Instead, Marco represents all that is soulless about the complacent hucksterism of America. Everything that he does

---

3. Sensing the formal connection between the three plays, John Henry Raleigh groups them as "the exotic historical" (ctd. in Berlin 135).

recalls the regalia and the spirit of "our modern Knights Templar, of Columbus, of Pythias, Mystic Shriners, the Klan, etc." (2.390). Yes, of the Masons.
We are terribly fond of costumes.

The Fountain, a play about the quest of Juan Ponce de Leon for the Fountain of Youth, is a more romantic play than Marco Millions, but its satiric
elements aim at a fanatical church determined to destroy the Native American life. The various fountains of the play and the poetry associated with the
fountains insist upon a symbolic reading of the quest that culminates in
Juan's dying words: "One must accept, absorb, give back, become oneself a
symbol. [. . .] Fountain of Eternity, take back this drop, my soul" (1.448).
This, then, is a soul, if he is willing to surrender it. These words confirm
those of the chief Nano that "the way is long" (1.416). The quest is long because its terminus lies on the other side of death; but before anyone can
come to grips with that death it must be imagined, fully and deeply, as
Marco Polo cannot do (1.380).

Imagining your death in Lazarus Laughed is very different from the invention of death that lies far back in the origins of civilization (1.310). Lazarus has
died and come to life, so he laughs at every invention of death and rides into
Athens and Rome as though he were Dionysus (1.307), not because he wishes
to but because the civilization insists that the god it expects must appear.
Crassus is more cautious when he supposes that "there is a god in it somewhere" (1.322), though Lazarus warns him to be careful about the invention of
gods. The world of Rome, however, is determined to prove that death is death
and nothing more, and thereby the perfect instrument of repression, just as the
church had insisted in The Fountain. The ambivalent instrument of this punishment in Lazarus Laughed is Caligula, a man who is "almost malformed, with
wide, powerful shoulders and long arms and hands, and short, skinny, hairy
legs like an ape's" (1.299). Nevertheless, as brutalized as his body is, he is human, and thus we return to the quests of Jones and Hank.

In The Emperor Jones the main character believes in sheer bravado that
he is escaping the effects of his rule that is now falling apart; the truth is that
he is pursuing a quest of his own fearful racial experience. The complacence
he exudes in the first scene is hollow, belied by a past of which he is mostly
unaware. It is neither the silver bullet nor the political unrest that kills him;
his body and soul kill him, the baggage he carries to the third and fourth
generation. At the beginning of The Hairy Ape Hank has the same complacence as Jones, both men being gifted with a physical charisma. In a phrase
that recurs often in the play, he insists that he belongs; but the rhetoric of

the play's eight scenes, the same number as in *The Emperor Jones*, insists that he does not belong and neither does anyone else who is born (3.251). Both plays propose a quest, but each ends in a regressive motion that despairs of the quest. Despite whatever gifts we have, we shall not know who we are.

To turn to the quests in Lovecraft, Wilbur's is one that many of Love-craft's readers have attempted to repeat or to imitate or, failing these at-tempts, to simply daydream of. He searches for a book, a good edition, not a fragmentary or ragged copy but as though that were possible for the thing it-self. For the *Necronomicon*. Throughout the books of the as-of-yet-unrealized Cthulhu Mythos there is no book its like. When we still had card catalogues it was easy to insert a card that bore the necessary provenance and Dewey number; I am sure that enterprising readers, despite the forces of order in the catalogue departments, find it not difficult today to impregnate the digital catalogues with the presence of the book for which Wilbur died. His quest is tragic and perhaps naive—his language is at least naive but no more so than the language of Hank—but he is a very idealistic young man. The final ob-ject of his quest, of course, the reason he is set upon his logocentric digres-sion, is to nurture his twin; again we see how self-abnegating his is—though we must never lose sight of the fact that in order to accomplish his quest he is also a matricide. He kills his white bitch.

The major figure in Lovecraft conducting a quest is Randolph Carter. He does not at first in "The Statement of Randolph Carter" understand that he is on a quest. He is in fact in a rather anomalous position; though for five years he has been Harley Warren's closest friend he insists or confesses that Warren "dominated me, and sometimes I feared him" (MM 300). Though every indi-cation in the dream that formed the basis of this story suggests that Carter is an alter ego for Lovecraft, he plays a supernumerary role and at the climax fails to save his friend "who held the key to the *thing* [*sic*]" (302), whatever that *thing* might have been. Whatever the quest may have been, which he in-sists to the "inquisition" (299) of the authorities he knew nothing of, the death of this friend toward whom he has ambivalent feelings must fill him with a sense of incompletion and failure. The continuation of the saga in "The Silver Key" and "Through the Gates of the Silver Key" replay this story as a work of profound guilt that has apparently not yet been worked through, as though this sort of guilt could ever be worked through: send Daddy into the bowels of the earth and let him die there. Warrens were at first the killing grounds of small animals and later meant cubbies or labyrinths. The trauma of the father in the grave, "the end of my experience" (305), will not cease.

In "The Unnamable" we learn that Carter is an author of "lowly standing" (D 200) who resorts too often to a rather general vocabulary, and so the story becomes a quest for the source of such words. Carter and a friend are discussing the matter. His friend has a very different aesthetic; he believes in "the solid definitions of fact or the correct doctrines of theology—preferably those of the Congregationalists, with whatever tradition and Sir Arthur Conan Doyle may supply" (200–01). The last phrase suggests that the friend does not quite have the courage of his convictions; his aesthetic is a mish-mash of Protestant timidity and contemporary spiritualism of the more moronic sort, a man who shares "New England's self-satisfied deafness to the delicate overtones of life" (201). O'Neill would have agreed with the judgment.

The two stories, despite their retrospective interest, are trifles with little sign of the extensive development Lovecraft gives them in his later works, *The Dream-Quest of Unknown Kadath* and the two Silver Key stories. In contrast to the first two stories *The Dream-Quest* is no longer external; it is internal, and thus the quest is solitary, though Carter meets several friends and guides, many of them not human or no longer so. Their presence is one gauge of the tone of the work that vacillates between an awe at beautiful sights, an awe that many might consider too facile since the beauty is too general or too repetitive—a bit too much onyx and marble—; a horror toward which the narrative gestures but that is seldom brought home to the personal state of Randolph Carter or the reader; and an overriding tone of understated irony and studied distance, frequently through well-chosen verbs and adverbs. Despite the fanfare of the first page and the complexity of the final eight pages, the self-references and the light touch leave the reader with the impression that his quest cannot be for anything important.

To correct this impression we need to see that the quest has two aspects. One is the city described in the first pages, compacted from a catalogue of significant imagery: walls, temples, colonnades, bridges, fountains, gardens, streets, trees, urns, statues, gables, concluding in the statement, "It was a fever of the gods; a fanfare of supernal trumpets and a clash of immortal cymbals" (MM 306), a phrase that shall be repeated at the end of the narrative. All this imagery invites the reader to play the ancient game that Plato invented, the utopian city as a symbol of the individual or super-individual, a game played by modernists such as Joyce in *Ulysses* and *Finnegans Wake* and Williams in *Paterson*. This city/body is the opposite of the city/body of Sarkomand and Thok that I have elsewhere argued represents the body of death

("Landscapes" 225); the ideal city contains imagery of death, the urns and statues, but in it they are sublimated to an ideal beauty.

The second aspect of the quest is more intimate, triggered by the poignancy and suspense of almost-vanished memory, the pain of lost things, "glimpses of a far, forgotten first youth" (MM 306–7). These are the suggestions, not sufficiently carried out here but to form the basis of "The Silver Key," that align themselves with Proust's program and that make sense of Lovecraft's admiration for the French novelist, whose protagonist like Carter is also "à la recherche" for a lost time. The quest is basic to both enterprises. Lovecraft was not to read Proust until two years had passed, but he was ready to read him.

The plot of the novella is more structured than it seems, depending on a series of parallels between the first half of the quest and the second. The battle of the cats and the moonbeasts in the first half is balanced by the battle of the doglike ghouls and the moonbeasts in the second half. The river Skai (pronounced "sky" I believe) is balanced by the river Oukranos (perhaps to be associated with the great river Okeanos in Greek myth). The nightgaunts associated with the great mountain Ngranek at the end of the first, where they tickle Carter mercilessly, aid him at the end of the second half by flying to the enormous mountain upon which Kadath rests. In addition to these structural correspondences, the resonance of the narrative is increased by the description of Dylath-Leen (die, loth, lean), its "blur of smoke," its "tall black towers" that make it look "in the distance like a bit of the Giants' Causeway," and its "dismal sea-taverns" and streets in which throng "the strange seamen of every land on earth" (MM 315). If Carter's marvelous city is a compound of all the romantic cities of New England, these details make it easy to think of Dylath-Leen as the image of a demonized New York.

The Dream-Quest shares an important image of Randolph Carter with "The Silver Key," perhaps since they were written at the same time. In both he is a pilgrim (MM 348, 417). For a writer in New England this is not an idle word. William Bradford had called the Puritans aboard the Mayflower pilgrims, having in mind this passage from Hebrews:

> These all died in faith, not having received the promises, but having seen them from afar off, and were persuaded of them and embraced them, and confessed that they were strangers and pilgrims on the earth. For they that say such things declare plainly that they seek a country. And truly, if they had been mindful of that country from whence they came out, they might have had opportunity to have returned. But now they desire a better coun-

try, that is, an heavenly: wherefore God is not ashamed to be called their God: for he hath prepared for them a city. (11.13–16)

We keep in mind here the quests in O'Neill that accuse life of insufficiency and look beyond it. The quest is more complicated in Lovecraft because at the end of *The Dream-Quest* Randolph Carter wakes up and springs from bed, happy to meet the morning on Beacon Hill; yet that is not enough since in "The Silver Key" he leaves Boston to return to his childhood home and to be lost there. In "Through the Gates of the Silver Key" he tries to prove that he is not dead and to return home once more, but this is rather difficult since he no longer bears his human body. Each of these stories testifies to the directionality of the quest that transforms the quester.

V

Way-ay, I'm bound away
Across the wide Missouri. (O'Neill 2.6)

Joseph Conrad, especially in *The Nigger of the "Narcissus,"* had a great influence on O'Neill's ocean mysticism (Gelb 273f.); he was ready to understand the ocean that he crossed in his tramp steamers in a particular way. Conrad gave him a vocabulary for that experience, one that he necessarily shaped to meet the language of the various simple men in the crew gathered together from so many different countries in the world, English, Swedish, Irish. "The scum of the earth," as the Duke of Wellington fondly expressed it. Conrad's novella gave him the plot for the first play of the Glencairn cycle, *Bound East for Cardiff,* and O'Neill's fascination with the diverse company, the moral weight of such a company, can still be found in *The Iceman Cometh.* In addition, a few words of the cook in *The Nigger of the "Narcissus,"* "Did you ever see them down in the stokehold? Like fiends they look— firing—firing—firing down there" (114), may have suggested the hellish imagery of the first scenes in *The Hairy Ape.* Lovecraft's experience is more scientific; in his *Defence of Dagon* he refers to a physiographer that he plucks from his library. But his experience is also dependent on his dreams in a way that O'Neill's seems never to have been; and Lovecraft had read *Twenty Thousand Leagues Under the Sea.* O'Neill's experience lies on the surface of the waves; Lovecraft's lies below.

Leaving aside such literary materials, both men have a strong relation with the sea, having grown up beside it. There is this difference, however. Lovecraft always lived by the sea and seems to have always hated it—at least he hated seafood—whereas O'Neill only lived beside it in New London during the summer when his father retired there from the season; O'Neill, that is to say, was something of an occasional visitor, not a tourist, because he knew the people of the town, but never quite an inhabitant either. He was an outsider and an insider at the same time. He made full use of being there, however, often taking out a small sailboat to dream away the hours at that wonderful, lapping distance from land. When a young man he had a much more intimate relation with the sea as an able-bodied seaman on a variety of tramp steamers; years later he loved to display his shirt, ABS, well earned. On board those ships he got to know the sea and the men that work upon the sea, so his first successful dramas are the one-act plays that form the cycle *S.S. Glencairn*. From these experiences his use of the sea became quite complex.

In examining this theme, however, we need to treat Lovecraft's and O'Neill's attitudes toward the sea as two distinct moods that arise from the vantage point of the character, whether on the full main far from land or whether on shore looking out to sea. We shall see that Lovecraft treats the ocean as a place of sheer terror, but his mood is very different ashore in "lanes up which fragrant sea-winds sweep at evening" (*D* 276). In an idyllic moment as the group about to attack Curwen's farm looks back at the Providence they mean to save, "steeples and gables rose dark and shapely, and salt breezes swept up gently from the cove north of the Bridge" (MM 141). Later in that evening "the strong freshness of the sea" protects many from a stench that reeks from the attack (144). This is the mood that permeates the wonders of "The White Ship" because the narrator of that story, a lighthouse keeper, insists, "More wonderful than the lore of old men and the lore of books is the secret lore of ocean" (*D* 36)—O'Neill would have agreed. When Randolph Carter mounts the hill to his ancestor's home he can see "hints of the archaic, dream-laden sea" far off on the horizon (MM 415). This mood permeates several of the sonnets in *Fungi from Yuggoth*, from early in the cycle until late in the cycle: "The Port," "The Bells," "Expectancy," "Nostalgia," and "Harbour Whistles" (AT 67–77) make gestures toward the great ocean of terror far from land, but they also express the sense of loss, of something long forgotten out there that we still almost remember and that the voice of the poems cannot surrender.

O'Neill's earliest plays take place on a tramp steamer plying between the Caribbean and England. In *Bound East for Cardiff* the scene is the forecastle in which one of the crew is dying, but we are made aware of the ship and the ocean beyond because its whistle blows throughout the play to indicate their position in the fog, a sound that is to echo through the last act of *A Long Day's Journey into Night*. The men curse the fog and comment upon the "dirty weather all dis voyage" and think of ships that went down in such weather in the past (1.481); the dying man for whom they are so solicitous particularizes their own condition. This foghorn serves a more subtle purpose, the same that we see in *The Emperor Jones* in which the tom-tom "starts at a rate exactly corresponding to a normal pulse beat—72 to the minute—and continues at a gradually accelerating rate [. . .] to the very end of the play" (3.184). We may wonder whether this physiological intention in its literal interpretation is ever perceived as such by an audience, but the steady call, whether tom-tom or foghorn, certainly adds to the rhythm and effect of the work. The only effect that Lovecraft can call on in his stories that might be similar is the steady repetition of the leitmotifs.

The Moon of the Caribbees is a romantic one-acter that takes place on deck under a full moon, "a melancholy Negro chant" (1.455) heard in the distance that suggests to the crewmen death and burial (1.456); and the song recurs at the end of the play. The action has two currents, the one the anticipation of the crew for the arrival of the women from shore with booze and the other the remorse of Smitty for whom the song triggers memories that he would rather forget. The donkeyman makes a good guess at his problem: "She said she threw you over 'cause you was drunk; an' you said you was drunk 'cause she threw you over" (1.467). The human problem is insoluble. No Senta reaches out her hand.

The sea is very much a presence in *Anna Christie* though none of the acts take place out on the full sea. Chris, though, who has been a seaman all his life, curses the "ole davil sea" throughout the play, so much so that he becomes something of a bore to the others. It is the symbol of all that has gone wrong in his life; he says to his daughter in an attempt to justify his life, "Ay don't know why but dat's vay with most sailor fallar, Anna. Dat old davil sea make dem crazy fools with her dirty tricks" (3.21). The attitude of the play is more complicated than his refrain seems to indicate. Only a few minutes after he has accused the ocean he praises it: "Yust water all round, and sun, and fresh air, and good grub for make you strong, healthy gel. You see tangs you don't see before. You gat moonlight at night, maybe; see steamer pass; see schooner make sail—see everytang dat's pooty" (3.23). The second act, however, opens on a dense fog and "the doleful tolling of bells" (3.25) and closes with Anna going to bed with Burke to Chris's shock: "Dat's your dirty trick, damn ole davil, you!" (3.40). The ocean behaves like the madam of a brothel; and Chris concludes the play on a note that uses these images once more: "Fog, fog, fog, all bloody time. You can't see vhere you vas going, no. Only dat old davil, sea—she knows!" (3.78). He had protested earlier, "No! Dat old davil, sea, she ain't God! (3.29), but she is God at the conclusion. The sea is the mother goddess who destroys us.

This is not, however, Anna's perspective. For her the fog is first mysterious. She stumbles trying to find the words for this experience she has never had. It is "funny and still. I feel as if I was—out of things altogether" (3.25). The fog allows her to fall in love with the ocean long before she falls in love with Burke: "It makes me feel clean—out here—'s if I'd taken a bath" (3.26). With a greater insight she realizes that here, in the fog on the sea she feels old: "It's like I'd come home after a long visit away some place. It all seems like I'd been here before lots of times—on boats—in this same fog" (3.28). There are several ironies in the play, but they never qualify this homecoming that O'Neill returns to in A Long Day's Journey into Night.

He needed, however, to meditate on the sea much longer before he could write that play. For a short moment in Strange Interlude Nina Leeds sinks into the meaning of her pregnancy as she sits in her seashore suburb that promises so little: "life is. . . and this is beyond reason . . . questions die in the silence of this peace . . . I am living a dream within the great dream of the tide . . . breathing in the tide I dream and breathe back my dream into the tide . . . suspended in the movement of the tide, I feel life move in me, suspended in me . . . no whys matter . . . there is no why . . . I am a mother . . . God is a Mother . . ." (1.91–92). She does not only affirm herself as the Goddess that gives birth and the Goddess that opposes the patriarchal God represented by her father and lover; she affirms the ocean as the Mother Goddess, the only place in her earthly experience that makes sense of her as she prepares to give birth.

In the trilogy Mourning Becomes Electra the Aegisthus figure Brant evokes the romantic ocean again, perhaps in an attempt to seduce Lavinia: "And they live in as near the Garden of Paradise before sin was discovered as you'll find on this earth! Unless you've seen it, you can't picture the green beauty of their land set in the blue of the sea." Lavinia, however, expects nothing less from "the son of a low Canuck nurse girl" (2.24). The dream is brutally cut off before it finds expression. He speaks more truthfully to Lavinia's mother Christine when he dreams of the ship he wants to buy: "She's as beautiful a ship as you're a woman. Aye, the two of you are like sisters. If she

was mine, I'd take you on a honeymoon then!" (2.39). This is a peroration to
the sea and the craft that rides it we never find in Lovecraft. The climax to
this language is to be found in the center of the trilogy when Orin dreams of
the islands that he read of in Melville's *Typee*: "I read it and reread it until
finally those Islands came to mean everything that wasn't war, everything
that was peace and warmth and security" (2.89–90). The problem with this
passage is that it modulates into an Oedipal dream of the mother: "There
was no one there but you and me. And yet I never saw you, that's the funny
part. I only felt you all around me. The breaking of the waves was your voice.
The sky was the same color as your eyes. The warm skin was like your skin.
The whole island was you" (2.90). The only answer to this dependence in
the play is to drive the mother to suicide. The third play addresses the islands from a strictly Puritan point of view. Now Orin sees them as a place of
open sin that seduced his sister to dance: "Oh, she was a bit shocked at first
by their dances, but afterwards she fell in love with the Islanders. If we'd
stayed another month, I know I'd have found her some moonlight night
dancing under the palm trees—as naked as the rest!" (2.145). This passage is
a demonization of the paradise, faulted and venal as it was, that the men of
the *Glencairn* in their true innocence found in the Caribbees. The Mannon
family of *Mourning Becomes Electra* lost that innocence somewhere at the establishment of the Calvinist reformation.

These themes of the fog, its danger and temptation, and of the ocean
that takes you into itself to dissolve your identity, are taken up most persuasively in *Long Day's Journey into Night*. They are expressed by Mary Tyrone
and her son Edmund, the two characters who have the greatest ambivalence
toward each other. Mary at first says that she hates the foghorn (17), and so
she does, but only because she loves the fog that becomes the symbol in the
play of her morphine addiction that muffles the pain of the past. To her servant Cathleen she says, "It hides you from the world and the world from you.
You feel that everything has changed, and nothing is what it seemed to be.
No one can find you or touch you any more" (98). But throughout this act
and the next the foghorn continues to sound regularly, alerting the audience
to attend to the pain and not to let go of it because it is finally the pain that
tells the truth in the play.

But not quite. Edmund's reaction to the fog is rather like his mother's but
played out in a different key. Facing the news that he has tuberculosis, he
takes a long walk through the fog, where

everything looked and sounded unreal. Nothing was what it is. That's what I wanted—to be alone with myself in another world where truth is untrue and life can hide from itself. [. . .] The fog and the sea seemed part of each other. It was like walking on the bottom of the sea. As if I had drowned long ago. As if I was a ghost belonging to the fog, and the fog was the ghost of the sea. It felt damned peaceful to be nothing more than a ghost within a ghost. (131)

He has pushed the experience as far as possible, but he does it as a poet, not as a person lost to an addiction. Though he is determined in this scene to be drunk, he is not drunk yet; and the truth of the scene is that he and his father are at last talking to each other on an authentic, vulnerable level. Later in the act he has another experience of the sea to relate, how he lay on a bowsprit at night, watching the water spuming beneath him, "and for a moment I lost myself—actually lost my life. I was set free! I belonged, without past or future, within peace and unity and a wild joy, within something greater than my own life, or the life of Man, to Life itself! To God, if you want to put it that way." He then recounts several other experiences connected with the sea that contain the same message of "the peace, the end of the quest, the last harbor, the joy of belonging to a fulfillment beyond man's lousy, pitiful, greedy fears and hopes and dreams." But always, he concludes, the experience passes "and you are alone, lost in the fog again, and you stumble on toward nowhere, for no good reason" (153). The oceanic experience is only valid so far, but his mother's words at the end does not invalidate it. Though a part of its meaning is that he is a person "who must always be a little in love with death" (154), he is determined to fight for his life. He is a ghost within a ghost who has set his major stake on life and joy. Though he stammers, as fog people must, that stammering is his "native eloquence" in which he finds himself most truly (154).

Lovecraft hated the sea, but he also realized its attraction. "Dagon," "The Temple," and "The Call of Cthulhu" are at their core all pretty much the same story, concerning a profound attraction that the sea, represented by the various aliens, exerts upon different men. Shortly after the publication of "Dagon" he wrote a series of letters in its defense, something he never did for any other story. Another version of this story appears in the late story "The Shadow over Innsmouth," where the attraction has become so profound that the anonymous narrator decides on the last page to find his grandmother and ur-grandmother who are calling him from the depths. In this story the decadent cult the Esoteric Order of Dagon enters the Lovecraftian network of pseudo-references. On the part of the Innsmouth people this is a conscious, blasphemous allusion to the passage in the bible that tells of the fate of Samson: "Then the lords of the Philistines gathered them together for to offer a great sacrifice unto Dagon their god, and to rejoice: for they said, Our god hath delivered Samson into our hand" (Judges 16:23). But Samson pulls down the temple upon them and kills more at his death than he had killed throughout his life. More specifically, Milton identifies him in *Samson Agonistes* as "thir Sea-Idol" (l. 13) and more specifically yet in *Paradise Lost* as a "Sea Monster, upward Man / And downward Fish" (1.462–63). Part fertility god, part fearful duality, Dagon functions in Lovecraft's work as a symbol of the sea that attracts, tempts, and destroys. Thus he returned to the original story "Dagon" and confirmed the central position of the motif in his work.[4]

It is a coincidence, but for us not an insignificant coincidence considering the enslavement of Mary Tyrone to morphine, that "Dagon" opens and closes with the narrator's confession of his own addiction to the drug, thus admitting the possibility that the story's reality is based upon a paranoid hallucination. Nevertheless, if the narration does record an hallucination the contents of that hallucination possess meaning; and one meaning, despite Lovecraft's denial in his long work *In Defence of Dagon* (MW 150), is the upheaval of the First World War. The submarine, commanded by a noble German, has come out of the depths that the creature at the end of the story ascends from; and the apocalypse at the conclusion, "when the land shall sink, and the dark ocean floor shall ascend amidst universal pandemonium" (D 19), an apocalypse counter to the promise of Revelation that "there was no more sea" (21:1), promises an ultimate horror of nothing but sea and nothing but the horror of the creature in its abyss.

Before that moment, however, the narrative center of the story is a confrontation with the bottom of the sea, its essence. The narrator wakes up under a brilliant sun to find himself not in his boat but "half-sucked into a slimy expanse of hellish black mire which extended about me in monotonous undulations" (D 15). How he has left the boat he has no idea and does not seem to wonder, being more oppressed by the solitude and stench; we must assume that he wished to leave the boat, but his reasons are obscure. He begins a trek through the monstrous desolation until in some days he is stopped one night beneath a full moon by "a far-flung body of water [. . .], winding out of sight in

---

4. Will Murray reminds us that Merry Mount was for a short time named "Mounte-Dagon" and that images of Dagon, if those are indeed images of Dagon, graced a number of gravestones in Boston after the fall of Merry Mount ("Dagon" 67–70).

both directions" (17). But after he has seen a mysterious monolith covered with its various deformed pictures and the creature that has "flung its gigantic scaly arms" (18) about it, he returns to the present and the morphine that "has drawn me into its clutches" (19). What is the reality here? The upheaval of the war, the morphine that behaves in his body and mind as though it were that one-eyed Polyphemus, the landscape that is utterly marine upon which his boat first floated aimlessly, or the landscape that is utterly abyssal, which is to say utterly unearthly? These different moments tend to collapse into one-another. A part of this collapse is the narrator's comparison of his trek through the abysm to Satan's "hideous climb through the unfashioned realms of dark-ness" (16). He is as monstrous as the creature. The reference to Doré later in the story (18) recalls that Doré is in fact the illustrator of Milton's *Paradise Lost* and of Coleridge's *The Rime of the Ancient Mariner*, which the young Lovecraft had enjoyed and which influences some of the language of the story. Coleridge, for instance, emphasizes the stark contrast between the solar vision and the lunar vision and challenges the Mariner to find beauty in the water-snakes; this story insists that there is no beauty at all to be found in the crea-ture at the bottom of the sea.

There is as it were a postscript to this story, the extensive defense of it that Lovecraft wrote in response to a variety of criticisms it excited in the amateur press. On the one hand he outlines the realism of the story, an aes-thetic justification that he returned to often in his later stories, most em-phatically in "Pickman's Model," and on the other hand he suggested that the story was based upon one of his dreams (MW 149–50). More remarkably his description of the sea-floor "raised from its age-long sleep in the darkness of ancient waters" and his insistence that no horror is worse than *"solitude in barren immensity"* bring us up again against his tacit understanding of the un-conscious that should be rich, overflowing in the abundance of the sea, but is not; it is empty. Then most remarkably the essay proceeds to a lengthy de-fense of his materialistic philosophy that seems prolix unless we agree that it does express his understanding of the story. This landscape, trapped in muck and endless horizons, is his symbolic correlative of the materialistic universe.

In "The Temple," written three years later, the narrator is now a U-boat captain, Karl Heinrich, but not of the noble sort found in "Dagon," though Karl Heinrich insists often upon the nobility and strength of his Prussian heritage. The man is something of a decadent, for he comments on how "picturesquely" a ship that he has just torpedoed sinks (D 59). But though he is a decadent he is resolutely rational—no morphine or hallucination here, not until the end when he has taken a sedative and twice imbibed so-dium bromide.

The trigger of the action is a small ivory carving of "a youth's head crowned with laurel" (D 60) that the crew has wrested from the pocket of one of their victims, perhaps an Italian or a Greek. The man seems con-nected to the immense numbers of dolphins and visions of drowned men that pursues the U-boat as it is carried south by a strange current. Several allusions are fused in this material, the story of Arion saved by a dolphin, the story of Coleridge's Mariner once more, and possibly certain moments in Samuel Loveman's *The Hermaphrodite*. The climactic moment that takes place in mid-ocean halfway between the Caribbean and the bulge of north-west Africa, after the captain has killed all his crew because they are not strong enough to endure the apparently supernatural events that confront them, is his discovery of a temple in long-lost Atlantis with decorations that feature "processions of priests and priestesses bearing strange ceremonial de-vices in adoration of a radiant god" (67) that resembles the head carved in ivory. Except for the temple the city is in ruins, its "mud-choked streets" (68) leading down to a river that of course no longer exists as a river since this landscape is at the bottom of the sea.

The captain admits that much of his experience as the submarine slowly loses power and the lights inside and outside dim is strung together by dreams and hallucinations. A strange light *"as from a mighty altar-flame"* (D 71) now pours from the temple; and so he decides, since there is nothing else left to do, that he will put on his diving suit once more "and walk boldly up the steps into that primal shrine; that silent secret of unfathomed waters and uncounted years" (72)

These two stories are at once very like and very unlike. Yes, they concern a marine upheaval and exploration of the sea-bottom, an ancient civilization and an ancient god. But how different the gods seem to be! One is mon-strous, the other "radiant," perhaps a god like Apollo. Polyphemus is the son of Poseidon, the patron god of Atlantis (Plato 113c), but monstrous as Poly-phemus is some mythographers like Robert Graves connect the Cyclops, the ring-eyed, with the cult of the sun (1.32). Whatever is monstrous in the threat of the ocean lies within two domains, that of power and that of the omniscient sun. "Dagon" is chiasmic in structure, "The Temple" quite linear, driving south and driving down into darkness; but both end in the sugges-tion of a hallucination. Between a monstrous energy and a rational omnis-cience there is no choice but madness.

A great difference between the two stories and "The Call of Cthulhu" is one of scale, only the third part of the later story taking place in an ocean landscape. The narrator hears of the encounter at second hand and recounts the story told by the manuscript that Captain Johansen has left after his death in indirect discourse, but this narrator, who is now dead, confesses, "When I think of the extent of all that may be brooding down there I almost wish to kill myself forthwith" (*DH* 150). His reaction is very like that of the other two narrators.

There is no need to dwell at length on this narration. Once more an undersea earthquake heaves to the surface of the waves to be discovered by the unfortunate Johansen and his crew. The mud is once more omnipresent; the substance of the land is transformed into chaos. The river of the other two stories has been transposed to the first part where we learn that Dr. Angell died "whilst returning from the Newport boat" (*DH* 126) and to the second part where Cthulhu is celebrated in "the swamp and lagoon country to the south" of New Orleans (136). Cthulhu, a hybrid creature like Dagon, "slavered and gibbered like Polypheme" (153). There is a sharp contrast between the bright sun and the blackness inside the door that dims the sun as though "that tenebrousness was indeed a *positive quality*" (152). This passage probably recalls once more the Miltonic lines: "A Dungeon horrible, on all sides round / As one great Furnace flam'd, yet from those flames / No light, but rather darkness visible" (*PL* 1.61–63). Perhaps most remarkably the Louisiana cultists call the creature "the great priest Cthulhu" (*DH* 139), reiterating the theme of the first two stories that the scene of the creature is numinous as well as an object of terror; it combines awe and fear. The narrative also insists that the creature is from the stars; it resides at the top of a mountain beneath the sea, but its ultimate locus is elsewhere. Like "Dagon" the structure is chiasmic; its beginning and ending in the death of the narrator frames dreams and madness. Since that which we fear in the sea transcends every human category, it seems simplest for the human imagination to locate it in death.

"The Shadow over Innsmouth" synthesizes elements from these stories in remarkable ways. It is not that the ocean floor rises; rather, the inhabitants of the sea come on land to preach a new religion. The narrator never sets foot on the bottom of the sea in the course of the narrative, but that bottom of the sea that represents an enormous power utterly inimical to human life is brought home to him as the narrative proceeds; and at the end of the novella, as at the conclusion of "The Temple," the narrator decides to enter

the numinous realm at the bottom of the sea because here, even more powerfully than in "The Temple," that realm is truly perceived as glorious, despite Zadok Allen's words, "That's whar it all begun—that cursed place of
wickedness whar the deep water starts" (DH 329). In the imagination of the
narrator a great light already shines in the darkness. Though he dives down,
as he intends to, into the "black abysses" with the help of a cousin, he is
convinced that he and his cousin shall find there "splendours, [. . .] wonder
and glory" (367). The light that had been external in the earlier stories has
become internal here, a part of the narrator's own being. The cousin functions as an objective and intensive sign of the truth of this experience; it is
not he himself who experiences this condition but another man, one of the
family, who does also; and the salvation of the abyss is granted to them both.

VI

Rattle his bones. Over the stones. Only a pauper. Nobody owns. (Joyce,
Ulysses 6.332–33)

To survey what we have dealt with so far: these themes of addiction and
abstinence and the price that either of them exact; of the suppressed aggression of the mother and the presence of the terrible old man, always an emi-
nent threat; of the sea, its beauty, its temptation, and the horror that lies in
its abyss; and of the quests that the characters must undertake at a risk to
their souls—these various themes culminate in the theme of death, a theme
that goes beyond the temptation that suicide presents to the harried soul.
Quite simply, both writers imply in a variety of ways that we do not need to
die unless pushed to it by the horror of our own inexplicable guilts because
we are dead already; this life, such as it is, is a living death without purpose
or goal and a moral imperative lies upon us to acknowledge this. The recognition and confession is traumatic but must be undergone.

This is a theme they share with other authors. Swedenborg tells a story of
how he once met a man with whom he had a pleasant conversation about the
nature of spirits until he found himself forced to tell the man "that he was now
a soul, or spirit—which he might know from his being now above my head,
and not standing on the earth—and to ask whether he could not perceive
this? He fled in terror, crying, "I am a spirit, I am a spirit" (¶ 447). This story
represents the shock in the most extreme manner. The individual engaged in a
pleasant conversation simply cannot accept his death. The evidence in any

case is ambiguous, if that evidence is simply one's elevation from the earth. It is the same evidence Aeneas sees in the step of the woman that meets him after the storm and gives him good tidings. Suddenly her step ascends, just that amount that one sees in classical vases, some six inches perhaps, "et vera incessu patuit dea" [and the true goddess stood revealed in her step] (*Aen.* 1.405). The man that Swedenborg met is in shock, but he may in time realize that he is one with divinity, already lifted up from the earth.

Something of the same sort of shock occurs at the end of Ambrose Bierce's short story "An Inhabitant of Carcosa" in which a man realizes that the grave before him is his, though the "exacting roots" of a great tree have robbed the grave of the body that lay within it, and that the city in ruins that he has just explored is his city (54). Not only has he died; the entire city through which, in the title of the story, he gains his identity is dead also, and the resounding phrase, "the ancient and famous city of Carcosa," meaningless (54). Even his shadow, the symbol of the soul, no longer exists. The shock is muted but palpable.

Charles Williams's novel *All Hallow's Eve* opens in a leisurely chapter about a young woman who is wandering the streets of London one evening, the same streets Eliot had walked when he met his compound ghost. When she meets another young woman, a friend although not such a good friend, together they slowly, casually realize that they are dead. What, then, are they to do with this knowledge? There is nothing to do but get on with it.

A fourth version of this moment is to be found in a dream that Freud relates and interprets, that we may regard as an incomplete commentary upon the narratives that we have presented. This is the dream of an anonymous young man: "Father is dead, but has been exhumed and looks badly. He goes on living, and the dreamer does everything to prevent him from noticing that fact" (*General Introduction* 158). This seems to be a very simple dream, but its relevance to the moments we have related, moments controlled through the genres of religious vision and fictions of various sorts, is immediately clear. Father may look badly but he does not seem to notice the fact—perhaps he does not want to notice the fact—and the son, the dreamer, is utterly complicitous in trying to save the father from that realization.

Freud's analysis of the dream is complicated by the dreamer's toothache that leads to the anxiety of whether the dead tooth should be taken out just as the father should be taken out and exposed to the air or whether an onanistic anxiety is exposed here. But this dead tooth has no immediate application to the dream as we have it or to our own concerns. Freud seizes upon that phrase, "he goes on living," to suggest the unconscious rancor it conceals and expresses. The young man, despite his best wishes, wants and needs the father to die, but the old man will not yield and maintains his control upon the son; this ambivalence is bound up in the Oedipus complex that Freud had already touched upon in *The Interpretation of Dreams* and that this passage expands (157–58).

Another aspect of this material is suggested in the epigraph to this section. Mr. Bloom finds an old song that expresses his own isolation given the deaths of his old father and his young son. Uttered within the *Hades* episode it implies that Mr. Bloom is one of the living dead, a state that renders him more acute to the presence of spirits around him, including that eternal conundrum, all the more impenetrable for its lingo, "Now who is that lankylooking galoot over there in the macintosh?" (6.805). This is no place to list the several destabilizing forces in the novel, but one of them is surely Mr. Bloom's sense of disconnection to the man who begot him and to the son he begot.

The Outsider is already dead—that is given from the conclusion of the story—but he still takes flight. I have often paid attention to the tragedy the story relates, which I do not wish to deny here. But the penultimate moment of the story is a triumph in that the Outsider takes flight. We may interpret that flight as we will: whether it represents a triumph of the father or of the son as the father; an orgasmic moment that is revealed as such through Freud's symbolic understanding of flight as symbolic of "general sexual excitement" or of "erection dreams" (*General Introduction* 127); or in Plato's language an ascent of the individual to a participation in the life of the gods. The symbol operates in both directions. If you must die, and you must, something in that moment elevates the self. Plato knew it and Lovecraft knew it, and given the language Freud developed in *Beyond the Pleasure Principle* he knew it also. Though the body of the Outsider still rots, it does not rot to the state of incoherence that Edward Derby suffers in "The Thing on the Doorstep," and thus the Outsider realizes that he is free from the ultimate trammels of the body. Derby, on the other hand, wakes up from his mad dream of freedom to find himself in a dead, rotting, buried body.

This theme in O'Neill goes beyond a simple ghost story like the one-act *Where the Cross Is Made*, in which the three dead crewmen appear. More subtle is the atmosphere expressed at the end of *The Moon of the Caribbees*, "the haunted, saddened voice of that brooding music, faint and far-off, like the mood of the moonlight made audible" (1.474). Dr. Johnson derives "haunt" from the French *hanter*, to frequent, to obsess, and makes "to frequent" the primary meaning, adding then, "It is eminently used of apparitions or spectres that appear in a particular place" ("Haunt"). A haunting is an obsession connected to a particular place and, I would add, a particular time. *Webster's Dictionary* derives the word from the Anglo-Saxon *hâmettan*, "to house," from *hâm*, "home" ("Haunt"); to haunt is to find one's self in one's true home. In his dedication of *Long Day's Journey into Night* O'Neill wrote to his wife, "[. . .] *I mean it as a tribute to your love and tenderness which gave me the faith in love that enabled me to face my dead at last and write this play—write it with deep pity and understanding and forgiveness for all the four haunted Tyrones*" (7). Given the haunted Tyrones I would extend the meaning to include words to this effect: to be haunted is to obsess over something not understood, to feel that powers larger than the self direct one's actions. O'Neill had read Freud and agreed with Freud's reading of the unconscious, but he was also aware of the economic anxieties in American life; his father's life had instructed him in those anxieties, and he allowed Tyrone to express them. So from the beginning of his career to its end these various hauntings take place.

Early in *Strange Interlude* Nina's father protests that she "can't live with a corpse forever" (1.9), but alas, as the next eight acts demonstrate, she can. In the second act she responds to her father's death in these thoughts: "I'm sorry, Father! . . . you see you've been dead for me a long time . . . when Gordon died, all men died . . . what did you feel for me then? . . .nothing . . . and now I feel nothing . . . it's too bad" (1.27). A variation on this theme appears in her reaction to the Evans' home in northern New York that "isn't haunted by anything at all—and ghosts of some sort are the only normal life a house has—like our minds, you know" (1.49); but later she discovers that the house is haunted by the congenital madness that has afflicted the family for generations and that even now her husband's aunt is shut up in the top floor, rather like Mrs. Gardner in "The Colour out of Space" (1.59). We need our ghosts, and whether we wish it or not they will abide with us. Nina's mother-in-law reveals this haunting in order to persuade Nina to have an abortion; Nina's consent adds another haunting to the count. But we need our hauntings no matter how much the contemporary homes try to gloss our gothic past.

The last play in the trilogy *Mourning Becomes Electra* has the blunt title, *The Haunted*, in part because O'Neill is determined to suggest the curse that pursues the characters in the *Oresteia* and to put a modern face on it; but the haunting has begun in the second play. Orin says, under the influence of his dead father who led his private soldiers in the Civil War, "I hardened myself

to expect my own death and everyone else's, and think nothing of it. I had
to—to keep alive! [. . .] My mind is still full of ghosts. I can't grasp anything
but war, in which he was so alive. He was the war to me—the war that
would never end until I died" (2.75). I think that it is clear from what we
have already said about "The Rats in the Walls" that this passage is much
more about the First World War than about the Civil War, much more
about the experiences of O'Neill's audience in the 1920s. At the end of the
third play the characters still alive do not believe they are alive. Orin says to
Hazel, his only hope of escape from the guilt of being the cause of his
mother's death, "Remember only the dead hero and not his rotting ghost"
(2.164). Immediately after this passage, after Hazel has left, Orin approaches
his sister and suggests that she is the reincarnation or the ghost of the sexual
woman in the past of the family. When Lavinia rejects him and he kills himself she at last admits that there is no escape from the past of the family.
"The dead! Why can't the dead die?" (2.174) she asks and has herself nailed
into the house to live with the ghosts until her death. The play is an odd
blend of the realistic and the hyperbolic as O'Neill works at adjusting the
Greek material to a realistic mode; but as a study in haunting it is a preparation, perhaps before O'Neill knew what he had to do, for the great haunting
in *Long Day's Journey into Night*.

In his dedication of the play note the emphasis with which O'Neill speaks
of writing it *"with deep pity and understanding and forgiveness for* all *the four
haunted Tyrones"* (7). There is good evidence that in the real time that followed the time of the play, August 1912, O'Neill did achieve a reconcilia-
tion with his father and mother. The problem was his brother, who vanished
into alcoholism, and himself who had to face the residual mourning that occupied the rest of his life and drove him to write the play; but that mourning
could only be achieved through pity and understanding and forgiveness. Pity
is a natural act, once a person has surmounted the anger that the four characters express volubly; but there is no forgiveness without understanding,
and understanding strikes me as the main point of the play.

What needs to be understood is the past. In that past the father lost his
ideal image of himself, the possibility of ever becoming a great actor because
he sold his soul for the easy success of "that God-damned play [he] bought
for a song," to which he became a slave (149). The success made him lazy,
never willing to learn another play but the one that the audience desired
from him, the "great romantic part" it offered (150). He went along with the
audience and turned his back on tragedy; and even when he discovered that

now he was inside his own tragedy, the great American tragedy of success, he could not return to what he might have been. In effect, he is a ghost of himself that knows thoroughly what he has lost. "Why this is hell," he might well say, "nor am I out of it." At the end of the play Mary says a number of times, with increasing bewilderment, that she has lost something: "Something I need terribly. I remember when I had it I was never lonely nor afraid. I can't have lost it forever. I would die if I thought that. Because then there would be no hope" (173). Whatever language we use to identify what she has lost will be necessarily metaphoric. In her language it is clear that along with her loss of faith she has lost her soul, and her damnation is one that she has elected, the night-fog of the morphine that protects her from physical and psychological pain. Through the comprehensive eyes of the author the audience needs to understand this loss that, in the rhetoric of the play, can never be redeemed.

What have their sons Jamie and Edmund lost? Most obviously they have lost their parents. Jamie lost his mother when he first saw her with the morphine syringe and intentionally lost his father in order never to feel that pain of disappointment again; but he follows the example of his mother in finding the perfect narcotic to deaden the pain. Edmund, however, has lost his mother before he was born in the early death of his other brother who in reality was called Edmund. In giving his character this name O'Neill is acknowledging to himself that he is dead, though the creation of his plays gives him the means to redeem that death.

We have already looked at the Outsider as the outstanding example of a character already dead. But several other characters in Lovecraft's work are dead already. One of these is of course Joseph Curwen, who is really nothing more than the faint blue dust mentioned at the beginning and end of the novella; but he does his best to feign life, first through the portrait he has made of himself. One of the functions of art is to give life, or at least a semblance of life. For Curwen the portrait is the vehicle that carries him from death to life, from non-existence into a sort of existence; but "the cellular structure of the tissue [. . .] exaggeratedly coarse and loosely knit" that hangs on his body betrays him (MM 108). Death hangs on him in the same way it hangs on Hickey.

Delapore, the narrator of "The Rats in the Walls," is such a haunted character also. An old man as the story begins, he has lost his father and the information that his father might have given him and lost his son too. He lives and dies in Mr. Bloom's world, disconnected from the past and the future. The last of his line he is obsessed by his line and distills it, returning to the place of its beginning where the natives regard him with more than distaste. He must seem to them a ghost, a revenant of the bad old times, and they are quite right when we consider the climax of the story in which he becomes the cannibal that his ancestors had always been. At the beginning of the story he does not realize that he is dead; and I do not believe that at the end of the story we should let the asylum hide from us the fact that he is a haunt indeed, now forbidden the home he had made for himself and come home to. We have often in the past suggested that his language as he plunges into the past is a language that Lovecraft filched from a variety of sources, but it is quite possible that this is a language that Delapore has filched because he has no other language for the death that he now lives.

The narrator of "The Call of Cthulhu," "The Late Francis Wayland Thurston, of Boston" (DH 125), presents a peculiar case, for though he is certainly alive as he recounts his initiation into the facts of the Cthulhu cult, the subtitle of the story announces his death; and in the last pages he is quite convinced that he shall die soon. It is not simply that he admits that "I do not think my life will be long. As my uncle went, as poor Johansen went, so I shall go. I know too much, and the cult still lives," and, as he supposes in the last paragraph, "Cthulhu still lives too" (154), in that state pronounced in the famous couplet from the Necronomicon, "That is not dead, which can eternal lie, / And with strange aeons even death may die" (141), which at the least lets no one dead escape from the possibility of being dead and aware of that death—not of eternal life but of eternal decomposing death, the kind of death that the Outsider leads. His condition lies in the damnation he describes in the first paragraph of the story. Given the kind of mind he has, no mercy has been shown him; he has pieced together a story that should either drive him mad or make him "flee [. . .] into the peace and safety of a new dark age" (125). Since he can do neither, it is better to accept the death in which he already lives.

The narrator of "The Shadow over Innsmouth" presents a peculiar case also, for it is not so much that he is dead at the beginning of the story as that he is living a merely normal life that is shortly to erupt into a more than natural life—we cannot say a supernatural life—that he joyously accepts. From outside his narrative, however, we must judge him dead, a man who has descended into the waves with his insane cousin whom he has either persuaded to descend with him or who already shares his conviction that the only life to live is beneath the waves. They share Edmund Tyrone's conviction, though with much more exultation than he, that it is best to be the ghost of a ghost.

But the great death in Lovecraft is revealed by that significant title, "The Thing on the Doorstep." We have already investigated several aspects of that story, its impulsions upward and its collapses downward. I want to look now at an aspect of the story that covers all the previous instances, the mere fact that it is about a thing, not a corpse or a cadaver, not even carrion, but a mere thing. What is a thing? Heidegger asked the question within the context of Kant's *Kritik der Reinen Vernunft*. Such investigations are anathema to Lovecraft, but there it is; we need to know what is on the doorstep, even if it is only a thing.

Heidegger is not asking about the nature of a corpse, though we cannot avoid the imagery of the corpse. The question is much more basic; if a corpse is a thing, if it has entered into that state of all other things, what is this existence that death has accentuated? Bound up with that question is the problem of the mind/body relation. So much of the story implies the separation of the mind from the body, at least the separation of consciousness from the body, the fantasy that "The Whisperer in Darkness" also implies; it is as though the story were acting out the Cartesian mind in the machine. On the other hand, the moments at which the consciousness of Asenath uproots Derby's mind and usurps his body implies something very different as Daniel Upton watches: "The face beside me was twisted almost unrecognisably for a moment—as if all the bones, organs, muscles, nerves, and glands were readjusting themselves to a radically different posture, set of stresses, and general personality" (*DH* 290). This language suggests a very close relation of the mind and body, so close that no part of the body remains apart from the mental component; even the glands, the governors of the various bodily processes, must accommodate themselves to a different mind. I do not think we can resolve these two kinds of language; the story is determined to affirm the separation of the mind and body and their intimate identity.

What, then, is this thing that is already possessed of this double nature? Playing upon the German word for an object, a *Gegenstand*, Heidegger insists upon this double nature of a thing. It is that which stands opposite to the subject, coming to the subject at the same time that the subject projects it through the anticipations of the Kantian categories; and it is that that stands in its peculiar constancy, betraying in this constancy not only its spatial nature but also its temporal nature (*What Is a Thing?* 137–40), owing to which a thing, any thing, is a particular, singular thing (18) that affects and resists other things (32–33). As Barth insists, though with more pathos, no being exists, much less no subject, without its temporal and spatial boundaries through which though it seems imprisoned it finds its true abode in which it can labor and work out its own salvation (3/2.683–87). Every thing insists upon itself. This thing, however, this thing on the doorstep, for all its spatial and temporal particularity, is not quite a singular thing for it has several voices competing for its presence.

Perhaps the most individual detail about this thing is the piece of paper it holds out, "a large, closely written paper impaled on the end of a long pencil" (*DH* 301). This may be the most unbelievable moment in the story, for a reader must ask at a certain point whether it is conceivable that a creature that can only say "glub-glub," that seems to have difficulty with a phone, and that knocks with the doorbell and knocker "uncertainly, [. . .] *trying to keep to Edward's old signal*" (300), can use a pencil at such length, successfully employing the old fine motor skills, albeit leaving a script that is "so awkward, coarse, and shaky" (301). The improbability is overruled by the fact that writing is overwhelmingly important to Lovecraft, as we see in the climactic moment of several of the stories (Waugh, *Monster* 18–19); more to the point, this pen acts out Heidegger's comment that to use a thing (and for a thing to use itself) we must become familiar with it (*What Is a Thing?* 70–71), as Derby is so familiar with the pen.

On the other hand, this detail though it is inconceivable bears something important for a reader to consider. The alliteration of the passage, holding out emphatically the "paper impaled on the end of a long pencil," underscores this importance. So we notice the impalement. Impaling (shades of Vlad the Impaler, the historical antecedent of Dracula) is a singularly cruel execution, the instrument being thrust into a man's anus or a woman's vagina; the sexual aggression is very much a part of this story. This pencil is thrust into the white womb that receives and delivers our words. The impaled paper is the white womb that gives birth to the letters on the page. If it were not for the paper the words as written words could not exist; they are dependent on the paper, just as Edward Derby is first dependent upon his mother and then upon his wife. Most people undergo the mania of the *causa sui* project, the attempt on the part of every individual to insist upon absolute independence, the self-creation of the self despite the fact of death (Becker 66, 115–24); but in Derby the project had failed before it had achieved very much at all, only a few intimations of decadence, a few poems not badly written, in revolt from his mother who does not have the grace to object to that revolt, and so it failed. Only in his relation to Asenath did it at first seem that he might be able to achieve the project; but it turned out that he was much too dependent upon her too. So now, desperately dependent after he killed her, he is dying as her body, heavy upon him, is dying also. No wonder, then, that with his phallic pencil he impales the white womb.

A thing that we radically distrust holds out our words in order to explain itself, and we find ourselves forced to use words in order to clarify the meaning of a thing. It is difficult, however, to understand a narrative that doubles back on itself and recasts what we think we know of the human constitution. We are often when reading Heidegger chagrined at his use of puns and odd constructions, but his style expresses his own conviction that it is only through words, our close comprehension and acknowledgement of them, that we can come to an understanding of the thing, the *Gegenstand*, that confronts us: "The truth [. . .] is not that our thinking feeds on etymology, but rather that etymology has the standing mandate first to give thought to the essential content involved in what dictionary words, as words, denote by implication" (Heidegger, *Poetry* 175). We cannot do without the building blocks of meaning, just as we cannot do without the thing on the doorstep and its pencil.

We have a certain revulsion, however, at coming to an understanding of the thing. It resists us actively; it is threatening, uncanny, and it stinks. It has a hand in its own actuality, in its *Wirklichkeit*, which is evidence of the work that must be worked upon it in order to bring out its presence fully (Heidegger, *What Is a Thing?* 191, 239). It is, however, at work on itself, desperately, heaving itself out of its own grave in order to bear witness as a thing on the doorstep that its fate is directly pertinent to what it is to be human; it is an active part of the dialogue we undertake in these matters (*Poetry* 174–76). But none of this is to deny the fact that it is dead; that, indeed, is the great point. So much in Lovecraft's work haunts this point, returning frequently to the place where every human is always already dead.

But final as that seems, it is not quite all, not as far as the rhythm of the narrative is concerned, which weaves back and forth among various times, looking back in such despair to the constitution of the self that remains unascertainable and looking ahead to the state of the thing when the authorities arrive, its puddle, and to Upton's decisive action with the pistol. This is the same rhythm that we analyzed in "The Outsider" as the protagonist fell into and back from the mirror (Waugh, *Monster* 116–17). Heidegger insists that despite the close relationship between the subject and the object, between the first-person narrator and the thing on the doorstep, between me and that, something still remains open in our relationship; and in this relationship we move forward, into that openness, and back, thrown back, for every reaching forward casts us back (*What Is a Thing?* 242–43). No doubt this is a gnomic language that has already caused much dispute; I am only interested in saying that our haunted state renders us obsessive, moving away from and back to the object that reveals us as we are, and that this motion finds no conclusion, despite the pistol, as Lovecraft knew very well in the rhythm he constructed in the last pages of this story.

I at first took up the question of O'Neill and Lovecraft because of Lovecraft's fervid admiration for the dramatist and because of their life as New England authors; but I soon became interested in their display of the same constellation of themes, the obsessive rage for alcohol, the anger at the mother that Lovecraft needs to muffle in a variety of polite ways, though it reveals itself clearly in the character of Lavinia and the rage for the father and his insistence upon his terribilitá. Anyone living in New England is forced to adopt an attitude toward the sea, so it is not surprising that the sea is a major symbol and space in their works. There is an immense difference between the two men in the tone of their lives. Until O'Neill needs to restrain himself or die he lives as a man driven, thrown into rage, whereas Lovecraft lives as a man restrained and constrained from his early years. Only very slowly, very slowly indeed, does he loosen the reins on himself. But both men are obsessed.

One thing I hope is clear from our final comparison between Lovecraft and O'Neill, that just as O'Neill is deadly serious and thereby America's first tragic playwright Lovecraft is also deadly serious. Within the limits of the weird tale, and also outside those limits, he earnestly means to address the modern condition, and thereby he remains, despite his various clumsy mannerisms of which he was acutely, awkwardly aware, endlessly engrossing as we watch him composing a narrative that lives and only lives truly in the life that is dead. Its landscape is the landscape we examined in our first pages, the blasted heath, the burning desert, and the trenches of the Great War. Or it lies in a muddy upheaval of the ocean. Nothing is more barren, but that is where he finds our life.

The arguments with life that no one can avoid he had in plenty, the argument with the terrible old man, wielding his age and his thunder from Sinai or from a place on the other side of Sinai, and with the mother. A generation before Philip Wylie, Lovecraft sensed the war between the mother and the son and aggressively underook that war; it is not a pretty sight, but it was undoubtedly necessary for the sake of his psychic recovery and balance.

But, at the end, any victory he won in those battles was futile. Life remains a death in life. You are a thing, nothing but a thing that despite its condition suffers and understands it. It was all very well to be a reed and a thinking reed, as Pascal would have had it; but now the subject is a heap of rotting thingness. We saw, however, that somehow the word was involved in this condition, that it was impossible to suffer the condition, much less understand it, without the intervention of the word that, as Heidegger would have it, goes before us and after us, reaches before us and reaches after us, a tentacle—thank you, Lovecraft—into the emptiness that surrounds and empowers every thing that is the thing as thing (Heidegger, *What Is a Thing?* 242–43). We may be more than that, but we are certainly that.

So, as I said from the beginning of this book, I have come to speak for H. P. Lovecraft. Not to speak for him for myself, not myself only, but as best I can for all who are interested in his world and his fate. If we are to speak for him we also need to speak against him, recognizing that he continues, in his constancy as Heidigger would have it, to be there, resistant to anything we have to say. So I have not exhausted this speaking. Lovecraft has much more to say, and we cannot avoid it; we need many more to speak for him, but he is already in so many ways a monster of voices.

In Swan Point Cemetery

At last I have assurance. His bones lie
to disarticulate beneath this stone
and looser lie. His earth accepts its own
unearthed decomposition casually,
flesh of our flesh, but makes us recompense;
all dissolution operates the bleak
engine that runs the year and does not break,
bees stop our mouths in gold from Providence.

His better part he leaves to our disputes,
a sublimate, odd prolegomena
against the seawind blustering in tonight;
till anonymities in grey-striped suits,
nothing new-fangled for them, enter, weigh
and bear us off to place us to his right.

Works Cited

A. Works by Lovecraft

Lovecraft, H. P. *The Ancient Track: The Complete Poetical Works*. Ed. S. T. Joshi. San Francisco: Night Shade, 2001.

———. *At the Mountains of Madness and Other Novels*. Ed. S. T. Joshi. Sauk City, WI: Arkham House, 1985.

———. *Collected Essays III: Science*. Ed. S. T. Joshi. New York: Hippocampus Press, 2005.

———. *Dagon and Other Macabre Tales*. Ed. S. T. Joshi. Sauk City, WI: Arkham House, 1986.

———. *The Dunwich Horror and Others*. Sel. August Derleth. Ed. S. T. Joshi. Sauk City, WI: Arkham House, 1984.

———. *The Horror at the Museum and Other Revisions*. Ed. S. T. Joshi. Sauk City, WI: Arkham House, 1989.

———. *Letters to Alfred Galpin*. Ed. S. T. Joshi and David E. Schultz. New York: Hippocampus Press, 2003.

———. "Letters to Lee McBride White." Ed. S. T. Joshi and David E. Schultz. *Lovecraft Annual* 1 (2007): 31–64.

———. *Letters to Richard F. Searight*. Ed. David E. Schultz and S. T. Joshi, with Franklyn Searight. West Warwick, RI: Necronomicon Press, 1992.

———. *Miscellaneous Writings*. Ed. S. T. Joshi. Sauk City, WI: Arkham House, 1995.

———. *Selected Letters*. Ed. August Derleth, Donald Wandrei, and James Turner. Sauk City, WI: Arkham House, 1965–76. 5 vols.

B. Biographical and Critical Writings

Benefiel, Candace R. "Shadows of a Dark Muse: Reprint History of Original Fiction from *Weird Tales* 1928–1939." *Extrapolation* Vol. 49 (Winter 2008): 450–65.

Buchanan, Carl. "'The Terrible Old Man': A Mythof the Devouring Father." *Lovecraft Studies* No. 29 (Fall 1993): 19–31.

Burleson, Donald R. *Lovecraft: Disturbing the Universe.* Lexington: University Press of Kentucky, 1990.

———. "On Lovecraft's Themes: Touching the Glass." In Schultz and Joshi, *An Epicure in the Terrible.* 135–47.

———. "Prismatic Heroes: The Colour out of Dunwich." *Lovecraft Studies* No. 25 (Fall 1991): 13–18.

Cannon, Peter. *H. P. Lovecraft.* Boston: Twayne, 1989.

Clements, Nicholaus. "Lovecraft and the Early Leiber." *Lovecraft Studies* No. 41 (Spring 1999): 23–24.

Connors, Scott, ed. *A Century Less a Dream: Selected Criticism on H. P. Lovecraft.* Holicong, PA: Wildside Press, 2002.

Eckhardt, Jason. In conversation. 21 August 1999. Oral.

Faig, Kenneth W., Jr. *The Unknown Lovecraft.* New York: Hippocampus Press, 2009.

Fife, Ernelle. In conversation. 12 November 2004. Oral.

Gayford, Norman R. "The Artist as Antaeus: Lovecraft and Modernism." In Schultz and Joshi, *An Epicure in the Terrible.* 273–97.

Hazel, Faye Ringel. "Some Strange New England Mortuary Practices: Lovecraft Was Right." *Lovecraft Studies* No. 29 (Fall 1993): 13–18.

Hitz, John Kipling. "Some Notes on 'The Rats in the Walls.'" *Lovecraft Studies* No. 40 (Fall 1998): 29–33.

Howard, John. "A Universe Shot Through with Invisible Forces: *Our Lady of Darkness* as a Lovecraftian Novel." *Ghosts & Scholars* No. 20 (10 March 2004). Web.

Joshi, S. T. *The Evolution of the Weird Tale.* New York: Hippocampus Press, 2004.

———. *H. P. Lovecraft: A Life.* West Warwick, RI: Necronomicon Press, 1996.

———. "Introduction and Notes." In H. P. Lovecraft, *The Call of Cthulhu and Other Weird Stories.* Ed. S. T. Joshi. New York: Penguin, 1999.

———. *A Subtler Magic: The Writings and Philosophy of H. P. Lovecraft.* 1996. Berkeley Heights, NJ: Wildside Press, 1999.

Joshi, S. T. *Lovecraft's Library: A Catalogue.* Rev. ed. New York: Hippocampus Press, 2002.

Mariconda, Steven J. "H. P. Lovecraft: Reluctant American Modernist." *Lovecraft Studies* Nos. 42/43 (Autumn 2001): 20–32.

————. *On the Emergence of "Cthulhu" & Other Observations.* West Warwick, RI: Necronomicon Press, 1995.

Montelone, Paul. "'The Rats in the Walls': A Study in Pessimism." *Lovecraft Studies* No. 32 (Spring 1995): 18–26.

Murray, Will. "Behind the Mask of Nyarlathotep." *Lovecraft Studies* No. 25 (Fall 1991): 25–29.

————. "Dagon in Puritan Massachusetts." *Lovecraft Studies* No. 11 (Fall 1984): 66–70.

Price, Robert M. "A Biblical Precedent for 'The Colour out of Space.'" *Lovecraft Studies* No. 25 (Fall 1991): 23–25.

————. "Erich Zann and the Rue d'Auseil." *Lovecraft Studies* Nos. 22/23 (Fall 1990): 13–14.

Schultz, David E., and S. T. Joshi, ed. *An Epicure in the Terrible: A Centennial Anthology of Essays in Honor of H. P. Lovecraft.* Rutherford, NJ: Fairleigh Dickinson University Press, 1991. Rpt. New York: Hippocampus Press, 2011.

Waugh, Robert H. "Landscapes, Selves, and Others in Lovecraft." In Schultz and Joshi, *An Epicure in the Terrible.* 220–43.

————. *The Monster in the Mirror: Looking for H. P. Lovecraft.* New York: Hippocampus Press, 2006.

————. "The Stuctural and Thematic Unity of *Fungi from Yuggoth.*" In Connors, *Lovecraft: A Century Less a Dream.* 153–77.

C. General Works

Abbate, Carolyn. "Erik's Dream and Tannhäuser's Journey." In Arthur Gross and Roger Parker, ed. *Reading Opera.* Princeton: Princeton University Press, 1988. 129–67.

Abrams, M. H. *The Mirror and the Lamp: Romantic Theory and the Critical Tradition.* New York: W. W. Norton, 1958.

Addison, Joseph. *The Spectator.* Ed. Donald F. Bond. Oxford: Clarendon Press, 1965. 5 vols.

Adler, Alfred. *The Individual Psychology of Alfred Adler: A Systematic Presentation in Selections from His Writings.* Ed. Heinz L. Ansbacher and Rowena R. Ansbacher. New York: Harper & Row, 1964.

Adorno, Theodor. *In Search of Wagner.* Trans. Rodney Livingstone. London: Verso, 2005.

————. *Minima Moralia.* Trans. E. F. N. Jephcott. London: Verso, 1978.

Aldington, Richard. "In the Trenches." In Walter, *The Penguin Book of First World War Poetry.*

Alt, Carl, ed., with Robert Riemann and Eduard Scheitemantel. "Anmerkungen" in Johann Wolfgang von Goethe. *Werke.* Vol. 4. Berlin: Deutsches Verlagshaus Bong & Co., n.d.

Andersen, Hans Christian. *Eventyr og Historier.* Odense: Skandinavisk Bogforlag, 1976. 2 vols.

Anderson, George K. *The Legend of the Wandering Jew.* Providence, RI: Brown University Press, 1965.

Apuleius. *The Golden Ass [Metamorphoses].* Trans. W. Adlington. Rev. S. Gaselee. London: Heinemann/Loeb Classical Library, 1935.

Aquinas. *Summa Theologiae.* Madrid: Bibliotecas de Autores Cristianos, 1955. 5 vols.

Ashbery, John. "Fuckin' Sarcophagi." In *Can You Hear, Bird?* New York: Farrar, Straus & Giroux, 1995.

Augustine. *De Civitate Dei.* 5th ed. Ed. B. Dombart and A. Kalb.Stuttgart: Teubner, 1993. 2 vols.

Auden, W. H. *The Enchaféd Flood; or, The Romantic Iconography of the Sea.* New York: Vintage, 1967.

Barck, Oscar Theodor, Jr., and Hugh Talmadge Lefler. *Colonial America.* New York: Macmillan, 1958.

Barth, Karl. *Kirchliche Dogmatik.* Zürich: Zollikon, 1932–65. 4 parts in 12 vol.

Bachelard, Gaston. *The Poetics of Space.* Trans. Maria Jolas. New York: Orion Press, 1964.

Baudelaire, Charles. *Oeuvres complètes.* Ed. Y.-G. Le Dantec. Paris: Librairie Gallimard/Bibliothèque de la Pléiade, 1954.

Bauer, Hans-Joachim, ed. *Briefe von Richard Wagner.* Stuttgart: Reclam, 1995.

Becker, Ernest. *The Denial of Death.* New York: Free Press, 1973.

Beethoven, Ludwig and Joachim Popelka. *Fidelio.* Frankfurt am Main: Ricordi, n.d.

Bierce, Ambrose. *The Complete Short Stories.* Ed. Ernest Jerome Hopkins. Lincoln: University of Nebraska Press, 1984.

Blind, Karl. "Wodan, The Wild Huntsman, and the Wandering Jew." In Galit Hasan-Rokem and Alan Dundes, ed. *The Wandering Jew: Essays in the Interpretation of a Christian Legend.* Bloomington: Indiana University Press, 1986. 169–89.

Blocker, Jack S., Jr. *American Temperance Movements: Cycles of Reform.* Boston: Twayne, 1989.

Bousfield, H. T. W. "Spring Song." *English Review* (April 1916): 313.

Bradford, William. *Of Plymouth Plantation 1620–1647.* New York: Modern Library, 1981.

Breton, André. *Manifestes du surréalisme.* Paris: Gallimard, 1977.

Brinnin, John Malcolm. *Dylan Thomas in America: An Intimate Journal.* Boston: Little, Brown, 1955.

Browning, Robert. *The Complete Poetic and Dramatic Works.* Boston: Houghton Mifflin, 1895.

Bruno, Giordano. *Gli eroici furori.* Intro. and com. Nicoletta Tirinnazi. Milan: Ricordi/Biblioteca Universale, 1999.

Burns, Robert. *Complete Works.* Philadelphia: Lippincott, 1875.

Byfield, Bruce. *Witches of the Mind: A Critical Study of Fritz Leiber.* West Warwick, RI: Necronomicon Press, 1991.

Byron, George Gordon, Lord. *The Vision of Judgment.* In *Don Juan and Other Satirical Poems.* Ed. Louis I. Bredvold. New York: Odyssey Press, 1935.

Calderwood, James L. *If It Were Done: Macbeth and Tragic Action.* Amherst: University of Massachusetts Press, 1986.

Carlisle, Lois, and Davida Richardson, ed. *Fourth Year Latin: Selections from Virgil, Ovid, Catullus, Martial, and Horace.* 1933. Boston: Allyn & Bacon, 1948.

Carpenter, Humphrey. *The Inklings: C. S. Lewis, J. R. R. Tolkien, Charles Williams and Their Friends.* Boston: Houghton Mifflin, 1979.

———. *Tolkien:* Boston: Houghton Mifflin, 1977.

Catullus. *Carmina.* Ed. R. A. B. Mynors. Oxford: Oxford University Press, 1958.

Champlin, Edward. *Nero.* Cambridge, MA: Harvard University Press, 2003.

Chaucer, Geoffrey. *The Student's Chaucer.* Ed. Walter W. Skeat. Oxford: Clarendon Press, n.d.

Chesterton, G. K. *The Man Who Was Thursday: A Nightmare.* New York: Ballantine, 1971.

Cicero. *Orationes.* Ed. Albert Curtis Clark. Oxford: Oxford University Press, 1909. 4 vols.

Clark, Norman H. *Deliver Us from Evil: An Interpretation of the American Prohibition.* New York: W. W. Norton, 1976.

Clarke, Susanna. *Jonathan Strange & Mr Norrell.* New York: Bloomsbury, 2004.

Coleridge, S. T. *Biographia Literaria.* Ed. J. Shawcross. London: Oxford University Press, 1962. 2 vols.

Crowley, Aleister. "Hymn to Pan." Web. Accessed 7 October 2009.

Dahlhaus, Carl. *Richard Wagners Musikdramen.* Stuttgart: Reclam, 1996.

Dante Alighieri. *The Divine Comedy.* Trans. Henry Francis Cary. Programmed Classics, n.d.

Davenport-Hines, Richard. *Gothic: Four Hundred Years of Excess, Horror, Evil and Ruin.* New York: North Point Press, 1999.

De Quincey, Thomas. *The Collected Writings.* Vol. 10. Ed. David Masson. London: A. & C. Black, 1897.

————. *Selected Writings.* Ed. Philip van Doren Stern. New York: Modern Library, 1949.

Donne, John. *Complete Poetry and Selected Prose.* Ed. John Hayward. Bloomsbury: Nonesuch Press, 1929.

Doyle, Arthur Conan. *The Complete Sherlock Holmes.* Garden City, NY: Garden City Publishing Co., 1927.

"The Dream of the Rood." In Rolf Kaiser, *Medieval English.* 3rd ed. Berlin: Rolf Kaiser, 1961. 95–98.

Dumas, Alexandre. *Le Comte de Monte Cristo.* Ed. Gilbert Sigaux. Paris: Gallimard, 1998. 2 vols.

Eckermann, Johann Peter. *Gespräche mit Goethe.* Ed. Fritz Bergemann. Baden-Baden: Insel, 1981.

Eliot, T. S. *The Complete Poems and Plays 1909–1950.* New York: Harcourt, Brace, 1958.

Empson, William. *Milton's God.* London: Chatto & Windus, 1961.

The Encyclopaedia Britannica. 11th ed. Edinburgh: A. & C. Black, 1875–98.

Faas, Ekbert. *Retreat to the Mind: Victorian Poetry and the Rise of Psychology.* Princeton: Princeton University Press, 1988.

Felsenstein, Frank. *Anti-Semitic Stereotypes: A Paradigm of Otherness in English Popular Culture, 1660–1830.* Baltimore: Johns Hopkins University Press, 1995.

Fiedler, Leslie. *Love and Death in the American Novel.* New York: Stein & Day, 1966.

Flaubert, Gustave. *Salammbô.* Paris: Éditions de Cluny, 1937.

Forster, E. M. *The Machine Stops and Other Stories.* Ed. Rod Mengham. London: Andre Deutsch, 1997.

Foscolo, Ugo. *Tutte le poesie.* Ed. Ludovico Magugliani. Milan: Rizzoli/Biblioteca Universale, 1952.

Freud, Sigmund. *A General Introduction to Psychoanalysis*. Trans. G. Stanley Hall. New York: Boni & Liveright, 1920.

———. *The Interpretation of Dreams*. Trans. James Strachey. New York: Avon, 1965.

Fussell, Paul. *The Great War and Modern Memory*. London: Oxford University Press, 1977.

Gaer, Joseph, ed. *Rhode Island: A Guide to the Smallest State*. Boston: Houghton Mifflin, 1937.

Gager, John G. *The Origins of Anti-Semitism: Attitudes toward Judaism in Pagan and Christian Antiquity*. New York: Oxford University Press, 1983.

Gibbon, Edward. *The History of the Decline and Fall of the Roman Empire*. Ed. J. B. Bury. 1909. New York: AMS Press, 1974. 7 vols.

Gilbert, Martin. *The First World War: A Complete History*. New York: Henry Holt, 1994.

Gilbert, William Schwenck, and Arthur Sullivan. *Ruddigore; or, The Witch's Curse*. In *The Complete Plays*. Garden City, NY: Garden City Publishing Co., 1938.

Goethe, Johann Wolfgang von. *Werke*. Ed. Erich Trunz. Hamburg: Christian Wegner, 1948. 14 vols.

Goodman, Paul. *Towards a Christian Republic: Antimasonry and the Great Transition in New England, 1826–1836*. New York: Oxford University Press, 1988.

Gough, John B. *Sunlight and Shadow; or, Gleanings from My Life*. Hartford, CT: A. D. Worthington, 1881.

Grahame. *The Wind in the Willows*. Oxford: Oxford University Press/World's Classics, 1983.

Graves, Robert. *The Greek Myths*. Baltimore: Penguin, 1955. 2 vols.

Green, Roger Lancelyn, and Walter Hooper. *C. S. Lewis: A Biography*. New York: Harcourt Brace Jovanovich, 1976.

Grimm, Jacob. *Deutsche Mythologie*. 4th ed. Graz: Akademische Druck- und Verlaganstalt, 1968. 3 vols.

Grimm, Jacob and Wilhelm. *Die Märchen*. Munich: Wilhelm Goldmann, 1964.

Guggenheimer, Heinrich W., and Eva H. Guggenheimer. *Jewish Family Names and Their Origins: An Etymological Dictionary*. New York: Ktav, 1992.

Hansen, Walter. *Richard Wagner: Biographie*. Munich: Deutscher Taschenbuch, 2006.

Harrison, Jane Ellen. *Themis: A Study of the Social Origins of Greek Religion.* 2nd ed. Cleveland: Meridian, 1962.

———. *Prolegomena to the Study of Greek Religion.* Princeton: Princeton University Press, 1991.

Hawthorne, Nathaniel. *The American Notebooks.* Vol. VIII in The Centenary Edition. Ed. Claude M. Simpson. Columbus: Ohio State University Press, 1972.

———. *The Marble Faun; or, The Romance of Monte Beni.* Vols. IX and X in the Old Manse Edition. Boston: Houghton Mifflin, 1900.

Heidegger, Martin. *Poetry, Language, Thought.* Trans. Albert Hofstadter. New York: Harper & Row, 1975.

———. *What Is a Thing?* Trans. W. B. Barton and Vera Deutsch. Chicago: Henry Regnery, 1967.

Heller, Terry. *The Delights of Terror: An Aesthetics of the Tale of Terror.* Urbana: University of Chicago Press, 1987.

Hillman, James. *Revisioning Psychology.* New York: Harper Perennial, 1992.

Homer. *The Iliad of Homer.* Trans. Alexander Pope. In *The Poems of Alexander Pope.* Vols. VII and VIII. Ed. Maynard Mack. London: Methuen, 1967.

Horace. *Opera.* Ed. Edward Wickham. 2nd ed. Ed. H. W. Garrod. Oxford: Oxford University Press, 1912.

Hesiod. *Theogonia, Opera et Dies, Scutum.* Ed. Friedrich Solmsen. *Fragmenta Selecta.* Ed. R. Merkelbach and M. L. West. Oxford: Oxford University Press, 1970.

Hoffmann, E. T. A. *Hoffmanns Werke.* Ed. Viktor Schweizer. Leipzig: Meyers Klassiker-Ausgaben,1896. 4 vols.

Howe, Elisabeth A. *The Dramatic Monologue.* New York: Twayne, 1996.

Hughes, Linda K. *The Manyfacèd Glass: Tennyson's Dramatic Monologues.* Athens: Ohio University Press, 1987.

Johnson, Samuel. *A Dictionary of the English Language.* 4th ed. London: W. Strahan, 1773. 2 vols.

Jones, David. *In Parenthesis.* London: Faber & Faber, 1963.

Joyce, James. *Finnegans Wake.* New York: Viking Press, 1960.

———. *Ulysses.* Ed. Hans Walter Gabler. New York: Vintage, 1993.

Julius, Anthony. *T. S. Eliot, Anti-Semitism, and Literary Form.* Cambridge: Cambridge University Press, 1996.

Juvenal. *Saturarum Libri V.* In *Persi et Ivvenalis Saturae.* Ed. W. V. Clausen. Oxford: Oxford University Press, 1959.

Keats, John. *The Poems of John Keats.* Ed. Jack Stillinger. Cambridge, MA: Harvard University Press, 1978.

Kipling, Rudyard. *Verse 1885–1918.* Garden City, NY: Doubleday, 1921.

Lawrence, D. H. *The Letters.* Vol. 2. Ed. George J. Zytaruk and James T. Boulton. Cambridge: Cambridge University Press, 1981.

——. *St. Mawr.* In *The Short Novels.* Vol. 2. London: Heinemann, 1956.

Leed, Eric J. *No Man's Land: Combat and Identity in World War I.* Cambridge: Cambridge University Press, 1979.

Leiber, Fritz. "A Bit of the Dark World." In *Heroes and Horrors.* New York: Pocket, 1980.

——. *The Dealings of Daniel Kesserich: A Study of Mass-Insanity at Smithville.* New York: Tor, 1997.

——. *Our Lady of Darkness.* New York: Berkley, 1977.

——. *The Second Book of Fritz Leiber.* New York: DAW, 1975.

Lewis, C. S. *The Lion, the Witch and the Wardrobe.* New York: Collier, 1970.

——. *The Magician's Nephew.* New York: Collier, 1970.

Lucanus, Marcus Anneus. *La Guerra civile: Farsaglia.* Intr. and trans. Renato Badalì. Torino: Garzanti, 1999.

Lukacs, Georg. *The Historical Novel.* Trans. Hannah and Stanley Mitchell. Boston: Beacon Press, 1963.

Lucretius. *De Rerum Natura.* 2nd ed. Ed. Cyril Bailey. Oxford: Oxford University Press, 1922.

MacCallum, Hugh. *Milton and the Sons of God: The Divine Image in Milton's Epic Poetry.* Toronto: University of Toronto Press, 1986.

Macaulay, Thomas Babington. *Lays of Ancient Rome with Ivry and The Armada.* Boston: Roberts Brothers, 1883.

McDonald, Beth. E. *The Vampire as Numinous Experience: Spiritual Journeys with the Undead in British and American Literature.* Jefferson, NC: McFarland, 2004.

McGouldrick, Paul F. *New England Textiles in the Nineteenth Century: Profits and Investments.* Cambridge, MA: Harvard University Press, 1968.

Machen, Arthur. *The Hill of Dreams.* New York: Knopf, 1923.

——. *Tales of Horror and the Supernatural.* New York: Pinnacle, 1971. 2 vols.

Magee, Bryan. *The Tristan Chord: Wagner and Philosophy.* New York: Henry Holt, 2001.

Manilius. *Astronomia/Astrologie.* Trans. and ed. Wolfgang Fels. Stuttgart: Reclam, 1990.

Marlowe, Christopher. *Five Plays*. Ed. Havelock Ellis. New York: Hill & Wang, 1956.

Marschner, Heinrich. *Der Vampyr: Romantische Oper in Vier Aufzügen*. Web. Accessed 30 November 2005.

———. *Der Vampyr*. Lib. [Wilhelm August] Wolhbrück. Perf. Roland Hermann, Arleen Auger, and Donald Grube. Bavarian Radio Symphony Orchestra and Chorus. Cond. Fritz Rieger. CD. German Opera Rarities. 1974.

Marvell, Andrew. *The Complete Poems*. Ed. Elizabeth Story Donno. Harmondsworth, UK: Penguin Classics, 1985.

May, Thomas. *Decoding Wagner: An Invitation to His World of Music Drama*. Milwaukee, WI: Amadeus Press, 2004.

Melville, Herman. *Moby-Dick; or, The Whale*. Ed. Harrison Hayford and Hershel Parker. New York: W. W. Norton, 1967.

Meyer, Stephen C. *Carl Maria von Weber and the Search for a German Opera*. Bloomington: Indiana University Press, 2003.

Middelkoop, Norbert. *De Anatomische Les van Dr. Deijman*. Amsterdam: Amsterdams Historisch Museum, 1994.

Milton, John. *Complete Poems and Major Prose*. Ed. Merritt Y. Hughes. New York: Odyssey Press, 1957.

Morison, Samuel Eliot. *The Oxford History of the American People*. New York: Oxford University Press, 1965.

Mucci, John. "Heinrich Marschner." Web. Accessed 31 October 2005.

———. "Heinrich Marschner and His Vampyre: Program Notes for the 2001 Lyric Opera of Los Angeles Production." Web. Accessed 31 October 2005.

Murray, Margaret Alice. *The Witch-Cult in Western Europe*. 1921. Oxford: Oxford University Press, 1962.

Murrin, Michael. "The Multiple Worlds of the Narnia Stories." In Schakel and Huttar. 232–55.

The New Encyclopædia Britannica: Micropædia. 15th ed. 2002.

NNDB. "Carl Maria von Weber." Web. Accessed 6 January 2010.

Nodier, Charles. *La Fée aux Miettes, Smarra, Trilby*. Ed. Patrick Berthier. Paris: Gallimard, 1982.

———. *Oeuvres dramatiques*. Vol. 1. Ed. Ginette Picat-Guinoiseau. Geneva: Librairie Droz, 1990.

Ovid. *Ars Amatoria*. In *Amores, Medicamina Facei Femineae, Ars Amatoria, Remedia Amoris*. Ed. E. J. Kenney. Oxford: Clarendon Press, 1961.

————. *Metamorphoses*. Ed. W. S. Anderson. Stuttgart: Teubner, 1991.

O'Neill, Eugene. *Long Day's Journey into Night*. New Haven: Yale University Press, 1962.

————. *The Plays*. New York: Random House, 1955. 3 vols.

————. *Ten "Lost" Plays*. New York: Random House, 1964.

Owen, Wilfred. *The Collected Poems*. Ed. C. Day Lewis. New York: New Directions, 1964.

Pardoe, Ro, and John Howard. "Fritz Leiber's *Our Lady of Darkness:* Annotations." *Ghosts and Scholars* No. 21. Rev. 2003. Web. Accessed 10 March 2004.

Pardoe, Rosemary. "*Our Lady of Darkness:* A Jamesian Classic." *Ghosts & Scholars* No. 20. Web. Accessed 5 March 2004.

Pegram, Thomas R. *Battling Demon Rum: The Struggle for a Dry America, 1800–1933*. Chicago: Ivan R. Dee, 1998.

Peter, Andritsch. "Der Vampir in der literarischen Verarbeitung." Web. Accessed 2 November 2005.

Philadelphia Inquirer 174, No. 158 (6 June 1916): 15.

Pieper, Josef. *Begeisterung und Göttlicher Wahnsinn*. Munich: Kösel-Verlag, 1962.

————. *Hoffnung und Geschichte: Fünf Salzburger Vorlesungen*. Munich: Kösel-Verlag, 1967.

Plato. *The Collected Dialogues Including the Letters*. Ed. Edith Hamilton and Huntington Cairns. Princeton: Princeton University Press, 1963.

————. *Opera*. Ed. John Burnet. Oxford: Clarendon Press, 1900. 5 vols.

Plutarch. *The Lives of the Noble Grecians and Romans*. Trans. John Dryden. Rev. Arthur Hugh Clough. New York: Modern Library, n.d.

————. *The Obsolescence of Oracles*. In *Moralia*. Vol. 5. Cambridge, MA: Harvard University Press/Loeb Classical Library, 1936.

Pokorny, Julius. *Indogermanisches Etymologisches Wörterbuch*. Bern: Francke, 1959. 2 vols.

Polidori, John. "The Vampyre." In Adèle Olivia Gladwell and James Havoc, ed. *Blood and Roses: The Vampire in 19th Century Literature*. London: Creation Press, 1992.

Pope, Alexander. *The Dunciad*. In *The Poems of Alexander Pope*. Ed. John Butt. New Haven: Yale University Press, 1963.

————. *The Dunciad in Four Books*. Ed. Valerie Rumbold. New York: Pearson Education, 2009.

————. *Homer's Iliad*. New York: Hurst & Company, n.d.

Pope, John C., ed. *Seven Old English Poems*. Indianapolis: Bobbs-Merrill, 1966.

Proust, Marcel. *Remembrance of Things Past*. Trans. C. K. Scott Moncrieff. New York: Random House, 1934. 2 vols.

Reaney, P. H. *A Dictionary of British Surnames*. 2nd ed. Ed. R. M. Wilson. London: Routledge & Kegan Paul, 1976.

"Rhode Island General Laws 11-20-1." Web. Accessed 15 June 2009.

"Rhode Island General Laws 11-20-2." Web. Accessed 15 June 2009.

Rickword, Edgell. "Trench Poets." In Walter, *The Penguin Book of First World War Poetry*.

Rilke, Rainer Maria. *The Complete French Poems*. Trans. A. Poulin, Jr. St. Paul: Graywolf Press, 1986.

———. *Gesammelte Gedichte*. Frankfurt am Main: Insel-Verlag, 1962.

Roberts, Warren. *A Bibliography of D. H. Lawrence*. London: Hart-Davis, 1963.

Rosenberg, Isaac. *The Collected Works*. Ed. Ian Parsons. New York: Oxford University Press, 1979.

Ross, Alex. "The Unforgiven." *New Yorker* (10 August 1998). 64–72.

Russell, Francis. *The Shadow of Blooming Grove: Warren G. Harding in His Times*. New York: McGraw-Hill, 1968.

Rutilius Namatianus. *De Reditu Suo*. In *Minor Latin Poets*. Ed. and trans. J. Wright Duff and Arnold M. Duff. Cambridge, MA: Harvard University Press/Loeb Classical Library, 1954.

Sassoon, Siegfried. "Aftermath." In Walter, *The Penguin Book of First World War Poetry*.

Schäfer, Peter. *Judeophophobia: Attitudes toward the Jews in the Ancient World*. Cambridge, MA: Harvard University Press, 1997.

Schakel, Peter J., and Charles A. Huttar. *Word and Story in C. S. Lewis*. Columbia: University of Missouri Press, 1991.

Schivelbusch, Wolfgang. *Disenchanted Night: The Industrialization of Light in the Nineteenth Century*. Trans. Angela Davies. Berkeley: University of California Press, 1988.

Scholem, Gershom. *Kabbalah*. New York: Dorset, 1987.

Schubart, Christian Friedrich Daniel. "Der ewige Jude: Eine lyrische Rhapsodie." Web. Accessed 7 October 2009.

Seneca, L. Annaeus. *Epistulae Morales*. Vol. 3. Ed. Richard M. Gummere. Cambridge, MA: Harvard University Press/Loeb Classical Library, 1962.

———. *Historiarum Libri*. Ed. C. D. Fisher. Oxford: Oxford University Press, 1911.

———. *Tragoediae*. Ed. Otto Zwierlein. Oxford: Oxford University Press, 1986.

Shakespeare, William. *Mr. William Shakespeare's Comedies, Histories, Tragedies, and Poems*. Ed. Richard Grant White. Boston: Houghton Mifflin, 1883. 3 vols.

———. *The Norton Shakespeare*. Ed. Stephen Greenblatt. New York: W. W. Norton, 1997.

Shattuck, Roger. *Proust's Binoculars: A Study of Memory, Time and Recognition in* A la Recherche du Temps Perdu. Princeton: Princeton University Press, 1983.

Smith, Jr., Lyle H. "C. S. Lewis as a Maker of Metaphor." In Schakel and Huttar. 11–28.

Smith, Ryan K. *Gothic Arches, Latin Crosses: Anti-Catholicism and American Church Designs in the Nineteenth Century*. Chapel Hill: University of North Carolina Press, 2006.

Society of Architectural Historians. *Providence Board of Trade Journal*, 1895. *Providence Architecture*. Web. Accessed 2 October 2005.

Spenser, Edmund. *Poetical Works*. Ed. J. C. Smith and E. de Selincourt. London: Oxford University Press, 1912.

Spurgeon, Caroline. *Shakespeare's Imagery and What It Tells Us*. Cambridge: Cambridge University Press, 1952.

Stevenson, Robert Louis. *The Works*. New York: Charles Scribner's Sons, 1895–1901. 26 vols.

Summers, Montague. *The Vampire: His Kith and Kin*. New Hyde Park, NY: University, 1960.

The Supreme Council of the Thirty-third Degree. *Morals and Dogma of the Ancient and Accepted Scottish Rite*. Charleston, NC: L. H. Jenkins, 1919.

Swedenborg, Emanuel. *The Heavenly Arcana*. Vol. 1. Boston: New-Church Union/Rotch Edition, 1918.

Tacitus. *Annales*. Ed. C. D. Fisher. Oxford: Oxford University Press, 1906.

Tennyson, Alfred. *The Poetic and Dramatic Works*. Boston: Houghton Mifflin, 1927.

Thompson, Francis. *Complete Poetical Works*. New York: Modern Library, n.d.

Tolkien, J. R. R. *The Hobbit*. New York: Houghton Mifflin, 1966.

———. *The Letters*. Ed. Humphrey Carpenter. New York: Houghton Mifflin, 1981.

———. *The Lord of the Rings*. Ed. Douglas A. Anderson. New York: Houghton Mifflin, 1987.

———. *The Monster and the Critics and Other Essays*. Ed. Christopher Tolkien. New York: Houghton Mifflin, 1984.

———. *The Return of the Shadow: The History of The Lord of the Rings Part I*. The History of Middle-Earth, Vol VI. Ed. Christopher Tolkien. New York: Houghton Mifflin, 1988.

Tucker, T. G. *Etymological Dictionary of Latin*. Chicago: Ares, 1985.

Vaihinger, Hans. *Die Philosophie des Als Ob*. 10th ed. Leipzig: Felix Meiner, 1927.

Verne, Jules. *Vingt mille lieues sous les mers*. Paris: Livre de Poche, 1980.

Virgil. *Opera*. Ed. Frederick Arthur Hirtzel. Oxford: Oxford University Press, 1900.

Wagner, Richard. *Gesammelte Schriften*. Ed. Julius Kapp. Leipzig: Hesse & Becker, 1914. 14 vols.

Walter, George, ed. *The Penguin Book of First World War Poetry*. London: Penguin, 2006.

Weber, Carl Maria von. *Der Freischütz*. Ed. and trans. Natalia MacFarren and Th. Baker. New York: Schirmer, n.d.

Webster's New Collegiate Dictionary. Springfield, MA: Merriam, 1960.

Weigall, Arthur. *Wanderings in Roman Britain*. London: Butterworth, 1926.

Westernhagen, Curt von. *Wagner: A Biography*. Trans. Mary Whittall. Cambridge: Cambridge University Press, 1981.

Wilde, Oscar. *Works*. London: Spring Books, 1963.

Wills, Garry. *Witches and Jesuits: Shakespeare's* Macbeth. New York: Oxford University Press, 1995.

Wilson, A. N. *C. S. Lewis: A Biography*. New York: W. W. Norton, 1990.

Žižek, Slavoj. "Foreword." In Adorno, *In Search of Wagner*. viii–xxvii.

CPSIA information can be obtained at www.ICGtesting.com
Printed in the USA
BVOW011654280312

286301BV00006B/29/P